Planning, Developing, and Marketing Successful Web Sites

Jason Miletsky

THOMSON

COURSE TECHNOLOGY

Australia • Canada • Mexico • Singapore • Spain • United Kingdom • United States

THOMSON

™

COURSE TECHNOLOGY

Planning, Developing, and Marketing Successful Web Sites
by Jason Miletsky

Managing Editor:	**Production Editor:**	**Editorial Assistant:**
Jennifer Locke	Danielle Power	Christy Urban
Senior Product Manager:	**Marketing Manager:**	**Cover Designer:**
Margarita Leonard	Angie Laughlin	Joseph Lee, Black Fish Design
Development Editor:	**Associate Product Manager:**	**Manufacturing Manager:**
Amanda Brodkin	Janet Aras	Denise Sandler

Disclaimer
Course Technology reserves the right to revise this publication and make changes from time to time in its content without notice.

The Web sites and companies mentioned in this book are subject to change from time to time as necessary without notice.

This publication is designed to provide accurate and authoritative information regarding the subject matter covered. It is sold with the understanding that neither the publisher nor the author are engaged in rendering legal, accounting, or other professional services. If legal, accounting, or other expert advice is required, the services of a competent professional person should be sought.

ISBN 0-619-03563-3

BRIEF

Contents

TABLE OF Contents

CHAPTER ELEVEN
More on Marketing: PR and Nontraditional Promotions　　307

CHAPTER TWELVE
Customer Service and Putting It All Together　　333

Preface

Planning, Developing, and Marketing Successful Web Sites will provide you with an understanding of the conceptualized method with which Web sites are built, branded, and marketed. As the Web sheds its novelty status and gains value and importance as a legitimate means of engaging in business and communication, it becomes critical to take the proper steps in Web site development from the start, rather than fixing mistakes later. Web sites are less a combination of programming and design elements than they are the result of careful planning. The vast majority of Web sites are designed with the objective of building and promoting business.

Planning, Developing, and Marketing Successful Web Sites explains the non-programming elements that go into creating a successful Web site by first reviewing the successes and failures of the past and making predictions for the future. We review various types of sites, how to derive revenue from each type of site, variations in technology and design, workable navigation, and how to brand and market a site for continued success and customer efficiency in the long term.

The Approach

Planning, Developing, and Marketing Successful Web Sites is a practical guide to planning, developing, and managing a winning Web site. The book focuses on using technology appropriately in the business environment, with an emphasis on the successful integration of both business and technical elements. Rather than focus on one or two business Web site examples, Planning, Developing, and Marketing Successful Web Sites takes a broad look at the Web as a whole. The book is divided into three general sections: the first part covers the various types of Web sites that can be used in a business environment. The second part delves into the production process, taking a broad view of technology, identifying the market, and exploring factors that contribute to successful graphics and navigation. Finally, the third part of this book describes the creation of a brand and methods for marketing a Web site and keeping site visitors satisfied.

Organization and Coverage

Planning, Developing, and Marketing Successful Web Sites and the elements that comprise each chapter will help you achieve the following objectives:

- Understand the Web as it relates to both Web-only and traditional businesses
- Identify and realize potential for generating revenue over the Internet

- Learn the dynamics of market research as it corresponds to Web site development
- Outline functional navigation for a Web site for efficient organization of content
- Understand what is meant by "branding" and the role that the brand plays in Web success
- Understand marketing to help drive traffic to a Web site
- Become familiar with the customer experience on the Web and elements that are needed to attract visitors and keep them coming back to your site

In **Chapter 1**, you will learn about the recent history of the Web, beginning with its popularization as a commercial tool. Through an analysis of the boom and bust period that affected the U.S. economy beginning in the mid-1990s, you will examine the errors and achievements of the early Web pioneers. Potential growth and Web site establishment into the future rounds out this introductory chapter. **Chapter 2** reveals the many different types of Web sites, concentrating on those that are used for business purposes. You will discover what makes each type of site unique, and the positive and negative aspects that may be associated with the development of each. **Chapter 3** provides insight into the planning of a Web site, including what type of content is needed and early customer service considerations. You will also gain an understanding of the target market for each site, why understanding that target is important, and the ways in which a Web site developer might go about determining who its market is. **Chapter 4** reviews ways of generating revenue over the Web, along with some of the problems and potential associated with each method. This chapter also provides a glimpse of the current state of advertising on the Web. **Chapter 5** describes the personnel and skills that go into creating a business-oriented Web site and explains why a team of people is typically necessary. The various aspects of Web site development that need specialized skill sets are described as well. Chapter 5 provides a discussion of internal vs. external (outsourced) site development. In **Chapter 6** you look at the importance of sound navigation and graphics usage. Considerations include how much or how little of these design elements should be used for various types of site and on which pages. This chapter also discusses the importance of creating a solid schematic for organizational purposes, how information should be categorized, and how to create a functional navigation tool that allows Web site visitors to easily access that information. **Chapter 7** explains the importance of testing your site, from both technical and visitor satisfaction perspectives. This chapter addresses both the topics that need to be tested as well as methods for testing. **Chapter 8** covers the concept of brand – what it is, why it's so important, and how to properly develop it for your Web site. **Chapter 9** outlines site features, called sticky elements, that sites can use to attract and retain visitors. **Chapter 10** covers both online and offline advertising efforts to help promote your site, while **Chapter 11** covers the public relations and nontraditional marketing methods that can help build audiences. The importance of public relations both on and off a site as a function of both marketing and building brand awareness are covered in this chapter. Finally, in **Chapter 12**, you will learn how important customer satisfaction is to the life of a Web site, and what elements can be integrated so that visitors have a positive experience on your site. Chapter 12 provides a brief summary of the key topics of the book and explains their integration.

Features

Planning, Developing, and Marketing Successful Web Sites is unique in its field because it includes the following features:

- **Chapter Objectives** The beginning of each chapter will provide a bulleted list of the objectives you will reach and the concepts you will have mastered within the text.

- **Chapter Summaries** Each chapter concludes with a Summary that concisely recaps the most important concepts in the chapter.

- **Key Terms** A list of key terms at the end of each chapter allows you to identify the language of the Web.

- **Review Questions** Approximately 15 questions follow each chapter. These multiple choice and fill-in questions help readers test their comprehension of chapter content.

- **Hands-on Projects** Two or three projects at the end of each chapter let you put your knowledge to practical use. These projects are conceptual in nature and require practical application of the content within in each chapter. A running case that continues throughout most of the chapters of the book requires students to work with in-class partners to develop their own plans for a fictional Web business and the creation of its various elements. Other projects require formation of opinions based on analytical thought and research, often requiring use of the Internet as a tool for reaching conclusions. These projects help you understand the chapter concepts so that you can apply them outside the classroom. The projects are ideal for use as the basis for class discussions or as written homework assignments.

- **Online Companion** The Online Companion is a set of Web pages maintained by the publisher for readers of this book. The Online Companion complements the book and contains links to Web sites mentioned in the book and to other online resources that further illustrate the concepts presented in the book. The Web is constantly changing and the Online Companion is continually monitored and updated for those changes so that its links continue to lead to useful Web resources for each chapter. You can find the Online Companion for this book by visiting Course Technology's Web site at www.course.com and searching on *Planning, Developing, and Marketing Successful Web Sites*.

- **Online Companion References in Text** Throughout each chapter there are Online Companion References that indicate the name of a link included in the Online Companion. Text set in bold, sans-serif letters ("**Amazon.com**") indicates that there is a like-named link in the Online Companion. The links in the Online Companion are organized under chapter and subchapter headings that correspond to those in the book. The Online Companion also contains many supplemental links to help students explore beyond the book's content.

- **Glossary** A comprehensive glossary compiles the key terminology along with definitions. The glossary is a handy learning and reference tool.

Teaching Tools

When this book is used in an academic setting, instructors may obtain the following teaching tools from Course Technology:

- **Instructor's Manual** The Instructor's Manual has been carefully prepared and tested to ensure its accuracy and dependability. The Instructor's Manual is available through the Course Technology Faculty Online Companion on the World Wide Web (call your customer service representative for the exact URL and to obtain your user-name and password).

- **ExamView** This textbook is accompanied by ExamView, a powerful testing software package that allows instructors to create and administer printed computer (LAN-based), and Internet exams. ExamView includes hundreds of questions that correspond to the topics covered in this text, enabling students to generate detailed study guides that include page references for further review. The computer-based and Internet testing components allow students to take exams at their computers, and also save the instructor time by grading each exam automatically.

- **Classroom Presentations** Microsoft PowerPoint presentations are available for each chapter of this book to assist instructors in classroom lectures or to make available to students. The Classroom Presentations are included on the Instructor's CD.

About the Author

Jason I. Miletsky is CEO and creative director of PFS Marketwyse, Inc., an advertising, marketing, and production firm specializing in brand development and communication for both traditional and cyber campaigns. PFS Marketwyse clients include JVC, BASF, Derek Jeter's Turn 2 Foundation, and Lucent Technologies.

Additionally, Jason is an associate editor for *Digital Output* magazine. He speaks at seminars and universities—including NAB (National Association of Broadcasters), Strategic Research Institute, and Pratt Institute—on topics such as electronic commerce, brand building, and successful marketing.

ACKNOWLEDGMENTS

Above all else, I need to thank development editor Amanda Brodkin. Amanda has been far and away the most professional, patient, and influential editor with whom I have ever had the privilege to work. I would similarly like to thank Jennifer Locke, Danielle Power, Janet Aras, Christy Urban, Angie Laughlin, Denise Sandler and everyone else at Course Technology who made this book happen. I would especially like to thank to Margarita Leonard.

Thanks to reviewers David Brownfield, Mount Saint Clare College; Mary Garrett, Michigan Virtual University; and Charlyne Walker, Florida International University. Each reviewer's comments and feedback played a role in helping the book evolve, and I appreciate the time that they took and the effort that they put in.

Thank you to my friends, family, and associates, especially Marv, Donna, Chris, Ida, Jackie, and most especially Jamie.

This book is dedicated to Dennis and Deirdre, without whom I would not have had the knowledge to even begin writing this book.

Jason Miletsky

1

THE WEB ECONOMY'S WILD RIDE

In this chapter, you will learn about:

♦ The main reasons that business on the Web grew so quickly

♦ The reasons that Web sites experienced huge losses in the late 1990s

♦ The global economic factors that contributed to the Web economy's downturn

♦ The role of brands in Web site success

♦ The differences between online and mass media advertising

♦ The rush to invest in sites that were conceptually flawed

♦ How traditional businesses entered the online marketplace

♦ What to expect in the future for Web business

Imagine you are going up in a very fast elevator. If it's powerful enough, you will get a slight head rush from ascending so quickly. Now imagine that as the elevator reaches its maximum speed, there's a lurch, an ugly sound of twisting metal, and a sudden, unexpected freefall as you hurtle down the shaft toward the ground below. That feeling is an approximation of what it's like to own an advertising, marketing, or production firm in the economic environment around the turn of the 21st century. As the CEO and cofounder of PFS Marketwyse, an agency with expertise in custom digital media campaigns, I have been immersed in the creative, technical, and marketing development of more than 100 Web sites since 1994. The combination of lightning-fast technological advancements and a roller coaster of an economy have made the business of Web site management exciting, frustrating, challenging, rewarding, and, at times, nauseating (though not necessarily in that order). This book explains successful Web site creation from the perspective of one who's been there. Chapter 1 describes the various economic and technical developments that led to the bursting of the Web bubble.

A QUICK TOUR OF THE WEB LANDSCAPE

"Ladies and gentlemen, this concludes your rollercoaster ride through the World Wide Web. Please excuse the sudden, unannounced stop. After the safety bar has been raised, we invite you to exit the rollercoaster to your left, and spend the evening with us in our newly constructed *Land of Skepticism* tour." Such has been the tumultuous ride of the New Economy. From dot-com company employees and owners to stockbrokers and buyers, the future of the cyber world is uncertain at best.

What Goes Up Must Come Down

After years of hype, the medium that would replace television has taken a dramatic turn. Even as **electronic commerce** (**e-commerce**), or online business, increases to record levels, the **Web start-ups** (businesses that exist only online, also called **pure-coms**) that first appeared to change the face of commerce are trading their home pages for "out of business" signs. **Dot-coms**, a broader category of online business, encompass both pure-com sites and sites run by traditional marketers.

Toward the end of 2000, following the strangest U.S. presidential election in modern history, interest rates and gasoline prices were on the rise. Companies that were starving for new employees only a few months prior suddenly changed course and began announcing massive layoffs. Earnings predictions were revised downward. Like any bust that follows a boom, these were days of mixed emotions. The widespread fear of recession among both corporations and the general population was somewhat offset by the odd contentment that the people who made billions on paper were as vulnerable as everyone else.

So what happened? For a time, it seemed that business on the Web was unstoppable. Companies were scrambling to get on the Web—the general attitude was "be there or be at a severe disadvantage." Traditional advertising agencies, unused to this new medium, rapidly tried to forge partnerships with upstart Web site development firms or to create internal Web programming shops. They did this rather than lose accounts to **production houses**, or small creative agencies that specialized in Web site production. Having a "dot com" next to your name practically guaranteed success; not having one got you branded "old fashioned" in the industry media.

The Party's Over

One day, in the middle of the third quarter of 2000, the pure-com market (followed soon by the economy as a whole) started to crumble. Suddenly, being an Internet-only business went from being a badge of pride to a near liability. Pure-coms scrambled to rebrand themselves to avoid negative ramifications of Internet association—as evidenced by Jfax.com changing its name to **j2 Global Communications** (www.j2.com) and ShopNow.com switching to **Network Commerce** (www.networkcommerce.com).

These companies wanted to differentiate themselves from the likes of Pets.com, Furniture.com, MotherNature.com, PlanetRX, and others who led the industry, spent hundreds of millions of dollars, and then abruptly closed their doors.

Heavy hitters like **Priceline.com** saw their stocks drop from a 52-week high of around $104 to just over $1 per share, and they announced massive layoffs. Stock for eToys.com plummeted from a 52-week high of around $32 per share to just over $.20, and as a result, eToys.com had to close its U.K. offices and lay off many employees. Even **Amazon.com**, the poster child of start-up success who made others believe they could do it too, saw its stock, which peaked around $250 per share, settle at $12. Amazon's revenues of over $3.5 billion have generated over $1.5 billion in losses, leaving many people to wonder just how much longer the site will be around.

The pure-coms weren't the only companies to suffer in the late 2000 slump. Major tech players such as Lucent Technology and Cisco Systems also experienced significant stock drops in light of revised earnings expectations. The sudden shift in the technology segment of the economy—which has, since the Industrial Revolution, led the economy upward—left the immediate future of the new economy (and the overall economy) in question.

Many Causes

So what caused the tumble? There were many causes: the venture capital money that funded many start-ups began drying up, the Federal Reserve's planned slowdown of the U.S. economy was not as effective as anticipated, and the high-flying, tech-rich NASDAQ stock market began a dramatic downturn.

Making matters even worse, the growth and expansion of the computer industry that had helped fuel the economy of the 1990s suddenly began to dry up. Even the European markets, which were relatively untapped compared to American computer markets, were slower to grow than many experts anticipated.

Figure 1-1 shows data for the NASDAQ for January 1996 through January 2001. You can see how the market nose-dived in the fourth quarter of 2000.

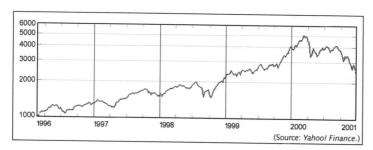

(Source: *Yahoo! Finance.*)

Figure 1-1   Point gains by the NASDAQ, early 1996 through January 2001

The NASDAQ chart illustrates the initial demand for and belief in pure-coms and related tech companies (including those that provided Internet service, site development skills, or the manufacturing of necessary equipment) starting in early 1997. It then shows a sudden abandonment of them, proven by the sudden drop in the market's index average. The dot-com sites developed by traditional marketers were typically just a function of their parent company and were not listed separately on stock indexes.

This new situation begs these questions: What happened to the pure-coms to make them fall from grace? How did they go from being the new American dream to an economic liability? Can they rebound, and, if so, will the Internet landscape ever be the same? In addition, where, in all of this, were the traditional marketers? How were traditional businesses dealing with and surviving on the Web? Most importantly, how can today's problems be avoided in the future, and what can we expect tomorrow?

With the benefit of hindsight, it is possible to identify many reasons that led to trouble for the pure-coms. These problems include economic conditions beyond pure-com control, lack of brand development, bad ideas, consumer oversaturation, and general lack of experience. The next sections discuss the many issues that contributed to the end of the seemingly unstoppable rise.

GLOBAL SHIFT

In many respects, the struggling dot-coms were mere victims of circumstance. Economics classes will probably be talking about the third and fourth quarter of 2000 for years to come. It is important to understand at least a general picture of what the world is like in the New Economy vs. its Old Economy predecessor before we can really investigate and comprehend what happened to Web commerce. Understanding the economic environment is vital to gaining a true picture of how Web commerce will survive.

A Changing Economy

Prior to the middle part of the 1900s, the economic environment known as the **Old Economy** was a setting in which fewer than 5 percent of American households owned stock. Those who did own stock were generally a specific type of conservative white-collar investor. Regardless of who was doing the trading, the market was always the buoy in rough waters—a source of stability even during times of economic recession. Changes in the market, either up or down, were always measured in points—rarely in percentages. The stock reports were available in a few editions of a daily newspaper, and buy/sell orders usually involved consultation and a phone call to a broker. Snap decisions were hardly part of the equation.

The **New Economy** of the 1990s and beyond is an environment of instant data, endless opportunity, and instantaneous decision-making in which the average American is an informed and active participant. Circumstances and conditions we've never faced before are creating a haphazard set of economic rules that we struggle to understand and work within. However, before any of them can be studied, we should take an overall look at the landscape of late 2000.

An Upward Spiral

For most of the 1990s, the United States enjoyed intense economic growth. In 1999 alone, the Dow was up 25 percent, and the NASDAQ climbed an unbelievable 85 percent. New homes were selling faster than they could be built, computers had infiltrated more than half of U.S. homes, and the Internet was, in the early 1990s, starting to generate a lot of buzz.

Commercialized growth of the Internet spawned new types of companies that the world had never seen before. These included pure-coms, consultancies, Internet service providers (ISPs), and production houses. Existing tech companies like IBM and AT&T had new crops of customers, and consumer demand for computers skyrocketed. Amazon.com (an online retailer that began selling books and later expanded into selling music, electronics, home furnishings and other items) roared onto the scene in 1995, and its success convinced anybody with an idea that if Amazon.com could sell books over the Web, they could sell music, clothes, imported herbal remedies, and so on. These high-tech trailblazers scoffed at **brick-and-mortar** stores, which are retailers doing business only in physical locations.

With the promise of a new medium (the smart money at the time was betting that Internet usage would eclipse television usage), everybody wanted a piece of the action. The NASDAQ became home to the new crop of tech players, including nearly every publicly traded pure-com, and consequently, its indexes inflated higher than ever. Even as market experts and stock analysts warned during the early days of the boom that a correction was imminent and the Federal Reserve issued repeated warnings about the dangers of inflation in an over-heated market, the stock indexes continued to rise. Stocks rose so dramatically that it seemed that the growth of the economy was the only topic the media were reporting. The media attention itself fueled the market further, which in turn fueled more media attention, and so on. Investors continued to pour money into many pure-com start-ups that, with inexperienced executive officers and often flawed business models, were getting in way over their heads.

New products, mostly high-tech gizmos such as MP3 players and Palm Pilots, hit the market in a rapid, constant blitz, taking advantage of an extraordinarily high consumer confidence and seemingly endless wealth. It seemed that the only major problem facing corporate America in the late 1990s was an extreme lack of skilled workers. With stock prices skyrocketing, consumers and corporations were finding new wealth to spend, creating a demand for goods across the board. Companies, hungry to meet the demand for new products and services, took advantage of the low interest rates and borrowed money for expansions. These expansions created a need for qualified workers to fill newly created positions so that growth could be maintained. Soon, the market for employees was saturated. With the unemployment rate hovering under 4 percent for most of the late 1990s, employers went to great lengths to find and retain qualified employees to help spur further growth.

The high demand for employees is what kept the Federal Reserve nervous about potential inflation. Before too long, corporations would have to increase salaries to lure and maintain new workers, and they would, in turn, raise the prices of their goods and services to cover their increased salary expenses. That was the (rational) economic theory. However, companies dealt with their employees without raising salaries. This helped keep inflation down. Instead of offering more cash, publicly traded companies offered enticing stock options, which were what the workers *really* wanted. Smaller firms often promised their employees that they would go public (offer stock in a public offering) in the near future and that shares of stocks and options would be distributed generously. Most companies installed creative quality-of-life improvements to keep employees without having to add more dollars to their paychecks.

Figure 1-2 shows the unemployment rates coupled with the inflation rate for the second half of the 1990s.

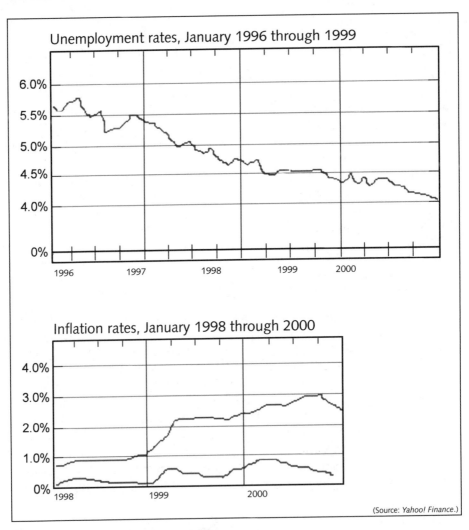

Figure 1-2   Unemployment and inflation rates

Figure 1-3 shows the stock prices for a few key pure-com companies that went public during those years.

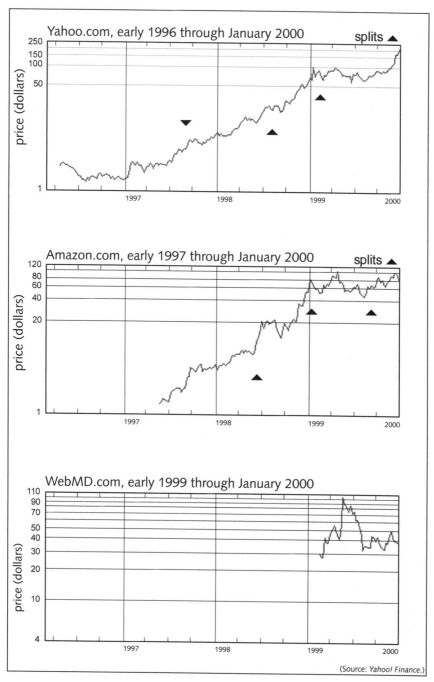

Figure 1-3   Pure-com stock prices

Like other companies eager to hire and retain talented employees, my own agency began offering attractive extras to help entice workers; we installed a full game room and lounge in the office and initiated a "come when you want, leave when you want" policy. We expanded creative freedom and scheduled field trips to ball games and amusement parks. The approach seemed to work. Although salaries weren't significantly increased, only a few employees left the agency to work for competing firms, while many of the others were recommending their friends for positions that we had open.

Then came the year 2000. The fear of a Y2K meltdown was unfounded, and threats to disrupt New Year's celebrations didn't materialize. Unfortunately, that was the last of the really good news for a while. As 2000 moved along, the economy did not experience much more of a change in the first quarter than it did in 1999. A few pure-coms failed, but those failures weren't cause for major concern. At the pumps, gas prices jumped suddenly—nearly doubling in some areas to nearly $2 per gallon. People complained about it, and the media made a slight issue of it, but it wasn't *that* big of a deal. The really big news of 2000 was that the Federal Reserve, under chairman Alan Greenspan, started to orchestrate an economic slowdown by raising interest rates. It was then that the wild ride ground to a halt.

The Downward Slide

In the fall of 2000, news came that Pets.com shut its doors. That was the first real indicator that something had gone terribly wrong in the Web's business environment. Pure-coms, far from being money machines, had *real* expenses to deal with and were vulnerable to losses. Then another pure-com died. And another. It was impossible not to watch with fascination; it was ugly and entertaining at the same time.

Not long after Pets.com's demise, eToys.com (a pure-com that sold children's toys online, and one of the few **e-tailers**, or online retailers, mentioned in the same breath as Amazon.com and eBay.com) released news that its 2000 holiday sales would be half of what it expected and its current cash would last only a few more months. Suddenly, the industry wasn't entertained—it was alarmed. If eToys.com could fail, what did it mean for the rest of the sector?

The downward slide was gaining momentum. Lucent Technologies' stock plummeted as bills from failing pure-coms and other expanding businesses went unpaid, and **Microsoft** (www.microsoft.com) reported that it would not hit expected earnings for the first time in a decade. The economy for the third quarter of 2000 grew at 2.2 percent, the slowest rate in years. Following a hotly contested presidential election, the word "recession" started being mumbled by stunned corporations, by stock-rich households, and, more loudly, by the media. The "soft landing" that the Federal Reserve had orchestrated wasn't going quite as planned.

This new set of economic circumstances, coming so quickly after the hot electronic commerce takeoff, sent investors running scared. As a result, stock prices plummeted, hurting even the most solid dot-coms.

Figure 1-4 shows the individual stock charts of the pure-com companies examined in Figure 1-3, with data through 2001.

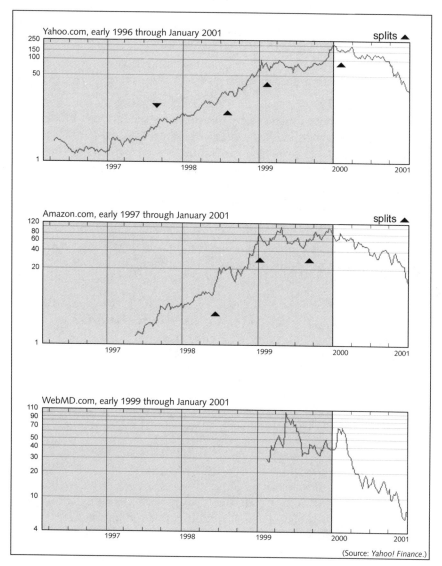

Figure 1-4 Pure-com stock drops in 2000

As a broader indication of the economic slide, the Standard 100, an index consisting only of dot-com and tech stocks, gained 28 percent in just the two months between January 2000 and March 2000. However, the Standard 100 had an overall loss of 69 percent between January and November of the same year. Even more alarming is the fact that electronic commerce companies that received venture capital funding in the fourth quarter of 1999 had a median value of $108 million, but just six months later they had a revised median value of $21.5 million—down about 80 percent.

Solutions to recent problems will likely come from sweeping and specific economic changes. These changes will eventually turn the tech and broader markets around, but they never will restore the dot-com mania of the end of the millennium.

Now that we've set the economic scene for the dot-com downturn, we should examine some of the New Economy conditions that contributed to it.

CONTRIBUTING FACTORS

Unlike the Old Economy described in the previous section, the New Economy is an economic environment in which the majority of American workers are participants. This situation, along with factors such as consumer consumption and increased access to information, helped spur the rise and fall of the dot-coms.

The New Economy Environment

Mutual funds, company 401k plans, and increased general interest due to rapid gains in the stock prices got more people involved in the market, and by the latter days of 1990s, nearly half of all American households were invested in stocks. Discussions about stocks moved from the smoky rooms of upper crust lounges to the dinner table of the common worker.

Information has become easier than ever to get. CNBC, CNN, and others provide real-time stock quotes during the day, and as a result, **day trading** (the act of buying stocks and selling them that same day after making a quick profit) became a widespread phenomenon. Executing a trade was as easy as jumping on a Web site. It was far easier and less expensive than consulting with a broker.

The repercussions of easy and instantaneous access to data certainly contributed to the downturn in the economy, as it brought not only too many (inexperienced) people into the stock market, but also spurred dizzying market heights that could not be maintained.

The real market dollars that at one time were an indicator of expectation and a forecast of how a company would fare in the future (stocks often rise and fall based on how well the stock traders *expect* a company will do in the short or long term) were being diluted with dollars that treated the NASDAQ as though it were little more than a roulette wheel. The effect of all this is still being analyzed. Data sources played an important role in building the New Economy, and later, the economy suffered because of easy access to data.

Most significant in the New Economy is the extreme volatility of the market and this volatility's impact on the public. Investors viewed companies that gained or lost 1/8 of a point as boring and unable to keep pace with a world in which a decent meal could be cooked in a microwave. With the introduction of pure-coms, it wasn't uncommon for many stocks, and the markets in general, to gain 15 percent, 25 percent, 50 percent, or even more in a single day. Most new pure-coms that went public (and many rushed to go public, ready for it or not) were instantly snatched up by eager investors who didn't want to miss out on the next eBay. Markets were measured not by their points, but by their percentage gains. Record-breaking highs were occurring with thrilling frequency.

All this excitement had a downside. With so many people invested in stocks, the market became less a source of stability and more a measure of the economy in general. When the market was up, people felt richer, even if the wealth was only on paper. (In 1999, with the NASDAQ up 85 percent for the year, household assets had climbed by $5.5 trillion over the same time frame.) Confidence was up, so consumers spent more.

When the pure-coms began collapsing, the market went with them. Between March 2000 and January 2001, $2.5 trillion of consumer wealth vanished. Consumer confidence vanished and spending habits changed.

Regardless of whether a country is really in a recession, the economy can be a victim of self-fulfilled prophesy. Consumer confidence is the single most important factor in maintaining momentum in the economy. Heightened confidence built the pure-coms; lack of confidence tore them right back down again. The same trend is true for the general economy.

Amazingly enough, the slide in the market and the talk of a recession didn't immediately hurt the unemployment rate, which at the beginning of 2001 remained around 4 percent, which is consistent with the rate for the previous 12 months. Although layoffs made headlines throughout 2001, it seemed that companies that fought hard for employees were reluctant to give them up after so much effort, and those workers who were laid off found new work almost immediately. This trend is in opposition to Old Economy activity, in which a slower economy meant longer unemployment lines.

In fact, the latest numbers show that over 145,000 new jobs were *created* in the midst of all this talk of layoffs, although most of these new jobs were created by biotech and pharmaceutical firms, which were Wall Street's new darlings. At the same time, nearly 65,000 tech workers lost their jobs. With nearly 55 percent of all tech-related employees (especially those at the pure-com companies) receiving at least a portion of their compensation in the form of now-worthless stock options, a lot of people who still had jobs were suddenly finding it more challenging to make their next rent payment. Later, though, the unemployment rate began to rise (mid-2001 figures showed the unemployment rate rising to 4.5 percent and approaching 5 percent rapidly) as the tech sector's economic woes spread to other sectors, particularly retail. Non-tech industries felt the pressure of a consumer public with fewer dollars to spend.

Not Much Left to Buy

By all appearances, American consumerism is at an all-time high. We've got our DVD players and our CD burners. Our Palm Pilots are tucked away in laptop computer bags, next to our e-mail-reading cell phones and MP3 players. Driving home in our SUVs is a cinch, thanks to computerized navigation systems. Once home, we can watch any one of hundreds of channels beamed in by the satellite dish on the roof, or we can surf the Web on our Pentium IV computer with 128 MB of RAM, a 4 GB hard drive, a video card, and a nifty game of Solitaire. The marketing wizards, including product manufacturers, retailers, and advertising agencies, outdid themselves. They sold the world every electronic gizmo they could think of, and whether it was tool or toy, we bought it.

There's nothing wrong with our purchasing habits, except that at the same time that investors demanded profits from the pure-coms, the range of "must-have" items seemed to have reached a point of saturation. The Web itself was the impetus for massive growth, computer upgrades, technological advancements, and a dire need by corporations to invest in new equipment. Tech companies released scores of new software programs to help companies streamline billing processes, serve their customers online, and become more efficient. At the same time, computer and electronics manufacturers targeted the consumer markets with everything that the average user would need to take advantage of the Web: faster computers and peripherals, hand-held items for wireless Web use, and the list went on. Soon after the Web became more of a staple and less of a novelty, companies and consumers had fewer reasons to purchase new products or upgrade existing systems. There was little need for a faster computer. (How fast does it need to be when your average user just surfs the Web or types a paper in Microsoft Word?) There was no apparent doom if you didn't upgrade to Windows 2000: Windows 98 worked just fine, thank you. As with all cycles, the boom created by the popularization of the Web and personal computing was subsiding.

Across the board, from businesses to consumers, the marketing gurus of the tech surge learned one hard lesson—with so many chips and wires, the most important component is obsolescence, and that's the one component they forgot to include. Even as newer, better, faster models hit the market, there seemed to be no way to convince a product-fatigued populous that there was anything wrong with the older, slower models they already had bought.

The lack of new purchases led to a severe reduction in earnings for both pure-com companies and traditional marketers. Microsoft's introduction of Windows 2000 epitomized the consumer lack of interest in new products; even the promise of new European markets didn't help the underwhelming Windows 2000 launch. Chip manufacturers saw downward revenue slides as computer sales dropped, and network solution companies were faced with a corporate world that was suddenly less eager to upgrade its existing network.

Was marketing *too* good, or were the new products and upgrades just not good enough? One way or another, tech companies had to develop new and more "must-have" features to penetrate an otherwise disinterested market.

Beyond economic factors, many dot-coms—and especially pure-coms—grew so quickly that they didn't have time to develop a primary element that is vital to success: brand. The next section addresses the implications of inadequate brand development.

DISREGARDING THE BRAND BASICS

With millions of dollars of venture capital money at their disposal, many pure-com sites unveiled large-scale advertising campaigns to drive traffic to their sites. However, a combination of inexperience (on the part of both site directors and their ad agencies, who were unused to marketing to Web audiences) led most sites to waste a good portion of their money making a pitch, but not building a brand.

A **brand** (discussed at length in Chapter 8) is the promise that a Web site, company, product, or service makes to its customers. Logos (which are frequently confused for the brand) are one of the brand components, along with tag lines, colors, font styles, and other elements that serve as the basis for brand recognition. The brand itself is intangible. One of the hard lessons of marketing is that it is rare for a brand to be built over a very short period of time. Television ads, no matter how radical, innovative, or memorable cannot provide the same promise and reputation that a strategic campaign, quality products, and a simple matter of time can.

The promise itself is what consumers come to expect from the companies from which they purchase. **Nike** (www.nike.com), for example, doesn't just make sneakers; it promises comfort, style, and increased athletic performance. You might not consciously process these messages when you buy a pair of Nike hightops, but the brand message is there—innate, subconscious, and built into the product's identity.

The brand itself is, in all cases, bigger than the product or service. The brand contains the message (what consumers can expect from and associate with the company, product, or service), and it's what consumers remember and believe. However, the brand is only as strong as the product or service it represents. If the product doesn't keep the promise, or if the performance is not what's expected, the brand becomes a smokescreen that consumers will see through immediately. If you buy a pair of Nikes for $100 and watch them fall apart within a month, or if they cause blisters on your feet, you might consider it a fluke and still go and buy another pair. However, if it happens a second time, there's probably nothing that Tiger Woods or Michael Jordan can say that will make you buy another pair of Nikes. In this case, the brand did not live up to its promise, and the product performance brought the brand down.

Dot-Coms and Branding

Failure to deliver on brand promises is where many of the pure-coms went wrong. Massive amounts of money thrown at expensive advertising campaigns does not equate to brand development. Remember the Pets.com sock puppet? That campaign won practically every advertising award possible. Now Pets.com is gone, having burned through approximately $110 million, and its most valuable remaining asset is that old sock. The puppet, while cute and funny, didn't represent anything, nor did the site itself offer consumers anything that they couldn't get elsewhere (with the exception of the increased shopping convenience already inherent in the Web). Providing some unique aspect to a consumer is an important feature that any company, product, or service must have. It is known as a **unique selling position (USP)**.

Rather than spend so much money on expensive ad campaigns, many sites would have been wiser to retain their funds, spend more on shipping and distribution systems, and build site enhancements to keep visitors coming back. Sites were slow to realize that marketing to existing customers is far less expensive than trying to recruit new customers. For some sites, that lesson came too late. At the time that most of the pure-coms were receiving their funding, it seemed that the well of venture capital-sponsored good fortune would never dry up. Thus, traditional brand-building practices could be disregarded. Many start-ups behaved as if an abundance of ads to drive people to their sites was all that mattered. In time, these sites helped prove that despite all the innovations they offered, some established, well-entrenched practices could not be replaced. Customer service, public relations, a well-organized marketing strategy, uniqueness in offering, and quality of service were all part of the overall brand, and brand counted.

Brands take time to develop, and the strategy behind them needs to be long-term—not overnight. The pressure of investors and venture capitalists, an untried new medium, intense media hype, and a general lack of experience prevented pure-coms from executing traditional brand practices. Instead, they turned business development into the corporate equivalent of an Olympic sprint for profitably. Although a strong brand can't guarantee success, the lack of one can almost guarantee failure.

THE PERCEIVED FAILURE (AND MISCONCEPTION) OF BANNER ADVERTISING

To the great surprise of many advertising veterans, Web site banner advertising is more effective than its mass media counterparts. Dot-com management often needs convincing and reassurance that their advertising dollars are not going to waste in **banner ads**, the thin horizontal or vertical ads that appear at the edges of many Web pages. (Since 2001, other types of Web ads have made an appearance, but the banner ad remains the most widely used.) A majority of data available prior to 2002 seems to indicate that people recognize banner ads more often than they recognize TV ads. *Jupiter Media Metrix*, a data collection and reporting firm, reported that general consumers are over 3.5 times more likely to retain and recall the message and brand associated with a Web banner ad than with a TV commercial.

Unfortunately, although brand recognition is the real value behind banner ads (in terms of value to the marketer), many marketers new to the Web are eager to quantify advertising success by measuring **click-throughs**, which is the number of times Web site visitors click an ad to link to the advertiser's site. If the click-through rate is low (currently, click-through rates are approximately 0.5 percent), then, according to the new conventional wisdom, the banner ad campaign is not working. However, the inherent value of brand recognition builds value far beyond that of a measured click-through.

Recognition Versus Action

How often do you actually get up from your couch to buy a can of Coke because you saw an ad with a dancing polar bear? Not often, because the TV ad is not a call to action for that very moment. Rather, it's a **brand recognition effort**, which is an attempt by an advertiser to plant the brand name in your head and make you associate that brand with a feeling, lifestyle, or philosophy. The advertiser hopes that when it comes time for you to make a beverage choice, you'll choose theirs.

Now consider another kind of television commercial in which you hear this type of message: "Get 26 hit songs on two cassettes or one CD, for the low, low price of only $19.95. This item is not available in stores and will be offered for a limited time only, so call now. Credit card orders are accepted; sorry, no C.O.D.s." This type of commercial is a **call to action.** Brand isn't a component of these ads. Instead, calls to action require an immediate customer response to be successful. Enough people have to pick up the phone and order the product to offset the cost of production, distribution, and the commercial itself.

Watch enough TV and you'll notice that there are far more commercials that fall into the first category than the second. Television has survived and prospered as an industry because it is an advertising/branding medium, not a call-to-action forum. Call to action ads have their place on TV for national companies (such as the direct sale of music or specific household items that are not sold in stores) as well as for many local companies like cafés and restaurants that use (primarily) cable outlets to pitch themselves to a local audience.

If *every* TV ad was a call-to-action ad, the audience would be asked to make a new purchase with every ad that it saw. Eventually (and rather quickly), the money that the audience has to spend on impulse items (items that you buy at the spur of the moment) would be unavailable. *Some* call-to-action ads would succeed, but by and large, most would fail, and television as an advertising medium would be deemed a failure.

On the brand-recognition side of advertising, the marketing people at Anheuser-Busch really have no concrete way of knowing whether you'll ever buy a beer because of its Budweiser talking frog campaign or how much any commercial in particular has really influenced your purchasing decisions. Anheuser-Busch doesn't expect you to get up off your couch to drive to the nearest store to buy a Bud as soon as you see the commercial. Instead, its goal is to build the brand. As long as the ad does that, the ad can be considered a success. Television, as an advertising medium, enjoys the same distinction. At first, this fact seems inconsistent with one of the earlier lessons that you learned about the Web and the mass-media advertising methods used by many of the pure-com sites. Their jump to television brand-style advertising hurt them instead of helped them. How can that be, if we now are singing the praises of brand-style television ads? Later in this book, you will learn about the differences and see how different types of messages and marketing need to occur at various stages of a Web site's life.

Online advertising differs from mass media advertising in how it is quantified; it is not easy to determine the effectiveness of Web advertising as a branding medium, and it is all too easy to track the click-through rate. Because the click-through rate is low, many advertisers consequently consider online advertising to be ineffective. As you'll see in later chapters, this assumption is not necessarily true.

REVENUE MODELS

Among the several reasons for starting a Web site, the main objective is usually to make money. There are various methods to bring in revenue online, including:

- Selling advertising
- Selling information
- Selling products or services

Chapter 4 of this book outlines online revenue generation in detail, and includes coverage of some alternative means of turning a profit—few of which are plausible. Of all the methods that are used to raise money, online retail sales, known as **business-to-consumer** electronic commerce (**B2C**), comprises the largest percentage of sites.

Financially, B2C e-commerce is the most amazing of all business models. By all indications, most sites should be generating a profit by now. However, a July 2001 article in *The Industry Standard* showed that of 43 publicly traded online retailers, nine had gone under completely and 10 had been acquired from traditional marketers (in each case, the selling was done in the face of collapse). Of the remaining 24, only four had managed to squeeze out a modest profit, with one of those being the standout Web success story that is eBay. Many of the remaining 20 were, at the time of the report, warning investors that they had only enough cash on-hand to remain alive for a few more months and were requesting that the NASDAQ not delist them.

The paradox in the situation is that even in the face of widespread negativity by mass media and stock market indexes, Internet traffic has continued to rise, gaining nearly 30 percent in 2000 with almost 63 million users by the end of February 2001. Shopping has increased, too, and is consistently finding newer, higher levels. More importantly, the amount spent per order is on the rise; as of February 2001, Web shoppers were spending almost $146 per order on average, up from $107 per order at the end of 2000. At this rate, B2C e-commerce will account for nearly 4.5 percent of the U.S. gross domestic product by 2002. Yet, as *The Industry Standard* report documents, pure-com electronic commerce sites aren't showing a profit.

Online sales are obviously hot and still growing rapidly, but distribution problems often cost sites more money than anticipated, and the price they pay for each new customer may prove to be astronomical. Amazon.com is one of the few start-ups to actively seek as much if not more revenue from existing customers than from new customers. Most

1

of the sites that sought to imitate Amazon.com's business model, however, have failed or are on the verge of failing. Of the pure-com e-commerce sites that are either profitable or coming close to turning a profit, all have at least one of two things in common: they either follow eBay's model of being nothing more than facilitators of transactions (they hold no inventory and become simply the intermediary between two parties), or they service only a niche market.

SOME IDEAS JUST DON'T WORK

Merchants noticed that Amazon.com could sell books online—a *lot* of books. Somewhere, some manager theorized this: "If Amazon.com can do it with books, then surely we can make a fortune opening www.wholesalefishnetstockings.com. People will come in droves! And they'll line up to invest in us, and we'll make millions, and be featured on the cover of *Fortune* magazine for finally bringing the world what they've been waiting for—a cheap and easy way to buy fishnet stockings."

It might sound cynical, but the truth is that a lot of really, really bad ideas got funded and went public. It didn't take long for investors and the public to realize that many of these sites didn't live up to their initial potential.

Mercata.com

Shown in Figure 1-5, Mercata.com was a truly innovative Web site that spent heavily on advertising in an effort to drive traffic. The site worked off the concept of group buying, which is the idea that the more people buy a product, the lower the price becomes. You could watch the price of a Mercata item drop as shoppers from across the globe drove prices downward.

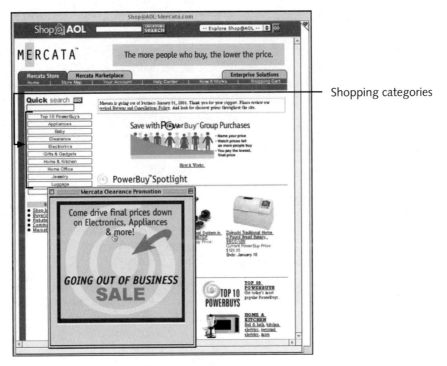

Shopping categories

Figure 1-5   Mercata.com group buying site

It sounded good in concept. Mercata had a few shortcomings, though. It was difficult or impossible to find a large enough group of shoppers who wanted to buy the latest and greatest gadget all at the same time. Another problem was that nobody wanted to be the person who bought the first product. It was better to wait until somebody *else* made the first move and then take advantage of the resulting lower price. Mercata.com closed its site at the end of January 2001.

PNV.com

Illustrated in Figure 1-6, PNV.com was a portal site for truckers. Apparently the makers of this site didn't realize that you can't surf the Web by plugging a laptop into a vehicle's cigarette lighter.

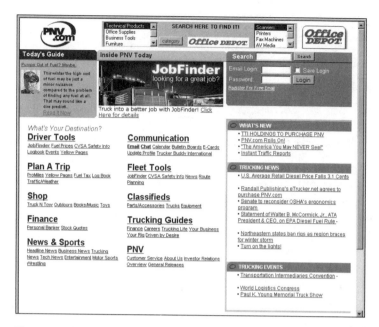

Figure 1-6   PNV.com—a portal for truckers

HaggleZone.com

HaggleZone.com was a great site to play in. Unfortunately, it was no fun for shopping, which was its intended purpose. Visitors would choose the product that they wanted to buy. Then, they would select a salesperson to buy it from, choosing from among a few icons of people's faces. There was really no difference between them, except in the way that they looked. Buyers then were asked how much they wanted to pay for the item they were purchasing. You could name any price that you wanted. For a top-of-the-line DVD player, you might offer $10. The salesperson would respond with a text message, something along the lines of this: "You're kidding, right? Look, I like you, so I'll give you the DVD player for just $400." The buyer then offered $30, and got a similar response, but this time the site came down a few more dollars. This would go on for a while until the buyer and salesperson came to an agreement. It was really very cute—the first time. Customers found the process irritating in the long run.

Other Ideas Whose Time Never Came

The stream of outlandish ideas never ends, as illustrated by the following list of pure-coms that are either having trouble or have gone out of business:

- Refer.com: Online referral service.
- Driveway.com: Another in a slew of online file management sites, Driveway stood apart because it had a really bad name.

- Stamps.com: Stamps over the Internet.

- AllAdvantage.com: One of many "pyramid schemes that tries to pass for legitimate business" companies.

- PersonalGenie.com: Marketers of "wish-fulfillment" technology; reading the site just one more time still doesn't explain what the site does.

- QuickDot.com: E-mail, instant messenger, and the other "best ways to stay in touch" didn't do anything more than AOL did years ago, and AOL did it better.

In any industry, there are ideas that seemed great at the outset, but that failed to have any real staying power. Some ideas are so bad that people look back and scratch their heads in wonder. Every industry has seen its share of bad ideas. In this instance, at least, the New Economy showed itself to be surprisingly similar to the Old Economy—something New Economy players found dismaying.

UNFORESEEN ISSUES IN ELECTRONIC COMMERCE

As the Web has slowly gained commercial success, a few economic theories became popular among site developers and marketers:

- If you build it, they will come.

- The Web lets small players compete equally with the monster corporations.

- Getting into a Web business is relatively cheap.

Not surprisingly, not one of these early "Webisms" proved true. You can build it, sure, but they won't come unless you advertise. Advertising costs money that keeps the small players from competing with the big budget sites. Lastly, from the site developers' perspective, there is almost no aspect of the Internet that is cheap for companies trying to make money. Warehouses, inventories, personnel, and marketing efforts all add up to a hefty cost of doing business, and that's before the most fundamental cost of the site is taken into consideration: the site itself. Creation, maintenance, upgrades, and other components of a major, publicly funded site takes more than two programmers in a garage (even if the site may have started that way).

The Web Got Ahead of Itself

During the 1999 pure-com boom, it was generally believed that online purchases would quickly account for a significant percentage of all retail sales. In fact, as of the first quarter of 2001, online sales accounted for only about 1 percent of all retail sales.[1]

For 2000, first-time Web shoppers outpaced experienced online buyers in terms of both numbers and average dollars spent. This can be interpreted to mean that experienced buyers are not making repeat purchases on the Web.

[1] Source: *The Washington Post*, Sept. 4, 2001.

As stated earlier in this chapter, Americans are consumption-happy. So why weren't we ready to do more Web business? The reasons are myriad, but there are three main issues at play:

- Poor service and high prices
- Too much to choose from
- Inconsistent technology

Poor Service and High Prices

From shopping carts that were difficult to use to forms that were too long to fill out (or required information that users did not want to provide, such as home phone numbers), many sites did not provide the convenience necessary to make users give up the benefits of going to an actual store.

More alarmingly, 45 percent of U.S. shoppers abandoned their shopping cart before the final purchase, due to high shipping costs.[2] Conversely, 55 percent of online shoppers have said that free shipping would entice them to visit a site more often.

To be fair, many sites have been forced to charge high shipping costs due to the popularity of **spider sites**. A spider site, such as **MySimon.com**, searches the Web for user-defined products and provides a list of the sites that offer the lowest price for that product. To be listed on these sites, many e-tailers lowered the prices of the products they carry—often below a level of profitability. They try to make up the loss by charging higher shipping fees. Some sites, such as Amazon.com, offer specials and promotions, reducing shipping costs for purchases over a certain level. But not all sites do that, and those that do still have trouble turning a profit on those purchases.

Increasingly, many sites are offering 24-hour, toll-free customer support to put a live person at the Web shopper's disposal. This is a step in the right direction to combat the criticism that Web retailers have received in terms of service.

Too Many Choices

Is more always better? Not always. Go to any hardware store or Home Depot to find a shower head. You'll probably find yourself standing in front of a shelf, choosing from about a dozen different products. Now go online and look for shower heads. There are hundreds of them. Who needs that kind of selection? Overwhelmingly, buyers have turned away from an excess of choice, abandoning their intended purchase because of "selection fatigue." Shoppers have become accustomed to having retail stores narrow down the choices for them. It will take some time to get used to having every last product available at the click of a button.

Site navigation and the ability to better confine a search for increased convenience are issues that e-tailers will need to deal with for Web sales to increase. Chapter 6 covers navigation in depth.

[2] Source: *CyberAtlas.*

Technology Discrepancies

As the Web gained commercial popularity in the mid-1990s, people accessed the Internet with what were then the primary options: 9.6-kilobytes-per-second (Kps) or 14.4-bps telephone modems. Those rates were slow relative to what people have since gotten used to, but sites were simpler then.

As Web use exploded, Web users diverged into two groups: people using the Web at work and people using it at home. The gap in connection speeds between the two locations has grown into a veritable chasm. In fact, of the 122 million Americans who have Web access from their homes, only 3.1 million have high-speed DSL or better Internet connectivity. Modems of 36.6 bps are still the average connectivity tool for home users.[3] At the same time, business users are more accustomed to faster connection technologies, such as ISDN, DSL, and T1 or T3 lines. Site designers, although designing for both markets, create sites intended for users with higher bandwidths (faster connections), which offer more development flexibility.

Now that we have examined consumer-oriented issues related to Web retailing, we will investigate the role of traditional business in the evolving Web marketplace.

ENTER THE EXPERIENCED BUSINESS PLAYERS

While the start-ups were dominating the Web world, investors, journalists and interested businesspeople looked at the established companies and wondered why they were barely visible in the online world. Although in retrospect many were far smarter to wait it out, at the time when pure-coms were getting tens of millions of capital dollars for what promised to be a commerce revolution, the established marketers seemed to have been caught snoozing. **Barnes & Noble** and **ToysRUs**, long-established brands and retailers, should have been the immediate, undisputed Web leaders in their categories, but each came in a distant second to start-ups **Amazon.com** and eToys.com, respectively. And where were **Wal-Mart** and **Kmart** and all the print catalog players that could have used the Web to their advantage? The big players suddenly became dinosaurs. Stodgy old corporations didn't understand the Internet, and they couldn't compete with the creative wizards who were the new stars of Wall Street.

 At the height of the Internet craze, I personally spoke at dozens of seminars, criticizing the established marketers for not jumping on the bandwagon sooner.

Maybe these old-timers knew something. In the rubble of start-up collapse, the Internet horizon boasts a new landscape. The old dinosaurs are gaining momentum through the same slow-and-sure brand-building techniques that led to their offline success. Their established brands and larger coffers provided many advantages that the pure-coms didn't have.

[3]*Jupiter Media Metrix*

Brand Loyalty and an Established Market

The most important factor in the online success of the established retailers is that traditional businesses enjoy brands that have penetrated consumer's consciousness over the course of decades, not just months. That brand recognition brings with it a high level of trust. After experiencing poor service and slow shipping times from dot-com retailers during the 1999 holiday season, consumers shied away from unknowns and sought more solid ground. They found that solid ground with the established companies, and the established companies delivered.

The integration of a dot-com address with the established firms' brick-and-mortar sites only added to consumer trust. If you are going to buy an electronics item, will you buy it from HaggleZone.com, an unknown company, or from **CircuitCity.com**, which has actual stores you can visit if you are unhappy with your online purchase? As more and more people are factoring in post-purchase satisfaction with their desire to shop on the Web, users are gravitating to the traditional marketers. Ideas and good intentions just can't compete with experience and strong branding.

Deeper Pockets

As discussed already in this chapter, many of the pure-coms are running out of money. The inability to turn a profit, coupled with sinking stock values and reduced marketing budgets, has caused such a strain on the pure-coms that many won't survive for more than a few months.

A few of the traditional marketers have succumbed to a dropping economy. Northeast discount chain Bradlees went under at the end of 2000, closing all of its stores, as did the large mid-Atlantic supermarket chain Grand Union. Most significantly, 128-year-old Montgomery Ward closed its doors in 2000, unable to compete in a new economy for which it never prepared. Although a few traditional marketers have closed up shop along with many of the pure-coms, those failures are the exceptions. Wal-Mart, Kmart, Staples, and others have launched dot-com operations, but they can rely on more traditional resources of revenue to weather any storm. In some cases, the dot-com addresses of the traditional marketers have been thriving, helping to compensate where the brick-and-mortar revenues have lacked. The diversification of revenue and a longer history of earnings has provided the "dinosaurs" with the cash that the upstarts lack.

Distribution Facilities and Experience

EToys.com made its first major blunder during the 1999 holiday season when it failed to deliver merchandise to thousands of customers who were expecting orders in time for Christmas morning. The leading online toy retailer found itself the ridiculed subject of news articles in which the media focused on the kids who woke up to no gifts at Christmas. A year later, the addition of two gigantic (and very expensive) warehouses for inventory and delivery weren't enough to overcome the ghost of Christmas past; shoppers avoided the eToys.com site during the 2000 holiday season, making it the site's last season of operation. EToys.com closed up shop in 2001. The eToys.com name is still around, however. The eToys name, the site's most valuable remaining asset, was purchased in 2001 by K-B Toys.

Other pure-coms have run into similar trouble. Even Amazon.com, with its multiple facilities, can't seem to optimize distribution. By sending the wrong product to the wrong customer, or more often, by sending multiple items in separate packages but only charging one shipping price, it's estimated that Amazon.com loses about $2.30 per order.

Established marketers like **Circuit City**, **Barnes & Noble**, and **JCPenney** streamlined their distribution processes years ago. Some of these have already experienced tremendous success as catalog merchants, so for them, selling over the Web was just a way to reduce printing costs, not a whole new experience. (In the case of JCPenney, online success is coming in the wake of many brick-and-mortar locations closing.) The Web learning curve is far smaller for these businesses than for start-ups, as is the financial investment, giving the traditional marketers a significant advantage.

Although there is no way to prove it, I'd take an educated guess that if the introduction had been the other way around, with the traditional marketers entering the Web scene first, they might not have fared so well. People love an underdog, and the Web was (or so people thought) an environment where newcomers could compete on an equal field with the big players. The fact that many pure-coms collapsed on their own has turned the established marketers into saviors rather than oppressors.

Easier, Less Expensive Marketing Avenues

Established companies already have marketing dollars worked into their annual budgets as they continue brand awareness campaigns. Integrating a Web component into that budget becomes a campaign enhancement, rather than a standalone project for those companies. Further, mailing lists of established customers already exist. Older brands can parlay these lists into Web traffic.

Brick-and-mortar locations are aggressively used to lead audiences to their affiliated Web sites. Walk into any Barnes & Noble café and you will see multiple instances of the bn.com URL address, as well as special discounts offered only on its site.

WHAT'S IN THE FUTURE?

Technology plays a huge role in the success or failure of Web businesses. When it comes to technology, and the Internet in particular, a week can be equal to a lifetime. New products can be introduced and new markets developed in a fraction of the time of traditional markets. The best minds in business have tried to predict the future. Some made millions while others went broke. In the 1980s, no one could have predicted the speed with which technology developed. At best, we can use past and current events to paint a likely picture of the Internet world that lies ahead. The one universal truth that we can safely assume is that the Web will only get bigger and better. It just won't take the path that most people expected it to.

Beyond that somewhat obvious assumption, what else can we hypothesize about the Web's future? How will future Web developers, programmers, and marketers survive in the coming years? More than survive, how will they *succeed*? What current problems will be solved, and what new hurdles will appear? The next four sections take a stab at anticipating what's in store for the Web.

Hype Will be Replaced by Substance

In the early craze of Web development, wacky ideas became multimillion-dollar enterprises for overenthusiastic investors. The speed and accessibility of media reports fueled this modern revolution. As the hype of the Internet and the frenzy over pure-com start-ups has faded, only the strongest and best in a category survive. The shake-up has left investors skeptical about Internet profitability, and few will be ready to jump on a new public stock offering just because it has "dot com" after its name.

In place of the frenzy will be stronger, more reliable Web businesses with clear, manageable business models. If the profitable sites are not owned by traditional marketers, they will likely be funded by them or affiliated with them. Partnerships similar to the **ToysRUs/Amazon** affiliation, developed for the 2000 holiday season, will be the standard.

The ToyRUs/Amazon partnership marked a potential turning point in Web marketing. Both companies were a little beaten up as a result of mishandling deliveries during the 1999 holiday shopping season. (ToysRUs, although receiving bad press, was not punished by consumers like eToys.com was, largely due to the former's long-established brand identity.) This partnership had each company doing what it excelled at, with Amazon.com taking orders and ToysRUs filling the orders.

In addition, shoppers will have more options for using both a retailer's Web site as well as its brick-and-mortar location. These electronic and physical presences will work together more frequently for service, support, ease of product return, and so on.

Convenience Will Increase While Prices Will Decrease

Web sites must—and will—introduce increasingly creative methods for providing online customer service. Whether it be through real-time chat sessions, 24-hour phone access, faster e-mail response rates, or even dedicated help desks at cobranded brick-and-mortar retail locations, Web businesses will develop dramatic improvements in how they serve their clientele.

At the same time, Web developers will not want to see their market reduce as price buyers shrug off convenience factors for lower brick-and-mortar prices. Through more and better-advertised specials, cobranded agreements, and better internal distribution practices, e-tailers will quickly find a way to reduce shipping costs and pass those savings along to valuable customers. This cost reduction will not only bring back the disenchanted, but also help recruit new Web shoppers as well.

Increasing Business-to-Business Commerce

The continued growth of the Web will be fueled by an expanding business-to-business segment (discussed in detail in Chapter 2). Companies will continue to include value-added Web provisions into their corporate revenue models. Devoted to servicing the business sector, these **business-to-business** electronic commerce sites (or **B2Bs**) understand the value of time-saving convenience over high art and site complexity, and they will be the solid foundation on which Web growth will be based.

Merging Old and New Technologies

The bandwidth discrepancies between home and business Web users will reduce, but the change will occur more slowly than users might wish. Regulation and government incentive will eventually push local phone and cable companies into providing faster residential connections at attractive prices. Cable resources, and the inevitable integration of TV and the Internet, will bring newer, more engaging advertising possibilities for marketers.

Consider a television show like *Seinfeld*: Far from being a show about "nothing," this show was about everything—everything that could be sold, at least. In practically every episode, viewers watched Jerry and the gang in his apartment as he paraded past boxes of Honeycombs cereal, Milton Bradley board games, and Superman figurines. The show was, in essence, one big product placement.

As TV and the Internet converge, and as products like TiVo catch on (TiVo is a continuous recording system, allowing viewers to pause live TV and bypass commercials with the touch of a button), television will look a lot more like *Seinfeld*. Product advertising will take the form of in-show placements rather than standard 30-second spots.

Product placement will become a popular advertising vehicle, and it won't stop at just showing the product on screen. In the future, as Jerry walks past his box of Honeycombs, a viewer will be able to push a button on his or her remote control or keyboard and go directly to the Post Web site, where he or she can browse for more information or order the special Honeycomb box with the *Seinfeld* cast on the front.

This integration, while exciting, will bring more than just new possibilities. It will bring veritable nightmares for Web designers, who will be forced to design for both TV screens *and* computer monitors. Designers who suffered through the introduction of Microsoft Internet Explorer (IE) will remember the headaches that accompanied designing for both Netscape Navigator and IE. Compared to designing for both TV and computer, the Netscape/IE problems will seem like a weekend at Club Med.

CHAPTER SUMMARY

❑ The rise, fall, and uncertainty of business on the Internet is enough to make anyone just a little motion sick. As the Web comes of age and the shakeout leaves many of the original players dead and forgotten, the financial world is learning a few lessons about the Web and the New Economy. The stock market has become a part of common culture, and fortunes rise and fall with popular opinion. Financial markets lost faith in pure-coms that took too long to show a profit, leaving the pure-coms strapped for cash with nowhere else to turn for financing. This situation, combined with Federal Reserve actions and diminishing consumer innovations for increased spending, brought the tech market crashing down in late 2000.

❑ Dot-coms are changing before our eyes. Traditional marketers are making a big splash on the Web, leveraging their established brand identity, deeper financial pockets, and easier marketing avenues for better Web potential. The Web will become a haven for traditional marketers, as business-to business-sites become more popular.

❑ For the consumer, the differences between shopping on the Web versus traditional retail operations include the immediate satisfaction, privacy, and pricing advantages offered by the latter. The most important factor—increased convenience—ultimately, will drive the success of Web sales. Increased customer convenience will need to be enhanced to compensate for high shipping costs as the dot-coms make their way into the next phase of development.

KEY TERMS

banner ad
brand
brand recognition effort
brick-and-mortar store
business-to-business electronic commerce (B2B)
business-to-consumer electronic commerce (B2C)
call to action
click-through
day trading
dot-com
electronic commerce (e-commerce)
e-tailer
New Economy
Old Economy
production house
pure-com

spider site
unique selling position (USP)
Web start-up

REVIEW QUESTIONS

1. Tech companies such as Lucent Technologies saw their earnings and profits drop in 2000 partially because _____.

    a. competition became fierce, driving hardware prices down

    b. failing and cash-strapped pure-coms weren't paying old bills or buying more products

    c. poor internal management led to weaker sales

    d. they poured millions into their own Web sites that never turned a profit

2. List three reasons why traditional marketers have a better chance of survival than do pure-coms.

3. The establishment of a meaningful brand typically takes _____.

    a. more money than time

    b. more time than money

    c. more television ads than print ads

    d. a really cool logo

4. From the mid-1900s to the late 1900s, the number of American households that were invested in the stock market _____.

    a. doubled

    b. remained steady

    c. rose to approximately half

    d. rose to approximately 80 percent

5. In the New Economy, high stock prices equate to _____.

    a. high consumer confidence

    b. high interest rates

    c. high unemployment rates

    d. All of the above.

6. Many of the pure-coms and tech companies are (or were) listed on the _____ exchange.

1

7. In the future, it's likely that Web commerce will be dominated by
   _____.

   a. pure-coms

   b. government agencies

   c. traditional marketers

   d. No one group will dominate.

8. What is the primary reason that price shoppers at B2C sites often abandon their purchases?

9. Successful banner advertising on the Internet is typically measured in
   _____.

   a. number of visitor views

   b. number of survey respondents who claim to recognize an ad

   c. percentage of visitors who click-through

   d. number of minutes visitors stay on the site

10. One of the fastest growing segments on the Web has been _____.

    a. B2B

    b. B2C

    c. sports sites

    d. banner ad placement sites

11. Recent banner ad click-through rates are approximately _____.

    a. 5 percent

    b. 2.5 percent

    c. 1.5 percent

    d. .5 percent

12. It is likely that many pure-coms will not survive in the long run, partly because
    _____.

    a. they are running out of products to sell

    b. the bandwidth discrepancy between work and home has hurt their markets

    c. with stock prices down, they are running out of cash

    d. the cost of doing business continues to escalate.

13. Describe one of the primary reasons that Web commerce became popular so quickly.

14. One of the surprising aspects of the New Economy is that _____.

    a. unemployment rates have been largely unaffected by the slumping economy

    b. venture capital is easy to come by

    c. global oil prices are inversely related to American interest rates

    d. fewer families are invested in the stock market

HANDS-ON PROJECTS

1. This chapter describes some Web sites that were questionable ideas from the start. Do some online research and find three business sites that you believe are conceptually unsound. List the URL of each site and write a paragraph explaining why you think each site is lacking.

2. Examine three of the following eight Web sites:

   www.pepsi.com

   www.sony.com

   www.dominos.com

   www.tonka.com

   www.hersheys.com

   www.nabisco.com

   www.levi.com

   www.nytimes.com

   Each of the eight sites has done a good job of providing a brand message that is consistent with its brick-and-mortar counterpart. Write a paragraph for each of the three sites you selected. In each paragraph, explain the following:

   ▫ The promise conveyed by the company's brand

   ▫ Visual similarities between the online and brick-and-mortar images

   ▫ Ways in which the Web site provides brand messages that go above and beyond those provided by the brick-and-mortar images

3. You are the CEO of Superworld, a Wal-Mart-like discount merchandiser. You believe it is time for your company to develop a Web presence. What are the three top challenges faced by Superworld in developing a Web site? Write a total of 500 words briefly explaining these challenges.

2

TYPES OF WEB SITES

In this chapter, you will learn about:

♦ Determining your Web site's purpose

♦ The two primary categories of business Web sites

♦ Brochure, account management, content, and direct gain Web sites

♦ Differences between Web business and traditional business

♦ Advantages and disadvantages of integrating traditional businesses and the Web

♦ Target audiences and their impact on site construction

Now that you are familiar with the ups and downs of the Web economy and probabilities for what lies ahead, we need to take a close look at exactly how sites differ from one another. Everything that you'll do for your site—from your site development team to the way you market it—will rely on the type of site that you are building.

Chapter 2 explores the different types of sites, emphasizing the impact that a site's content and purpose have on its development. You then will learn about target audiences and examine the factors that make a Web business different from a traditional business.

GETTING STARTED: TAKING YOUR IDEA LIVE

It is easy to confuse a Web site for a business, but a site is not the business itself. The business *runs* the Web site, and it handles any legal issues, marketing issues, investor relations, personnel problems, and other daily chores associated with running a company. A site, especially a pure-com Web site, is rarely the product of an idea and a few hours of programming time. (Although this has happened successfully on occasion, it is not the standard operating procedure.)

There are many things that need to get done just to get the business started. Even before handling the tedious, standard-issue chores such as getting the corporation legally registered, coming up with a name (as well as a domain name for the site), setting up a bank account, and so on, you need to develop an idea, an objective, and a needs assessment, which includes a business plan. These three tasks are outlined next.

Honing the Idea

Coming up with an idea is not as easy as it may sound. If the site being developed is for an established marketer, the idea is already there: the company's products and services will be presented on the Web. Even if the company in question is a very small company—say a five-person shop that designs and distributes its own greeting cards—it may decide that it might make more money by either adding a Web site or moving the entire business onto the Web and selling directly to end consumers instead of selling to stores. Either way, the idea was already there—it came from the already-established business.

If the business is not already established—in other words, if you are launching a pure-com—the road is a bit tougher. You need to develop an idea for the site that can both fill a need in the market and make a profit. Ordinarily, an idea for a site comes from information or talents that the developer already has. For example, if you happen to be a talented basketball player, you might develop a site that provides tips on becoming a better player, as well as in-depth looks at some of the professional players in the sport. A site that relies on your expertise makes a lot more sense than a site that offers, for example, travel tips when you have, in fact, no unique knowledge in that area.

The site subject should be one that the developer not only feels he or she knows better than most people, but also that fills a need in the market. For example, if you find that Michael Jordan already has a site that provides free information on becoming a better basketball player, there may not be a need for any more information on that topic from any other players. After all, who is better able to give advice on the subject than the greatest player of modern times?

Defining Your Site's Objective

The obvious purpose of building any type of business site is to make money. But that's not enough in terms of a vision. There are many other goals to take into consideration.

Do you have dreams of growing the company into a huge corporation that will one day fight its way into the Fortune 500, or is the company not intended for growth at all? Are you looking for it to just bring in a steady income? Maybe the goal is simply to be the biggest or most well known within a particular niche industry, or maybe the company is to be built with a goal of earning a quick profit and sold within a couple years. Depending upon what the ultimate goal is (and the goal may change over time), the site and the company may be developed to reflect that goal. For example, a company that wants to grow and have long-term staying power may conserve its funds and grow slowly, allowing its brand to develop over time, while the company that is looking to be attractive enough to sell itself to a larger company may pour more money into marketing for a quick profit.

Needs Assessment

What your site needs in terms of resources ultimately depends on its objective. Resources can include designers, developers, marketing, inventory, and content. And that's just for the site. That doesn't include any office space, salaries, supplies, and so on, for the business. All of this takes money.

The amount of money you will need depends on your ultimate goal as well as your ability to raise funds. You can form a company and a Web site on a **shoe-string budget** (which is a very low amount of money). For example, many small companies are formed and run right out of the owner's home. But not every site can be run out of a basement. B2C retail sites intended for growth and meant for general audiences will need warehousing, distribution, and other features, just as an online magazine, or **e-zine**, will need reporters or some other source of updated content. If that is the case, it is not unlikely that millions of dollars will be needed to get the project up and running—as stakes and goals go up, so does the price tag. Marketing alone can cost millions just to drive people to the site, with even more dollars needed to build a safe and secure site, to house the site, to hire and retain the right employees, and so on.

Companies that are seeking high levels of funding need a **business plan**, which outlines the site concept, market, anticipated revenue structure, marketing, strategy, and technology plans. Although all companies should have at least a rudimentary business plan, it is an absolute necessity for a company seeking outside funding. Typically, companies seek outside funding either from banks, in the form of loans or investments, or from venture capitalists. **Venture capitalists** provide the financing that is needed for growth. They furnish money in various phases, known as **rounds**, as needed. In return, the venture capitalists usually take a large share of stock in the company, possibly hold a seat on the board of directors, and expect to see a plan for the company to **go public** (become listed on one of the major stock indexes so that their shares can be traded on the open market) within a relatively short amount of time. By going public, venture capitalists can sell their shares on the open market for (hopefully) significantly more than they paid for them, while at the same time the company can sell some of its shares on the open market to receive additional funding from individual or institutional investors.

The business plan needs to outline and highlight the important aspects of the company and the Web site, as well as the finest details regarding the site's purpose, what it will provide or sell, what need it fills in the market, what kind of audience it can expect to gain, what competitors it expects to have, how the site intends to acquire and retain an audience, and the timeframe under which it expects to turn a profit. This latter point is the most important, culminating in a spreadsheet that (usually) shows three-year projections for expenditures (a plan of how you will spend the venture capitalist's money) compared with revenue growth. Although it's seldom admitted out loud, three-year projections for a start-up pure-com company are hardly worth the paper they are typed on. There are few ways to accurately estimate three years' worth of expenditures and revenues in a media that is still brand new and with market conditions so volatile. Considering the state of many publicly traded pure-coms, it is safe to say that few of them accurately predicted their three-year forecasts. The business plan may range from as few as 10 pages to as many as a few hundred, and typically, it is written by a business consultancy that has experience with the business plan procedure. Although there are variations, most business plans contain the following information:

- **Executive summary**: A summation or overview of what the company and its associated Web site will do and how the company anticipates growth.

- **Market overview**: A review of market conditions, including market size and the life cycle (anticipated duration of prosperous times and slow growth periods within the market).

- **Service**: A description of the Web site, including highlights of any specialized sections, explanation of how it will serve the market, what it will do, and what opportunities there may be for growth and future expansion. This area needs to detail the reasons why users would come to the site and, even more importantly, why they would come back.

- **Revenue streams**: A description of how the site intends to generate revenue, whether from B2C retail sales, banner ad sales, other means, or a combination thereof. Investors will need to know exactly how the site intends to earn money so that they can be sure of a positive return on investment. Expansion opportunities for increased revenue in the future are also explored in this section.

- **Company**: A review of the company, including its **mission statement** (a brief statement of the company's goal and what it stands for), its current status (whether the company is already in existence and is looking for funding to advance to the next level), and biographies of the executive team. Most companies, regardless of how many employees they have, live or die by the experience and decisions of a few key figures. Investors want to feel confident in their abilities.

- **Strategic plan**: An explanation of how the company intends to compete with any similar companies vying for the same market, what makes it unique, how it will position itself, and what type of phased-in development plans it has to introduce future growth.

- **Marketing plan**: Although full marketing details may not be known at the time that the business plan is drafted, many investors will want at least a few broad statements outlining how the company plans to bring the site to market. This section addresses online marketing, radio, TV or print advertising campaigns, public relations campaigns, and any other promotions. The marketing plan describes how the brand is to be built, as well as the geographic target area for the marketing launch. (Advertising does not always happen on a national level. It may first be introduced in a few key geographical areas.)

- **Technology plan**: A review of the technology—programming and equipment—that will be needed and used to make the site work, as well as the efforts that will be made for fulfillment. This includes automated systems for product tracking, packaging and delivery of product, and so on. For a content-only site, this may mean a review of how new information will be obtained and quickly posted on the site on a regular basis.

- **Financial section**: This final area provides a spreadsheet that itemizes all anticipated costs and revenues, typically over each of the next three years. Current market conditions and any relevant historical data are used as a basis for these estimations.

Once the business plan is written, you present it to people and companies who may be in the position to provide funding. You use any funding attained to get the company and the site started or grown beyond its current point.

GENERAL TYPES OF WEB SITES

Although there are seemingly endless ideas and products offered on the Web, nearly all sites can be grouped into just a few broad categories and subcategories. Chapter 1 focused mostly on retail, or B2C sites, with particular emphasis on cyber retailing to general consumers by pure-com sites, but there are many other types of sites. Figure 2-1 shows the breakdown of the types of sites that exist on the Web.

The three top-tier site categories are as follows:

- **Business sites**: Business sites are created either as entities unto themselves, such as a pure-com, in which the Web is the only or original source of business, or are created by an established company.

- **Information/help sites**: Some sites, usually organizations with a .org domain name suffix, simply provide relevant information to interested readers. Government sites that guide you through tax forms, nonprofit sites that give information just for the taking, and other sites that exist to provide a public service without anything expected in return can be found all over the Web. Figure 2-2 shows an employee overview page from the site for the New Jersey Job Bank. A potential employee creates the page using an online form, and the page is fairly typical for an information/help site in that it is very simple and utilitarian. These sites typically lack complex navigation, interesting graphics, or enhanced interactivity. Black text on a white background with blue, underlined hyperlinks is the standard. Lack of budget and specific audience needs are the usual reasons for the starkness of these sites.

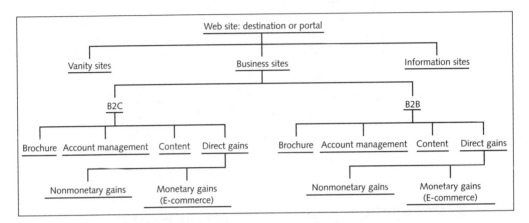

Figure 2-1   Types of Web sites

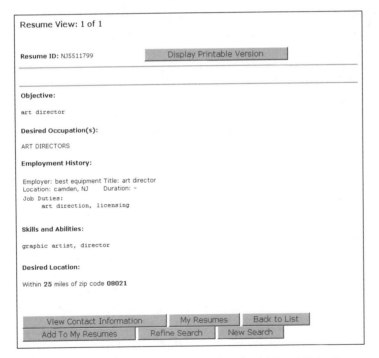

Figure 2-2   The New Jersey Job Bank information Web site

- **Vanity/hobby sites**: As the name implies, these are sites built by people who want to display pictures from their family vacation, post their resumes for potential employers, create an online chat room just for fun, and that sort of thing. Figure 2-3 shows a vanity site from AOL's personal home page area that includes poetic musings and pictures of the site owner's cars. This type of site has no business purpose and is almost always set up by a novice programmer. The spelling errors on the page are evidence of the amateur nature of the site. These sites typically have an excess of graphics and animations, poor layout, and a lack of refinement.

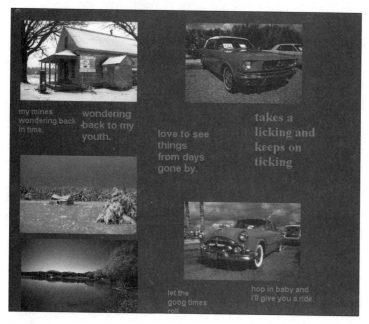

Figure 2-3 A vanity Web site

Because this text focuses on the business of Web sites, this chapter will cover only the business Web site category.

BUSINESS SITES

If you study Figure 2-1, you will notice that the B2B and B2C categories have identical subcategories. The content, layout, and the audience may differ within each category. The next section explains the B2B and B2C categories and some of the differences between them.

Unlike the dot-com sites of established marketers, pure-com Web sites have a virtually blank canvas upon which to create. You create a pure-com's brand around its site design and structure, as it would appeal to the target market (covered later in this chapter). Traditional, established marketers, however, do not have such a luxury. To remain consistent with their established brand image, they need to create their site in such a way as to remain true to their existing brand. For example, a fine art gallery known for its use of white space and sophistication would damage its overall brand with a bright yellow Web site with big green letters and a link to some cool interactive games. Similarly, a company known offline for its impeccable service would hurt its reputation if the site were not implicitly easy to navigate and had poor customer service attributes (examined in detail in Chapter 12). The pure-com companies don't have established brand awareness, but they also don't have the limitations that traditional marketers face when designing and developing a site.

Business-To-Business Web Sites

B2Bs are one of the fastest growing segments on the Web. Recall from Chapter 1 that among the predictions for the future was that the Web will be dominated by B2B sites. This it not a particularly tough prediction to make, when you consider that:

- Web users spend significantly more time online at work (on average, 21 hours per month) than they spend online at home (on average, 10 hours per month).[1]

- Internet connectivity is significantly faster in the workplace than it is in the home.

- 90 percent of electronic commerce conducted in 1999 involved B2B sites. In 2000, B2B sites generated revenues of $433 billion,[2] whereas B2C electronic commerce generated $38 billion in revenue that year.[3]

Figure 2-4 shows the revenue generated by B2B sites and B2C sites for 2000, alongside predictions for 2005.

The chart projects a dramatic rise for B2B earnings. While the overall revenue generated from B2B sites is vastly outpacing that of their B2C counterparts, the average sale price in a B2B transaction is much higher than the average sale price of a B2C purchase, because businesses are purchasing networks, steel, and other high-ticket items—not the latest Stephen King novel. Still, we can't ignore the significance and potential in the B2C sector.

Companies have started to realize that far from being an artistic canvas, the Web is a tool that can be used for time and money savings and for corporate benefits. e-STEEL.com, shown in Figure 2-5, is a Web site that caters to corporations buying large quantities of raw steel.

Businesses such as Ford Motor Company can use this site as a resource to check prices, read industry news, or place large orders to realize price reductions. Because it's on the Web, anybody can get to the site (although access is limited without registration), but there is little for the casual Web surfer to do there.

[1]Source: *Nielsen/NetRatings.*

[2]Source: *E-Commerce Times*, June 22, 2001.

[3]Source: *PC World*, Sept. 25, 2001.

2

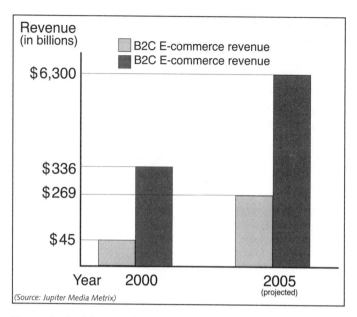

Figure 2-4   Disparity between B2B and B2C electronic commerce revenue

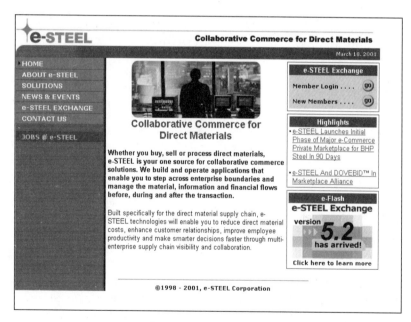

Figure 2-5   e-STEEL.com corporate business-to-business Web site

Because most B2B sites deal with corporate decision makers who race through life at the speed of the modern world, many of these sites have led the way in the recent design revolution toward simplicity and understatement. Although these sites are not completely devoid of design and art, aesthetics play a less important role than do navigation and ease of information gathering. In terms of design, however, most B2B sites, especially those with operations outside the cyber world, take special care to keep the site consistent with their existing brand identities. B2B sites usually offer fewer opportunities for the visitor to be sidetracked, because the company behind the site is respectful of its customers and their time. The sites, however, often go out of their way to provide information that would be useful to their visitors, even if that information has nothing to do with the message of the site itself. A corporate architectural firm, for example, might provide timely stock updates or weather reports on the home page of the site. This type of information is fairly cheap to include, although sites have to be careful not to overdo it.

From a sales perspective, a B2B site faces specific challenges. Depending on what it is selling, and to whom it is selling (other businesses, distributors, or retailers), the B2B site must be prepared to accept and fill orders ranging from small shipments to huge crates to complete an order. Increased business from the site may require more and better distribution equipment and a specialized staff to help fill orders.

Business-to-Consumer Web Sites

B2C sites seem to be in the limelight more often than their B2B cousins. B2C sites sell directly to the end consumer—you, me, and the masses who spend money on products, services, information, and entertainment. These sites typically have larger audiences than B2B sites due to a broader market appeal. Although the revenue generated from B2B sites is significantly greater than what B2C sites generate, B2C sites spend more in terms of overall marketing. This trend is expected to continue, as illustrated in Figure 2-6. Although the spending gap will narrow, real dollars spent will continue to be greater for B2C sites as they struggle to claim a portion of Web users' shopping dollars.

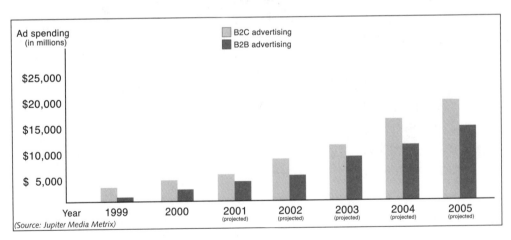

Figure 2-6   Total ad spending by category

The next sections describe the four site categories that are common to B2B and B2C Web sites.

Brochure Sites

Brochure sites are typically **static**, meaning they do not change on a regular basis and do not allow visitors to make direct purchases. Reading a static site is much like reading the electronic version of a printed brochure, with levels of interactivity ranging from none at all to a complex searchable catalog or sales office locator. The content on the site is not likely to change much or often, and regular repeat traffic is unlikely and usually unnecessary. Typically, the main purpose of the brochure site is one of the following:

- To generate an e-mail or a phone call from the site visitor so that a sales or service representative can follow up with him or her

- To maintain the comfort level of existing customers through online offerings, such as product specifications, warnings, uses, guarantees, or account status

- To alleviate some of the time constraints on human employees by answering common questions online

B2B Brochure Sites

Figure 2-7 shows the Web site for **ASCO** (www.ascovalve.com/home/main_frameset.htm). Although the site is relatively large in terms of pages and searchable catalogs, it exists primarily to generate interest in its products. In addition, it relies on human interaction to close the sale. In the future, this site will add a bulletin board system for engineer support and an online chat area for daily customer service. It's unlikely, however, that this site will ever offer the ability for end users to make direct purchases, although it is conceivable that the company may eventually allow its distributors to order inventory through the site. (Allowing the end-users of ASCO's products to make direct purchases would undermine its network of independent distributors, which could be financially disastrous, not to mention contractually illegal.)

Figure 2-8 shows another brochure site, this time for **Yukon Graphics** (www.yukon-graphics.com), a small but successful print shop in northern New Jersey. A much smaller company than ASCO, this site is a bit more typical of what you'd expect from a small local or regional company that doesn't rely on the Web as a main component of business development. The design is relatively simple, as is typical of brochure sites. Brochure sites also usually include a guest book in which site visitors can fill out a form.

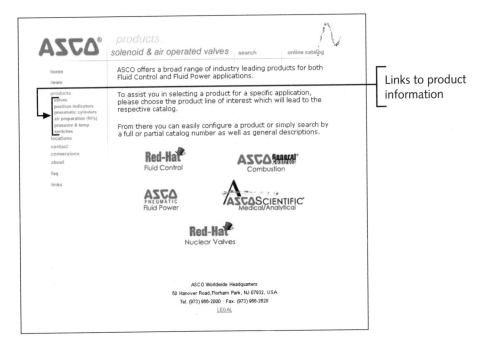

Links to product information

Figure 2-7   An interior page from ASCO's brochure Web site

Figure 2-8   A relatively simple but attractive brochure Web site

B2C Brochure Sites

It might seem odd for larger, more retail-oriented companies like **BMW** or **Post** to invest in brochure sites. These companies eagerly promote their sites though advertising, yet many of the sites have nothing to sell, don't support outside advertisements, and even go out of their way to develop games and interactivity to keep users on the site longer. Why?

Web sites for companies such as **Coke**, **Pepsi**, **Burger King**, and others fall into the brochure category because although they are not selling anything directly, their sites have a higher purpose. Unlike Yukon Graphics, discussed earlier, which wants companies who visit the site to pick up the phone and retain them for upcoming printing needs, Pepsi doesn't expect you to drop the mouse, run to the refrigerator, and grab a can of soda as soon as you land on its site. In fact, much of the Pepsi site is centered around online games, movie trailers, music news, and other fun stuff that is unrelated to soda.

For these companies, the Web acts as an additional branding vehicle. Pepsi is the "choice of the new generation," and so you are invited to come onto the site, play the games, and stay as long as you want. In fact, Pepsi doesn't care if you don't read any of the well-hidden information about the products. What really matters to the company is that while you're reading about the upcoming Tom Hanks film, you'll still see the Pepsi logo in the corner and subliminally make the connection between Pepsi and the fun things you enjoy in life. That connection builds brand value that ideally leads to increased sales.

Account Management Sites

Account management sites let people supervise their personal financial, utility, and other types of accounts. Banking on the convenience factor (pun intended), online banking is a rapidly growing component of electronic commerce. People can check their accounts, transfer money from one account to another, order checks, and conduct other banking chores from their computers. Using password-encrypted information, general consumers can manage their lives on the Web. They can pay utility bills, order groceries, check their credit card balance, or execute stock trades. The ability to manage their private accounts with a vendor is a win-win situation for businesses and consumers; consumers see their lives as being made easier, and businesses create a marriage with their customers, making it that much harder for the customer to jump ship and find another seller.

Within the account management category of electronic commerce is a subcategory of particular interest. Online auctions, dominated by **eBay** and shown in Figure 2-9, are really what the Web is all about: giving people the ability to conduct product or information transactions among themselves with relative ease and enjoyment. Although (for the most part) individuals who post products or offerings on an auction site (sellers) don't usually have actual dollars invested in maintaining significant inventory, they are still managing an account. Sellers supply a product and coordinate the final transaction, including payment and shipping. The site, for bringing the buyer and seller together, typically charges a percentage of the sale price.

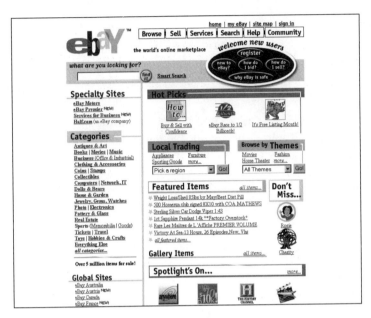

Figure 2-9   eBay, the runaway Web success story

Unique Challenges for Account Management Sites

Two obvious challenges face account management sites: the issues of privacy and the minimal risk of computer error. Site managers need to implement technology that keeps customer accounts away from prying eyes and ensures that mistakes won't occur during transactions. A more difficult task for the site is convincing users that the site is actually safe to use.

The Web, although no longer a novelty, is still new enough to be outside many people's comfort zones when it comes to managing an entire account. Making a credit card purchase online is not too far of a stretch for most shoppers, because many people are accustomed to using their cards over the phone. But considering the difficulty online banks and other entities have had recruiting new users, it's safe to say that even if the technology exists and is shown to be safe, the concept of electronic account management will continue to be a hard sell, and only time will change the way people feel about these sites.

Content Sites

To attract and maintain traffic, **content sites** try to offer something unique in terms of information, or content, which is usually updated on a regular basis. Specialty e-zines may offer timely news content updated frequently, while sweepstakes and game sites offer ongoing contests to keep visitors coming back. Web search engine sites, such as **Google** (www.google.com), which is shown in Figure 2-10, give users information and links to other sites on the Web.

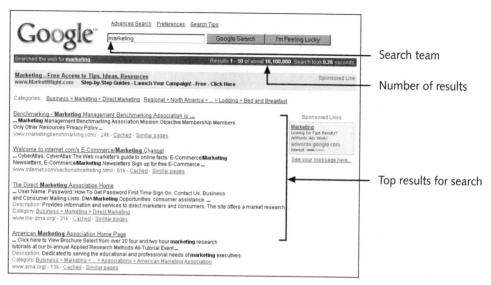

Figure 2-10 Search engine Web site

Figure 2-11 shows **OnlineBoardwalk.com**, a site that builds revenue through online advertising, yet has no updated information at all. Instead, this site offers prizes for accumulated high scores on 3-D animated boardwalk games. The site requires visitors to click banner ads and directory listings to earn credits. These credits can be used by visitors to play the games and add to their accumulated score. Advertisers pay a premium to be seen on the site because there is a built-in incentive for user click-through and a high level of return visits.

Both B2C and B2B content sites generate revenue primarily by selling advertising space on the site. Advertising space usually includes standard banner ads, but is not limited to them. Page or channel sponsorships, directory listings, affiliate programs, and similar strategies provide content sites with a variety of ways to increase their bottom line. In addition, these sites may gain revenue through subscription sales or paid memberships for access to certain content. Revenue sources are explored in more depth in Chapter 4.

Although some sites have tried to earn revenue through subscriptions or paid memberships, few, if any, have succeeded. However, the idea is currently popular—sites are withholding some information for access only by priority users (translate: people who pay for it). To make their advertisers happy, these types of sites have to deliver high and increasing traffic amounts on a regular basis. More traffic means more eyeballs viewing advertisements.

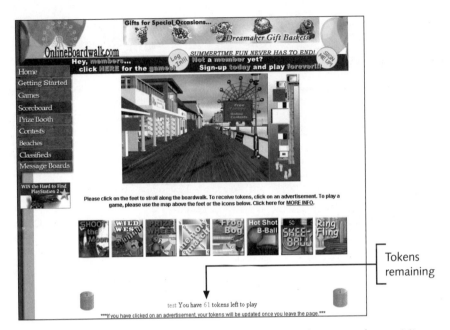

Figure 2-11   OnlineBoardwalk.com uses games and prizes to keep visitors coming back

Unique Challenges for Content Sites

To be worthwhile, your content site must display changes with considerable frequency. This is especially true for news-oriented sites, which surfers visit to receive updated information. Take **ESPN.com** (www.espn.com), for example. Because it offers frequent updates of scores, players, teams, and so on, the site often changes its content two or three times a day by updating the scoreboards and articles. To a Web surfer, the frequency of updated information equals a greater incentive to visit more often, which means that the site can charge more for advertising space.

That's all well and good for ESPN.com, which is in the center of the sports world and has easy access to information. ESPN.com, with its affiliation to the ESPN television network, print magazine, restaurants, and merchandising, probably has deep enough pockets to hire a room full of data entry workers and can afford to lose some money on the site—for a little while, anyway.

What about smaller sites that don't have the kind of properties or resources that ESPN.com has? How do smaller content sites manage? Well, to begin with, content on most sites doesn't need to change twice per day. However, the unfortunate reality is that for a shot at success, content will need to change at least once per day, or the site will look stale. Weekly publications might work for print magazines, but regular, daily updates are the rule on the Web for a steady audience.

Nonfunded start-ups (those that have not been funded through venture capitalists, banks, or other business-related sources) with limited capital may have to break the rules and accept weekly content updates as the standard. Growth of these sites will be significantly slower, and repeat traffic will be much tougher to retain. Similarly, niche publications (the kind that deal with very specific segments of an industry, such as an e-zine dedicated to model train enthusiasts or a humor e-zine such as TheOnion.com) may also enjoy the privilege of updating on a weekly basis while experiencing overall growth.

Thus, the most important and dire need for a content site is the content itself. Where does it come from? Content can be gathered by employees or developers of the site, purchased, or acquired through an affiliate program.

Another unique hurdle for content sites is the *quantity* of content: there has to be enough content spread over enough pages within the site to make the site profitable. A one-page content site that displays all of its content on one page, for example, only has that one page on which to sell advertising. Ad banners are typically placed only at the top or bottom of a page and sometimes down one of the sides. There isn't much demand for ads in the middle of a page, and it wouldn't make your site very attractive if they were placed there, anyway. As you can guess, a one-page site is not a very profitable venture.

So here's the catch: more content can equal more pages, which can equal more advertising dollars. But more pages also calls for a more sophisticated database from which to mine the information and a reliable navigation system. Suddenly your simple little content site has gotten a lot more sophisticated and complex. Site navigation now comes into play. You will learn about navigation in Chapter 6. Navigation on a content site will often deliberately direct visitors to a specific page or area of the site to accommodate certain advertisers or fetch higher banner ad prices.

Lastly, content sites have a particular challenge in that more than any other type of site, they need to keep very close track of traffic for each page. Understanding where the audience goes on a site, which paths they take, where they enter and exit, how long they spend on any particular page, and other traffic facts are required to set ad rates for the site and to keep advertisers happy. Powerful **ad serving programs** (programs that place and track banner and other types of ads on specific pages within a site) also need to be developed to ensure that the advertising is handled properly. You will learn more about this technology in Chapter 11.

Direct Gain Sites

Direct gain sites seek to earn something directly from the user. This type of site can be either nonmonetary or monetary, depending on what the site is trying to gain.

Nonmonetary Gain Sites

Although everything in business at some point boils down to money, not all companies use their site to gain revenue. **Flack + Kurtz** (www.fk.com), for example, seeks to make direct gains from its Web site (shown in Figure 2-12), but it is not selling anything directly over the Web. Instead, this global engineering firm uses its Web site to show off its portfolio and specific attributes of the company. Although the site does not offer electronic commerce features and does not update itself to feed updated newsworthy information to its industry,

Flack + Kurtz's site is only a cousin to the standard brochure site. What separates it into a different category is the purpose of its existence: it seeks to make a direct gain—not money, but new employees. Engineering students have a lot of options when it comes to choosing a company to work for, and Flack + Kurtz needs to do what it can to convince graduating engineers to work for the firm. This is the objective of the site.

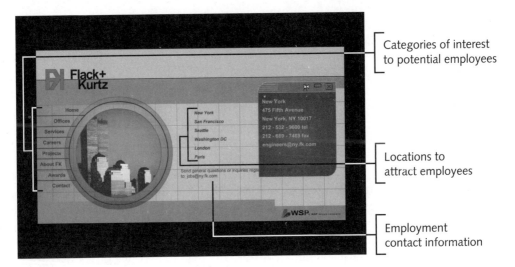

Figure 2-12   Flack + Kurtz's direct gain Web site

To make the company appealing to potential employees, the site not only targets students, but allows them to search for available positions at Flack + Kurtz and submit a resume online. In addition to its intended direct gains, the company realizes indirect gains because the site saves the costs of other, more traditional recruitment methods.

The particular audience (college students) was a main factor in determining the look and feel of the site, as well as how the job search and resume posting areas were developed.

Monetary Gain Sites

Monetary gain sites, better known as retail or electronic commerce sites, offer visitors products or services to purchase online. These types of sites have gained the most media attention in recent years, with players like Amazon.com, Drugstore.com, and others offering wide, specialized catalogs of products. Updated offerings, sales, and promotions keep visitors coming back, while customer service programs become a vital component in the success of an electronic commerce site.

The size of an electronic commerce site can range from very large, like Amazon.com or Walmart.com, to very small, like the antique soda bottle seller with a small store hosted by Yahoo!. Just like in the real world, specialized products have far less competition for customers than do more general-use items, but they also have a much smaller market of people finding their site. General products such as electronics and books appeal to a large market, but face massive competition.

More and more companies are expected to engage in electronic commerce transactions, and the number of companies capable of selling online is expected to grow significantly as well. In fact, while only 14 percent of companies had the technology to allow transactions from their sites in 1999, that number is expected to jump to between 30 percent and 40 percent, with an incredible 80 percent to 90 percent of companies expected to buy online. Small firms will most notably experience a difference in commerce habits, jumping from a relatively low share of 8 percent engaging in electronic commerce to an anticipated 72 percent doing so by 2003.[3]

Online vendors have learned that while it may be technically *possible* to sell most anything online, it's not yet all that practical. Nontangible offerings, such as travel services, have pulled in large electronic commerce dollars and continue to gain momentum. Certain durable goods, including clothes, books, toys, and electronics, have also proven to be big sellers, as have flower and gift delivery services. Larger products, such as cars, have not had as much luck, although not from a lack of effort. (Although direct sales of new vehicles over the Web haven't exactly broken any records, the Web has been a formidable ally to dealerships, as many shoppers will research a vehicle online before traveling to a dealership.) Perishable goods like food have also been weak sellers, with the noted exception of Boston Market's online turkey dinner orders during Thanksgiving 2000. Even sites that allow users to make purchases of perishable goods at a discount (like Priceline.com's "name your own price for groceries" campaign) failed to generate interest among shoppers. Apparently, few shoppers really wanted to use the site for relatively small savings each time they went grocery shopping.

Unique Challenges for Monetary Gain Sites

Retail sites probably face the toughest challenges on the Web because of their need to keep inventory and because of the potentially heavy competition they face, but, if successful, these sites can reap the greatest rewards. As with account management sites, retail sites need to promise and deliver privacy and security for buyers' personal information. Convincing the buying public of this has become easier for retail sites than for account management sites, as buying online has slowly permeated into our collective comfort zone.

Retail sites face fierce price competition. The Web makes comparison shopping easier, creating competitive pressure on retailers. As you learned in Chapter 1, this competitiveness has hurt some sites. Some Web retailers, attempting to attract users with low product prices, set the prices lower than was profitable. To make up for this loss, many sites compensated by charging higher-than-normal shipping costs, which were not figured into the total purchase price until close to the end of an order. Nearly half of all Web shoppers have reported abandoning their shopping carts at the last possible minute due to high shipping fees.[4]

In addition, like the content sites, retail sites have to keep their catalogs updated with new product lines, specials, and sales to retain consumer interest. This is not always an easy task, and it involves maintaining an inventory and frequently rearranging site content.

[3]Source: *eMarketer*, July 19, 2000.

[4]Source: *CyberAtlas.*

BEYOND PROFITS: ADDITIONAL MOTIVATIONS

Beyond the primary reasons that companies create Web sites are a few secondary drivers, including file distribution, improved customer service, public relations, media relations, and even competitive pressure, which is the publishing of a site because the competition has one.

A quick glance at the structure laid out in Figure 2-1 might suggest that Web sites are restricted to one category or another, but that's far from reality. Many sites have mixed purposes and are an amalgamation of several categories, offering multiple ways of generating revenue.

Figure 2-13 shows a page from the **Discovery.com** Web site (www.discovery.com). A complete hybrid, this site offers visitors up-to-date information, drawing target audiences to the site on a regular basis. This regular traffic allows the site to earn revenue by selling ad space throughout the content pages. At the same time, Discovery.com has leveraged its audience even further by building a retail section to increase earnings. The difficulties that face both content and retail sites are grouped to make this site more difficult to maintain than a site with only a single objective, but the potential gains are much greater. Discovery.com enjoys one additional (major) benefit in that it can and does cross-promote itself with its non-Web entities, such as the Discovery Channel (available on cable television) and its chain of brick-and-mortar Discovery stores. Each of these areas alerts customers to the other affiliated areas, and that helps generate interest in alternative Discovery properties.

Links to Discovery affiliates

Figure 2-13   The Discovery.com hybrid Web site

How Web Business Differs from Traditional Business

2

Given a choice between ordering a book from the comfort of your chair or getting out of that chair, driving to the mall, parking, finding the book on the bookstore shelf, standing in line to pay for the book, and then returning home, how would you prefer to make your purchase? For most people, the primary reason for shopping on the Web is convenience.

There are many factors beyond advertising and convenience that influence people to make purchasing decisions. The following tables list some of the factors that make up the shopping experience and describe how business on the Web can differ from traditional business. We'll examine these tables for both retail buying and for content-oriented sites.

Table 2-1　Comparison of Web and traditional retail shopping factors

	Web	Brick & Mortar
Accessibility	Very accessible. Users can compare one store against another with the click of a button.	Relatively inaccessible. Users have to travel to store using cars or other means. Comparison shopping is not as easy and more time consuming.
Selection	Seemingly unlimited. For any given product, the Web can provide a far wider selection than can ever be looked at. Could be a benefit to some, but most shoppers report that it is too much.	Limited to what any particular retail outlet puts on its shelves. Stores act as a filter for poor products.
Immediate satisfaction	Except in cases of downloads (MP3s, software, and so on), immediate satisfaction is nonexistent.	Except in cases where things need to be shipped or delivered (like furniture), shoppers receive the immediate satisfaction of leaving with their purchases.
Price	The initial impression was that price shoppers could go to the Web for bargains. Actually, shipping costs often erase any savings and prices are often higher after shipping is factored in.	Shipping costs for most products don't exist, because buyers simply walk away carrying their purchases.
Privacy	Buyers need to provide information ranging from name and address to credit card numbers and sometimes telephone numbers. Customer lists may be sold, resulting in excess junk mail and e-mail.	Shoppers typically don't have to divulge private information about themselves to make a purchase.
Social interaction	Virtually no social interaction, except through chat rooms.	Buyers get to be around actual people, although crowds can be irritating and cause delays.

Table 2-1   Comparison of Web and traditional retail shopping factors (continued)

	Web	Brick & Mortar
Service	Help menus and intuitive interface are the only assistance. Otherwise, you're on your own.	Salespeople are on hand to help you with your purchase. Service can be spotty, though.
Pressure	Virtually none. If you don't want to buy, you simply click off the site.	High-pressure sales people sometimes become a nuisance or make shoppers feel uncomfortable.
Waiting time	Go straight to the head of the line. If a site's shopping cart and checkout areas are good, making the final purchase should be easy.	Possibility of having to wait in line behind slow or bothersome shoppers.
Returning items	Usually have to send any returns back through the mail, sometimes at the shopper's expense. This is slowly changing with Web sites run by traditional stores.	Can make returns simply by going back to the store from which a product was purchased.
Business expense	For the e-tailer, unique costs include creation of the site itself. Pure-coms have the additional expense of building the initial customer base through expensive advertising.	Unique costs include building or renting retail location. Although advertising is needed, existence is promoted by visible location.

Table 2-2   Comparison of Web and traditional magazine/news distribution aspects

	Web	Brick & Mortar
Accessibility	Information is very easy to find.	If specific information is not delivered, it must be sought out (at the book store, newsstand, and so on).
Price	Information can usually be found for free.	Pay per publication.
Convenience	Unless it's printed, information needs to be read on screen, wherever the computer is.	The news goes where you go.
Readability	Text on a monitor can be hard on the eyes.	It's easier to read words on paper than on screen.
Access to related data	Just a click away, either to a new page within the publication or to a new publication altogether.	Turn the page, but you must stay within the pages of the publication you are reading.
Multimedia	News may contain audio or video clips to support the text.	Sorry, no multimedia.

In addition to the factors outlined in the tables, there are other aspects that are unique to Web sites. Some of these include the less obvious issues that many pure-coms didn't take into consideration when estimating the costs in their initial business models. For example, early beliefs that Web sites were inexpensive to build and that inventory could be kept to a minimum turned out to be false.

The Traditional Retailer

Consider a typical retail clothing store at a mall (for the purposes of this example, it doesn't matter whether the store is independently owned or part of a chain). The store needs to make sure that the products it offers are new and that the clothes in the window change often enough to keep shoppers interested. Store management also must stay on top of the latest fashions. The store keeps on hand as many units of each product as it can comfortably hold, and when the product is sold, it is not restocked. As for the store's physical environment, the interior design might change occasionally, but that change is usually little more than lights, new pictures on the walls, or very rarely, a fresh coat of paint. It's extremely unusual for the entire architecture to be rebuilt. Salespeople are on site to help customers, and because you don't find too many clothing stores standing by themselves in the middle of a forest, the store can rely in part on walk-in traffic.

The Web Retailer

The early commercial developers of the Web thought that they'd have it easy in comparison to traditional retailers. The storefront in the mall was expensive—a cost that could be avoided on the Web. Early Web retailers believed that inventory could be kept to a minimum. The site would keep some products on hand, but most Web shoppers wouldn't mind waiting a couple of weeks for their product to be delivered.

It looked good on paper, but the reality was entirely different.

Surprisingly, Web businesses face many of the same challenges that the traditional retailers do, but often to an exaggerated extent. Like the traditional clothing store, the Web retailer needs to keep its product offerings fresh as well. But while this means changing the window displays every few weeks for the traditional retailer, it could mean freshening the site once every day or two for the Web retailer. Web shoppers can visit a site with far more frequency than they can a mall store, and they get bored quickly if the site is not kept updated.

The traditional store does not need photographic representations of its products, either; salespeople just open the boxes of products, put the items on the shelf or hangers, and that's it. It's a simple job for the part-time high school employee. The Web retailer, on the other hand, must acquire images of the clothes (if they are not provided by the manufacturer, then photos have to be taken) and download the images along with all other vital product information (price, size, and so on) into a database appearing on the site.

The architecture of the site is also a challenge. Design trends seem to change faster in the virtual world than they do in the real world, and sites may frequently need to undergo design changes to keep the pages looking fresh and modern. General design concepts for sites have changed from colorful and confusing to overburdened to minimalist, all in about 18 months. These changes take time, money, and headaches to implement.

Technology also changes rapidly. Online retailers often find that as their sites finish one phase of development using a technology such as Flash (described in detail in Appendix A of this text), the next evolution of site design calls for the incorporation of more modern programming languages.

Web space is not cheap, either, especially as a site grows and needs to feed an expanding client base faster without collapsing. In many cases, maintaining a large, commercial B2C site can be just as expensive as paying rent in a mall. While the cost for a simple brochure site that uses less than 20 MB of space is usually under $50 per month (paid to the Web hosting company if the site is not self-hosted), the costs are dramatically steeper for larger, more public retail sites. Fully secured servers (secured both technologically from hackers and literally behind locked cages for protection) at hosts that have enough power to handle heavy traffic, never go down, and maintain high delivery speeds may cost tens of thousands of dollars per month. Other costs include **mirrors**, which are exact duplicates of a site located on separate servers that can take the site's place in case of power failure or other problems that may cause the site to be down or lose valuable information. Costs also include regular equipment upgrades, maintenance fees, and surcharges for traffic overages.

Inventory for early Web retailers turned out to be a problem as well. Items that were sold out did not automatically disappear from a Web site's page. Users continued ordering them. At the same time, the novelty of Web buying wore off fast, and shoppers expected quick delivery of their purchases. Shoppers had, after all, been lured to the Web initially by the promise of convenience that included having 24 x 7 access to goods. This raised expectations of fast turnaround times. So, unlike the traditional retailer who just holds inventory until stock runs out, the Web retailer needs to maintain a far larger inventory (which creates a cost for warehouse space, warehouse equipment, and employees to manage inventories) than it likely intended, with more advanced distribution systems to move products quickly.

Finally, Web businesses incur all of the costs associated with maintaining customer support services to compensate for the lack of real-life sales people. Other unanticipated expenses include the high price of marketing efforts to drive people to the site in the first place. Marketing will be covered in detail in Chapter 10.

Hope for Web Retailers

All of these conditions paint a pretty bleak picture of the Web, at least as far as starting a business goes. Are there any differences that make a Web business worthwhile? The truth is that starting a new site without a major brand affiliation will continue to be extremely difficult. Even being affiliated with major brands might not always help when technology changes so fast. Take **Listen.com** (www.listen.com), for example.

The site made headlines as the first pure-com Web site for downloading MP3 music files (for a price). It had the support and funding of every major label in the recording industry. Then along came Napster. All the money in the world wasn't going to help Listen.com get customers when Napster was giving music away for free. Listen.com had to change its business plan, and, as you read this, it may already be defunct. In 2001, Napster lost its highly publicized court battle, which saw metal band Metallica and other musicians pleading the case before Congress that Napster basically allowed people to steal their music by downloading copyrighted songs without paying for them. Napster was forced to block hundreds of thousands of copywrited song files from being downloaded, but the damage to Listen.com was already done. All this happened in an environment in which online sales of music grew 233 percent from 1999 to 2000.[5]

Despite the initial obstacles, there are some major factors that play in the Web's favor. The number of Web users continues to rise, and expenditures by online shoppers are growing faster than expenditures by traditional shoppers. In addition, during 2000, Web shoppers spent more on average per purchase than did traditional shoppers.[6]

Besides better rates and statistics, the Web enjoys benefits that traditional retailers do not. These include the ability to do business 24 hours a day and reduced risk of liability. A Web retailer never has to worry about a customer slipping in Aisle 4 and suing for millions of dollars.

One of the popular benefits that marketers like to mention—the fact that their products or services are available to a global audience—is misleading, though. While it's true that regional marketers can more easily access a larger audience throughout the United States and into Europe, expecting a truly global audience is unrealistic; in fact, of the 300 million Internet users worldwide, approximately 56 percent of those are in the United States.[7] That doesn't comprise a truly global audience, although an extended reach is certainly a benefit.

Business on the Web is still in its infancy. As technology starts to plateau following the dramatic ups and downs of the latter half of the 1990s into the early 2000s, and after the initial problems described in this chapter are reduced or eliminated, the Web will be a smoother place for businesses to exist and thrive.

The next section investigates the differences between online shopping and shopping in the "real world." Although individual preferences vary, the deciding factors in shopping overwhelmingly come down to price and convenience. As you will learn, shoppers have different expectations for electronic and brick-and-mortar shopping experiences, and Web shopping can become a complex game of give-and-take.

[5]Source: *eMarketer*, 2000 summary.

[6]Source: *eMarketer*, 2000 summary.

[7]Source: *E-Commerce Times*, Sept. 19, 2001.

MERGING BRICK-AND-MORTAR FIRMS WITH DOT-COMS

The early days of the Web pitted the New Economy against the Old Economy. The pure-coms of the New Economy burst onto the business scene with energy and enthusiasm, and the Old Economy didn't know what hit it. But after the dust settled, the Old Economy marketers persevered, showing the brightest sparks of promise for Web profitability.

Old-school businesses have been picking up some new tricks. The traditional marketers are beginning to construct a **click-and-mortar landscape**, which is a retail environment that combines the best of what the New Economy has to offer with the trust and security that the Old Economy has already established.

Combining a brick-and-mortar site with a Web business is not as popular as marketers might expect. The initial integration is an obvious one. Shoppers who make purchases over the Web from a site run and owned by a traditional marketer could be assisted at any of the brick-and-mortar outlets. For example, shoppers could return or exchange products if necessary. This is an amazing advantage over the alternative, which is returning products to the electronic commerce site through the mail at the shoppers' own expense.

Although survey after survey shows that consumers want more integration between brick-and-mortar stores and their associated Web sites, consumers are not yet taking advantage of those businesses offering this integration. However, this will likely change as more traditional marketers make their presence felt on the Web.

Marketing integration opens up the field to more creativity, such as in the case of Ben & Jerry's ice cream. Each container of Ben & Jerry's uses valuable real estate to promote a special voting section of the company's Web site. This section allows consumers to rate specific fringe flavors on a scale of 1 to 5 and then vote on whether the flavor should be continued.

This type of integration works on multiple levels. It allows Ben & Jerry's to test how closely its customers read the containers, to determine how many will actually go to the Web site, and to gather important insight into which flavors are resonating with its audience. Will Ben & Jerry's sell more ice cream because of this effort? Maybe, but it's unlikely that gaining new customers is even the point. Rather, the effort helps Ben & Jerry's to further expose customers to the brand in an interactive, communal atmosphere.

The click-and-mortar models have great potential for retailers, allowing marketers to leverage both their existing brands and the power of the Web. Of total marketing dollars spent on Web advertising, companies that have integrated their brick-and-mortar existence with their dot-com entities have not only spent more money on banner advertising and other Web-based advertising, but also will continue to far outpace traditional marketers and pure-coms for years to come. Figure 2-14 shows a chart indicating that click-and-mortar retailers are willing to spend ad dollars to promote their efforts because of their strong potential for success.

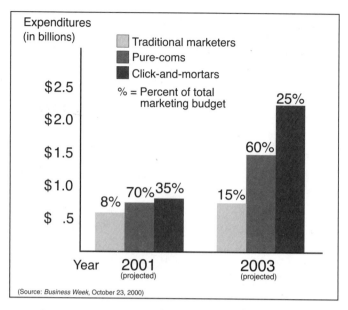

Figure 2-14   Web advertising expense comparison

THE WEB USER'S PERSPECTIVE: UNDERSTANDING VISITOR NEEDS

As Web surfers become more sophisticated and using the Web becomes an everyday function instead of an infrequent novelty, it is becoming clear to researchers and marketers that consumers have distinct and universal reasons for doing business, seeking information, and engaging in transactions over the Web. While the Web was originally shaped by the creative vision of designers and programmers, it now reflects the needs of those who use it, rather than those who create its content.

Although there are a number of reasons why consumers use the Web, convenience is by far the leading factor. Online shoppers give up the ability to hold the product in their hand or use a product at the time of purchase for the convenience of shopping from the comfort of their home or office. People who visit news sites sacrifice the ability to read the news anywhere as they would with a paper source. What they expect in return is access to more timely updates, more vibrancy in images, or multimedia enhancements that would be impossible to deliver on paper.

The convenience factor created by the advent of the Web in turn creates an impetus for further Web growth. This snowball effect is based on the following general principles:

- Making purchases or doing research by computer in your home or office is more convenient than driving to a store, mall, agency, library, or other location.

- Immediate physical results of Web shopping are nonexistent. Electronic shoppers forego the ability to hold, wear, feel, or test a product before purchasing it. They also don't have physical possession of a product at the time of purchase. Software purchases are the exception to this rule. In addition, the ability to "carry" a content-related item such as a magazine, while technically possible in the digital domain due to wireless features, PDA downloads, and e-books, is not, as of 2001, very popular. This will change as those features become more streamlined and generally accepted.

- Special Web value pricing is negated either by widely advertised sales in traditional brick-and-mortar locations or undesirably high shipping costs.

On average, retail sales grow over time. However, offline retailers will gradually lose market share to online retailers because convenience will become increasingly important to shoppers, and they will spend more dollars online rather than offline. However, the importance of convenience will grow incrementally because of other Web factors coming into play. For example, as more people get faster connections, the convenience that the Web offers them becomes greater. Similarly, as fewer people fear the Web (and become more comfortable entering their credit card numbers into Web forms), Web retail growth will increase. At the same time, as sites improve customer service and navigation, charge less for shipping, and ensure quick delivery of products, more people will find the Web a convenient place to shop and research information. As long as more people realize the convenience of the Web, and the Web continues to make improvements in what it offers, Web business will continue to grow, and dollars channeled to electronic commerce will continue to cut into overall retail spending. It is inevitable, however, that this growth will eventually plateau, with Web retail growth rising or falling along with overall retail growth. The leveling off of Web e-tailing growth is inevitable as long as the immediate results of traditional retailing still holds value to the consumer.

Site planners must take into consideration the convenience factors that will make their own Web sites grow.

DETERMINING THE TARGET MARKET

Very few Web sites can expect to be online and attract *everyone* to their site. It is impossible to have universal appeal to every potential shopper. Instead, each site, depending on its offerings or the information that it provides, caters to a specific group of people that shares common traits. Some of these traits, called **demographics**, may be geographic location, age group, career choice, or income. Other traits, called **psychographics**, are based more on personalities, hobbies, and desires. The group that a Web site tries to attract is its **target market**. To be appealing to a target market, a site must have a good idea of the preferences of potential customers so that it can develop appropriate promotions. For example, the personalities and lifestyle similarities of people that would surf a NASCAR-oriented site are likely very different from those of people who would visit a site about opera. Knowledge of the market translates into a site's ability to devise an effective **marketing strategy** (the strategy that a site or company employs for gaining more customers and revenue) for increasing product sales.

Because hyperlinks make it far easier for potential clients to check out competition in the cyber world than they might otherwise do in the brick-and-mortar world, **customer retention** (the measure of how long a customer remains on your site and how often he or she returns) is a vital component in the long-term success of any Web site. This retention can only come through an intimate understanding of both the market demographics (including age, income, and geography) and the psychographics (such as favorite places to travel, favorite activities, hobbies, and interests).

Research Data: Demographics

Market research companies know that determining the composition of any audience can be difficult, time-consuming, and expensive. Companies analyze their potential audiences using a generally accepted set of characteristics, or variables. These variables tend to be general and depend on whether the site is geared toward consumers or businesses.

Standard Consumer Demographics

The following constitutes an abbreviated list of some demographic information a site might seek from individuals that comprise its target market. This information is used to help design and develop the Web site so that it will ultimately be more appealing to the audience that it seeks:

- Age (median age and predominant age group)
- Family size (marital status, number of siblings, number of offspring, and so on)
- Education level
- Income (median income and income range)
- Gender (percentage male versus percentage female)
- Occupation (type of work and number of years with same employer)
- Nationality
- Race
- Religion
- Geographical residence

Standard Business Demographics

The following are some facts that a B2B Web site developer might seek about the kind of companies that would be most likely to use its site. Keep in mind, however, that a *company* itself does not surf the Web or make electronic commerce purchases. One or more individuals within the company make the decisions and do the buying, so it is often just as important for a B2B site to gather the traditional demographic information (as in the previous list) as it is to gather information about the company:

- Size of sales

- Profitability (percentage of businesses that are profitable and range of profit)

- Publicly or privately held (percentage of each)

- Number of employees

- Type of company (products versus service and percentage breakdown of product or service type)

These broad categories provide the basic facts that any Web site developer must know about its audience to develop a successful site. The data can have a bearing on everything from the language used on the site to the colors chosen for the background.

Taking Demographics Further

Better understanding into the psychology of the target market helps developers to streamline the design and layout of the site and to integrate marketing and advertising strategies, develop content, and determine strong potential affiliate partners for cross-promotional efforts. These psychographic variables can be minimal or extensive, depending on time and budget.

Audience Psychographic Variables

You can use the information gathered from the following list to understand the personality of the target market and develop a site to appeal to that personality. For example, this information may help to determine whether the site should be highly interactive and charged with graphics and energy, or more staid and relaxed. It can also help determine which advertisers would most likely benefit from advertising on the site, assuming that the site accepts advertising.

- Types of hobbies

- Vacations (places traveled and number of vacations taken per year)

- Recreational sports played

- Luxury items owned

- Number of general-use items (cars, sneakers, and so on) purchased last year or over the last three years

- Minutes per day spent on the Web

- Web use location (percentage from work versus percentage from home)

- Types of sites visited

- Dollars spent on online retail over the last six months and over the last year

- Top five favorite Web sites
- Biggest Web complaint

This type of information is vital to both creating and marketing your site, and while understanding the audience should be an ongoing process in one form or another, it's particularly important at the outset of production. Without this information, you will be creating blindly, with only a random chance at targeted success. For example, consider a Web site that sells outerwear and accessories to an audience of 14- to 19-year-old females. Without doing any market research at all, the site developers may design the site using colors, text, images and content that they assume, through common sense, would appeal to girls and women in that age category. However, deeper, more organized research of the target market may reveal some startling concepts. For the category of products being sold, site developers would likely want to market and develop the site to appeal to 20- to 25-year-old women—a few years beyond their target market. The reason is that the research would probably show that 14- to 19-year-olds want to look and feel like they're 20 to 25 years old. In addition, the research might also show that the one sure way to lose the audience completely would be to focus too much on the product line. Hard sales won't work with this demographic. Instead, the research might show that a different approach should be taken, such as forecasts of next week's plot for the current "hot" TV show, gossip about music stars, and tips on dating and dealing with parents. The sales complement the broader appeal of the site.

Unfortunately, many smaller companies and sites are anxious to begin making money immediately and forego the market research aspect in favor of quicker results.

Gathering Information

You should gather as much information about your prospective audience as you can. Typically, site developers who appreciate the value of audience profiling will not take on the responsibilities of these tasks themselves, but instead hire professionally trained and experienced agencies to do this research for them.

Even if you hire an outside agency, it's important for you to understand at least the basics of the research methods and how the results are derived. Understanding the audience is too important a task to hand over to an agency without being able to check that its information is accurate (or at least that it was gathered in such a way that the findings could be trusted).

Researchers employ various methods to collect audience data and then analyze it so that it can be useful in developing and promoting the site.

Some of the more popular methods include:

- Personal interviews
- Mail, Web, or telephone surveys
- Focus groups

Personal interviews and surveys involve the use of survey questionnaires. Focus groups are more informal and conversational in tone and will be covered later in this chapter. Each method involves determining a **sample** (a few representatives) of the target market on which to start your research.

To find the group that will best respond to your site, you should conduct research on a random group of people that includes all ages, races, genders, religious affiliations, and socioeconomic categories. You then solicit their opinions on the products, services, or information that you have to offer. Obviously this is not always possible, as budgets and time constraints often limit research. You can probably narrow down your initial audience to omit people who wouldn't be likely to need or want your Web site's offerings. For example, a site that sells expensive antique furnishings probably does not need to involve children or low- to lower-middle income individuals in the study to realize that those groups can be excluded from the target audience.

 If you've ever done everything in your power to avoid taking a class in probabilities and statistics, reconsider your hesitation. This type of course is the foundation of good market research and provides an understanding of how to associate a random or selected sample of people to a larger population.

Conducting Personal Interviews

Personal interviews can be conducted multiple ways, depending on your Web site's needs. For example, if you work for a B2B Web site that provides services to human resources (HR) professionals, you may benefit from scheduling personal interviews with HR employees from a cross-section of companies. If you work for an existing traditional company, you would conduct personal interviews with your existing clients to learn what they would desire and respond to on your site. Large general-product retail sites can conduct informal personal interviews with surveyors talking to random people outside of malls, on city streets, and so on.

The benefits of personal interviews include higher response rates (compared to surveys), the ability to answer questions that the interviewee may have, more in-depth information, and the ability to improvise questions based on respondents' previous answers. The negative aspects of personal interviews include interviewees who get bored or restless with a survey that lasts too long and interviewers who unwittingly lead their prospects by subconscious facial tics or body movements. Worst of all is high expense. Personal interviews can take a lot of time from training the interviewer, to traveling to the prospective interviewee (including renting space to conduct interviews), and to conducting each interview individually.

Most personal interviews that are arranged in advance are done for free by the interviewee. Your site may choose to provide interviewees with free benefits from the Web site when it launches or to give a small gift such as a t-shirt or hat with the Web address on it. These offerings are usually nominal and are given as a token good-will gesture. Random interviews at malls may require compensation for people who participate and can include items such as coupons to local stores, prepaid calling cards, or cash upon completion of the interview.

Mail, Web, and Telephone Surveys

Surveys usually are more difficult to conduct than interviews or focus groups because junk mail and telephone solicitations have deterred many people from responding to these efforts. Considering that a successful rate of return for any direct response mailing is just over 2 percent, getting enough responses from a random mail sample to build a useful audience profile may be difficult. Similar situations exist for Web surveys, which require efforts by Web marketers to drive traffic to the survey to get results. Another major problem with Web surveys is that participants have more time to think over their answers than they do in live forums, possibly muddying first-impulse responses. The downside of delayed reactions is offset by the fact that participants may be more honest due to the anonymity of the method.

Other benefits of Web surveys include the ability to reach people who would be otherwise difficult to reach through more personal methods (perhaps because they live in remote areas or simply don't want to sit through an interview). Surveys also provide less chance of the interviewer biasing the participant. The overall cost and time spent on these efforts are far less than personal interviews.

Setting up a Survey

Unfortunately, setting up a survey isn't quite as easy as jotting down a few random questions. You must follow a specific process to get meaningful results. The general steps taken for survey development include the following:

1. **Determine the objectives**: What are you trying to learn? Is the research mostly for advertising the site or for developing the site? Is it more important to know the demographics of your audience, the psychographics, or both?

2. **Develop the questions**: Some questions, such as age, geography, and income, will become standard for practically every survey that you use. Other questions should be more specific and targeted, depending upon both the target audience and the type of site you are developing. For example, a site that is providing information on family cars will likely write many of their survey questions to address the respondents' prior car buying and owning experience and type of information they would have liked to have known before buying their car. Their responses would likely affect the type of information that is presented on the site.

3. **Find survey respondents**: In what is possibly the most difficult step of surveying, surveyors need to find people to answer their questions. This means not only locating the right *type* of people, but finding enough people who will be willing to take the time out of their day to answer the questions. Depending on the site and the subject matter, the people asked need to be representatives of the *perceived* target market (the market demographics that site developers most logically expect will visit their site) as well as a good cross-section of those who fall outside of the perceived target market. For

instance, in the car information site example that was used in the previous step, it might make sense for surveyors to go door-to-door in neighborhoods that have a large number of families with family-style cars or to stand at the door of certain car dealerships. Don't stop there, though. Since the site provides information about family cars, the buyers of which are the heads of households, you might not think that there would be any reason to bother questioning kids and teenagers for this market research. But there might be. It's entirely possible that the kids, especially the teenagers, have a large amount of influence on what vehicle their parents buy for the family. That influence may need to be addressed in the Web site.

4. **Analyze the data**: Once collected, you need to organize the data and study it, tallying the percentages of responses. For example, you'll need to determine the percentage of respondents who were between 25 and 30 years old, the percentage of respondents who make purchases over the Web, and so on. Then you must cross-reference and analyze the results to highlight useful findings. You might find that 67 percent of all respondents under the age of 30 have done online vehicle research in the last month, but that only 18 percent of those were male. This information can later be used during site development to create features that take advantage of these facts.

Another important part of the survey is asking the right questions. Forming the survey questions is not an easy task. While it may seem that developing the survey should be as simple as writing a few questions down on paper, the truth is that for the results of a research effort to be meaningful, the questions need to be asked in a way that allows the user to give unbiased and relevant information. For example, consider the following two survey question examples. Each asks the same thing, but uses a different method to extract respondent information:

Q. 1: Did you find this Web site useful? (Please check one)

____Yes

____No

Q. 1: How useful did you find this Web site? (Please circle one of the following):

Extremely Useful

Very Useful

Moderately Useful

Not Very Useful

Not Useful At All

The second question provides more insight and information as to the Web user's experience with the site, while the first question limited the respondent to one of two choices. The "yes" or "no" choices are vague and not very helpful. Although yes and no questions have their place in surveys, they are better off being used for factual matters (such as "Have you visited this site within the last 14 days?") instead of subjective ones (such as "Do you like this site?"). Now consider another example:

Q. 17: Most people enjoy making purchases online and believe it is a convenient way to shop. On a scale of 1 to 5 (5 being "Yes, I completely agree"), how would you compare your agreement with these people? (Please circle one):

5   4   3   2   1

Q. 17: Compared with buying products through traditional retail outlets (such as you may find in a mall), how would you compare the convenience of online (Web) shopping? (Please circle one):

Much more convenient

A bit more convenient

About the same

A bit less convenient

Much less convenient

In this example, each question allows the respondent a wide range of responses, but the first question is far more leading. The respondent is led to believe that from the outset, other people have already responded favorably to the issue of online shopping. This phrasing creates a bias in the question that diminishes the value of the answer; the respondent may respond favorably simply because he or she does not want to feel left out or in the minority. The second question, on the other hand, allows the respondent to express an opinion without being prejudiced.

Focus Groups

Focus groups are among the more dynamic methods of collecting data and one of the few that departs from the survey-use style of questioning. Focus groups are conducted by gathering eight to 15 people in a room around a conference table with a moderator leading them in discussion about various topics. Very often, the people in the focus groups are not told more than the basics of the subject matter (like knowing that the topic may revolve around produce, for example). This is done to make sure that they are not biased in their thoughts when entering the conversation. In fact, the moderator (an experienced professional who knows how to ask questions without leading the group's answers) will often ask many questions that have little or nothing to do with the subject matter so that he or she does not give away the actual topic or the name of the company that is conducting the focus group. Giving even the company name away can severely prejudice people in the group (for example, Ford Mustang enthusiasts might be immediately biased and partial if they walked into a focus group they knew was being conducted by Chevrolet).

Focus groups typically run about two hours, with different demographic categories of people segregated into different groups. For example, men aged 19 to 24 might be in one group, while men aged 25 to 34 might be in another. Participants are typically paid a fee that can range between $20 to $100 per hour for being part of the group. It is also traditional to provide refreshments during the session.

Like in surveys, focus group questions are carefully developed beforehand by either the site developers, or, more often, an outside agency, and the moderator is typically trained to get conversations started and ensure that everyone participates. Because there is so much spontaneous information that can surface during these efforts, focus groups are usually run behind a two-way mirror. Group participants, although they are aware of the circumstances, cannot see that on the other side of the mirror is a camera recording their actions. Research professionals can review the tape to analyze the conversation, body language, and voice inflections of the participants.

How Audience Profile Affects a Web Site

Once you have gathered data about your target audience's preferences and needs, you can use that information to shape your Web site. Knowing your audience from both a demographic and psychographic standpoint gives you insight into the types of layout, colors, images, and content to which your visitors would best respond. Most importantly, understanding your audience will help shape the core message and personality of the brand for long-term market penetration. In the final analysis, it's the brand's job to sell the product or service, and it's the site's job to help build the brand.

Pepsi's Web site is a good example of a site that reaches out to its audience in a way that plays on the likes and interests of the "new generation" that the company targets. Although it is a well-branded site with the logo on every page, Pepsi knows that it's unlikely to retain visitors for very long or keep them coming back if the main feature of its site is the calorie count for a 12-ounce can of Diet Pepsi. In fact, it's almost diffi-cult to find specific information relating to Pepsi products—but, then again, providing information about the products isn't really the point of the site. Instead, the site's main purpose is to simply reinforce the brand. What *is* easy to find on the site is plenty of information on current movies and musical acts, complete with biographies and concert tour dates. Pepsi knows that to maintain its brand image and to reach its target market of young adults, it must be less self-focused and more of a resource for the content in which its audience is interested.

ASCO, whose site is shown in Figure 2-7, features a site with streamlined, no-frills information. The company opted for this style because its customers are mainly engi-neers who want to gather information quickly without distractions. However, ASCO realizes that its audience is human and does have interests outside of the site topic, and thus the site has sponsored online contests for concert tickets, appealing to another aspect of its audience profile.

Although earlier you learned about the hazards of venturing too far outside the core message (such as having stock quotes on a site that assists gardeners), understanding your audience as well as your reasons for site development and the core message of your brand will help you know where these boundaries exist. What, one may ask, do movies and music have to do with cola? Technically, nothing. The site helps establish the essence of the brand, largely based on the personalities of the target market (as determined by extensive research), and that brand is what keeps consumers trusting enough in the company to continue purchasing its products.

Not all sites are or should be strictly brand-building sites. As you learned earlier, there are many reasons for a site to exist, although regardless of that reason, you should never ignore the brand.

CHAPTER SUMMARY

- ❐ Taking an idea from concept to live site requires specific planning. Online businesses face a frontier that in many ways is similar to the traditional business environment, with its requisite brand building and consumer retention considerations, but in many other ways, Web business is quite unique. Despite original beliefs that Web businesses were relatively cheap to run, it turned out that the benefits to the consumer (convenience and selection) do not offset some of the negative aspects (including increased competition, a need to build a brand practically overnight, and unforeseen business costs). However, the increased savvy of both retailers and shoppers and the pace of technology advances signal good things for online business.

- ❐ The two main categories of business Web sites, business-to-business (B2B) and business-to-consumer (B2C), each have four subcategories: brochure, account management, content, and direct gains. All of these types of sites have unique hurdles and benefits that need to be understood by site managers. Brochure-style sites help in branding and customer acquisition while still relying on basic human interaction to generate revenue. Account management sites rely on visitors feeling safe with their online account data to help marry them to the company and keep them retained for a long period of time. Content-oriented sites rely on visitor traffic to gain revenue through advertising sales. Retail, or direct gain, sites face an uphill battle in maintaining inventory and distributing products on time and at low cost while battling fierce competition. However, they are buoyed by the fact that online shopping continues to grow even in hard times.

- ❐ Traditional merchants endeavor to provide a best-of-both worlds experience to their customers by integrating online shopping with traditional service in click-and-mortar sites.

- ❐ Sites gather information about their audiences using interviews, surveys, and focus groups, and then shape the site to appeal to those audiences. Understanding your site's characteristics and audience and acknowledging how it differs from a traditional business are key factors in achieving Web success.

KEY TERMS

account management site

ad serving program

business plan

click-and-mortar landscape

content site

customer retention

demographics

direct gain site

e-zine

go public

marketing strategy

mirror

mission statement

monetary gain site

psychographics

round

sample

shoe-string budget

static

target market

venture capitalists

REVIEW QUESTIONS

1. Maintaining inventory is an expense that _____.

   a. retail sites don't have to worry about because they are Web based

   b. retail sites didn't originally believe they would have to worry about, but now spend money to manage

   c. traditional retailers can only afford if they integrate their business with a Web site

   d. brochure sites are dealing with on an increasing basis

2. Three of the benefits of Web shopping are _____.

3. In general, which of these statements about prices for products on the Web is true?

   a. Prices found on the Web are typically the same as prices found offline.

   b. People originally thought that prices for products would be higher on the Web, but found that they were actually lower.

   c. People originally expected that prices for products on the Web would be lower, but found they were actually higher due to shipping costs.

   d. People had no expectations about Web prices and don't really factor cost into their decisions.

4. Web marketers looking to reach consumers in Asia in the beginning of 2001 could expect to reach _____ percentage of the population.

5. The term B2C means _____.

6. _____ rely most heavily on basic human interaction to generate revenue.

   a. Vanity sites

   b. Brochure sites

   c. Retail sites

   d. Content sites

7. Between 2001 and 2003, traditional marketers expect to change their Web ad expenditures as a percentage of their overall marketing budget by _____ percent.

8. According to the graph in Figure 2-14, the _____ segment typically spends the greatest percentage of its marketing budget on Web advertising.

9. Although B2B sites generate significantly more revenue than B2C sites, it's important to remember that _____.

   a. there are a lot more B2B than B2C sites on the Web

   b. B2B sites get more media attention than B2C sites

   c. businesses have better Web connectivity than most homes

   d. the average price for a B2B electronic commerce purchase is far greater than the average price for a B2C electronic commerce purchase

10. Why do large, traditional marketers like Pepsi create brochure sites?

11. Name two specific challenges faced by most account management sites.

12. Sites that generate revenue through advertising rely on _____ to raise prices and retain more advertisers.

   a. heavy traffic levels

   b. targeted traffic of specific demographics

   c. neither a nor b

   d. both a and b

13. _____ is an example of a nonmonetary direct gain from a Web site.

   a. A college getting more student applications through its site

   b. A bank receiving letters to the Webmaster, complimenting the site

   c. A museum winning multiple "Best Web Site" awards from various institutions

   d. A toy store selling more products online than offline

14. Between 2000 and 2003, the percentage of small companies that provide retail services on their sites is expected to _____.

   a. increase by 16 percent to about half of all small companies

   b. drop by 12.5 percent to about half of all small companies

   c. increase by 20 percent to about a third of all small companies

   d. increase by 36 percent to about half of all small companies

15. Total ad spending by B2B sites is consistently _____.

   a. greater than total ad spending by B2C sites

   b. less than total ad spending by B2C sites

   c. roughly the same as total ad spending by B2C sites

   d. increasing

HANDS-ON PROJECTS

1. You and two classmates want to start a pure-com business with the hope of creating a large nationally recognized brand. Among the three of you, you have some basic programming capabilities and some design talent, but not enough upon which to build a thriving corporation. Even worse, you have very little start-up money to fund any sort of venture. It seems that all you have is an idea. There's no question that you and your two partners will need to get some investment money to get the company off the ground. Team up with two classmates to develop the business plan. What kind of an idea can you come up with for a Web site? Will it be a content-based site or deal in B2C electronic commerce? What will be the topic, and what kind of services will it offer? (For example, it could be a site that helps high school students find out more about various colleges, a dating Web site, or something else.) Outline and describe what the site will do, and explain why you have collectively decided on that idea. Come up with a name for your company. Develop a plan that addresses the following issues:

   a. Who is your target market? Using the criteria described in chapter, create a mock demographic analysis of what you believe your audience would look like, statistically. Using this information, how would you propose that you create or develop your site in order to reach that market? In other words, what type of content or features would you have in your site that would attract this particular audience?

2

b. Go on the Web, and check out three sites that would be competitors of your particular site. What does each of them have in common? What does each offer that the other doesn't? Based on your idea and your anticipated market, which site would you expect to be your primary competitor? How will your site differ from the sites you have found on the Web? What advantages or disadvantages will your site have?

This information will be the basis of a business plan. In future chapters of this book, you will refer to this "company" and build upon the business plan.

2. Categorize the following sites based on the types outlined in the chapter. What is the main purpose of each Web site?

- **www.nabisco.com**

- **www.pfsmarketwyse.com**

- **www.rockwell.com**

- **www.slate.com**

- **www.webtrends.com**

- **www.redken.com**

- **www.buy.com**

- **www.efloralz.com**

Write an explanation of the purpose of each of these sites and print out pages from each site to support your determination.

3. Looking at the packaging on different products that you buy on a regular basis or the direct mail ads that arrive at your home, find a company that integrates its traditional business with its online presence. Answer the following questions about the company:

a. What are the advantages of the integration for the consumer?

b. Would this method influence you to visit the site or purchase more products?

c. What does the integration tell you about the brand?

3

PLANNING THE SITE

In this chapter, you will learn about:

- The three perspectives from which you should plan your Web site
- Nine keys to meeting customer needs
- In-house site development versus outsourcing
- Using time lines and style guides
- How to maintain brand integrity on a Web site
- The lowest common denominator for your site's technical requirements

Every project you undertake—from booking a vacation to running a business—involves planning from multiple angles, and building a Web site is no exception. In general, Web site developers need to plan the site (after its purpose and audience have been established, as discussed in Chapter 2) from three angles: user, business, and technical. How you plan the site can largely determine whether the site succeeds or fails.

INCORPORATING VISITOR NEEDS INTO A WEB SITE

Web site users want and expect many things from sites and become more demanding as they become more knowledgeable and sophisticated. Following are the top nine elements that visitors expect from Web sites:

1. Valid, up-to-date content

2. Sound navigation features

3. Quick downloads

4. Better prices

5. Simplified shopping

6. Entertainment

7. Personalization

8. Security

9. Improved customer service

As much as is reasonable, you should incorporate these elements into the sites that you develop. Specialized elements relating to your specific site and audience will need to be considered on a site-by-site basis, but the following guidelines generally apply to all sites.

Valid, Up-To-Date Content

People tend to apply different expectations to the Web than in other areas of life. If you walk past the magazine rack in a bookstore on a Thursday, you'll likely see most of the same magazine covers that you saw on Tuesday, and that wouldn't phase you. Stores offer only a certain number of magazines, and through experience, you've come to know that new issues of each title will be delivered on a weekly or monthly basis.

In contrast, the Web's magazine rack is seemingly infinite—sources of new information are endless. No set schedule of updates has been established for Web sites. In fact, many of the early e-zines or retail outlets often updated information infrequently and sporadically. Unpredictable and delayed updates cause users to become skeptical about a site. With so many others from which to choose, why bother going back to one without a standard and regular release of new information?

General news sites and broad category e-tailers, such as **MSN**, **CNN**, or **Amazon.com**, update content on a daily basis—or even more often when news is breaking. Although it comes at a great expense, a daily freshening is the standard that other content-oriented sites must maintain to compete. Less-traveled content sites that offer unique information can get away with updating content on a weekly basis (or even less often) without losing visitors.

Sites that don't rely on repeat visitors for revenue, which include many brochure-style sites for smaller companies, don't need to be updated as often, although for brochure sites quarterly updates are still recommended to keep them from becoming stale.

Provide Valuable Content

Because it needs to be updated so often, content itself, whether it be new product information on a retail site or the most updated news story for a certain audience, is one of the most valuable and sought-after commodities on the Web. Knowing what *type* of content to gather and how to present it are important aspects of planning your site. For example, suppose you run a Web site that provides visitors with information about snow skiing. Obvious topics include tips from experts, reviews of popular mountains and resorts, and new product updates and reviews. To be a viable site, you need to find the information. How will you know when K2 has manufactured a new, more aerodynamically improved ski with lighter bindings? You will need to have this information to report it on your site, and you will need someone of an unbiased nature to review it. To gather that information, you could hire full-time journalists to think up story ideas, do product trials, write reviews, and so on. Their job may also include notifying K2 and other ski manufacturers about the site. They also might solicit press releases (discussed in Chapter 11) so that the site is notified on a regular basis that there are new products being introduced.

Another option is to hire freelance reporters, who work on a project-by-project basis on stories and features. Freelancers are paid by the article. Smaller online publications find this method more economically sound because it costs them less overall. They pay more per article, but they save in other salary and tax-related costs.

A third option for gathering information is to find a content partner. For example, say you know of a travel Web site that has a team of journalists on its staff. With winter coming up, the travel site will begin reporting on ski resorts. Your ski site, in a partnership agreement, may pay the travel site for use of this content. You save salary costs but pay a licensing fee for the content. The downside of this arrangement is that the same content will appear on more than one site.

In addition to finding content, site developers also need to determine what kind of information to include on the site. Rarely is a site created on a topic that has clearly defined boundaries. For example, would the skiing information site need or want to report about the skiing death of actor/congressman Sonny Bono? Would skiing enthusiasts automatically think that your site would be the best source of information on that particular topic and be disappointed if it wasn't covered? Should the site not bother with stories like that one and instead stick to reviews, updates, and skiing tips? It's not a simple decision. Providing such information makes the site seem more topical and gives visitors a reason to come back often. However, it may be difficult to present content of mass interest in such a way that visitors get greater value by reading about it on your site rather than by going to **CNN.com**. One way that the ski site could provide a unique perspective would be to report on Bono's accident and then provide expert analysis on what went wrong and tips for how the average skier could avoid a similar fate.

Sound Navigation Features

Imagine walking into a room. You turn around, and the door you just entered through is gone. You look for other doors, but don't see any. Finally, you find them—three of them that were hidden behind some plants and furniture. One of the doors leads you back to the place from which you just came. That's odd, considering that it's on the opposite wall. Another leads you to a room that seems completely out of place, considering the room that you're in. (It's like walking into a fine dining room from a dirty garage.) The last opens into a brick wall. Apparently it's just a door that doesn't lead anywhere.

If this were a real-life scenario, you probably wouldn't be in a huge rush to visit this house again any time soon. Web sites, especially retail and content sites, can have similar layout problems. From a visitor's perspective, they can be cumbersome and overwhelming. Links appear not only in the standard blue underlined text, but also as graphics and can be placed practically anywhere on a Web page. It's not uncommon for a site—even a small site—to have many links on every page; after all, linking from one page to another is one characteristic that popularized the Web in the first place.

In the commercialization of the Web and designers' desire for aesthetic achievement, buttons and button placement often fall victim to artistic concerns. Their real value as navigation tools is sacrificed. When a visitor comes to a site, he or she come for a specific purpose, either to conduct a transaction, be entertained, or gather information—not to admire the site's design. In most cases, the visitor wants to achieve the desired purpose as quickly and efficiently as possible. The links within a site should help, not hinder, that goal.

Developing a sound navigational structure for a site can be an exacting, complex, and difficult task, one in which an early mistake can cost a great deal of time and money to correct. Chapter 6 reviews the navigation of a site in complete detail.

Avoid Long Downloads

Imagine sitting in a fairly empty room, with nothing to do. There are no magazines or books to read, no television, nothing. The only thing in the room at all is a large, ornate hourglass. You can't leave the room until all the sand has fallen from the top to the bottom. So, for lack of anything better to do, you sit and watch, and sit and watch. It seems that the sand takes forever to fall. Although you can see the sand falling in a trickle, it seems to make no difference in the amount of sand remaining at the top.

Can you imagine how frustrating that would be? The Web is not much different. When a surfer comes to a Web site, he or she must wait for all the images to download. Each image, button, photograph, and body of text has to appear individually within the browser. If the user has a slow connection, or if the images are very large, downloads may take a long time; this procedure can be as frustrating as watching the sand through the hourglass.

3

There is one unmistakable difference between the hourglass example and the Web. In the hourglass example, you weren't allowed to leave the room until all the sand had fallen. On the Web, bored surfers can move on to any other site—including competitors' sites that may download more quickly. In our fast-paced society, moving on after a slight bit of boredom is not a threat, it's a reality.

One of the biggest challenges facing site designers today is the bandwidth discrepancy between Internet connections in people's homes and in their offices. By and large, as the Internet changed from a business luxury to a (perceived) necessity, corporate America has made the move to high bandwidth connectivity. Even 56-Kbps modems—considered fast by some standards—seem out of place in most modern offices, as DSL, ISDN, T1, T3, and cable connection have become standard options.

Recall that most home-based Web users access the Internet using 36.6-Kbps modems. Local phone companies do not aggressively market high bandwidth products for the home, and in light of little competitive incentive, local cable companies also are fairly passive about pushing their high-speed broadband technologies for home use. The purchase of major cable players by AT&T in the late 1990s also slowed the spread of cable modems into most homes (the opposite of its intent), due to legal tie-ups and discrepancies of local and interstate regulations.

These connectivity variances mean huge differences in the time it takes to download Web pages. For Web users connecting on phone modems, download times can be slow to the point of irritation.

Many developers have started to worry a little less about how heavy their Web sites are in file size for several reasons. First, more people report that their major use of the Internet is from work. Second, growth in the B2B segment means that more Web commerce is conducted for business, not consumer purposes. (B2B grew 24 percent faster than B2C during the second half of 2000[1].) Finally, design trends have become more subdued, providing users of 36.6-Kbps modems with faster download times than those of previous page styles.

Does that mean that you should go out and create graphics without any thought at all to their file size? Of course not. It just means that you have a lot more liberty to be creative. Toward the end of 2000, most developers still tried to keep **cumulative page weights** (the total file size, in bytes, of any Web page when the file size for all the page's graphics are added together) to less than 150 K.

Improve Prices

No one likes a nasty surprise. That's why you should do everything you can to keep item and shipping costs low. You learned in Chapter 1 that high shipping costs account for e-shoppers abandoning nearly half of all shopping carts before completing their purchases. Let your customers know early what shipping costs will add to their bottom

[1] Source: *PC World*, Sept. 25, 2001.

line. When low Web prices are not offset by widely advertised sales in traditional brick-and-mortar locations or by undesirably high shipping costs, the convenience aspect of online shopping increases in value. If Web prices aren't inflated by shipping costs, Web business will grow and revenue will rise, cutting into overall retail spending. Higher Web prices or higher shipping costs reduce the value of convenience to Web shoppers.

Shoppers will always be price conscious, even in prosperous times. To an extent, price shoppers will forgo some savings in place of added convenience. However, even for shoppers who buy based on convenience, the convenience factor needs to be significant to compensate for higher Web prices (or Web prices that are increased by shipping costs).

Prices for online sales will drop as Web sites, especially pure-coms, streamline their distribution systems to allow for more reasonable shipping costs.

Keep Shopping Simple

If waiting to buy *online* takes longer than waiting to buy *in line*, then consumers may as well go to the store for immediate results. Online retailers must ensure that both the shopping and checkout processes are as simple as possible to achieve convenience for shoppers. Three areas in which retail sites must make e-shopping a positive experience are:

- Giving access to specific products
- Providing an easy means of removing items from shopping carts
- Streamlining the checkout process

A fourth and equally important point is to allow consumers to track their orders after making their purchases. This need falls under the realm of providing better customer service and is detailed in Chapter 12.

Easy Product Access

Not being able to find a specific product is a common complaint of e-shoppers, and it is particularly common with advertised specials or limited-time offers. Visitors will see an advertised special that looks interesting and click it with the expectation that they can purchase it immediately. Instead, they are linked to a page with more advertisements for the product and an explanation of how it works, the benefits, and so on. Eventually, the final link for the advertised product is nothing more than a form to fill out for more information on how to purchase the item, which is a low attempt by the site developers to force contact information out of a consumer. The customer also might find an explanation that the product can be purchased only at the advertised price if other purchases are made first. This carrot-and-stick practice might work in a brick-and-mortar location (in which trained and experienced salespeople can try to divert the shopper's attention away from the advertised special and onto a more expensive item), but the Web is still a new medium, and standard advertising deceptions or lures are transparent at this early stage.

Offering too much selection just because it's easy to do can be as bad as making a desired product hard to get. Brick-and-mortar stores weed out the less desirable products due to limited shelf space and offer only those products they believe will most benefit their shoppers. Shoppers typically don't have a problem with this method. The fact that an exponential amount of choices are available on the Web for any product has been shown to confuse shoppers and drive them away from online shopping. An extensive study by PFS Marketwyse found that over 22 percent of online shoppers complain about having too many buying options.

Easy Product Removal

Many sites make it very simple for shoppers to put items into their shopping carts, but raise the level of difficulty when it comes to later removing those items. Until recently, **ToysRUs** was one of the largest perpetrators of this practice. Placing products in a shopping cart was a snap, but finding the cart and the "remove" button was more of a challenge. Was this a deliberate attempt to force a buy? Maybe not—it was more likely just an oversight. However, that didn't make it any more bearable, and consumer backlash caused site developers to revamp this aspect of the shopping experience. Be sure to provide your customers an easy out if they have a change of mind. They will appreciate it.

Streamline the Checkout Process

After a shopper has located the products he or she wants to buy, your site should allow him or her to make purchases quickly and easily. If possible, refrain from prying too much information out of users as a prerequisite for making a purchase. Obviously, certain information is necessary, such as shipping information and credit card numbers. Users expect to provide such information. Unfortunately, many online retailers don't stop there. Instead, they request additional data, such as a home or work phone number, information which may be outside of most visitors' comfort level. They also might require opinion surveys regarding personal shopping habits, which can be time-consuming and annoying. If the annoyance factor of these elements is too high, users often find it easier to shop elsewhere (competition is just a click away) or to end their Internet session without making any purchases.

Information is important, and users will provide it—when they are ready. Highly personal information requests or behavioral surveys are not uncommon or unwelcome on the Web, but make these requests optional rather than mandatory to maximize shopper happiness and site success.

Entertain Your Visitors

The Web has proven to be a haven for instant entertainment, with online games and short movies (animated or real-life) acting as growing sources for traffic retention. New technologies have made game playing and online shows more sophisticated, faster to download, and more entertaining. Flash, Shockwave, and 3-D development lead the way for these technologies.

Figure 3-1 show pages from **Shockwave.com**, a popular entertainment site. Users come to the site to play games (new games are updated on a regular basis) or to see serialized Flash movies. (Flash allows for smooth animation with relatively quick download times, among other valuable capabilities.) StainBoy, an increasingly popular Flash animated character created by Tim Burton (director of *Batman* and *Edward Scissorhands*), is shown in the figure.

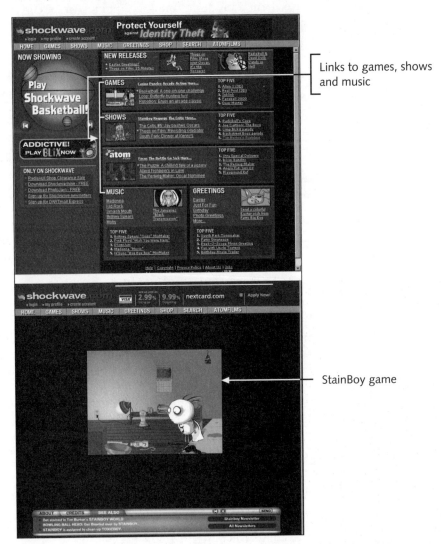

Links to games, shows and music

StainBoy game

Figure 3-1 Shockwave.com entertainment site

StainBoy is an early example of how Hollywood cashes in on the online entertainment phenomenon. The entertainment industry benefits as movie shorts shown on the Web gain in popularity, and movie production companies license their work to Web sites that want to use them to attract an audience. Additionally, actors, directors, and producers benefit from being retained by marketers who leverage their talents to create movies for their sites.

Studies show that sites offering entertainment retain traffic longer than sites that don't and have better rates of returning visitors[2]. Both of these facts are important features for online brand building.

One of the benefits of advanced online entertainment is that because it isn't cheap to implement, there is little risk of it saturating the Web any time soon. Entertainment doesn't necessarily have to be complex to be beneficial, and even simple entertainment can be well branded, as you will see in the next section.

Maximize Brand Value

Web sites like Shockwave.com aren't the only types of sites that benefit from entertaining their visitors. Corporate sites also use games to keep traffic on their sites. Not all corporations maximize the brand value of their online games. Coca-Cola, largely credited as one of the most brilliantly marketed companies on the planet, is surprisingly limited in terms of the online games that it offers. Figure 3-2 shows a game of darts on the **Coca-Cola** store site (cocacolastore.com). The game itself is fine. From a technical standpoint, however, it is unexceptional. What is lacking in terms of promotion is that the game is completely unbranded. There is no connection between darts and the Coca-Cola name or product. Instead, the company would have been better off developing a game in which players threw darts or balls not at a board, but at a row of Coke bottles on a ledge. The site should work the product into the game and keep the company name and logo in front of the user.

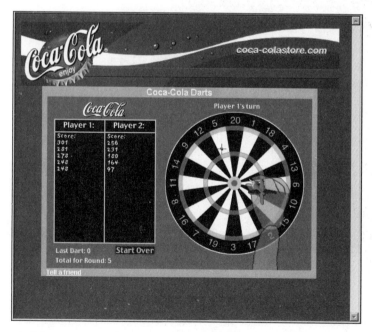

Figure 3-2   Coca-Cola's online dart game

---

[2] Source: *The Industry Standard*, February 2001.

Nabisco has done a far more successful job of branding its incredibly developed **NabiscoWorld.com** Web site, shown in Figure 3-3. Each game (and there are many) is branded to one or more Nabisco products. The QB Shootout football throw shown in Figure 3-3 may be just a standard game of throwing a football at a target for points, but it ties the product to active sports and allows for self-marketed banner ads.

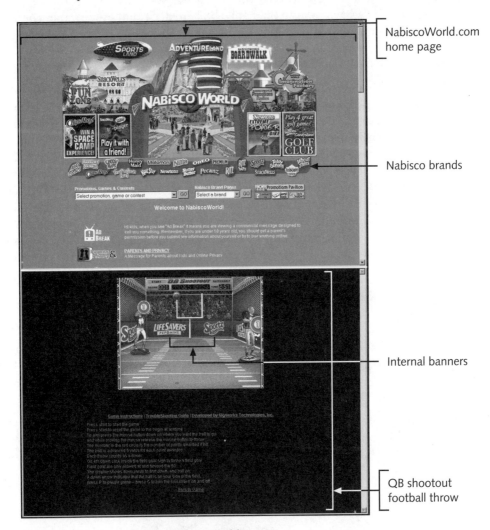

NabiscoWorld.com home page

Nabisco brands

Internal banners

QB shootout football throw

Figure 3-3   Games from NabiscoWorld.com

The wide variety and enhanced development of the games on the Nabisco site give people a reason to stay on the site longer. The branding identities that are associated with and interwoven throughout each game make that extended stay worthwhile for the company; in contrast, the unbranded Coca-Cola dart game keeps people on the site for no useful reason. The brand value of the Nabisco site is that it keeps the Nabisco name and products in the mind of consumers, and at the same time, it helps create an association between Nabisco, "fun," and "entertainment."

Maximize Game Value

Entertainment, if done correctly, can provide more than brand value, it can help increase online sales. The Coca-Cola dart game shown in Figure 3-2 provides no useful reason for existing. It is set up so that people can play just to spend time. However, considering that the site's goal is to sell Coca-Cola branded products (hats, shirts, memorabilia, and so on) online, the games could be used more wisely to help increase sales.

By implementing a database and some fairly complex programming, the site could allow visitors to play the dart game as often as they'd like and accumulate points. These points would be retained even after a user leaves the site or stops playing the game. Like the frequent flyer miles used by airlines, game players would be invited to play the dart game over and over again to accumulate more points, which could be cashed in for discounts on Coca-Cola store products. For example 1,000 accumulated points could be cashed in for free product shipping, and 5,000 points could be cashed in for a free Coke baseball cap. This type of strategy not only entertains, but also provides the potential for a company to earn revenue from integrated entertainment because some players will buy merchandise to take advantage of the free shipping, while others will make purchases to coordinate with the free cap.

Simpler Web Entertainment

Of course, scenarios like the one described above are expensive to implement. Not all Web sites are going to have the same budget that Coca-Cola has for marketing, and so they will be limited in the amount of entertainment that they can provide. Flash and Shockwave developers require high salaries, as do programmers who are needed to keep track of players and their scores in a database.

Entertainment can occur through simpler means and not only through complex programming. For lesser budgets, try adding a funny quote that you update regularly. Ideally, this quote would be from someone in your site's industry. You also could provide a survey with which people can interact with and then to which later they can return and see updated results. There are limitless ways to creatively add spice and levity to a site without spending lots of money or venturing too far from the core idea.

Personalization

The concept of personalizing sites for each individual visitor is gaining popularity. In Chapter 2, you learned about the value of market research and understanding the audience. It is important to realize that a group of people falling into a common demographic set will not share *exactly* the same tastes and interests. This is where personalization comes in. Personalizing a site can involve some intense programming (translate: expensive); however, it may be worth the cost.

For example, assume that your site is a general information Web site that offers main-stream news headlines, horoscopes, sports scores, and other basic information. Customization would allow a user to determine which of these items is most important to him or her. Through a user friendly interface, a visitor could set up the site so that each time he or she visits the home page, recent football scores, regional weather, a local traffic report, and a personal horoscope appear on the page. Another user visiting the same site could view different information more appropriate to his or her individual needs, such as the leading business news, specific stock quotes, and baseball scores.

The Web site shown in Figure 3-4 is the customization page for msn.com. **MSN.com**, one of the leading portals on the Web, offers visitors a lot of data when they first come to the site. Some of the information is relevant to individual site users, and some of it isn't. You can choose what information you want listed on the page—even if the content comes from other sites, such as Discovery or Forbes. You can also rearrange the order of the information on your msn.com home page, omitting certain content if you wish.

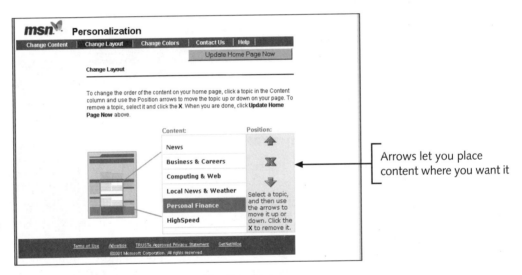

Figure 3-4   MSN.com site personalization features

Using Personalization Properly

Personalization of a site can exist in models different from the one used by MSN.com. **Amazon.com**, shown in Figure 3-5, personalizes its site by welcoming return visitors back by name and recommending books based on previous purchases. By doing this, Amazon.com smartly increases the amount of revenue it generates from existing customers, which is far less expensive than attracting new customers. Note, however, that there is a point at which personalization changes from an asset to a liability. Site developers must be aware of this distinction.

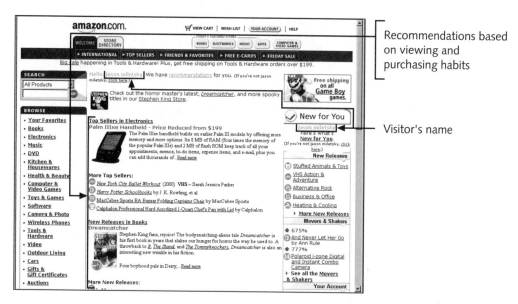

Figure 3-5   Amazon.com, the quintessential site for personalization

Although users want personalization and respond favorably to the pampering that comes with being treated like an individual and not a number, they are at the same time concerned with living under the eye of Big Brother. Marketers, especially on the Web, need to walk a fine line between individualizing and prying.

One of the ways useful sites make themselves indispensable to visitors is providing merchandise recommendations based on past purchases or research. Using cookies (small programs that are placed on visitors' hard drives and that track the pages they visit each time they surf the Web) or other customized programs, some sites collect data on visitors' activity. They record what pages they visit, how long they stay, what they buy, and so on. These sites greet returning customers with recommendations on products they might find interesting. These suggestions are educated recommendations developed from a customized study of each individual customer and are theoretically meant to help increase sales.

The successful use of personalization often comes down to proper wording and a basic understanding of human nature. For example, assume that you buy a book from Amazon.com about Michael Jordan. Upon your next visit, or through a direct mail advertisement, you are greeted with the message "If you like books about Michael Jordan, you'll love these books on the Chicago Bulls and stars of the NBA." Chances are that this type of personalization will be met with a good reception, and there is a higher likelihood that the effort may result in a sale.

Consider what happens when the wording of that message is changed slightly to read "*Since* you like books on Michael Jordan…" There's a big difference. This latter message might aggravate, annoy, and scare visitors.

The word "if" in the first method implies a *likelihood* that you like a specific topic, but it may just be coincidental that you happened to buy a book on the topic not too long ago. You might have purchased it as a gift for a friend who happens to be a basketball fan. The word "since" implies, "I've been watching you." It invades the visitor's privacy. Retailers, no matter how nice they may be, will never be considered the visitor's friend. Therefore, it's fine to get personal, but keep it safe and comfortable for the visitor.

Another, more subtle way of using customer movement information is to offer products on the home page that may be of interest to the returning visitor without using any marketing language to acknowledge that his or her movements have been tracked.

Keep Visitor Information Private

As suggested in the previous section, privacy is important to site visitors. Each new warning of a major virus alert or report of a major system breach by a hacker undermines the security that people need to feel when giving out private information. Slowly but surely, however, Web users are getting used to the idea of sharing certain sensitive information—such as their credit card numbers—with retail Web sites, especially with pure-coms that have either established their names (such as Amazon.com or Priceline.com) or traditional marketers that are starting to make their mark on the Web.

The other major privacy concern on shopper's minds is the threat of e-tailers distributing private information among themselves. Shoppers who provide their name, mailing address, e-mail address, and other personal information become part of massive mailing lists, which hold tremendous value to marketers who want to reach specific demographics. Many e-tailers make it clear that they will not sell private visitor information. However, to the dismay of many trusting shoppers, some pure-coms who ran out of cash and hit troubled times sold their mailing lists, even when their policies clearly stated they would never engage in this practice.

For your Web site to succeed, you must constantly assure customers that more and better privacy controls are being put in place.

Improve Customer Service

Many site developers believe that a FAQ (Frequently-Asked Questions) page answers all customer questions and that traditional customer service applications are unnecessary on the Web. Nothing could be further from the truth. Site developers are quickly coming to understand the important role customer service plays in the success of a Web site, and they are beginning to attract customers with the promise of better service. The foundation of customer service that has helped build traditional businesses is even more important on the Web, where consumers' comfort levels for online purchasing are still relatively low.

Customers want to know:

- How long will a product take to be delivered?

- How easy is it to return an item if I don't like it?

- What if I don't understand a technical aspect of the purchase? Is online help available?

Only quality customer service features that are obvious and easy to use can address these concerns and increase customers' comfort levels. Customer service issues are explored in Chapter 12.

FROM A BUSINESS PERSPECTIVE

So far in this chapter we've examined what consumers look for, expect, and respond to when they visit a Web site. All these elements need to be taken into consideration during the planning stages of the site. You must budget for costs related to each element that may not be obvious at first (these are illustrated in the business plan provided in Appendix B), consider time lines for development, and make sure that brand integrity is maintained throughout the site. It's not enough to just have an idea for a site. As we saw in Chapter 2, the business plan takes many variables into account before the first line of programming is even typed. When planning your site's business, you need to address many variables, including internal versus outsourced development, time line and schedule development, your style guide, and your branding, before focusing on consumer issues.

Internal Versus Outsourced Web Site Development

Anyone developing a Web site must decide whether to build the site **in-house** (by company employees) or to **outsource** it (hire out the development project) to a third-party developer. The decision usually comes down to at least two variables:

- Is the site your company's main source of business? For example, a pure-com that intends to generate revenue solely or primarily from its Web site would likely need to have people on staff create the site, as well as update and maintain it. The pure-come may work with outside consultants from time to time when necessary.

- How much growth is intended for the site? For example, if the site is being built by an established marketer as a brochure site and not intended for rapid growth, it may not be economically feasible to staff employees who won't have a lot to do once the site is up and running. If that is the situation, it may be more efficient to hire a third-party vendor to handle developmental duties.

If you decide to outsource production, design, or both tasks, you most likely will work with either a Web production shop, which specializes in Web site development and other technology development, or an advertising/marketing agency. Advertising agencies have been developing creative messages for clients since the late 1800s. The industry has grown from print ads to full cross-media campaigns including television, radio, roadside billboards, novelty items such as pens and calendars, and just about anything onto which you can stick a logo.

When the Internet became commercialized, it opened up a new advertising medium. At first, that's exactly what it was—a way for companies to advertise their sites without the same high costs charged by television, radio, print, and other media.

During its infancy, the Web spawned a whole new industry of service providers and Web developers to handle creation needs. Companies like **Razorfish** and **Organic** were the models for hundreds of stand alone Web development shops. Traditional advertising agencies have added Web-specific departments to compete with the Web development shops. These shops, in one form or another, work with client companies of all sizes to help get them on the Web. If you don't count pure-coms into the equation, over 70 percent of companies with Web sites have hired some sort of outside help for site design and programming.

Dot-coms or traditional retailers rely on advertising agencies or development shops for a good reason. The Web is a strange medium and not everybody understands it. Most people understand what a print ad can do. It sits in a publication and promotes the company or product. Companies also understand what they will get in television advertising: a specified number of seconds, produced in a specific format, that will air during certain broadcasts. Building a Web site, however, is different from these traditional marketing methods, and technology changes far more frequently than traditional media. It's hard to keep up with new developments. Therefore, education is a hidden cost in site development.

Site developers—whether in-house or outsourced—must understand the business as much as they do good programming. Smaller companies that don't understand branding or marketing often look to the developer to determine the message to convey on the site. Chapter 5 covers the internal versus external development debate in depth.

Planning with Time Lines

A **time line** is a projected schedule that helps to organize the many facets of work that go into creating a site. Because these facets may need the expertise of a lot of people, it's important to know when one phase of a project ends so that another may begin. Timing is extremely important when it comes to the programming and design of any type of Web site. Except in the instances of brochure-style sites (in which deadlines may be less important), it's likely that many issues will be affected by the timely development of your Web site. For example, content may be time-sensitive, press releases may need to be distributed, or a marketing campaign may need to be launched. The success of all these efforts depends on keeping to a strict deadline for completion.

3

The first step in creating any Web site is to develop a **schematic** for the site. Schematics, which are covered more thoroughly in Chapter 6, usually consist of a rough sketch that approximates the site's various pages and navigation structure. The schematic helps developers understand how difficult a site will be to develop, as well as how large the site will be. It also gives you a blueprint for construction, from which you can create your time line. Depending on the staff and talent available, it stands to reason that larger and more complex sites will need a longer time line for completion. Database-driven sites may take longer to build depending on complexity, as may sites that use Flash or other interactive technologies.

Your site should have a team of people dedicated to site development. All team members should have input on the time line to ensure that delegated tasks can be completed according to a mutually agreeable time frame. This is especially helpful if some team members are working on other projects at the same time. Don't guess at how long each section is going to take to program. Ask the programmers for their estimates, and then tack on a few extra days. Sites are delayed more often because of poor planning and overly optimistic deadlines than for any other reason. Chapter 5 describes in detail the elements of the site-building team.

Figure 3-6 shows a sample time line for **Flack + Kurtz** (www.fk.com). The main purpose of this site is to entice engineering students and make them want to work for Flack + Kurtz after graduating. To that end, the site needs to showcase the company as technologically advanced and give students the impression that Flack + Kurtz would be a fun and exciting place to work. At the same time, the site can't overlook the fact that potential clients likely will visit, so whereas the site has to make Flack + Kurtz look appealing from a student's perspective, it also has to look professional from a business perspective. The Flack + Kurtz site is a moderately complex site that includes original graphic design. (The design is made from scratch. This is an original creation, not a redesign of something already existing.) The site also includes Flash programming for an interactive interface, database development, and a back-end administrative area that allows the site to be easily and instantly updateable. The site is not being built in-house, but rather by an outside agency that is responsible for all components of development. Although the agency in this case may make recommendations, the client for whom the site is being built supplies all content.

1. Development and review of content with Flack + Kurtz	Week 1
2. Preparation and collection of all materials	Week 1
3. Sample design and comps	Week 2
4. Programming alpha phase (prototype, structure, and layout)	Week 6
5. Review period for Flack + Kurtz (3 days)	Week 6
6. Beta phase (additional elements, content, and design)	Week 9
7. Review period for Flack + Kurtz (3 days)	Week 10
8. Test launch on client staging server	Week 11
9. Bug fix and proper application functionality review	Week 12
10. Final launch	Week 12

Figure 3-6   A sample time line

This time line is broken up into weeks, with varying numbers of weeks distributed for different aspects of the project based on task difficulty, complexity, or tedium. The time line also allows for client reviews and in-house testing before the site is launched to ensure that no bugs exist when the site reaches the public.

To prevent your site from hitting unforeseen delays caused by inconsistencies in branding or other visual characteristics, it is extremely useful to define the look of the site using a style guide.

Style Guides

If you are developing a site for an established company (either yours or a client's), that company may require you to adhere to a **style guide**. A style guide is a set of rules that all external marketers, print developers, Web developers, and others have to follow so that the company is assured that its logo, colors, fonts, and other brand identity elements remain the same across various media. Consistency is an important part of brand development. The style guide typically provides guidelines that must be followed to maintain brand integrity. These guidelines may indicate the font styles to use, illustrate how to use the logo properly, which RGB mixes should be used for the corporate colors, and provide other specific direction. (RGB refers to red, green, and blue—the three basic colors used by computer monitors to mix millions of hues and shades. Appendix C provides a deeper look at how color works.)

Regardless of whether a style guide exists for the core brand, your development team should create a style guide specifically for the site that you are creating. A style guide provides consistency, which is especially important because of the unique layout and structure of the Web, and the fact that, unlike printed brochures, Web sites change frequently.

The Web style guide should address everything that could come into question, including:

- Font styles, sizes, and colors for headlines (primary headline, secondary headline, and tertiary headline)
- Font styles, sizes, and colors for body text
- Other text used (such as pointers to new information)
- Button and navigation bar colors
- RGB color breakdowns for title bars and backgrounds
- Attributes for images and text, such as the composition of drop shadows, glows, bevels, embosses, and outlines
- Margin widths and column widths

As the Web becomes more image oriented and as many text features such as headlines are created as graphics, it is important to keep a record of specific Web details. It will not only help you and your team when it comes to making changes later, but also it will prevent confusion down the road.

Brand Integrity

As you've probably noticed, the concept of the brand plays an important role in this book. Nothing is more important to the long-term success of a legitimate company than the brand that it builds.

Not every company spends the time to care for its brand image the way that it should. Smaller companies, especially, tend to pay less attention to brand issues because they take time and money to develop. Many smaller companies don't understand branding enough to make the investment, understand it but sacrifice the long-term benefits of branding for more immediate (and short-term) profits, or simply don't have the budget to support brand development.

If you are involved in the development of a site for a company that has not taken steps to develop its brand properly (meaning it has a logo, but little else), at least make sure to maintain consistency with existing materials. For example, if an established company does not have a brand style guide, but it does have a corporate brochure that is dark blue with photographic images and serif font styles, don't build a Web site that uses mostly red with cartoon-style illustrations and a sans serif font. Consistency between media makes a company look more organized and professional. These are important qualities to potential customers.

Beyond some of the business considerations that need to be accounted for, the site needs to be physically programmed and designed to come to fruition. With so many programming languages and applications from which to choose, it's not always easy to determine the best and most efficient way to create a site, especially when future growth also needs to be considered. The following section reviews some of the elements that developers need to consider to build the site properly.

THE TECHNICAL PERSPECTIVE

As time and technology march on, the Web and Web surfers become more savvy and sophisticated. More and better options and alternatives become available to make the Web more useful—and more complicated. The fact that developers can't control or even know (beyond an educated guess) what type of hardware and software Web surfers are using to view sites makes developing sites a hit-or-miss endeavor. Unlike television, which takes an image and scales it up or down according to one ratio regardless of the physical size of the receiving television set, the Web looks and acts differently depending on the user's equipment and settings. Differences in browsers, monitors, platforms, resolutions, and connection speeds combine to create a complex set of variables. With these variations in mind, developers need to ensure that the widest possible audience can see and use the site.

The programming languages that are available have also grown in number as the Web has gained importance as a commerce tool. Languages and applications need to be chosen and tempered by developers based not only on what the site needs to do and provide, but also on how many potential users will be able to see the site properly. Developers also need to consider which language will likely remain popular in the future so that changes and upgrades can be made.

Because the Web is shaped by programming and technology, various aspects of each have to be carefully considered and understood at the outset of the site. This section goes into some of these aspects. Be aware that the topics covered here are only the tip of the ice-berg. Technology and the Web as a subject can't be contained within an entire volume of books, much less a relatively short section. Technology issues concerning the Web can be broadly based, ranging from how the Internet actually works to very specific details of various programming languages.

Establishing a Lowest Common Denominator

One of the main technical challenges of creating a Web site is to design a site that all visitors can successfully access. Variations in connections, local traffic, systems hardware, and other elements can mean huge connectivity variations among visitors. The solution for developers is to determine the site's **lowest common denominator (LCD)**, or the minimum set of variables that need to be programmed so that the largest audience possible can see the Web site.

As a result of conducting market research, you will learn how your target market accesses the Web, including the users' information download speeds, browser versions, and monitor resolutions. From this information, you can develop a technical profile of the low-end visitor. This profile is your LCD.

Web connection speed is becoming a nonissue for developers, as faster connection devices find their way into homes and businesses. Even though a chasm exists between the speed at which people can access the Web from home and from work, speed has increased greatly enough for both audiences to allow for greater flexibility in design. However, until all Web users have cable modem connections (or better) and the most current browser versions, it's important to set some general boundaries for design. Setting an LCD is a means of establishing these boundaries and can affect the types of images and the amount of alternative applications (such as audio files, Director movies, and so on) that will work on the site.

Based on the LCD, you should set a size for each page limit. The size limit must take into account the cumulative byte weight of all graphics. For example, you may determine that because your target market is using 36.6-Kbps modems, the individual pages of your site shouldn't exceed 100 K each when the file size of all graphics—background graphics, buttons and inline graphics—are totaled.

3

In 1998, it wasn't uncommon for many developers' LCD to resemble the following:

- 14.4 Kbps modem

- 640 x 480 dpi monitor resolution

- America Online 2.5 browser

By mid-1999, the LCD had changed to reflect the times, with more developers building sites for the following standards:

- 28.8 Kbps modem

- 640 x 480 dpi monitor resolution

- Microsoft Internet Explorer 3.0 browser

The LCD is a constantly updated standard. In fact, because of the access gap between home and work, many developers use two general LCDs, one for B2B sites and one for B2C sites. However, as users upgrade their systems, their Web connections and capabilities change; as a result, site designers often re-evaluate LCDs for each new site they build.

Currently, average LCDs are as follows:

B2B Sites

- ISDN connection

- 800 x 600 dpi monitor resolution

- Microsoft Internet Explorer 4.0 or Netscape Navigator 4.0 browser

B2C Sites

- 36.6 Kbps modem

- 800 x 600 dpi monitor resolution

- Microsoft Internet Explorer 4.0 or Netscape Navigator 4.0 browser

The only real difference between the two is the modem speed, but it's a major difference. Also of significance is that version 4.0 and higher of the Internet Explorer and Netscape browsers are listed in the LCD. Because these browser versions are compatible with Macromedia's Flash technology (each has the necessary plug-in preloaded for easy viewing), programming for a site is opened up to take advantage of this technology.

Programs and Languages

In the early days of Web commercialization, all that a Web site programmer needed to know was **Hypertext Markup Language (HTML)**. HTML is not a program, but a simple language made up of various tags that instruct browser software how to lay out a Web page for display on a monitor, where to find certain graphic images, and other pages to which to hyperlink.

Other programs that were very popular in the earlier days included Common Gateway Interface (CGI), a protocol used to create interactive Web site applications that allowed sites to process, distribute, and protect information. On the graphics front, Adobe's Photoshop was (and still is) the primary graphic design tool. Although because it is primarily a print developer's program, it can be difficult to use for creating graphics for Web sites. (Designing graphics for the Web requires different talents and knowledge than creating graphics for print use.)

Today the Web landscape has new programs, languages, and complications. In fact, tools and options available for Web creation have gotten so vast that whereas it used to be normal for smaller corporate sites to be graphically designed and programmed by the same person, today even small sites typically require a team of people, or at least a division of responsibility between graphic designers and programmers.

A wealth of programs and applications are available for site development. Each site uses a different combination of languages and programs, depending on the desired result. Appendix A provides description of some of the more popular ones.

CHAPTER SUMMARY

- ◻ Like any other challenging and detailed task, Web site development needs to be planned from many different angles if it has any hope of success. Specifically, you must consider the user's perspective, your business angle, and technical factors when planning your site.

- ◻ You must consider what Web users require of the site. At the same time, you should understand the specific target audience so that you can cater to their wants and needs. You need to take into account valid, up-to-date content, sound navigation features, quick downloads, better prices, simplified shopping, entertainment, personalization, security, and improved customer service when planning your site for universal acceptance. More specific content, design, and layout decisions can be made after audience data has been generated through surveys, interviews, or focus groups.

- ◻ From a business standpoint, it's important to maintain a working schematic blueprint of the site and to create a time line for production to keep the site organized and on schedule. Using a style guide (or creating one, if necessary) can be helpful in maintaining brand integrity.

- ◻ Thorough planning of your Web site, which entails considering all the factors described in this chapter, is one of the most important factors in the success of your online business.

3

KEY TERMS

cumulative page weight
Hypertext Markup Language (HTML)
in-house
lowest common denominator (LCD)
outsource
schematic
style guide
time line

REVIEW QUESTIONS

1. The main reason that content sites need to be updated often is that
   _____.

   a. information changes so quickly

   b. printed magazines and broadcast news update information as it happens

   c. there is a seemingly infinite number of competitive content sites on the Web

   d. they really don't have to be updated all that often—most people visit content sites infrequently

2. An easy way to show that you've updated a Web site is to _____.

   a. change the color of the home page

   b. insert a small line that reads "Last updated on:"

   c. let the visitor type a "last visited on" date

   d. insert a graphic that says "Updated!"

3. It is most important for Web site navigation features to _____.

   a. be well designed

   b. keep visitors on your site for as long as possible

   c. help visitors find what they're looking for on your site

   d. take the visitor to the home page

4. When taking into consideration a site's download time, developers need to pay attention to_____.

5. Selling the mailing list _____.

   a. is a great way to make money

   b. diminishes shoppers' faith in your site's promise to keep information private

   c. is common practice among B2C sites

   d. All of the above.

6. Which of the following statements about electronic commerce is not true?

   a. Making it more difficult to remove items from a shopping cart to increase sales is a good policy.

   b. Making items easy to find on a Web retail site is one key to success.

   c. People don't want to fill out very long forms just to buy a product from a Web site.

   d. High shipping prices cause nearly half of all Web shoppers to abandon their purchases.

7. An example of brand advertising on a Web game is _____.

   a. a pop-up banner that appears in front of the game before you start playing

   b. a program that takes the user directly to an advertiser's site after the game is finished

   c. a billiards game with an advertiser's logo printed on the surface of the pool table

   d. a horizontal banner that remains at the top of the game page

8. A Web site that allows personalized customization might _____.

   a. allow you to put the site's address in your "Favorites" file

   b. give you easy access to other Web sites

   c. make purchasing a product more streamlined

   d. allow you to change the way the home page presents information

9. What is one potential danger of Web site personalization?

10. Making a product recommendation to a returning Web visitor based on his or her previous purchases enhances _____.

    a. customer service and navigation

    b. customer service and personalization

    c. entertainment and personalization

    d. personalization and the provision of up-to-date content

11. What are two customer service issues that sites must address?

12. When planning a site, the _____ is crucial to a successful start.

    a. time line

    b. time plan

    c. launch plan

    d. master schedule

13. List three pieces of information you might expect to find in a Web style guide.

14. Why is it important to establish an LCD?

HANDS-ON PROJECTS

1. Continue the business plan that you started in Chapter 2 with your two partners. By now, you should have decided on the idea, you should know the demographics of your target market, and you should have an analysis of some of your competitors.

   a. Considering your audience and the type of site you want to develop, what steps can you take to make sure users enjoy being on your site and that they will have a good enough experience to come back?

   b. From a business perspective, what types of costs can you anticipate before site production begins? Would it be more feasible to hire out a third-party development company to build the site or to build the site in-house? What are the costs involved with each?

   c. Consider the type of site that you will be building. Refer to Appendix A to determine the types of programs and technology that will work best to create the site. Make a list of the programs and applications that would be best, as well as your reasoning why you have made those particular choices.

2. Look at several pages on three of the eight Web sites listed below:

   ❑ **www.cnn.com**

   ❑ **www.fedex.com**

   ❑ **www.ebags.com**

   ❑ **www.sony.com**

   ❑ **www.eonline.com**

   ❑ **www.bodyshop.com**

   ❑ **www.mustang.org**

   ❑ **www.target.com**

   Based on what you see, explain each site's style policies and develop a style guide for each site.

3. This chapter outlines nine key points that consumers look for and appreciate in a Web site. Search the Web and find a site that you believe has at least six of these qualities. Provide printouts and written evidence to support your belief that these qualities exist on the site. Finally, list the qualities that are missing from the site. How does their absence detract from the site and the overall brand? If you were a consultant, what would you recommend the site do to make the site better for the consumer? How would you recommend the missing elements be incorporated?

4

REVENUE AND ADVERTISING

> **In this chapter, you will learn about:**
> ♦ Basic approaches for business success
> ♦ Six models for making money online
> ♦ Four styles of Web advertising
> ♦ Methods to track advertising data

You have a great idea for a Web site. You know what you want it to do, what kind of site you want it to be, who your audience is, and what they will respond to. Yep, it's going to be a great Web site.

Of course, making money can be nice, too.

Over the last few years, the options for generating revenue with a Web site have increased tremendously. As you learned in Chapter 2, there are many different types of Web sites. Assuming that you have identified the type of Web site that you want to develop, you need a plan to turn that idea into a profitable venture. Early Web entrepreneurs held the high-flying belief that the Web was an ever-flowing river of green. Now, online businesspeople find themselves wondering, "Is there *anything* on the Web that works?"

This chapter outlines some of the requirements and pitfalls of making a Web site profitable. The chapter begins with an overview of basic business principles and requirements for a successful Web venture. We'll look at some of the standard means of generating revenue with a Web site, as well some new, creative ways (such as the new online advertising methods and reemergence of the once-defunct subscription plans) to bring in money. Finally, the chapter examines Web advertising in its various forms.

WHAT DOES WORK: THE VERY BASICS OF BUSINESS

Thus far, this text has illustrated many examples of sites that have failed to earn a profit and that subsequently have either gone out of business or teetered on the brink of doing so. It raises the logical question: What *does* work on the Web?

Any business, be it cyber or traditional, has to be built on a foundation of necessity—if there is no need or desire in the market for your product or service, you won't be able to sell anything, regardless of how much money you invest in it.

Suppose, for example, you decide to rent retail space right in the heart of Times Square in Manhattan. It's a huge facility that is visible to anyone within two blocks, and you spend lavishly to decorate it. Your multimillion dollar ad campaign reaches a massively large audience, and it wins awards for its ability to be clever and deliver a clear message. You might think that all these circumstances brought together would mean guaranteed success for your venture. However, suppose that the company that you opened in that expensive Times Square retail space was a typewriter and rotary phone sales and service company? Because so few people have either typewriters or rotary phones these days, you'd end up with a great-looking store, but no customers.

It's an extreme example, of course, but with a clear point: If the public doesn't demand the products or services you are offering, your products or services hold no real value in the marketplace. At the same time, if there is a demand for a product or service, there probably are other companies already in existence, competing with each other to service that demand. Thus, you must have something unique to gain **marketshare**, which is the percentage of the overall market for your industry that buys its products or services from your company. If you're going to start a fast-food hamburger restaurant, your food needs to be better, faster, cheaper, or in some other way different from McDonald's offerings to provide consumers any incentive to buy from you.

Opening a business online is no different. You need to find an opening in the market where demand is not being met, and fill that demand if you're to achieve any real level of success. If that demand is being met to any extreme, your entry needs to differ in some (even slight) way. Chapter 8 covers unique selling positions and how a brand can distinguish itself from others in the field.

One of the dangers of online business, however, is that sometimes technology allows so much flexibility that it may create demand when there was none. It can disguise itself as an opening in the marketplace when the need is not a true need, but a manufactured need. Consider WebVan.com, a start-up that promised to deliver groceries to your home on demand. Shoppers could visit the site, submit their shopping lists, and have their orders delivered to their front doors. It seemed to be a clear case where the Web could work wonders in a way that made people's lives more convenient. However, the fact that the technology *could* be manipulated to pull off such a venture led to the fatal mistake of thinking that there actually was a *need* for this type of service. Marketers who were accustomed to capitalizing on consumers' desire for convenience failed to realize that most people live relatively close to their grocery stores, and are willing—and indeed many prefer—to go to the store to see grocery items on the shelf in front of them, to compare product information, and even to make last-minute, impulse purchase decisions. The hard lesson that WebVan.com learned was an expensive one. There was nothing fundamentally wrong with the traditional shopping method to garner ongoing interest in WebVan's Web site. WebVan went out of business in 2001.

Finding a need in the market is the first step toward success. The second is to make sure that the demand is high enough and that the **profit margin** (the difference between what a product or service costs you to produce and how much you can sell it for) is high enough that your sales revenue can cover your expenses and earn some profit.

4

Suppose, for example, that you're going to be selling music CDs online. You arrange with the music industry's distribution houses to buy CDs at a retail price of $6 each. That's a reasonable price, so you buy 10,000 CDs that you'll warehouse (you'll need to have them onhand to ship when your customers order them). So, at this point, your total expenditures are $60,000 for inventory ($6 per CD × 10,000 units purchased = $60,000). On your Web site, you'll sell each CD for $13. If you sold your entire inventory, you would have sales of $130,000 ($13 per CD × 10,000 units sold = $130,000). This would generate a profit of $7 for each CD sold, or a total profit (sales minus costs) of $70,000 ($130,000 total sales - $60,000 inventory cost = $70,000 profit). To put it another way, you would have to sell just 4616 CDs from the 10,000 that you have in your inventory to break even (regain the money that you spent on inventory). Every CD you sold after that (of the remaining 5384 CDs in your inventory) would be pure profit. Not too bad, right?

Wrong. *If* the cost of those CD were the *only* costs of the company, that scenario wouldn't be all that bad—in fact, it would be ideal. More than half of your inventory, assuming you could sell it, would be pure profit. In the real world, however, life isn't that kind. Other costs to your company will inevitably be involved and unavoidable. To begin with, the site has to be developed, and there will be development costs aside from the **hard costs** (money paid to outside firms or entities) for the domain name, the merchant accounts, and so on. If you need to hire programmers, there will be a one-time cost for development, plus ongoing site maintenance costs. Even assuming that you (and maybe a few friends or partners) had the programming skills to develop the site on your own, the production of the site is not "free" from a realistic accounting standpoint. Instead, the costs of the site in this case are whatever you could have made per hour elsewhere times the number of hours that it took you to create the site. So, for example, suppose your programming skills could earn you $50 per hour working as a freelancer at a large company. If your own site takes you 600 cumulative hours to build, the site has cost you $30,000 in lost time, because that is the money you could have earned, but didn't.

You must also account for the costs of any office space that you'll need to run your business and the salary costs of any employees needed to buy new products, fulfill orders, answer phones, and so on. Warehouse costs (to store the inventory) must be added and so must phone bills, electric bills, office supplies, accounting fees, attorney fees, and of course, any marketing or advertising that you'll need to do just to get enough shoppers to your site to buy your inventory. All of these are the costs of doing business that companies must face to stay afloat and generate a profit.

So, let's assume that when all other costs are factored in, non-inventory costs come to another $5 per CD. That brings the total cost per unit up to $11 ($6 per CD + $5 in non-inventory cost). Suddenly your profit margin is only $2 per CD ($13 sale price - $11 total cost). That's less than 10 percent—a lot lower that the original scenario. In this case, if you sold out your entire inventory, you still would have **gross sales** (total dollars brought in from sales before costs have been subtracted) of $130,000. However, your costs will have risen to $110,000 ($11 cost per CD × 10,000 units), leaving a **net profit** (difference between sales and costs) of $20,000 ($130,000 gross sales - $110,000 total cost = $20,000). Put another way, you would have to sell 8462 CDs to break even (regain your investment), with only the remaining 1538 CDs representing profit.

Is that enough to get by? If all of the CDs are sold, the business can be deemed a success. You have not only covered your costs, but you also have generated extra income (profit). You would have a problem if only part of the inventory gets sold. Anything less than 8462 CDs sold would mean that the company would sustain a loss. To avoid these issues, your company could take a few steps. It could raise the price to $13.50 per CD or even higher if the market could bear it, or it could work something out with the wholesalers. Perhaps purchasing larger quantities of products would drastically reduce the unit cost of each CD and allow for a higher profit margin. You also could negotiate with wholesalers for lower prices, with long-term contracts promising those wholesalers exclusivity over a specific period of time. Other measures that could be taken by the site would be to offer other products to users, who are a captive audience on the site. You could sell t-shirts or other band memorabilia or try to obtain subscription dollars from site visitors who may wish to gain Web access to an exclusive newsletter, MP3 downloads, or other goodies.

However it's done, after you identify a need in the market and develop a plan to fill that need, you must strive to increase sales to their maximum levels while simultaneously seeking ways to reduce overall costs or adding new products or services from which to gain additional revenue.

THE STATE OF WEB REVENUE

Business plans of electronic commerce companies—those agendas for what a site is meant to do and how it intends to generate revenue—usually left no stone unturned. The marketing strategies were well thought out, and the financials (the spreadsheets projecting profit) were laid out by brilliant accountants. These plans boasted some of the most beautiful numbers ever put on paper—brand new companies run by fledgling CEOs would generate a gagillion dollars in just the third year of business. Very impressive!

Chapter 1 addressed many of the reasons why profitability and success have been elusive for pure-coms. At the same time, Web use and the rate of companies embracing the Web continue to grow at a spectacular rate. So what is going on? If there is no money to be made on the Web, and nobody except the traditional brands seem to have any success, why are so many companies bothering to try?

Media Hype

4

The primary reason for continued Web growth is that whereas the "failure" of the Web economy must be reported by the media, the reports are misleading on a grand scale. News reports can sensationalize topics to make them more interesting and salable. More often than not, the gloomier or more shocking the news is, the more fascinating it becomes.

This kind of media overexposure is not confined to politics or global disasters. Consider the media coverage of job layoffs at the beginning of 2001. For all the U.S. layoff-related news stories printed in January 2001, over half focused on the dot-com layoffs. However, the ratio of dot-com layoffs to nondot-com layoffs was nearly 30:1.[1] This means that if 31 articles were printed about U.S. layoffs, you might expect 30 of them to be about nondot-com layoffs, whereas only one would be centered on the dot-com problems. Instead, the dot-coms were the stars of 16 of those 31 articles.

The overall effect of this unbalanced coverage is panic and a widespread belief by the general public in something that is true, but only from one perspective. Yes, there have been a lot of Web layoffs and a lot of high-profile Web failures. Yes, profitability has been difficult to find for many revenue-generating Web sites. However, the focus that the media have paid to this topic has created the illusion that the Web is an utter failure. That illusion can become a self-fulfilling prophecy.

The failures and struggles that have been spotlighted by the media have been those of the highly visible companies, such as Amazon.com, eToys.com, and WebVan.com. These companies were media targets from their inception simply because they were the pioneers and because they received and spent huge amounts of money to make their ventures a reality.

Small Successes

Not every Web site is a globally recognized entity that needs hundreds of millions of dollars and dozens of distribution centers to operate. It's a different story for the smaller sites that don't gain as much media exposure. In fact, by the end of 2000, 61 percent of retail Web sites (both B2B and B2C) that generated revenue between $100,000 and $999,000 (for the year) were profitable. Of retail sites that generated revenue between $10,000 and $99,000, 57 percent were profitable, and 23 percent expected to be profitable before 2002.[2]

[1]Source: *The Industry Standard*, March 2001.

[2]Source: *Jupiter Media Metrix*.

Unfortunately, sites that generate less than $1 million in annual gross revenue tend not to make the papers very often, nor are they usually sold publicly on Wall Street. It still might be possible that the large, high-profile companies, through a combination of restructuring, time, and partnership with traditional brands, may someday see a profit, but smaller, unheralded sites are seeing their profits right now.

SOURCES OF REVENUE

The popular revenue models, including electronic commerce, subscriptions, and selling advertising space—with the exception of a few standout examples—have largely proven less than effective to date. However, that doesn't mean that they aren't viable or that they should be abandoned. Business on the Web still has a long way to go. It is likely that in the aftermath of the Web collapse, when the shake-out of weaker, less-viable sites is over, the Internet community will find a means of turning a previously depressed revenue model into a profitable one.

This section examines some of the methods that Web sites use to earn money, and it touches on some of the emerging ideas for the next generation of the New Economy.

Sites to Support Brick-and-Mortar Business

Can you think of any companies that don't have a Web site—even a bad Web site? If they don't currently have one, they probably have plans for building one. Of the types of sites reviewed in Chapter 2, brochure sites account for the largest segment of sites currently on the Web.

As you learned in Chapter 2, companies build brochure sites for many reasons. The site could be a way to promote the brand, or it could be a way to provide better customer service. The site may even exist because competitive pressure forces the company to have a site. Whatever the company's primary reason is, the bottom line is that like everything else, a company's site is intended to help gather new customers and retain existing ones. This is an important point to consider, and it is directly related to the primary rule of Web business: Without new and returning customers, there won't be any profits, regardless of the company's revenue-generating strategy. The probability of expanding the customer base depends on the industry, audience, and products in question. To be worth the money spent on it, each site must somehow contribute to generating new sales or to keeping clients from moving their accounts to a competitor.

Selling Over the Web

Retail Web sites, such as **www.crutchfield.com**, which sells audio and video equipment, and **www.talbots.com**, the women's clothier, gain the most commercial attention of all the types of sites. Traditional marketers are showing that there *is* a way to make money by selling on the Web. Most pure-coms are still trying to figure out how.

With a retail Web site, visitors do their product shopping from the comfort of their home or office. A **shopping cart** allows consumers to collect in a central place items that they may want to purchase. Shoppers place their desired products in a virtual cart, specifying size and quantity of items, if applicable. The shopping cart tallies the purchases, calculates any applicable sales tax, adds on any shipping costs, and presents the total to the customer.

4

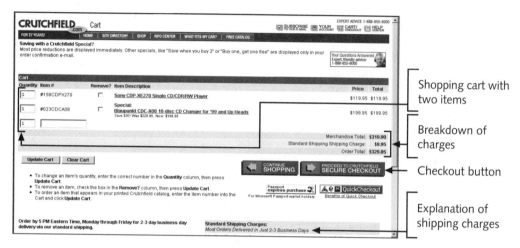

Shopping cart with two items

Breakdown of charges

Checkout button

Explanation of shipping charges

Figure 4-1   Crutchfield's shopping cart

Typically, e-shoppers have to use a credit card to make their purchases, providing card and personal information to the site through a secured online form. Many sites retain this information in a database so that the shopper does not have to complete the form on subsequent shopping visits.

Slow Growth

Spending by e-shoppers has been significant and growing.[3] Although the growth rate has slowed and has not reached the 20 percent of all shopping dollars once anticipated by industry analysts, online shopping does account for an impressive amount of consumer spending. Despite these positive signs, few sites have been able to come close to a profit.

As you have learned, problems with retail sites go beyond their tendency to charge high shipping fees. For example, pure-coms significantly underestimated the costs of starting and maintaining an electronic commerce site. They often forget how warehousing, distribution, site maintenance, and other factors cut into margins and profit potential.

Established Retailers Lead the Way

Traditional marketers are proving that experience in distribution and customer service, as well as deeper pockets and brand name recognition, can help make an e-tail effort

[3]Source: *The Industry Standard*, February 2001.

profitable. **ToysRus.com**, for example, breathed new life into online sales with its 2000 holiday results. Doing an estimated $174 million in sales for the months leading to the holiday, ToysRUs.com realized a profit of over $15 million. Although this was a drop in the bucket compared to the more than $1 billion in sales done by the company's brick-and-mortar locations for the same period, it was significant in that a highly publicized company that had seen its share of Web problems in past years was finally able to come into the black, financially. After a year of gloom and doom, any light at the end of the Web tunnel was a welcome sight for Web retailers.

Investing in Customers

To make a retail site work from the standpoint of generating a profit, marketers need to focus more on squeezing dollars out of current users and less on attracting new customers. Sites spend money to attract new customers, but research shows that new customers don't spend as much at sites as returning customers do. To curb spending while trying to increase revenues, you should concentrate on bringing customers back to your site and increasing the amount of their purchases. Direct mail campaigns (either through U.S. mail or e-mail) are less expensive marketing methods than mass media advertising through print or television and can use customer data acquired at the time of purchase. More important than their relative cost is the fact that these efforts reach an audience that already has expressed an interest in your site and products. Similarly, special "members-only" discounts, reduced rates for shipping, and other marketing strategies can be used to attract clients back to your site.

A key to Web success is to ensure that your site uses the power of the Web for what it does best: track and allow for intuition. Amazon.com is one of the best proponents of this tactic. Figure 3-5 in Chapter 3 shows how Amazon.com's home page greets returning visitors by name and makes recommendations on new books and products based on previous purchases.

You can expand on this kind of intuitive interactivity to help sell your site's offerings. For example, if a shopper is buying a lamp, he or she is going to need lightbulbs. Paper catalog purchases can't interact with the user to make that offer, but a Web site can. Salespeople in a brick-and-mortar location sometimes don't suggest the **up-sale** item (a higher priced item, or an accessory to the item that a shopper is interested in). However, the Web is the perfect medium to increase sales through intuition, and to increase revenue without spending more per customer.

A Flawed Business Model: Free ISPs

If online advertising had proven immediately successful for both advertisers and sites selling ad space, this section may have been titled "A Brilliant Business Model," but that is not the case.

Companies such as Juno, NetZero, and others had an idea. They'd give Internet access free to almost anybody who wanted it. This offer would save most users an average of

4

$20 per month that they'd be paying to an ISP, and they wouldn't have to pay any long distance bills to get online or stay connected.

So what's the hook? Users would have to view a few ads that would appear each time they logged on, and they would have advertisements visible at all times while they stayed online. This wasn't a problem. The only ads that got annoying or intrusive were the pop-up window ads that appeared when the user initially logged on, and those could easily be closed.

Because users weren't paying the phone bills for the calls (many were through an 800 number) and because many had installed second phone lines strictly for Web usage, they really had no incentive to log off. So some users just stayed on—all the time. Enough users did this to cause the phone bills of the free ISPs to skyrocket, making each quarter a larger financial loss than the last.

So what's a free ISP to do? Consider what happens when you run an "all you can eat" buffet and the local high school football team comes in and settles down. Five hours later, they'll still be going strong, but you've already lost tons of money from their meals alone. They're within their rights to keep eating. If you put a cap on how much food they can have, it's no longer "all you can eat." Tell them to stop and you're reneging on a promise that you made when they started—a promise that likely attracted them in the first place.

The buffet restaurant has one clear advantage that ISPs lack: If the food is good, the restaurant can raise prices. The free ISPs have no prices to raise for their users. Prices that they charge companies for advertising have been dropping dramatically, due to the fact that marketers were becoming unhappy with the low click-through rates of the ISPs' ads. The free ISPs could try to drive the abusers away by flooding them with so many ads that they would voluntarily leave. This isn't the greatest publicity move, though. The ISPs could also put a limit on how many hours are designated as "free" hours, and then charge a flat or per-minute rate for any accumulated time after that period of time. However, at that point, a limited user would likely choose to go back to a flat-rate-per month ISP instead of having to watch the clock.

Clearly, with the drop in advertising and ad rates, the free-ISP business model doesn't work. Like so many other sites that relied on advertising dollars to account for all or most of their profits, the free ISPs had to find an alternate path to profitability.

Memberships and Subscriptions

In a **membership** or **subscription** revenue model, users are asked to become members, sometimes paying a price (typically per visit, per week, or per month) to gain access to certain information on the site. In many ways, membership fees are the equivalent of subscription fees: You pay for a magazine subscription, and, therefore, you gain access to the publication's content. Initially, the subscription model and membership fee model crashed and burned as users realized that they could easily find information free on one site that they had to pay for on another. Not many were willing participants.

The system of charging a subscription or membership fee has been resurrected in recent days. A reason for this revival is familiarity. The Web is no longer a novelty to users, nor is it a vast universe of endless information. Of course, information seems to be limitless on the Web, but users have started to see that relatively few sites really put any effort into providing quality information or updating it on a regular basis. Because it is so expensive for a site to update such a vast amount of quality content on a regular basis, visitors now may be more willing to pay for it.

Some sites have learned the lesson of compromise. Instead of making a site either 100 percent free or 100 percent payment-based, sites have started flirting with the concept of dividing content. Users can visit the site and gather a certain amount of widely distributed or general information for free. Paying members, however, have more options available to them, measured either in available content or interactive capabilities.

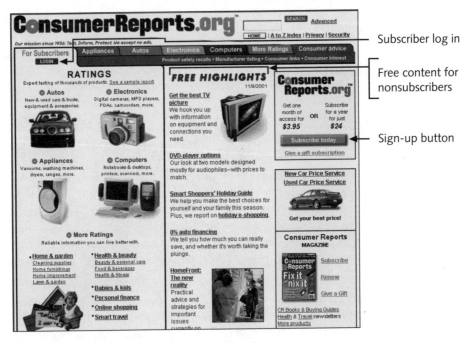

Figure 4-2   Consumer Reports, a membership site

Figure 4-2 shows the Web site for **Consumer Reports** (www.consumerreports.org), an online version of the print magazine. Part of the site's content is available to anyone who wants it, but other areas of the site are limited to users who have subscriptions.

Singles/personal sites are big proponents of multiple levels of memberships. Nonmembers can view other singles' pictures and profiles, but don't have access to contact information. The next-level members can post their own profiles and pictures online, as well as keep a mailbox on the site in which interested people can leave them notes. Finally, the highest level memberships (the most expensive) allow users to respond to messages and gain access to contact information.

Response to membership fees is more acceptable among Web users than it was a few years ago. However, it remains unlikely that the memberships and subscription fees will ever generate enough revenue to allow a site to profit from this alone. Instead, if it proves to work, memberships will only supplement Web ads or retail sales.

Commissions and Set Payments

As an alternative to charging membership fees, some sites generate revenue by acting as the facilitator in a transaction. These sites seek to establish a service that allows a group of buyers to get together with a group of sellers for the purpose of potentially engaging in a transaction. The site would then collect a commission or set payment for making that connection. If the site is successful, its revenue could be very high—there is relatively little overhead in facilitating a transaction, compared to electronic commerce sites that need to maintain an inventory. However, if the site is not successful, and fails to put buyers and sellers together, or those buyers and sellers fail to engage in a monetary exchange for goods or services, the site could wind up generating very little revenue.

Auction Sites

One site that has seen amazing growth even as many other pure-coms failed is **eBay**, the online auction site. Figure 4-3 shows the stock charts of eBay over the past few years, measured against the performance of Amazon.com for the same period.

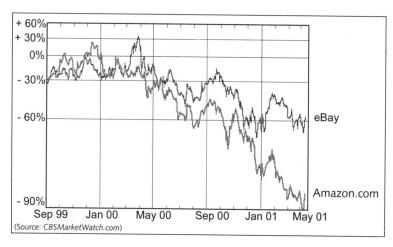

Figure 4-3   eBay and Amazon.com stock price comparison

The concept behind eBay is that a user who has something to sell can post the item on the site with a picture and description of the item. The seller sets the terms for payment (money order or certified check), shipping costs, and other handling details. The seller also sets the initial bidding price and determines how long the auction will last. Buyers search for items they want to purchase on the site and then place bids in amounts of money they are willing to pay for the items that interest them. When the auction closes, the highest bidder is obligated to purchase the item at his or her last bid price. eBay is illustrated in Figure 4-4.

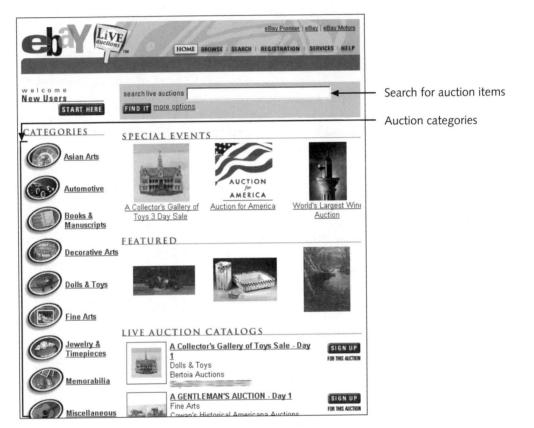

Figure 4-4 eBay auction site

What makes eBay an interesting case study is the fact that it has few imitators, despite its proven ability to make money. Although both eBay and Amazon.com both came out of the gates around the same time, Amazon.com has never come close to earning a profit. The vast majority of ideas funded since the introduction of these two sites went the retail route rather than the auction route. Sites like Yahoo! have added auction components to their own empires, but these efforts are afterthoughts more than anything else. What makes the initial rush toward developing retail sites rather than auction sites even more surprising is that of all the sites that are built to generate revenue, eBay most closely resembles the core concept of the Web: a convenient way for people to come together and easily exchange information on their own terms.

The best part about an auction site (for the site developers) is that, unlike with retail sites, there is no inventory to warehouse. There is no distribution for the site to handle, because the sellers are responsible for shipping their goods to the buyers. Any shipping charges are made known before the purchase is made. Because none of the products are direct from the manufacturer, each product listed is unique, so there is little competition among sellers. In addition, unlike content sites that need to gather new information and post it regularly, auction sites like eBay never have to worry about that. The site visitors provide new content.

With such a broad audience, different personalities and extreme behaviors from users will be a given, allowing auction sites to get plenty of free advertising in the form of publicity. eBay has gained plenty of headlines when people have tried to put a kidney or even a human soul up for auction. You can't buy that kind of advertising!

So how do sites like this make money? Varying models are based on a commission fee. In some cases, a site will use a "fee posting" model but will charge the seller to list items. This charge can be a set amount that can range from a dime per item up to $10, depending on the initial asking price. An auction site also can try to attract more sellers by using the "free listing" method, allowing them to post all items for free, but charging a small percentage of the final sale price should the item sell.

Each pricing method has its pros and cons. The free listings model significantly increases the amount of items up for bid, but also increases the amount of junk listed that nobody wants to buy. The audience could become lost in a huge selection of products, although percentage-wise, the site can expect many items to sell, and thus it will have more items from which to collect revenue. The fee-posting model will drive away a lot of sellers who do not want to pay for a listing because if the item does not sell, the seller loses money. However, the site is guaranteed to take in revenue from listed items regardless of whether they sell or not and, because there will be fewer undesirable items offered, the overall quality of the site offerings will be raised. Sellers are likely to sell many items in this environment and continue to post new items.

Auction sites can establish additional fees, including higher prices for items to be listed on the auction site's home page or featured in an e-mailed newsletter.

The location of an auction site's servers plays a role in the site's functionality. For example, eBay's servers are located in California, where reselling (also know as scalping) tickets to sporting events or concerts is legal. That's not the case in New York, however, where this practice is illegal. However, it's legal for a New Yorker with extra tickets to a Yankees game to post and sell his or her tickets on eBay because the actual transaction is being processed in California, not New York.

Other Types of Commission Sites

Auction sites aren't the only sites that make money through commissions and set rates (pre-established prices for listings or actions). Sites that allow users to buy and sell stocks or other securities online do so by charging either a small percentage of each transaction or a low standard fee for each transaction, regardless of how large. Users get the benefit of making transactions more quickly and more inexpensively than by using a traditional broker, but they lose the ability to get advice from a trained professional. Similarly, other sites that sell nontangible goods, such as airline tickets, like **cheaptickets.com**, also make money through commissions. In most cases, sites like this collect their commissions from the vendors for whom they are selling. For example, commissions earned from selling airline tickets are collected from the airlines, not the ticket buyer.

Selling the Mailing List

Web sites that collect personal user information, either through guest books or retail purchases, have databases of people that fit certain demographic profiles, complete with names and mailing addresses. **Mailing lists** are organized lists of people and their contact information, categorized into various demographic groups, which are used primarily for direct mail marketing efforts when advertising a site. Advertisers hungry for lists of potential customers seek these mailing lists, using them to reach specific targets.

Most sites promise users that their contact information will be kept private and not sold, although not every site adheres to this standard. Some do sell their mailing lists to outside companies. In fact, there have even been cases in which sites that promised secrecy sold their databases in the face of bankruptcy. Selling your site's mailing list is a bad way to make money, as it undermines the privacy that Web users desire and expect to feel safe making online purchase. Although some governmental regulations against spamming are in place, and new laws continue to be written, these laws often are ignored and are difficult to enforce. Laws that, for example, require e-mail marketers to provide viable links in their ads that allow recipients to request their names be taken off the mailing list are practically impossible to enforce. In fact, even if an e-mail ad does have such a link, it's advisable that recipients ignore it. Clicking it and requesting to be taken off the list only confirms to the marketers that your e-mail address is viable, and the marketer can either continue sending e-mail solicitations from a different address or resell the mailing list to someone else. Because of these methods, it is practically impossible for most Web users to know which marketers have sold their information. Still, respectable marketers rarely engage in these practices, especially if they have promised users that all personal information will be kept confidential. Beyond the questionable issues raised by selling mailing lists, the taint that it could create on a brand image and reputation may be irreparable.

WEB SITE ADVERTISING

Advertising on the Web means different things to different people. For marketers who purchase ad space on various sites, it is one of the main (if not only) source of driving traffic to their Web site. For Web sites that sell the space to advertisers, however, Web advertising is meant only to be a source of branding. This branding provides a highly visible space on sites so that site visitors can see the ads, and retain the name and message of the advertiser. It does not, however, have an emphasis on driving traffic directly to the advertiser's site.

Why is there a discrepancy, and why is this distinction important? It's important because the measure of success will vary based on the definition and expectation of Web advertising. Sites that sell advertising space on their pages often depend on that revenue as a main source of income. It's up to these sites to provide valuable content or services so that large audiences will be willing to come to the site on a regular basis. The audience is typically tracked through a combination of various Web tracking technologies (discussed later in this chapter), online surveys, and other means so that the site can determine the demographic makeup of the audience. If the audience is large enough, advertisers trying to reach those same groups will place their advertisements on those Web sites in the hopes of attracting new customers. The more advertisers a site can get, the more money it can make. Similarly, the larger the audience that a site can attract, the more money it can charge for its advertising space.

Because the nature of the Web allows for easy and instant linking to and from various sources of information, the ads that are placed also act as hyperlinks. For example, say that Lexus posts an ad on Yahoo!. Interested Web users who click the ad are immediately taken to Lexus's own site, where they can find further information about vehicles.

A **click-through count** tracks the number of visitors who click an ad. The percentage of Web users who actually click an ad is very low—only about 0.5 percent. Herein lies the conflict caused by two distinct viewpoints on the value of Web advertising. Advertisers who believe that the value of Web ads are measured only by how many people actually *click* an ad consider much of Web advertising a failure. Who cares how large the audience is that visits a site and sees an ad if they aren't clicking through to the site being advertised? Many marketers believe that failure to click through means that there is no positive return on the investment in the advertising space. Ultimately, this hurts the sites that rely on selling ad space as a primary source of revenue. If advertisers lose faith in the medium, they advertise less, and sites have to drop their prices, sometimes dramatically, to attract disgruntled advertisers. This reduction in revenue may hurt sites' ability to get quality, up-to-date content, which then reduces chances of attracting larger audiences on a regular basis.

Because of this food chain, sites that sell ad space take another view. These sites promote the position that Web advertising is not measured by the percentage of people that click through to the advertiser's site, but by the brand recognition that the advertiser receives when a large audience sees the advertisers message on their Web site—regardless of whether the ad actually gets clicked. The debate over how to measure Web advertising value continues, although there is no arguing that Web advertising has taken a deep and serious hit.

Advertising on the Web took a particularly harsh beating through most of 2000, as marketers bemoaned the poor click-through rate of their banner ads and sought something better.

Online advertising takes many forms, some of which have endured through the popularization of the Web. Others are more innovative. The primary forms of Web advertising include banner advertising, pop-up windows, interstitials, skyscraper ads, embedded ads, and sponsorships.

Banner Advertising

The most prominent form of online advertising, **banner ads** typically appear at the top of a Web page and remain there as long as the page is being viewed. Although the top of the page is the most common placement, some sites also place ads at the bottom of a page, along the sides, or even in the middle of the page. **CBSMarketWatch.com** is perhaps one of the more innovative sites on the Web when it comes to serving (displaying) ads. Figure 4-5 shows a page from CBSMarketWatch.com. Later in this section, we return to this site for further examples of Web advertising.

Figure 4-5 CBSMarketWatch.com uses banner ads

Audience Retention

Banner ads boast a higher viewer retention rate than radio or even television. In fact, 24 percent of people who use the Web more than 10 hours per week could remember a subject and company of a banner ad more easily than they could recall a television commercial[4]. Widespread surveys show that people who regularly surf the Web and regularly watch television tend to remember Web banner ads more often than they remembered the same information in television commercials. This shouldn't be too surprising. The average amount of time spent on a Web is approximately 44 seconds—14 seconds (nearly 50 percent) longer than most TV commercials. More important, people may easily bypass a television ad by getting up and leaving the room or using the remote control to change to another station. Banner ads work differently, however. A visitor remains on a page because it contains information that he or she wants to read. The banner ad at the top of that page can't be bypassed, even though it is not part of the

[4]Source: *Jupiter Media Metrix.*

information that the user came to the page to see. It remains in the visitor's peripheral vision until he or she clicks to a new page (or scrolls down and hides the ad).

Banner ads do have some limitations.. They are restricted, usually to a thin horizontal graphic bar that doesn't allow much room for anything more than a simple, quick message, unlike TV's standard 10-, 15- or 30-second format that uses video and audio to tell a more complete story. (Other banner ad shapes and sizes will be discussed later in this section.) Even more challenging is the fact that unlike TV ads, Web banner ads rely on instant action to be considered successful.

4

Tracking Banner Clicks

Banner ads have not generated the response that advertisers hoped for. In most cases, banner ads are a call to action. Unlike the call-to-action TV ads described in Chapter 1, however, they don't offer anything particularly time sensitive or otherwise difficult to find. There's nothing urgent about the "refinancing your home" message that one sees on a Web banner ad. Information on refinanced mortgages is fairly easy to obtain. A Web search or a trip to a bank will give that information, so few site visitors will interrupt reading the page that is open just to click a banner that can be visited later. Yes, there is a call to action, but there is no built-in urgency to the message.

Another deterrent to clicking through banner ads is that site visitors, overrun with junk e-mail, tend to be afraid of clicking a banner ad. Many users fear that even one click will open them up to all sorts of unwanted e-mail solicitations. This silent threat creates an even greater challenge to Web advertisers. Recall that the lack of privacy, the selling of mailing lists, and the abuse of mass e-mail are the main culprits behind the hesitation of Web users.

Although the prices for Web ads and the number of ads that we see every day are likely to decline, banner ads aren't going away. Eventually, prices will fall to a level that makes banner ads worthwhile for advertisers, even with the average click-through rate hovering around 0.5 percent. At present, advertisers feel that a 0.5 percent click-through rate provides a positive return on their investment. At the same time, the rate is not so low that a site selling space would be forced out of business.

Unfortunately, not every site will be able to reach that balance, and some will shut down because of it. With each site that closes its doors, the desirable space that is available for advertisers to purchase becomes reduced. Eventually, enough sites will be shaken out that the demand for space will match the space available at prices that are acceptable to both the advertiser and space seller. However, due to the cost of content and site upkeep, prices for ad space may fall so low that sites that once relied on nothing but ad revenue to earn a profit may need to seek out other sources of generating income.

Pop-Up Window Advertising

Relatively new and significantly more annoying than banner ads, **pop-up ad** windows appear when a user first logs onto a Web site. Figure 4-6 shows an example of how the site for **Shape** magazine (www.shape.com) greets its visitors with a smaller window than what appears in front of the main navigator window. This is typically a larger ad that can't be as easily avoided as banner advertisements. A site visitor has to move the window out of the way or close it completely to see the information on the main page. For advertisers, the downside of pop-ups is that the ad is not in front of a user's face at all times while a page is open, like a banner ad is.

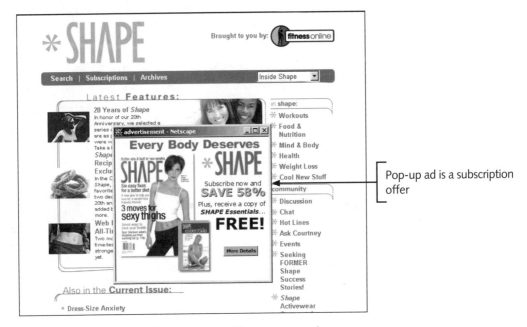

Pop-up ad is a subscription offer

Figure 4-6   Shape's Web site opens with a pop-up ad

Despite their shortcomings, pop-up ads have significant advantages for advertisers. In addition to being larger than their banner cousins, pop-up ads include a *forced* interactivity. When a visitor moves the pop-up window out of the way or even closes it, he or she forces the ad to center stage. This is a highly effective way to create a relationship between the user and the ad, even if that relationship is short-lived. Whether this forced interactivity will be considered such an annoyance as to have a *negative* overall effect on the brand is unknown. Pop-up ads are too new to have been effectively measured.

Other Web Ads

Although banner ads are still the most common of all ads, other types of advertising (beyond the pop-up window advertising that was discussed in the previous section) have started to appear in the hopes that they will increase click-through rates. To date, these ads are still too new to have any accurate measure of click-through success. However, at first glance, they seem to be merely larger or perhaps more prominent versions of the standard banner ad. New add styles include the following:

- **Skyscraper ads**: These ads run vertically down the side of a site. Although these are little more than the standard horizontal banner ads turned on their sides, it is arguable that they are a bit more visible and may stay in the site visitor's field of vision longer because they remain within the browser as the user scrolls for more information.

- **Embedded ads**: Embedded ads make a Web page look like a standard magazine or newspaper page. Within the article or area of content appears a (usually) square box that contains an advertisement. These give significantly more space to the message than standard banner ads provide, and they are directly in the field of vision while the visitor reads the content.

- **Interstitial ads**: So annoying that consumers have tried to stage boycotts of advertisers that use this method, these ads appear *behind* the browser window, and don't go away, even when you switch from one site to another. Often times a user won't even know the ad is there until he or she closes the browser window. Some interstitials, however, are not so hidden. They work in conjunction with pop-up window advertising. The interstitial gets placed behind a browser window, while another ad appears in front of the browser window. When the user closes the pop-up window ad, the interstitial then emerges from behind the browser and acts as another pop-up ad.

Brand Advertising

At long last, marketers have started to recognize the value of Web advertising in promoting their brands, acknowledging that click-through is not necessarily the best or only way to measure Web ad success. The transition is slow, and the main takers have been the traditional marketers, who are more interested in securing long-term recognition than driving short-term traffic.

Unlike a banner ad, a **brand ad** on the Web is almost like a product placement on a TV show, cleverly becoming part of the background in a subtle way.

Brand advertising is growing rapidly in the online gaming component of the Web. Figure 4-7 shows another page from **CBSMarketWatch.com**. Take a close look at the figure, or go to CBS.MarketWatch.com and look up any stock. Do you notice anything interesting about the advertising?

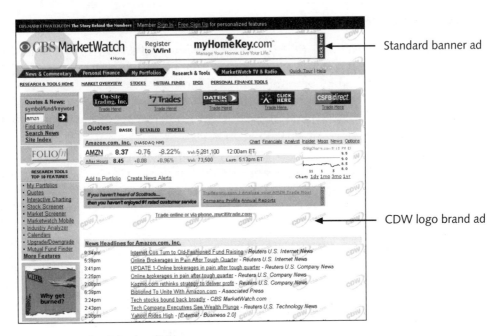

Standard banner ad

CDW logo brand ad

Figure 4-7   Brand advertising

Don't feel too bad if you don't notice anything. It's rather subtle and not very common. The banner at the top is standard, and the smaller ads for brokerage houses aren't anything new either. Take a close look at the background of the site. The wallpaper in the background is very light and is overshadowed by the information on the page. If you look closely enough, you'll see that the wallpaper repeats the logo for CDW, a computing solutions company. You can't click the logos. Most people don't even report noticing them, but they're there. Even if they are not recognized immediately, they filter into the viewer's mind on a subconscious level. This is one of the better examples of brand advertising on the Web and an early indicator that Web developers might be starting to put more value in Web branding and less value on click-throughs.

In the continuing struggle that sites face to push the brand value of banners over the click-through value, CBSMarketWatch.com, in 2001, was one of the first sites to forego the practice of providing advertisers with click-through statistics for their ads.

Marketers will develop increasingly clever ways to work a logo or an ad message onto Web pages. Companies that appreciate long-term strategy will take advantage of the Web's significant branding power and will reduce their emphasis on immediate gratification. This type of advertising opportunity will be especially important in the coming years as the impending integration of television and the Web takes shape.

Web and Television Integration

Although countries such as Japan have had digital television for years, bringing it to the United States has been a lackluster effort at best. The government's deadline for all stations to broadcast in digital has been repeatedly pushed back, as smaller stations (understandably) continue to complain about the high conversion costs.

When it does become available throughout the United States, digital television will bring with it a new way of being entertained, and it likely will change both the way people get their information and the way that information is created. In its most basic form, digital television will provide stations with a signal that is so strong that it can be used to show one, theater-quality image (by then, many homes will be equipped with flat screen, digital televisions capable of displaying these images) or nine or 10 subchannels. This means that NBC, for example, could move its other networks, such as MSNBC and CNBC, off cable and onto broadcast television. ABC could do the same with the Disney Channel, ESPN, ESPN2, MTV, VH1, and others. These networks would emulate ABC's past foray into Web/television integration a few years back, in which WebTV owners could click a button during the Academy Awards. The show would shrink to one-quarter size, and viewers would see Web-style information about the current and past awards ceremonies, with hyperlinks to other pages and Web sites, while watching the show.

As a result of many stations that were originally on cable abandoning cable for the new digital broadcast medium, cable will have fewer premium stations. However, cable—unlike broadcast—will maintain features for interactivity, with chat rooms (to discuss a TV show with other people while you're watching it), real-time surveys, and other features. In all likelihood, AOL (now one with Time Warner) will become the next big television network, taking advantage of cable modems and allowing total interactivity through television.

So what does all of this have to do with advertising and promoting the brand? Lots, and it will likely lead the way to a hybrid form of advertising that combines both the brand ad and the call-to-action ad. Take a specific episode of *Baywatch*, for example, that aired in 1998. In the episode, the cast was to take a trip on Princess Cruise Lines—a quirky story line, and a brilliant branding effort for the cruise company. The cruise company name, the boat, and the service were featured throughout the hour-long episode. The program became a call to action in the interactive areas of the show. Viewers who had a WebTV unit saw an icon onscreen, and, with the click of a button, reduced the show to a quarter screen. The rest of the screen showed an advertisement for Princess Cruise Lines, a way to request more information, and an offer to register for a contest to win a free cruise.

Although this type of brand advertising mixed with a call-to-action ad is still years away from being the standard, it does offer a strange glimpse of the future. Advertisers will more closely associate themselves with shows, pushing beyond the 30-second commercial format *and* beyond the standard ad placement format. Viewers, though, may be left with shows that are little more than serialized commercials, written more around a product and less around a storyline.

Sponsorships

Advertising that allows content to be brought to you by a specific company is called a **sponsorship**. Sponsorships usually preclude any other company from advertising on a certain page or section of a Web site. A Web page sponsor owns all the ad space available on a given page. In some instances, a "sponsored by" credit is provided to let the user know that the information is "brought to you by" the paying advertiser.

Tracking Advertising Data

Whether you are going to sell ad space directly on your site to advertisers or through a third-party company such as **DoubleClick** (www.doubleclick.com), which places and manages advertising on Web sites for clients looking for broad exposure throughout the Web, you must have precise measurements of the traffic to each page. Understanding the traffic will allow you to calculate the number of impressions each banner ad has. Each time an advertisement appears on any Web site is an **impression**. Advertisers can pay the sites on which they advertise in various ways. The three most common methods are cost per thousand, pay-per-click, and pay-per-purchase. Before we discuss these methods, we need to first learn how ads end up appearing in a browser.

Ad Rotation and Distribution

On the more technologically sophisticated sites, banner ads are rotated through an **ad server**, a program that manages the display of ads. This rotation means that each time someone new comes on the site, or each time the visitor clicks the "Refresh" button on the browser, the displayed ad may change. The ad server that creates the rotation keeps track of how many times the ad is shown, on which pages it has appeared, and how many visitors have clicked it.

Sites selling ad space on their pages don't always sell the space directly to advertisers. Large Fortune 500 companies use advertising agencies or media buying companies to determine where their ads should be placed and how much money to spend at a given venue. Smaller sites selling advertising often do so through companies such as DoubleClick. These companies charge a fee for their services or take a commission of any ad that they place on behalf of an advertiser. By using an outside company like this, you can populate your site with advertisers relatively quickly, but you will most likely lose the ability to set your own price for ads.

Cost Per Thousand

Cost per thousand, or CPM, is the most widely used structure for quantifying Web ad placement. Under this structure, an advertiser pays a site one set rate, typically between $20 and $80, for every 1000 impressions that the advertiser's banner ad has on that site. The advertiser directs the site to set a certain maximum number of impressions, perhaps spreading the impressions over a number of weeks or months. The ad server is programmed to record the number of impressions for the ad and limit the number so as not to exceed the maximum. The site must draw enough traffic to serve the ad enough times that the site can generate revenue. (If nobody sees a page, nobody sees an ad, and the site doesn't get paid.)

The *amount* of traffic on a site is not always as important as determining the *type* of traffic that visits your page. A search engine such as Yahoo! sees extremely heavy traffic on its home page, but that traffic is hardly targeted. It attracts people from all demographics with vastly different interests and backgrounds. Advertisers who have banner ads on the home page are paying to get their message out to as many people as they can, regardless of who they are.

What about specific areas of Yahoo!, like the health and medical channel? These pages see far less traffic than the home page, but certain advertisers will pay a premium for it—sometimes even more than they would pay to advertise on the home page. These pages are more valuable to advertisers because they know that the ad will be seen by people who have an interest in health and medicine. Theoretically, an ad for PlanetRx that appears on this page has a better chance of driving traffic to its own site because of the targeted nature of the viewing audience on the Yahoo! Health page.

Pay-Per-Click

With click-through rates at only 0.5 percent, advertisers are less willing to pay only for impressions. In the **pay-per-click** method, advertisers pay for their ads only when site visitors click them. This system allows advertisers to limit their risk by placing their banners ads on sites without paying huge costs if nobody clicks them.

Advertisers are willing to pay more for each click than for a simple impression, because each click buys them a potential new customer. Pay-per-click rates can be as high as $1 per click. Advertisers get the brand value of banners that aren't being clicked along with the clicks for which they pay. Unfortunately, sites that offer this specific advertising method have a hard time making money, especially when few users click an ad.

Pay-Per-Purchase

Not everyone who clicks a banner to make it to a site ends up making a purchase. To compensate for traffic that clicks an ad, visits an advertised site, but doesn't make a purchase, some sites offer the **pay-per-purchase** method. In this method, an advertiser pays nothing for the ad impression but pays a premium (usually a percentage of the sale) if a Web user makes a purchase from the advertised site. This method is used by advertisers to ensure that their banner ad efforts translate into actual sales. Sophisticated programming is used by the site that sells the ad space to track users and to record what they do after they enter the advertiser's site. Even if a user enters a site through a banner, leaves the site, and then comes back to it directly days or weeks later, various applications let the advertiser and the site know that the user initially clicked a banner to get there.

With this method, advertisers pay a percentage of the final sales price to the site on which they advertised. The percentage is usually between 5 percent and 15 percent of the gross sales price. Amazon.com is a well-known proponent of this method of advertising and is widely considered to have been the innovator of this advertising method. Small Amazon.com banners exist on practically any site that wants one—even small sites that are hobby-style in nature. Sites that post these banners get monthly accounting statements from the sites on which they are advertising. These statements let them know how much traffic the banner has driven to Amazon.com, how much of that traffic has made purchases, and how much money the site has earned with its banner.

Understanding Ad Traffic

Having detailed information of the traffic that you're bringing to your site is important, regardless of the type of site you have. However, understanding that traffic is probably most important for sites that intend to generate revenue through advertising. Specific traffic information helps you establish prices for specific pages and areas of content. It also is required by advertisers, who consider traffic when making decisions about advertising on your site.

To track traffic data, you probably will use a tracking program such as those offered by **WebTrends** or **IN2**. These products typically track established variables, although most are customizable to a certain extent. A brief list of some of the information you should be looking for and how each measurement is defined, is provided in the following list. Of course, the list that a Web developer might actually review could be extensively longer and more specific than what is provided here. General traffic terms:

- **Hits**: The term hits is often misused when it comes to measuring Web traffic. The number of hits on a site is not how many people have visited your site, but how many *individual items* have been downloaded from a site. For example, if your home page has seven buttons and five images, each time a person comes to that page, 12 hits are generated.

- **Page views**: One of the more important basic measures is the page view. Measured in total for any given month and as a weekly or daily average, page views tell you how many pages within your site have been visited. If two visitors come to your site in a day, and one visitor views eight pages and the other visitor looks at 12 pages, the total number of page views will be 20, with the average being 10.

- **Visitors**: Unique visitors indicates how many newcomers have made their way to your Web site. Many advertisers will want to see that a good percentage of your traffic is from unique visitors, an indication that the site is continually growing.

Other measurements include how many visitors have returned to your site once and how many have visited two or more times. Keep in mind that individuals may be counted twice in these numbers. For instance, if a visitor visits a site for the first time and then comes back to the site again a few days later, he or she would be counted as a unique visitor for the first visit, but would also be counted in the total for visitors who have come to the site once before. Visitor-specific terms:

- **Visitor sessions**: A visitor who comes to a site daily for updated information is counted as a unique visitor once, and then ends up on a list of people who have visited twice or more. Visitor sessions tell you how many times a visitor has actually viewed a site. If a user comes back to a certain site once a week, for example, that user is counted only once, but there have been seven visitor sessions—one for each time the user came and spent time on the site. Visitor sessions are often tabulated as monthly totals and as averages per day. Another important component is the average length of time each visitor remained on the site.

- **Path through site**: The path through site measurement tells you which paths are the most regularly traveled through your site. For example, you might find that in any given month, the largest percent of your traffic is going from the home page to the "today's tip" page to the "current events" page, and then to somewhere off the site.

Related information reveals the most popular introduction pages. Not everyone enters through the home page, especially if they have other pages bookmarked or find other pages through a search engine. Other information includes the least-visited pages, the top single access pages (pages in which people came and then left immediately), and the top exit pages (the last page that people most often see before they decide to leave the site). Other advertising metrics:

- Geographic regions: Depending on the site and the market, it's going to be important to understand from where in the world your audience is coming. This can be broken down by continent, country, state, or city.

- Activity by time: Time tracking measures the days of the week and the hours of the day that people are visiting or not visiting. This measurement is especially helpful if you are tracking a marketing campaign. Did traffic levels increase a day after your radio campaign broke? Did site traffic go down right after a sale ended? This information will help you plan your upcoming marketing agenda, as well as set prices for banner advertising.

- Advertising: Of course, one of the more pertinent pieces of information to existing advertisers is the click-through rate of their banner ads. Of all their ads, did different banners throughout the site or the same banners on various pages drive more traffic than others? Which pages drew the largest audience to their sites?

- Mixing it up: Of course, none of this information needs to stand alone. Traffic reports can be extremely long and complicated and take a lot of time to properly analyze. Besides additional information not listed here, reports will mix and match information for a more comprehensive report. For example, besides just knowing the number of unique visitors and the number of page views, a comprehensive report will tell you the average number of page views for each new user as compared to the average number of page views for regular visitors.

PAYMENT PROCESSING

After you have convinced a customer to spend some money at your Web site, you need to make it easy for the customer and his or her cash to part ways. Accepting payments online requires being able to accept and process credit cards, typically Visa, MasterCard, American Express, and Discover. Although there are other ways to accept payment, such as accepting personal checks through the mail, C.O.D (Cash On Delivery), or by sending a bill and waiting for payment, most retail sites utilize the credit card payment method. Credit cards allow the site to collect its money as quickly as possible and to be assured of payment. Other methods, especially billing and extending time for payments, are more likely to be used in B2B sites, which typically have larger average price tags associated with purchases. They may even establish ongoing accounts with the Web sites from which they are buying.

To allow Web visitors the ability to make electronic commerce purchases from your Web site, you'll need to establish a **merchant account**, which is an account with a bank or bank-affiliated entity that processes credit cards and allows for purchases to be made online in real-time (the time of purchase). There are two ways that you can do this: by owning your own merchant account or by paying another company a fee to use theirs. As each option has advantages and disadvantages, the one that you choose will depend on how extensive your site and company are.

For small companies or entrepreneurs who want to sell a limited line of products over the Web without the benefit of a large budget, it's typically more beneficial to pay an existing third-party company to use its merchant account. Many sites on the Web provide this service, such as **ECHO** (Electronic Clearing House Inc.) and **PayPal**. Although these two sites differ slightly on the exact terms, services, and costs, the way in which they work is typically the same. Using this approach benefits the small company and entrepreneur because it requires fewer start-ups cost than owning your own merchant account. In addition, these companies handle all customer service for you, refund fees to customers in the event of returned items, and end up costing far less in the event that a small volume of products are sold.

The shortcoming of this option is that the costs are higher per item sold, with most leasing companies charging between 9 percent and 12 percent of each sale. In addition, there is a lag time before money is collected (by the Web site owner from the merchant account owner), and you'll be limited to the third-party vendor's shopping cart system and server. This means that there is nothing you can do if the site goes down for any length of time, and you have less control over customer service and returned items.

In comparison to that method, if you're willing to spend more money in up-front costs, you can gain far more control by owning your own merchant account. Owning your own merchant account means having to find a merchant provider, typically a Web entity that has an affiliation with a specific bank, like **Authorize.Net**. The merchant provider may be established by the bank itself. The provider or bank supplies you with the necessary tools and programs for processing orders and collecting money directly from the credit card companies you choose (and that will work with you—this method is not for those with poor credit ratings).

The benefits of this method are several. You maintain control over your own site in the event that the server goes down, you maintain greater control over customer service, and there is less waiting time to collect your money. In addition, you aren't at the mercy of another company if it suddenly decides to increase prices or go out of business.

The fees associated with owning your own merchant account are different as well. You won't have to pay a high percentage of each sale to anyone. However, the credit card companies with which you work will collect from 1.99 percent to 3 percent of each sale, plus a transaction fee that may range from $.20 to $.50 per transaction. In addition, you likely will be charged a higher start-up fee, which, depending on the bank or provider, can be upwards of $1000.

Other fees that may be incurred include a statement fee, usually $10 to $15 per month, that provides a written record of all transactions, deposits, and returns made from your account. You also might pay a monthly fee, and a gateway fee for use of programs and software that allow the transaction to take place over the Web in real-time. This fee generally ranges from $15 to $40 per month. The fees are paid to the provider or bank that issues you your merchant account.

Lastly, when the merchant account has been established, you'll need to determine the type of method that will be used by shoppers to buy your products. Most sites use shopping carts, which are the most convenient method available for consumers to use and understand. This method is particularly useful and necessary when it comes to purchasing tangible goods online, as opposed to services. Just as important as the convenience factor, shoppers have come to equate shopping cart systems with a safe, secure means of making electronic commerce purchases. The alternative purchase method is to use an HTML-based form or CGI script to send orders and contact information (including credit card numbers) by e-mail. Although this method can work with some merchant accounts, it's not recommended for anything other than sites that are selling nontangible services, as opposed to actual products, or sites that are using another company's merchant account that doesn't allow for shopping carts. (There are many types of shopping cart programs and software available and plenty of viable languages for building a customized shopping cart system. However, not all hosts and merchant accounts can work with all types of programs.)

CHAPTER SUMMARY

❏ Unfortunately, making money on the Web hasn't come as easily or as steadily to many Web sites as they might wish. Although profits for high-profile companies have been minimal, smaller Web sites that generate less revenue and aren't typically publicly traded have had considerable success generating income.

❏ Any successful Web venture must begin on the foundation of a firm business approach. Multiple types of revenue streams are available for Web sites, including retail sales, advertising space, memberships, commissions, and auctions. From pop-ups, skyscrapers, and interstitial ads that supplement the traditional banner to a resurgence of subscription and membership models, Web sites have multiple options available to them to generate real value in their site.

❏ With the elements in place to generate revenue in one variation or another, Web developers take measures to track their audience and gain a complete understanding as to where visitors go and what they do on the site. This information, typically tracked and maintained by third-party programs, helps developers understand which parts of their sites are being visited most often, and by what types of people. With this information, future marketing efforts can be better targeted, and the site can evolve accordingly.

❏ Web developers must set up a merchant account to be able to process credit card payments. You can also use a third-party company to handle online payments. Most electronic commerce sites use shopping carts to allow their customers a convenient way to purchase items online.

KEY TERMS

ad server
banner ad
brand ad
click-through count
cost per thousand (CPM)
embedded ad
gross sales
hard costs
hit
impression
interstitial ad
mailing list
marketshare
membership
merchant account

net profit
page view
path through site
pay-per-click
pay-per-purchase
pop-up ad
profit margin
shopping cart
skyscraper ad
sponsorship
subscription
up-sale
visitor
visitor session

4

REVIEW QUESTIONS

1. Most business sites on the Web earn revenue by _____.

   a. selling items over the Web through e-tail sites

   b. creating brochure sites that are meant to make people pick up the phone and/or visit a brick-and-mortar location

   c. selling advertising space

   d. selling broadband Internet connectivity

2. The method for collecting items on a Web site that shoppers want to buy is typically called a(n) _____.

3. Which of the following statements is true?

   a. In 2001, online shopping was expected to account for 20 percent of all consumer retail spending, and actual Web spending far surpassed expectations.

   b. In 2001, online shopping were expected to account for 20 percent of all consumer retail spending, but Web spending didn't even come close.

   c. Online sales were expected to be the driving force behind generating revenue on the Web by the end of 2000, but ad sales have since outpaced retail sales as a revenue model.

   d. Experts agree that it would be practically impossible for a Web site to ever generate a profit through e-commerce.

4. Web sites are finding it most profitable to _____.

    a. change their focus to work only in the B2B sector

    b. increase sales through existing clients

    c. increase sales by acquiring new clients

    d. sell their mailing lists

5. CPM stands for _____.

6. From a branding standpoint, which banner payment method is the most cost-effective?

    a. the CPM method

    b. the pay-per-click method

    c. the pay-per-purchase method

    d. They're all about the same.

7. One of the main reasons that pop-up window advertising may be effective is _____.

8. Digital television will likely _____.

    a. put an end to the Web for general commercial use

    b. integrate television and the Web into one community

    c. eliminate the need for computers

    d. be too expensive for most people to afford

9. _____ is important traffic data for Web site developers to measure.

    a. Visitor type (demographic characteristics)

    b. Popular paths through the site

    c. Geographic areas of visitors

    d. All of the above

10. Subscription-based Web sites have gained in popularity (especially relative to their introduction a few years ago) primarily because _____.

    a. they are considered a novelty

    b. most sites provide a banner-ad-free version for paying members

    c. a large number of sites integrated their printed subscriptions with their Web subscriptions

    d. many sites will provide a certain amount of information for free, while providing more specialized, higher-quality information to members only

11. Setting up a merchant account will allow you to _____ over your Web site.

    a. accept credit cards

    b. accept money orders

    c. process B2B transactions

    d. take out business loans

4

12. What are two advantages to owning your own merchant account and two advantages to using another company's merchant account?

13. Every site, regardless of its revenue stream, should always take _____ into consideration.

    a. the brand

    b. the future of the Web

    c. the formation of a partnership with a traditional marketer

    d. offline advertising

14. If the cost of a banner ad on a popular site is $50 CPM and the banner is shown 100,000 times, the total price for the ad space is _____.

15. An example of an intuitive retail site is one that _____.

    a. brings you to the checkout area as soon as at least three minutes have elapsed since you last put something in your shopping cart

    b. allows you to easily remove items from your shopping cart

    c. provides access to a page with products that relate to products you are purchasing

    d. has links to sites that sell similar items, for price comparison

16. An impression is _____.

    a. a person who comes to your site

    b. a single appearance of an ad on a site

    c. the number of seconds an ad appears in a browser

    d. a reload of a banner ad

HANDS-ON PROJECTS

1. With your business partners, you will add the next part of your business plan. This time, consider the revenue issues of Web site that you want to build. In your business plan, determine the following:

    a. What is the main source of income that could be derived from your Web site?

    b. What, if any, are secondary sources of income?

c. What kind of prices would you charge for your offerings? In other words, if you'll be making money through selling ads, what pricing model would you use and at what rate? If you will be charging subscriptions, what will you offer, and how much will the subscription rate be? If your site is an electronic commerce site, what will your mark-up be per product?

d. Considering the costs that your site would incur (as you did in Hands-on Project 1 in Chapter 3), how much product will you have to sell to break even and to eventually turn a profit? Research the market in which your Web site will exist. How long will it take to generate this profit? Is the market strong or weak?

e. Finally, research at least two different tracking systems at different price points. What is the difference between them? Which will you use for your site?

f. Research merchant service account options. Select one and outline your decision-making process.

2. Go to **CBS.MarketWatch.com** and **www.msnbc.com**. Answer the following questions about the each site:

a. How many types of ads do you see on the site, and what types of ads are they?

b. Do different types of ads appear on different pages, or is it just a random mix? What reason could there be for one ad type to be in one section and another ad type to be in another section?

c. Which type of ads do you think are most successful from a click-through definition of success? What about from a branding perspective? Why do you deem these ads successful?

d. Do you notice any particular type of companies that seem to be predominantly advertising on the site? What about in a particular section of the site? What do the types of advertisers tell you about the audience that the site is most likely attracting?

e. Do some research and find out the payment method for these ads. Write a brief report on your findings.

5

THE TEAM: PEOPLE WHO MAKE THE SITE HAPPEN

In this chapter, you will learn about:
- The reasons that companies outsource their sites to agencies
- The challenges and benefits of working with clients and their sites
- The importance of team efforts in development
- The 15 roles that typically comprise a development team

Web sites come in all sizes. Smaller sites with limited interactive features (such as electronic commerce functionality, complex games, and chat rooms) that are created either for personal use or as brochure sites for small companies may be created by a single individual. In fact, at the outset of Web commercialization, it wasn't uncommon for one or two people working in their basement to design and program entire sites in a relatively short period of time. Today, some sites still are built solely by individuals. However, the growing variety of programs and tools combined with the increasing sophistication of Web users has made the creation of a viable business site by one person quite rare. The development of larger scale, business-oriented Web sites, regardless of site type, typically requires many team members working together.

INTERNAL VERSUS OUTSOURCED WEB SITE DEVELOPMENT

Companies can either handle development of the site internally, which means that company employees oversee and develop the site, or it can hire another company to build the site. Building a site internally means that the company itself takes on all the tasks associated with site development, including preliminary research, schematic development, graphic design, and programming. The advantages to taking this route include the following:

- Potentially lower costs than would be incurred by hiring an outside company.

- Subject expertise—you know your own products or services better than an outside company does, so there is no time lost in training someone who is not familiar with your product line.

- You can retain all creative control, which makes some people feel more comfortable.

Trying to build a Web site internally is easier for some companies than for others. A company that builds and markets software, for example, likely will have more people on staff who understand the programming necessary to build a Web site than would say, a car dealership. Similarly, very small companies of only a few people may also prefer to build their own site, which lets them save on the expense of paying outside vendors and which keeps them busy during slow times.

Keeping a site internal doesn't mean that only full-time employees are on the job. It's common in these cases for freelancers—workers who work only on assigned projects and who are not on the payroll—to be hired for a short period of time to accomplish certain tasks that the company can't do on its own. The advantages and disadvantages of using freelancers are reviewed later in this chapter.

The problem with trying to develop a Web site internally, however, is that except for relatively small, brochure-style Web sites that won't change very often, sites can vary in complexity. Simple HTML may not be enough. The site may require a database to house information and some sort of administration device to allow easy updates without rewriting any code. It may also need a shopping cart to allow electronic commerce purchases, search engines, online surveys, and other features. Aside from the fact that the company would need experienced programmers who know how to implement these features, the company would first need someone who understands that these and other features are needed for the site.

Suppose a company that decided to create a site internally (to save cost) wanted to have a shopping cart on its site. The person in charge of the company, or in charge of the site, would need to know far more than just "We want a shopping cart." He or she must know what type of cart works with the company's server and with its merchant account, what special languages will be needed, and what programs will be implemented to allow for product updates. If the person in charge doesn't know to ask these questions, he or she won't know what specific talents will be required to build the site properly.

Although keeping the creation part of the development process internal has some advantages, so too does hiring an outside company. Outside vendors that specialize in Web development are trained and used to doing just that. Web site design agencies or advertising agencies with internal Web site design shops (ideally) have the expertise needed to put a site together properly, allowing you to concentrate on your everyday work.

Just as important, vendors can likely create the site faster and more accurately than your own company could. The vendor should know the right questions to ask and have the knowledgebase to determine the most efficient means and programs available to create your site. In addition, there is a benefit gained from the fact that outside development companies are somewhat removed from your products and services. Often this outside perspective results in creative ideas for site development that you may not have considered, simply because you were too close to the subject matter.

On the downside of outsourcing is the added expense. Hiring an outside company may be far more expensive in the long run than if you kept production in-house. There is also a higher risk of discrepancy—contractual disputes that may result in a delay of getting the project completed. In addition, it stands to reason that if retaining creative control is one of the benefits of keeping development within your company, losing some creative control over the site is one of the disadvantages of hiring outsiders to do it.

WORKING WITH AN OUTSIDE COMPANY

In situations in which a company determines it is necessary or desirable to hire an outside company to develop its Web site, both parties will have different considerations that they'll need to address for the relationship to work. We'll take a look at how the relationship should form from the outset—what questions need to be asked and what issues can be anticipated from both sides. Keep in mind that there are no right or wrong answers to these questions. The point is to educate yourself about your vendor or client. What one client might find ideal in a vendor—such as vast experience in Fortune 500-site development—might be all wrong for another client.

Outsourcing from the Client's Perspective

Whether a company keeps the production of a site internal or hires out for it, the bottom line is that success relies on people. Business, especially creative business, is based on relationships as much as it is based on experience. One of the biggest misconceptions in business is that you can predict accurately how any one person will work or act based on information provided in his or her resume. Web site development often requires a large team of people and a hierarchy of positions. Although few like to admit it, creative people tend to have fragile egos that sometimes make it difficult for a team to function properly. Finding the right mix of people—in terms of talent, experience *and* personality—can be crucial to the success of a Web site.

That being said, the search for a vendor agency to build your site largely comes down to the people at the agency. Of course, there are other considerations to take into account as well, and as a client looking to accomplish a project in a timely fashion, you'll want to look for the following features in the vendor you choose:

- What is the breadth of the agency's experience? This can be measured in terms of years as well as the number of Web sites they have worked on. Established companies that have been around for a while may offer some benefits in terms of experience, while newer companies may be "hungrier" for the work and might pay more attention to your project.

- What is the agency's general type of experience? In other words, has it generally worked on B2B sites or B2C sites? For what markets have the sites it has created been built? Are these markets consistent with those you are looking to reach?

- What is the agency's proficiency with various programs and languages? Can it easily accomplish tasks using multiple language types, or is it specifically geared to create all sites in one of a few language options? Has the bulk of the agency's experience been with static brochure sites, shopping carts, database-driven sites, or other types?

- Can the agency provide you with an extensive URL list? A URL list acts as a great prequalifier to eliminate or qualify potential vendors *before* you waste time asking too many questions or reviewing them thoroughly. If you are unimpressed with the work they have done, there is no need to move forward with them. Watch out for URL lists that are sprinkled with many sites that are still "under construction" or accompanied by many excuses, such as "This is a site that we did, however the client insisted on the color scheme" or "This site is slow to download because the client needed the site in a rush, and there was little time to optimize the graphics." Too many excuses usually indicates a poorly run Web shop. Nearly every project will have hurdles and boundaries. A good shop will know how to create the best Web site given all these variables. In addition, look to make sure that there is significant difference in the design of each site and that the vendor is not selling just a "cookie-cutter" template to all its clients. Each site should be unique, given the product, industry, and market within which it is working.

- How large is the vendor? Is there a team of people that works on each project, or is the shop so small that everyone works on every project?

- Does the agency handle all aspects of the site in-house, or does it have to outsource for certain parts, like graphic design? Some companies only want to work with vendors that have all necessary personnel in-house so that creativity is not spread out too thinly. Other companies don't care if their Web development vendor hires other resources to help, as long as there is only one point of responsibility. As the company hiring out, you don't want to hear your vendor say, "We're sorry this part of the site doesn't work, but it's not our fault. The company that *we* hired messed it up." The company that you hire is responsible for the project and should not pass the buck when something goes wrong.

- Does the agency have its own servers to host your site? If it doesn't do hosting, can it recommend a good host?

- What is the agency's primary business objective? Is it strictly a Web site development shop, or is it a marketing agency that builds Web sites as one of its marketing services?

- Where is the vendor geographically located? With overnight delivery, e-mail, telephone, and even video conferencing available as forms of communication, it may not be necessary for your vendor to be located close to your company. Some clients, though, see more value in face-to-face meetings and require vendors to be headquartered within their local area. If the vendor you are hiring is not local, are its employees willing to travel for necessary meetings, and if so, do they charge for that travel time and expense?

- Will the agency provide you with client referrals? For some clients, it's enough just to receive written testimonials on other clients' letterheads. More often, especially for more complex and expensive projects, clients prefer to receive names and phone numbers so that they can ask past clients specific information, such as how easy it was to work with the vendor, the vendor's adherence to schedules and budgets, and the creativity and proactivity of the vendor in terms of providing solutions for the site as the work progressed.

- Can the agency provide you with financial information? This is usually done if the Web project is large and will take considerable time to develop. If the agency is a public company, its financial information will be easy to collect and pass on to you. If it is a private company, you may expect to see its earnings. You also should seek references from its accountants, bank, and at least two sub-vendors to ensure that the agency has credit in good standing. The purpose of this step is primarily to make sure the company is not currently having financial hardships and that it is not likely to go bankrupt or out of business while your project is being developed.

- Who owns the rights to the programming, the graphics, and all the project files? As a client, you should insist that after the project has been paid for, all copyrights and file ownership be transferred to you. Beware of vendors who offer to store and save all files and material for you. This will keep you married to that vendor and force you to return to it—even if you don't want to—should you ever want to make changes to the site. It's always best to maintain all original files in your own possession, if possible.

- How much will the project cost, and how is that figure derived? Does the development company or agency charge by the hour, by the project, or by some other way? Is it possible for the agency to break down the price so that you can see how much of the cost is for design, how much is for programming, and so on? Typically, the more broken down a price is, the better chance you'll have of getting the lowest price possible. Finally, what is the company's desired payment structure? Quite often, a vendor will require final payment be delivered on completion of the project.

■ Does the agency have any kind of maintenance guarantee or follow-up contract? If there is a problem with the database within the first month, will the vendor fix it for you, or does it need to be paid for again? If you want to enter into a long-term agreement so that the development vendor can keep making upgrades and changes to the site, what are the terms of that maintenance contract?

When looking for potential vendors, there are two obvious places to begin. The first is word-of-mouth, which is often the best way of finding a shop. The recommendation of someone you trust is a valuable commodity. The other way to go about seeking vendors is to surf the Web yourself, find sites that you like, and research which Web shops were responsible for the development of those sites. After you have found a number of shops to review (it is usually wise to look at more than one vendor), you can either speak to each shop in an informal client-vendor interview or issue a request for proposal (RFP) to each firm, detailing exactly what you are looking for. Specify a due date by which vendors must submit their proposals. The proposals should include answers to the questions outlined earlier, including pricing and expected time line for completion. As a client, you can either make your decision based on these RFP responses, or, for particularly large projects, use the submitted proposals to narrow the field to two or three finalists. Invite each of the finalists to make a formal presentation to describe why they should win the account. It is not unreasonable to ask that each presentation be accompanied by draft designs of what the proposed site will look like.

After the vendor has been selected, the client is expected to provide any necessary photographs (if there are product shots that are essential to the site) and background material and text. Some Web development shops have copywriters on staff or available for hire if no text is available. You will have to guide them in terms of content, however, especially if you service a complex industry. You also will need to provide all brand information. This will include digital versions of your logo(s), fonts for specialized styles, corporate color breakdowns, and other items.

You should expect the vendor to provide you with detailed time lines to benchmark points of project accomplishment as well as a schematic blueprint to follow for the navigation of the site. Don't expect as the site progresses that everything will always go very smoothly. There will inevitably be bumps in the road and issues to overcome. In an ideal situation, however, the Web development firm should become part of your extended business family, and the site should develop on time and with little hassle.

From a Vendor's Perspective

If you run a Web site development shop, you generate revenue by creating Web sites for various clients. In doing so, you must work with many types of personalities, each requiring a certain amount of finesse. Because of the Web's relative newness, its vast capabilities, and the fact that not everybody understands it from a technical perspective, you will often find yourself playing multiple roles. As a vendor, you are simultaneously the planner, programmer, designer, and consultant. In addition, you often will be the educator. Clients who do not understand the Web will often ask you questions that might seem ridiculous, such as, "If I want my site to act as a virtual ATM machine, can you rig it so that cash will dispense from the disk drive?" Patience in educating the client as to what is and is not possible is a must! You also will act as arbitrator, because it is likely that discrepancies will arise as to what changes and upgrades to the original plan are allowable under the terms of the contract.

It's easy to think that if you have a product or service, you can and should sell it to whomever is willing to buy it. However, when it comes to relationship services that may last for some time, not every client will be a profitable client. Consider the following issues when entering into an agreement with a client (some of these matters cannot be determined by simple question and answer sessions, but rely on information you gather from initial discussions):

5

- What is the purpose of the client's Web site? Is the company trying to build a brochure site, an electronic commerce site, or some other type of site? What are your experiences and capabilities in these areas?

- What is the industry and market that the client is serving? Is it a market with which you are familiar and an industry in which you will enjoy working? Although it may seem that money is money, money can not always compensate for the boredom potentially felt by you or your colleagues while designing a 600-page Web catalog of copper lug connectors for the fluid control industry (unless you find that topic stimulating, of course).

- What is the client's understanding of the Web? A high degree of understanding may help the development process, but it may also lead to significant intrusion by a client who wants to be "too involved" by overanalyzing your work or making programming "suggestions" as you try to make progress. A low degree of Web understanding may require to you spend several hours (for which you usually cannot charge) educating the client as to how the Web works or fielding an inordinate number of questions.

- How creative will the client allow you to get?

- Does the client have an organized brand that you can incorporate into the site?

- Does the client have all of the photographs and text necessary for you to use in site development?

- Does the client already have a database of information that you can use to create the site? If so, what database application is used? If not, does the client want one? (Not all clients will know whether they want a database, or for that matter, why they should have one.)

- Does the client have an established budget for the site (or have one that will be revealed to you)? If he or she does not, and the client is asking for multiple features or complex programming, you should consider presenting a proposal that breaks up the site into Phase One and Phase Two development areas, so that the client has a choice of spending more or less, depending on whether certain features can be delayed.

- How is the client's credit? This isn't a typical question you would ask the customer, but a quick check with Dun & Bradstreet or with the Better Business Bureau will reveal whether the client has credit issues with which you should be concerned. Even the most valuable account is not worth much if you don't get paid.

Pricing Your Services

When trying to come up with how much you will charge for the site, keep in mind that you face pricing competition from other firms and that the prices submitted by other firms for the same project may vary widely. The variation in price is due to a number of different issues that presently apply more to Web site development than to the development of other marketing tools (such as print documents). For example, each vendor may have a different idea for the programming tools needed for development, and one tool may be easier to use than another.

Clients may not understand the complexities of Web development and might ask for prices from shops that are not in the same league as each other. An established shop that has employees, a large office, significant overhead, experience enough to know that it has to allow a certain number of hours for fielding client questions, and the foresight to anticipate issues that will arise later on if a more complex development route is not taken at the outset, may charge, for example, $30,000 for the site to be developed in three months. A competing firm made up of three people in a basement with limited experience, but tremendous talent and drive, might charge under $10,000 for the same project. It also might pay more attention to the client. The smaller agency has less overhead to cover, and $10,000 is a lot more valuable to it than $30,000 is to the larger company. The lower price, though, is a tradeoff for less experience and a higher degree of risk (the vendor may not survive in the long term).

Some competitors may underbid a Web site depending upon the name of the client, even if that means losing money. Doing a Web site for Big Al's Cola isn't going to raise as many eyebrows as creating even a small Web site for Pepsi. A small, growing Web development shop may find it worth a temporary loss to work on the Pepsi Web site, which, by virtue of the name, will ultimately help the vendor to get and retain other large clients.

More goes into pricing a site than just the amount of labor hours that will be put into constructing the site. Vendors must anticipate the unknown. It is quite likely that additional hours will be needed to cover unforeseen circumstances, such as when the client changes his or her mind about a design, or in the case of the client's senior management demanding changes to the project. You will also need to cover hard costs in the shape of equipment costs, salaries, rent, and other charges. You must also weigh the costs of taking on a Web project on which you or your team members will ultimately not enjoy working. If it's a chore to create, nobody will be surprised when the results show it.

Other Considerations for Agencies

Finally, once you are retained by the client, there are certain things that you can come to expect and that will be expected of you. If the project involves design and layout as well as programming, the client will likely expect to see a number (usually three) of distinctly different drafts for the site. You should stipulate in a contract before work begins that there will be only a certain number of drafts provided and a maximum number of draft rounds. For example, after presenting first-round designs, you might create three, second-round versions of the client's favorite first-round design to close in on what the client wants. One final round of drafts may be presented for simple tweaks and alterations. Any changes that are needed past the allotted number of draft rounds may be subject to additional charges. As the vendor, you should insist that anything that receives approval—from layout drafts and schematic designs to the final site—should be signed off by the client. An e-mail approval is not enough (it does not hold up in court); you need an actual signature by the client that states he or she is accepting the material as presented. (Changes after sign-off are usually subject to additional charges.)

Working with clients is vital to any vendor company. The Web has its own set of rules and problems that can make working with a client challenging, but if you are aware of the nuances of each customer, you should be able to work together successfully to develop successful sites.

THE WEB SITE DESIGN TEAM

The Web site development process requires the expertise of many people in various roles and functions. Regardless of whether you are working in the Web department of a full-service advertising and creative agency or in a specialized Web site-only design shop, the general team components are the same. However, each company creates sites according to its own agenda, and each project involves varying numbers of participants (usually dependent upon deadline, site complexity, and budget).

The remainder of this chapter details the specific job functions that typically support Web site development. Keep in mind that some Web site development teams may have multiple individuals for any one position. For example, it's not uncommon to have one account executive, but dozens of programmers. It's also common for some development companies to assign one person multiple tasks. For example, an account executive might also take on project manager duties, or a graphic designer might also be the interactive developer.

It's also becoming more common for Web development houses to offer more, non-Web specific work, such as developing the marketing and advertising strategy to drive traffic to the site. The constant evolution of the Web has created an amalgamated market segment comprising a hybrid mix of marketers and developers.

Figure 5-1 shows a sample personnel hierarchy of a Web site development team within a vendor agency. The figure omits the upper-level executive and administrative staff.

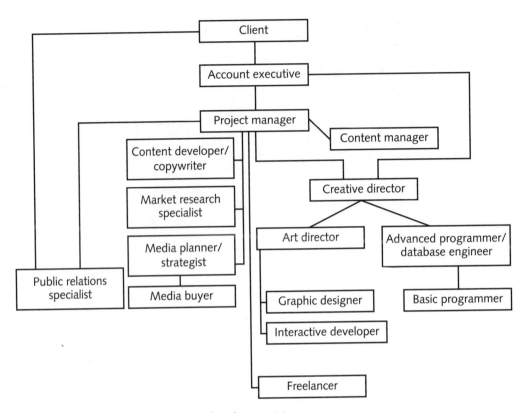

Figure 5-1   The agency Web site development team

Different companies will employ various team configurations depending on the extent of the site being developed. For example, a simple 10-page site with no interactivity hardly needs the vast team shown in Figure 5-1. If a client needs a very large site, but has already done the bulk of the research and marketing through another vendor, the development team will utilize a number of programmers and designers, but few (if any) marketing professionals. Whatever type of team on which you work, chances are that you'll find at least some of the following positions involved in a project:

- Account executive
- Project manager
- Content manager
- Content developer/copywriter
- Market research specialist
- Public relations specialist
- Media planner/strategist
- Media buyer

- Creative director

- Art director

- Graphic designer

- Interactive developer

- Advanced programmer/database engineer

- Basic site programmer

- Freelancer

5

Account Executive

If the site is being created for a client, then an **account executive** (often referred to as the AE) is almost always included on the team. The AE is the key figure heading up the team effort. The AE's job is a stressful and busy one, and the responsibilities are many.

In some agencies, the AE is responsible for making sales and bringing in clients. Other agencies have a sales department that generates leads and turns those leads over to the AE. In either case, once a contact is made, it's usually the AE's job to convince that client to work with the agency.

With the client contract signed, the AE assembles the team and is responsible for overseeing the entire project. This includes ensuring that the market research (as described in Chapter 2) is done properly and in a timely manner, checking that the production schedules are made and maintained, and overseeing any marketing that is to be done. The AE needs to be aggressive, patient, organized, and open-minded to pull off his or her function successfully.

The AE is the single point of contact between the agency and the client. Internally, he or she needs to receive regular updates on progress from other leaders within the team. The AE passes this information on to the client, updating the client about schedules, efforts, and accomplishments. Additionally, a successful AE needs to be the ubiquitous but subtle salesperson, always seeking new ways to upsell a client (for example, suggesting the addition of an online game or an expansion into a new market).

AEs are usually paid a combination of a base salary plus commission as an incentive to keep their accounts alive. Considering how difficult and time-consuming it can be to gain new clients, AEs typically reflect the marketing philosophy of many dot-coms: customer retention is more profitable than customer acquisition.

Account executive skill requirements are as follows:

- Good organization

- People/communication proficiency

- Strong leadership capabilities and the ability to distribute work among others and to make quick decisions

- Diplomacy in case of client complaints or contract discrepancies
- Propensity for sales
- Punctuality in keeping tasks on schedule
- Ability to maintain a balance between creativity and desire, and reality and client need

Project Manager

Reporting directly to the AE is the **project manager**, or PM, who handles the details (and there can be many!) of a Web site development project, including:

- Dealing with outside vendors, such as Web hosts and printers
- Working with the production and marketing professionals to keep them aware of schedules to ensure they are making progress and to keep deadlines
- Keeping track of all internal and client files
- Keeping the AE informed of progress for each aspect of development
- Keeping track of all hard costs, such as overnight delivery fees and long distance phone call charges that may need to be invoiced and paid by the client

The PM is typically the only person on the team who interacts directly with the AE, acting as the bridge between the AE and the rest of the staff (while the AE acts as the bridge between the company and the client). However, depending on the company, other team members, such as the public relations specialist, may report to the AE as well.

Clients, especially those who take their brand seriously, have numerous files that they'll need to transfer to the agency, including images, photographs, brand material, and any other information that will appear on a site. Some of this material will arrive in hard copy form, some as e-mail, and some will never arrive at all without constant reminders. The PM is responsible for collecting all material, organizing all material, and making sure that the right people within the teams receive the materials that they need.

Content management is usually handled by the project manager and can be a time-consuming and frustrating aspect of site construction. Large sites that have a vast amount of information can turn an ordinary desk into a tidal wave of paper, and changes to content can flood an e-mail box. Well-organized project managers must keep track of all files that come in from the client, as well as maintain an archive of all correspondence that occurs. (Archiving correspondence will help during the Web production process in the event that a discrepancy occurs.)

The PM also assists the AE in managing the team, making sure that timetables and deadlines are met, and ensuring that the project is moving in the right direction. The PM usually meets with the team on a regular basis for updates and reports details of these meetings to the AE.

The PM usually has the task of speaking with vendors, such as service bureaus, commercial printers, ISPs, and other outside parties who help bring the project together.

Project manager skill requirements include the following:

- Being extremely well organized

- Working well under pressure

- Having strong negotiating skills (for work with vendors)

- Having strong communication skills

- Having strong leadership skills (to enforce time frames and production requirements on the rest of the team) and having the ability to take direction well (from the AE)

- Being highly punctual

Team members reporting directly to the PM are the content developer, market research specialist, public relations specialist, media planner, and creative director.

Content Developer/Copywriter

The true value of any Web site is in the information, or content, that it provides to site visitors. A brochure site for a radio station, for example, may provide content such as biographies of disc jockeys, information about upcoming contests, and new music reviews. A brochure site for an accounting firm will want to highlight the experience of its accounting professionals, the types of services that it provides, and maybe even a few case studies to show how clients have benefited from its services.

Although all Web sites are built to deliver content in one form or another, not all clients have content to provide. The accountants who need a Web site might know generally what they want to say, although they may have nothing formally written down to appear on a Web site. They may not even think to write case studies—the inclusion of such useful features is usually suggested by the AE. In other cases, the clients may provide content that is written as its associates may understand it, but it's not necessarily written in a style that would appeal to its target market.

The **content developer** or **copywriter** is responsible for either deriving original content that is pertinent to the site and target market (usually by asking the client pointed questions or doing outside research) or adapting client-provided content for a Web audience. Any writing that is done or revised always gets sent back to the client for signed-off approval or for editing.

Note that the only examples used here are for brochure sites. Content sites that report timely news on a regular basis as the impetus for driving traffic and selling ad space typically provide their own content. The same is true for electronic commerce sites. They usually provide the necessary information about the products they are selling.

Content developer/copywriter skill requirements include the following:

- Strong writing ability
- Knowledge of multiple markets
- Strong research capabilities
- Ability to pick up new concepts quickly

Content Manager

The **content manager** is an assistant to the project manager. His or her main responsibility is to organize and distribute the sometimes massive amounts of content that can be part of a site. This can be trickier than one might think, as it's not uncommon for site categories to undergo multiple changes during the creation process, resulting in frequent changes to information content and placement. Content can change categories on a site, and it's important for one person to be responsible for organizing and regularly updating the content so that when the site programmer and designers are assembling the pieces, it is obvious what content goes where. The content manager also has to regularly delete or archive older content versions, so that no confusion arises when it comes time to assemble the site.

Content manager skill requirements include the following:

- Strong organizational abilities

Market Research Specialist

Unlike the content developer, who researches and writes about the client company itself so that Web visitors can get something useful from the site, the **market research specialist** determines who those visitors are going to be. It's his or her job to outline the demographics and psychographics of an audience so that promotional efforts and the site itself can be built to appeal to the widest possible market. The site planning tasks outlined in Chapter 3 are accomplished by the market research specialist, who writes and conducts all surveys, arranges any necessary focus panels, and then analyzes all collected data.

It is the market research specialist's job to make sure that the entire team understands the target market. The entire team needs to be familiar with the target market so that they can work together to create a site to which the target market will most likely respond. Weeks or months after the site has been launched, the market research specialist revisits the market through many of the same steps taken in the original market research (surveys, interviews, and so on) to determine whether the market is responding positively to the site. The market research specialist will learn whether the site is a success, which sections of the site seem to be more popular, and which sections are less popular. He or she then will recommend evolutions of the site based on this information.

On the marketing front, the market research specialist also works with the media planner to determine which media to use in promotion. With this information, the researcher can cross-reference the demographics of various media outlets against the client's targeted demographics.

Market research specialist skill requirements include the following:

- Strong communication skills
- Strong capability for data analysis
- Understanding of multiple markets
- Knowledge of statistical derivation and analysis
- Knowledge of traditional research tactics

Public Relations Specialist

Public relations, or PR, is such an important and unique aspect to an overall campaign that it's often segmented off and treated differently from the rest of the development process. In fact, because PR depends so much on relationship building, the **public relations specialist** is usually the only person on the team other than the AE to have direct contact with the client.

Public relations is a matter of getting the name of the site out in front of the public through non-advertising means. The PR specialist may send a news announcement, or **press release**, to specific publications about the launch of the site, in the hopes that an editor might pick it up and write a blurb, a mention, or a story. The idea of PR is to start people talking about the site—to keep the name constantly on the minds of the public.

Published articles are great, but a good PR specialist will also try to get the client featured in print, radio, or television interviews. Seminar appearances for a representative of the client company are also a good way to publicize the company. The PR specialist is responsible for preparing the client, who must respond appropriately to questions, appear confident, and handle tough situations with grace. The PR specialist also handles damage control, should something go wrong, such as with orders or customer service.

Because PR is so complex and an important part of promoting a Web site, more detail on the subject is provided in Chapter 11.

Public relations specialist skill requirements include the following:

- Strong understanding of public relations tactics and the media
- Strong writing skills
- Strong public speaking skills
- A personable attitude
- Ability to come up with solutions to problems
- Creativity (to see different angles of any situation)
- Strong command of the language

Media Planner/Strategist

If a site is not promoted through outside advertising means, such as print, TV, or radio ads, then it simply sits in cyberspace waiting for visitors to trip over it. What avenues should be taken to get the word out? The answer largely depends on the information the company wishes to relay to its audience and the budget with which a company has to work.

The **media planner/strategist** determines how the message is delivered to the prospective audience. There are a lot of options from which to choose. A print ad campaign with a direct mail component is one possibility, but should the direct mail effort last for three weeks? Six weeks? Should it be a printed piece or one of those cool business card-sized CD-ROMs? Should the campaign include a PR component to help build a brand and drive traffic to a site? These are the questions that the media planner/strategist answers to get the message out as effectively as possible.

The media planner/strategist is often responsible for determining affiliate partners for co-promotion. These efforts can help sites alleviate costs, reach a broader market, or even incorporate traded resources—such as content—that could improve the site.

Media planner/strategist skill requirements include the following:

- Strategic thinking
- Understanding of multiple media, media outlets, and the markets they reach
- Strong mathematical ability (to allocate budgets)

Media Buyer

If your client wants to promote its site using advertising, the **media buyer** works with the strategist in making sure that campaigns are brought to fruition through various media. In many cases, depending on the size of the agency, the media planner/strategist and the media buyer are the same person. Most agencies need only two or more individuals if the client has a large budget and requires complex media purchases.

The buyer is responsible for purchasing the desired space for the ads being developed based on the media planner/strategist's recommendations. This means buying time during specific shows or hours on television if a commercial is being produced, buying pages in publications for print ads, reserving time on roadside billboards, and so on.

Initially this process may sound like a fairly simple job, and in some cases it can be. A company in a niche B2B industry likely won't have massive consumer appeal, and the media purchasing will be quick and painless. For example, let's say that the site being developed is for a printed circuit board company, whose Web audience will primarily be engineers at computer-related companies. The ad campaign, aside from any direct mail efforts, may also include print ads, but no TV and no radio, because the client's market is so targeted. The print ads will appear in industry-specific magazines, some of which may even be published and distributed by industry associations. Buying advertising in this example is a simple process that won't even need a specific media buyer. A phone call and a check will be sufficient.

The situation is quite different for a full-blown, B2C, national ad campaign. The list price of a full-page, full-color ad in a top-tier magazine like *Time* or *People* is roughly equivalent to the value of a two-bedroom, two-bath house in central New Jersey. The price for TV? CBS got over $2 million for each 30-second spot it aired during the 2001 Super Bowl. These kind of prices make it more difficult to just pick up the phone and say "Hi, I'd like two spots during the Super Bowl, please. Do you accept Visa?"

Instead, a seasoned media buyer negotiates a price and secures placements for all the space and time that he or she wants to purchase. Meetings are established with account representatives from the target media outlets, and the agency media buyer enters into negotiations to achieve the best price and best placement on behalf of the client. Negotiations for time on commercial broadcasts sometimes depend on the guarantee of a minimum audience. Because there is never any sure way of knowing beforehand how many people will tune in to any particular show, media buyers will sometimes negotiate a clause that makes full payment contingent upon a certain rating level.

The more money that the media buyer has to wave in front of the account representative, the better his or her bargaining chips will be. Publications aren't likely to discount too heavily if there is no reason to believe that the media buyer representing the advertiser won't be back with more dollars to spend down the road.

If the agency's media buyer has experience (which translates into stronger relationships with media sellers), or has built a solid reputation with media outlets, buying media can be a lucrative business all its own. In theory, the idea is to bill the client the **rate card price** (the price that a media outlet prints as the cost of the ad space or time) while securing the space or time at an even lower price. The difference becomes the media buyer's profit. Often, media buying is outsourced to companies who do nothing but buy media and who therefore have significant leverage for better prices.

Media buyer skill requirements include the following:

- Strong mathematical ability (to allocate budgets)
- Strong negotiation skills
- Personability
- Highly organized work habits
- Knowledge of various media and their formats

Creative Director

The creative director is the artistic force behind the design and structure of the site. With an understanding of the audience from the research professionals and an understanding of what the client wants from the account executive, the **creative director** develops concepts and ideas on numerous fronts. It is perhaps one of the most complicated and enjoyable positions on the team of developers, and it takes a person with a unique mix of imagination, business experience, strategic skills, and understanding of human nature (both as individuals and as a societal whole) to accomplish the tasks successfully.

The creative director, or CD, is responsible for coming up with the **concept** of the entire project. The concept is the overall look, design, and atmospheric style of an idea. Figure 5-2 shows several site concepts for a company called I-many, with each design being proposed to the client as the CD's vision of a site that would best reach I-many's market. Notice the variations in graphics, site shading, and placement of navigation features.

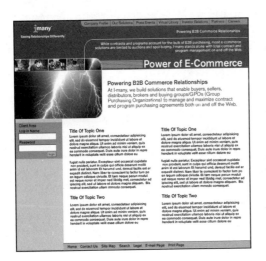

Concept 1

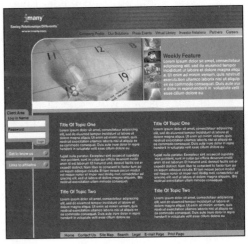

Concept 2

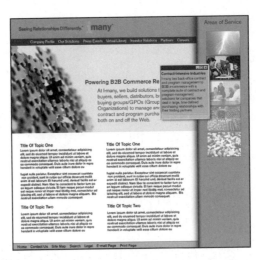

Concept 3

Figure 5-2   Three concepts for the I-many financial software site

I-many makes financial software for large companies, and therefore its audience is composed of decision makers who are high up on the corporate ladder. These people don't have a lot of time to spend searching the Web. They appreciate clean, direct, clear messages that let them know what the company does and where to find the information that they are seeking. To that end, each design was created to present the information as efficiently as possible while maintaining a certain aesthetic style and compatability with the overall I-many brand (in regard to general look and feel, colors, logo treatment, and so on).

In addition to developing the look of the site based on the client's determination of what the site does, the CD may also (along with the AE) make recommendations for site functions and content. For example, logical additions to I-many's site could include a link from the site that would send a specific page to a friend (in the hopes of drumming up referral business). It also could include a virtual library on the site to allow site visitors to quickly search for and find archived data about site-related topics.

Figure 5-3 shows two ad concepts for an Internet-based auctioneer of rare coins. The ads are meant to tout an upcoming auction, branded under the name Premier Plus. The auction will feature coins that are significantly higher in value than most of the other coins that the client offers in its traditional auctions, and the ad concepts were created to get that message across. To do that, the agency recommended sophisticated imagery and layout, rather than an aggressive ad that screamed "Really valuable coins!" However, the CD had to keep in mind that while the coins *themselves* were valuable and would appeal to a wealthier audience, the site that would host the auction (www.gregmanning.com) wasn't designed to accommodate these new coins. The layout of the site was far from upscale and sophisticated, as shown in Figure 5-4.

Concept 1   Concept 2

Figure 5-3   Premier Plus coin auction concepts

Figure 5-4   Host site for Premier Plus coin auction

Having a highly upscale ad that brings readers to a less-than-upscale Web site (in design only—the programming for the site is quite advanced) creates inconsistency, potentially injuring the Premier Plus brand. Therefore the ad concepts could be upscale, but only up to a point. Each needed to allow for a small bit of lightheartedness to better synchronize the two designs.

The samples shown in Figures 5-2, 5-3, and 5-4 are finished comps that have gone beyond the stage of creative direction. Although the ideas for those Web sites and ads came from the creative director, the details and design work most likely did not. Rather, the details for each comp came from the art director (who reports directly to the creative director), and the actual assembly was done by graphic designers. The creative director often sketches the concept indicating how the site or ad will look, what it might offer, how it will present its information and allow users to navigate through the pages, or in the case of advertising, what message might be employed to drive traffic to that site. Figure 5-5 shows a sample sketch that a creative director may give to an art director as a guideline for developing the home page layout of a site called Efloralz.com.

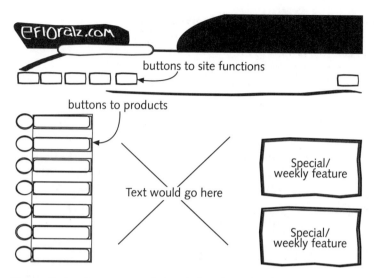

Figure 5-5 A conceptual sketch for the Efloralz.com site

Figure 5-6 shows how the art director and graphic designer turned the creative director's concept into reality.

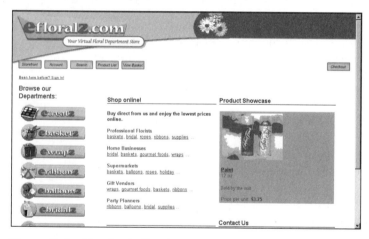

Figure 5-6 The final Efloralz.com site design

Creative director skill requirements include the following:

- High level of creativity

- Understanding of multiple media

- Understanding of how different markets may react to different imagery and copy

- Strong language and writing skills
- Ability to delegate and lead a team
- Artistic nature

Art Director

Working primarily on the graphics side of the agency, the **art director** typically reports to the creative director and works more closely with him or her than do the other people on the development team. A graphics expert in his or her own right, the art director oversees and directs the graphic designers in the creation and design of everything from the site itself to the supporting advertising, direct mail pieces, storyboards, and so on.

The creative director relays to the art director his or her vision of a site or a concept, including the kinds of elements it should have (for a Web site, this could mean a lot of white space, a very pronounced image on the left side of the home page, and so on). For an ad concept, the creative director describes the scene or imagery that should be achieved. For example, for the coin auction site example used in Figure 5-4, the creative director might tell the art director, "We want to promote the coins offered at this auction as being better than most other coins. Let's do something where we see a coin perched at the top of a column, like it's something special that people would revere." The art director then is responsible for developing the finer detail in the art as it relates to the creative director's concept.

The art director works with the graphic designer to decide how the ad should be developed. Should the column with the coin appear in the daylight or at night? Should it be small or large? The art director instructs the graphic designer on the finer details of how the ad or Web page should be designed.

Art director skill requirements include the following:

- Artistic nature
- Creativity
- Ability to lead a team as well as take instruction from superiors
- Knowledge about important design programs and production processes
- Attention to details

Graphic Designer

Graphic designers are responsible for building the interface and graphic elements used in Web sites. The responsibilities of the graphic designer can vary. The graphic designer might be a simple site builder who follows the orders of the art director, or the graphic designer might direct himself or herself under the guidance of the creative director. (In this latter situation, which is typically found in a smaller shop, there is no official art director—the graphic designer is responsible for taking concepts from the creative director and developing the final details.)

The typical responsibilities of the graphic designer include everything from scanning images and basic color retouching to the creation of original graphic elements. These elements include the button design, title work, background development, and main photographic and illustrative imagery. A good designer should understand the particular elements of Web graphics, such as formatting issues, how color works on the Web, download times (file size considerations), and resolution.

Table 5-1 shows and describes some of the Web elements with which graphic designers have to deal with when creating a Web site. More importantly, the graphic designer must understand what works and what does not work aesthetically in a browser window, which is often a sticking point for many print designers who try to make the leap into Web design.

5

Table 5-1   Graphic elements of a Web site

Topic	Details
Image resolution	The number of pixels that exist per every inch of a graphic. The more pixels in an image, the more detailed it will be (if the image is to be printed) and the larger the file size. For Web graphics, images never have to be higher than 72 ppi (unless high-resolution images are to be provided for media or others to download).
Monitor resolution	The number of pixels that will be displayed within a user's monitor. Three standard monitor resolutions are 640 × 480 dpi, 800 × 600 dpi, and 1024 × 768 dpi. At the higher resolutions, images on a screen appear smaller. Web designers need to consider which resolution their market will likely be using before designing a site. Based on the default settings by monitor manufacturers, 800 × 600 dpi tends to be the safest resolution for which to design.
Color	Designers use the RGB (Red, Green, Blue) color mode for Web graphics because monitors display all images by varying degrees of red green and blue light. See Appendix C for more information about colors. In addition, colors will appear different on Macs (the preferred platform by Web designers) than they do on the PC (the preferred platform by the business world). Typically, colors look a few shades darker on a PC than they do on a Mac. However, for very specific color needs, there is a crop of "Web-safe" colors that appear exactly the same on both platforms.
File formats	For most 2-D (static, non-interactive) graphics, files are saved as either JPEG or GIF images. (For more detail on these two formats, please refer to Chapter 6, Table 6-1.)
Download times	Graphics with heavier file sizes take longer for end users to download. Reduce the size of all graphics as much as you can by using features in your image editing program (such as Photoshop) of choice. Also, whenever possible, use the same images often from one page to another to reduce download time—once an image has been downloaded once, it need not be downloaded again.

Graphic designers often use programs such as Photoshop and Illustrator to develop graphics. Although some programs are more popular than others, there are enough applications and ways to create Web graphics that no one way is necessarily "better" than any other. A graphic designer's preference is based on his or her training, combined with the agency's preference. Although different programs are available, most employers will want their Web graphic designers to be proficient in at least Photoshop (an Adobe-made graphic design program) and Dreamweaver (a Macromedia program that helps assemble the layout of Web sites). In terms of hardware, most designers and design shops work in direct contrast to much of the business world. Graphic designers usually use Macintosh computers rather than Windows-based PCs. Macs deal with graphics programs better than their Windows counterparts. Although they have a reputation for crashing more often, Macs are more user- and designer-friendly, and they have developed a cult-like following among their fans.

Other, non–Web-related graphic design duties of the graphic designer include art for advertising, direct mail pieces, and other items that are used in the promotion of a site.

Graphic designer skill requirements include the following:

- Creativity
- Artistic nature
- Proficiency in Photoshop and Illustrator
- A working knowledge of Dreamweaver or similar program
- Knowledge about color and differences between print and Web design
- Knowledge about the Mac platform, with an understanding of how images differ on Windows-compatible computers

Interactive Developer

The demand for interactive developers has been on a steep rise, as sites have been increasingly incorporating Flash and Shockwave features. Both are programs made by Macromedia. Flash allows for fast downloading of animation over a Web site, with the ability for significant interactivity. Shockwave allows Director files (interactive and animated elements with a more photorealistic quality) to be available over the Web. Flash has become very popular on the Web, allowing developers to create sites outside the confines of HTML. It also allows dynamic page transitions, animations, and content to be presented quickly.

Developers need to understand the ways these programs work, and, because of the specific nature of each program, the **interactive developer** may be called upon to guide and direct the graphic designers in creating usable images for each program.

Because each program has increased in complexity through the last few upgrades, their capabilities have expanded. Typically, Flash developers need to know Java and other coding languages to get the most out of a program. Likewise, the interactive programmer needs an understanding of database development as well.

As most interactive developers will tell you, however, it can often be a lot harder to change a site or application created in Flash or Director than it is to change a site done in HTML or similar languages. Because both Flash and Director are timeline-based, changing one element often throws off many other elements that subsequently will need to be redone.

Interactive developer skill requirements include the following:

- Creativity

- Artistic nature

- Proficiency in Flash

- A working knowledge of Director and Shockwave

- A working knowledge of how interactive elements integrate with programming

Basic Site Programmer

The **basic site programmer** sets up the client's Web site, implementing the graphics elements as well as the content and hyperlinks into one cohesive page or site. The basic site programmer uses site development programs such as Dreamweaver and FrontPage to assemble the site, although in most cases a working knowledge of HTML, DHTML, and XML is needed as well.

The basic site programmer incorporates all the graphics provided by the graphic designer, as well as any interactive elements that are provided by the interactive developer, and then builds the framework for the site. This means that besides the page construction, he or she programs all the hyperlinks (according to the schematic of the site presented by the account executive) along with any simple feedback forms or e-mail links that are needed.

The basic site programmer handles the simple programming that is still necessary in the Web world. These programmers usually are junior developers who are fairly inexperienced and who don't know the more complex languages. These individuals are especially important on smaller, brochure-style sites for which more experienced programmers would be overqualified.

If the site is going to be more complex (including database integration, shopping cart creation, and search features) the basic site developer needs to interact with advanced programmers (described next) to integrate other languages into the site. Similarly, the basic site developer needs to work closely with graphic designers to ensure that graphics are created in the proper way so that basic construction is as simple as possible.

Basic site programmer skill requirements include the following:

- Mastery of HTML and other markup languages

- A working understanding of the other languages being used, their functions, and their capabilities

- Mastery of Dreamweaver or a similar program

- Understanding of graphics and graphics programs (to work with designers in making graphics that will work with programming and layout)

Advanced Programmer/Database Engineer

Chapter 3 and Appendix A list and describe some of the many programs that may be needed to complete a Web site. The technologies available to Web site programmers are constantly developing, and **advanced programmers** and **database engineers** need to be constantly aware of these new technologies. What's more, they need to know which languages to use in which situations, making certain that present developments won't hinder future site improvements.

Thinking ahead (in some cases, predicting the future) is often the most difficult part of programming. You can think of the construction of a site as a game of chess. If programmers don't think a few phases ahead, they may end up programming themselves into a corner that makes it hard to change things later.

Advanced programmer/database engineer skill requirements include the following:

- Skill sets vary depending on the employer or the sites. See Appendix A for a list of the languages and programs that may be needed.

Freelancers and Outsourced Resources

Because the size and needs of sites can vary so dramatically, it's not always necessary or cost-effective to keep a full staff of employees on payroll. Let's say, for example, that you are working on a site for a client who wants it to be written in Domino, which is a Lotus server program, and nobody at your agency knows Domino. It would be overkill to hire a full-time employee strictly for that project, unless that person could also do other job and would be useful in other areas. Instead, it may be more practical to **outsource**, or subcontract, the work to a company that specializes in Domino programming, or hire temporary help, in the form of a **freelancer**, to work until the project is completed.

From the agency point of view, contracting freelancers allows employers to save on employee taxes and Social Security payments, while providing access to designers who are hungry to work on new projects. What the agency gives up is the luxury of having a designer who gets to know a project and the client over time, which can add value to an account by creating familiarity with client's preferences, awareness of what he or she responds to, and knowledge of how both the client and the client's market evolve.

For the freelancer, the benefits are terrific. First, freelancers usually get a higher-than-average hourly rate for their work than a standard employee would receive, making the final paycheck for a project very attractive. Freelancers also (sometimes) get to work from their homes, and, if they want to go on a vacation, they just don't schedule any projects in that time. The best benefit of all for a freelancer is the diversity of the workload. Having multiple employers means that you're not stuck working for only one client or doing the same tedious task over and over again. As a freelancer, you might work on a Web site one day and a print brochure the next, each with a different target market.

Of course, benefits have their price, and freelancing is not without its problems. Getting paid can sometimes be more difficult than it is if you are a full-time employee. You'll also have to make your own arrangements when it comes to benefits such as medical, dental, or 401(k) plans. Psychologically, you may miss having the community atmosphere that exists in an office environment, and you'll need to be self-motivated to work from home while ignoring the beckoning of the refrigerator and television. Worst of all, when you're not working, you're not getting paid. Go for long enough without a project, and you might spend less time in front of a computer doing work than you spend in front of a TV watching talk shows.

5

CHAPTER SUMMARY

- Working on a Web site can be a complex task—so much so that sites often require a team of specialists. Companies that want or need a Web site of their own need to consider the benefits of either building the site in-house or outsourcing the work to an advertising agency, a creative agency, or a Web development shop that specializes in these tasks. Although creative control is maintained and less money is spent by a company that builds the site internally, a better, more efficient job may be achieved by hiring out to do this type of work.

- Like most other major tasks, developing a functional and successful Web site requires a strong team with complementary skills, responsibilities, and personalities. Team members include the account executive, project manager, content developer/copywriter, content manager, market research specialist, public relations specialist, media planner/strategist, media buyer, creative director, art director, graphic designer, interactive developer, basic site programmer, advanced programmer/database engineer, and, possibly, freelancers.

- Each member of the team, whether he or she works directly on developing a site or spends more time driving traffic to it, plays an important role in how the site comes together. However it takes shape, the team structure of Web design is the only way that a truly successful B2B or B2C site can come to life.

KEY TERMS

account executive
advanced programmer
art director
basic site programmer
concept
content developer/copywriter
content manager
creative director
database engineer
freelancer
graphic designer
interactive developer
market research specialist
media buyer
media planner/strategist
outsource
press release
project manager
public relations specialist
rate card price

REVIEW QUESTIONS

1. List three reasons why a company would want to keep its Web site development in house.

2. What are three reasons why a company would benefit from outsourcing its development to an outside agency?

3. Explain three facts that a client company would want to know about a potential Web site development agency. Why are these facts important for the client to know?

4. The head of the team at most agencies or production companies is the

   _____.

   a. creative director

   b. account executive

   c. project manager

   d. agency CEO

5. In fewer than 100 words, explain an account executive's responsibilities.

6. One of the most difficult aspects of creating a Web site for a client can be
_____.

   a. collecting the money that the client owes you

   b. introducing the client to the team

   c. upselling the client to a larger, more complex Web site

   d. educating the client about the Web's capabilities and limitations

7. In most agency situations, the overall concept for a site or a campaign is developed by the _____.

8. In which of the following tasks would you expect to find a public relations specialist involved?

   a. Writing the content for a brochure site that needs to capture a new audience.

   b. Determining an angle of interest about a site and pitching the angle to a magazine editor as a story idea.

   c. Reviewing the site's traffic log and determining which pages and content audiences seem to like best.

   d. Creating a concept for an advertising campaign to promote the site.

9. A media buyer can usually get lower prices for ad space if _____.

10. Employers will most likely expect their Web designers to know at least
_____.

   a. Adobe Photoshop

   b. Macromedia Director

   c. Macromedia Flash

   d. CorelDraw

11. Demand for Macromedia Flash developers has grown because _____.

   a. Flash provides easier streaming of video

   b. Flash is one of the better programs for working with bitmap graphics and allows faster JPG compression

   c. Flash allows for large scale animation and interactivity without a long download time

   d. Flash is cheaper to buy than Director and easier to learn than Photoshop

12. The market research specialist is most interested in _____.

   a. how many people visit the site through the home page

   b. the average length of time it takes for each page of the site to download over a standard modem

   c. how many people visit the site in the days after an ad campaign first breaks

   d. how the site development information is being relayed from one member of the team to another

5

13. What is the main reason agencies use freelance help?

14. The creative director most often conveys his or her ideas to the
_____

    a. art director

    b. graphic designer

    c. client

    d. president of the agency

HANDS-ON PROJECTS

1. Gather your business partners and the business plan you've been writing—you're going to add to it. Every business plan needs a biography of the key executives who are running the company, as well as how they will get the site developed.

    a. Write a 200-word biography for each person on your business team. Detail your individual talents, and describe which role each of you will play in the company.

    b. Obviously, there will be other people that will be needed to make your company work. Considering the type of company and Web site you plan to build, what are the minimum positions you anticipate will need to be filled? What are the special skill sets needed to successfully fill those positions?

    c. Determine whether you intend to hire out for the construction of your site, or whether you will build it internally.

        i) If you plan to build it yourself, do you need to reconsider the list of employees that you'll need to fill? What type of knowledge will your staff need to actually build the site?

        ii) If you intend to outsource the site, use the Web and research Web development companies. Based on the information presented in their sites, narrow your choices of vendors down to two. Describe why you have chosen these vendors as your likely Web site developers.

2. Pick a site of your choice. Based on viewing the site and its source code, describe which elements of the site were likely completed by people in different development positions. Using printouts, describe the role that you believe each professional played in the development of the site.

3. Find a Web site development company in your local area. Arrange an interview with the person whose job position to which you would most closely relate. Learn that person's day-to-day activities and how the team members communicate with each other to complete the site. From the interview, determine the team structure of the company and map it so that it takes the same schematic form as Figure 5-1.

6

ORGANIZING YOUR WEB SITE WITH NAVIGATION AND INLINE GRAPHICS

In this chapter, you will learn about:

♦ Organizing your Web site using navigation features
♦ Navigation tiers
♦ Building flexibility into your navigation structure
♦ Background graphics
♦ Inline graphics and buttons
♦ Six universal design tips
♦ Issues surrounding color usage
♦ Resolution issues
♦ Two primary file formats used in Web programming
♦ File size considerations

People visit Web sites to gather information, to conduct transactions, or to be entertained. Whether they are looking to make a purchase or just to read an article, surfers use the Web because content is expansive, convenient, and (usually) easy to find. The best content in the world can be boring without decent graphics, and content becomes completely pointless if it can't be found easily by site visitors. Navigation and graphics are among the first things that call attention to your site visually, and they can help make a lasting impression with your site visitors. It's up to you whether that impression is a positive one.

This chapter helps you understand the sometimes complex chore of setting up navigation features. You will learn how to structure your site for maximum user friendliness. You also will learn how to use graphics to aid navigation and to add interest to your site.

WEB SITE NAVIGATION

Have you ever tried to find your way through a really complex maze? It's challenging, and it's even fun to do if you have some time to spend. You know that there is a way to reach your final destination—in fact, there are probably a couple of ways to get there; some are pretty straightforward, while others take the scenic route. The maze may also have a lot of dead ends and paths that bring you right back to where you started.

These characteristics are fine for a maze, but not so great for a Web site. Dead ends, multiple paths to the same places, and roundabout ways of reaching certain data plague many sites and are a leading cause of frustration among Web site visitors. Site developers, often too busy with the management of the graphics and the aesthetic features of a site, frequently neglect the navigation and fail to create a user-friendly, sensible site hierarchy.

Regardless of the type of site you are developing, visitors are coming for one basic reason: to gather information. As a developer, your job is to make that information as easy to access as possible. The larger the site is, the more attention the developer has to pay to the navigation.

Site **navigation** refers to the elements that allow the user to "jump" from one page to another. These elements are referred to as **hyperlinks**. In the early commercial days of the Web, navigation features usually looked like regular text and were colored in blue and underlined. Clicking the blue underlined text allowed you to instantly access a page with related information.

Today, although some sites still use the blue underlined text for certain purposes, it's more common for sites to use graphic buttons or other images to link from one page to another. Because buttons and other hyperlinks can be less than obvious, and because some sites have a lot of information to relay, presenting a clear, organized navigation system is very important. When information is segmented into different categories, such as "Products," "Find a Store," and "Your Account," your site should have a navigational structure that allows each category of the site to be easily accessed from any other category.

The navigation structure that you create should be directly related to the amount of content that you have to provide. The larger the site, the more detailed the navigation structure should be. Content often will increase as you plan or build your site, potentially forcing you to change your navigation structure midstream.

Organizing and Presenting Content

Before you can begin to put your navigation together, you need to determine exactly what information you are going to provide, as outlined in your initial business plan (discussed in Chapter 2). What reasons would someone have to visit your site? Ask yourself why you visit other sites. Do you just wake up in the morning with a burning desire to check out **Hersheys.com**? Probably not. Determining *why* someone would come to your site is the first step in organizing your site's navigation. As with so many other aspects of e-business success, the reason relates to brand. This idea will be reviewed a bit more in Chapter 8, where we discuss the details of bringing the brand message to your Web site. The brand creates an emotional bond between the product or company and the customer, which leads to the question: How much of an emotional connection do people want between themselves and their chocolate bar? How important is it for them to chat with other Hershey's lovers online? Every site and every brand has a message that can be sent over the Web—you just need to determine what that message should be and how to best use the cyber medium to present it.

Too often, sites fluctuate between not having enough content to support having a site and having so much content that visitors are confused by it. As you plan your navigation, you should ensure that the content of each page meets a combination of the following descriptions:

- The page content is information that you want to provide to a potential audience.

- The page content is information that an audience would be interested in or would likely respond to (notice that what you may want to provide to an audience is not always what the audience will find interesting).

- The page content is information that you can easily acquire.

- You can update the content quickly without sacrificing the site's overall quality.

Once you have assembled your content, it's time to put it in order.

Organizing Your Site

Having multiple **tiers,** or levels, of navigation features on a site helps you organize content into logical segments. Technically, though, Web information (no matter how much there is) doesn't have to be segmented at all. Because the Web is limitless, there is no technical reason that all information can't be put on one page that scrolls on and on for as long as you need it to. *War and Peace*, for example, could be posted as one long page on a Web site.

Of course, what's possible isn't always what's practical. One long scrolling page would not only take a long time to download (especially if images are included), it would also defeat the purpose of the Web—to make information fast and easy to find through the use of hyperlinks. Not only that, but Web users don't take kindly to long, scrolling pages, and there is only so far that most viewers are willing to scroll before they give up and surf elsewhere. Therefore, you should segment all of a site's information into various categories and spread these categories over a tiered navigation system. Create a schematic of your site and its navigation features using whatever method you prefer: a hand-drawn sketch, a flow-charting program, or a word processor document.

Navigational Tiers

The main categories on a site comprise the **upper-tier navigation,** or the names of the buttons that (should) appear on every page of a site. These should be broad topics that logically can contain other, more-specific items of information.

We will use the fictional example of Chef Jay's restaurant to illustrate the considerations that go into creating a logical navigation structure. First-tier navigation features for the restaurant are not unlike the menu, in which main topics might include Appetizers, Salads, and Dinners. On Chef Jay's Web site, these categories constitute the first-tier navigation—the main categories. More specific items, such as mozzarella sticks, potato skins, and calamari, are listed under the category in which they most logically belong, in this case, Appetizers. These categories become the **second-tier navigation** of a Web site—the items that are directly beneath the upper-tier categories. This makes sense, as each of these items falls within one common heading: the word or phrase that they share. A schematic of the navigation to this point looks like Figure 6-1.

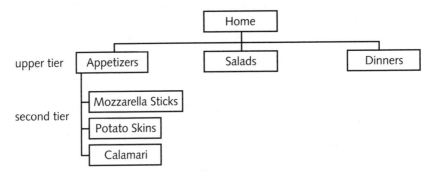

Figure 6-1   An initial schematic for the navigational layout of a site

Naming the navigation features is subjective and just takes a basic understanding of organization. Assume that the restaurant offers calamari as both an appetizer and as a dinner.

Figure 6-2 provides two schematics—one for each way that the site could be organized. In the top version, calamari appears once and is listed under both Appetizer and Dinners. In the second version, calamari (along with the other appetizers) is the main category, and Appetizer and Dinner are subpages within it. Neither version is *wrong*, but the set-up of the second version is limiting and doesn't really provide the information in the most useful way to the reader.

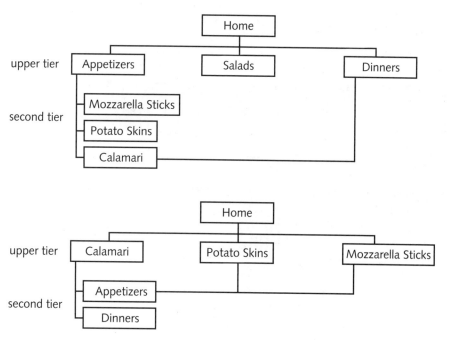

Figure 6-2   Two schematics showing alternate ways of organizing information

The secondary navigation level provides a listing of the various appetizers that are available, but what if there are different *types* of any one appetizer offered? Say, for example, calamari is served either mild, hot, or spicy. Each of these new choices is listed only under the calamari item, and if this menu were a Web site, it would be considered the third-tier navigation, and so on. Figure 6-3 illustrates how these tiers are structured in the updated schematic.

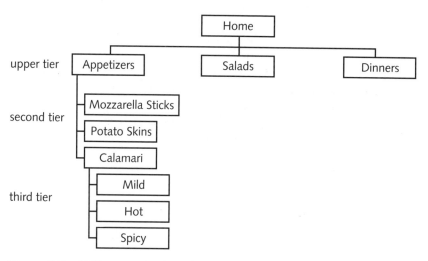

Figure 6-3   Differences in the schematic after the information has been updated

Only the upper-tier category items are visible on the site at all times, as shown on the home page of Chef Jay's site in Figure 6-4. Basic information is provided about the restaurant, and some graphics are presented on the home page.

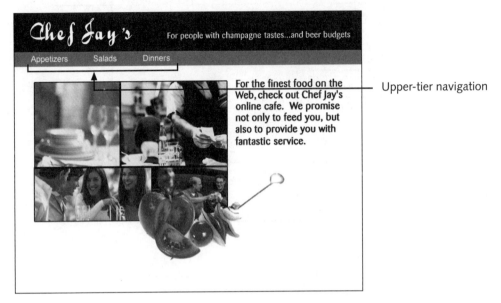

Upper-tier navigation

Figure 6-4   Chef Jay's home page with all the upper-tier categories visible at all times

Figure 6-5 shows how the site changes if the user clicks the Appetizers link. Notice that the information on the page now shifts from the restaurant itself to general information about Chef Jay's appetizers. Notice too that the upper-tier navigation hasn't disappeared—it's still there, but now another navigation device also exists—the second-tier structure. In addition, the word Appetizers is highlighted to remind the visitor where he or she is on the site. This new navigation option lets the user link to any of the appetizers on the menu. Finally, as Figure 6-6 shows, if a user clicks the link for calamari, yet another third navigation device appears (with links for Mild, Hot, and Spicy), while both the upper- and second-tier navigation buttons remain in place.

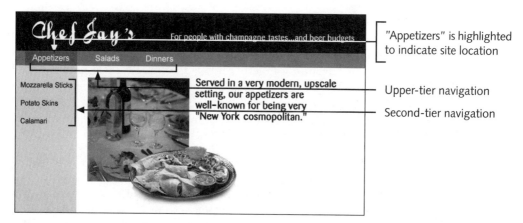

Figure 6-5   First-tier navigation and second-tier navigation within the selected category

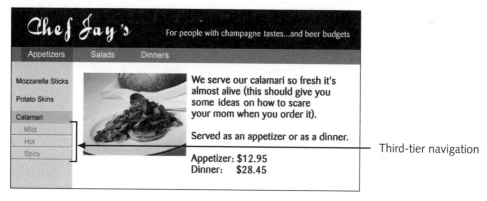

Figure 6-6   Navigation links for third-tier features with first and second tiers remaining visible

When More Content Makes the Site More Complex

Web sites are rarely ever completely finished. Instead, they are in a constant state of evolution and growth. Like almost any business, the restaurant featured in the previous section eventually will want to add more categories or organize its current content more efficiently.

Web site developers need to anticipate changes. Based on knowledge of the company for whom the site is being developed, and based on the market and industry predictions, it is possible to make some general guesses. As a developer, you need to think about how those changes may affect the navigation of the site. Changes may not only affect the individual content categories, but also could change the general navigation schematic.

Suppose that an art supply reseller is building a Web site. The company wants the site up and running for a blow-out sale at the store. However, it has only a few pictures of its products and doesn't have time to take any more before the sale. The company says that it has been working on putting together a more complete catalog, but it has been slow to actually do it. Thus you must build the site with what you have. As a result, the "Products" section would list the products available, but show shots of only a few of them. As the developer, you would be building the site in anticipation of a complete product database eventually becoming available.

Assume that six months after the site is launched, the art supply store has finished its product database. If you have planned well, you would have designed the site to include a database search field. You also would have programmed it to incorporate database integration so that the graphics and layout do not have to be completely redone to accommodate an improvement. The database integration feature is a pretty obvious one. However, what if the company's continuing market research learned that allowing aspiring artists to post their work to the site for public display would be a popular feature and an enticement for future visits? The site navigation should have been set up in such a way that adding a new category such as this would be a relatively simple process.

Now we'll return to the Chef Jay's example, taking it a bit further. Chef Jay's also serves specials, side dishes, desserts, beverages, and other items. You know these facts from your site planning activities. There are also non-food content items, including critic reviews, directions, and contact information, that may need to be included. Assume that the following content needs to be added to Chef Jay's Web site:

- Lunches (six subcategories)
- Desserts (five subcategories)
- Side dishes (four subcategories)
- Beverages (nine subcategories)
- Specials (the number of subcategories varies day to day)
- Critical reviews (three subcategories)
- Contact (one subcategory)
- Directions and map (two subcategories)
- Reservations (one subcategory)
- Information about the restaurant, including information on the owners, the history of the business, and the chef (three subcategories)
- Coupons (one subcategory)
- Parties and events (one subcategory)

These new categories should be enough to give visitors to Chef Jay's Web site the information they need about the restaurant. Later in this book, you will discover how specific content can be added for marketing purposes and how to encourage users to come back to the site on a regular basis. This content might consist of original recipes or contests. These elements are called **sticky** elements, because they provide a reason for the user to stay on the site or to make a return visit.

Categorizing New Data

The first real challenge in expanding a site is to determine which of the new content elements should be main category (upper-tier) listings and which should be subcategory (second- or third-tier) listings.

The schematic can take on a few different configurations, depending on how the site will be laid out, the audience, and how important it is for certain information to be provided when a user first comes to the site. Figure 6-7 shows a basic schematic in which all of the meals and food-related content is listed under a new category, titled Menu. (Only the few appetizers listed earlier are present here—looking at the schematic, you can imagine how large it will be when all the categories are completed.) You can see how the rest of the new content is distributed, with Directions and Reservations falling under the main category Contact, and each of the other items (Reviews, About Us, Coupons, and Parties) becoming new upper-tier category headings. Figure 6-8 shows how the Web site is set up according to the schematic.

6

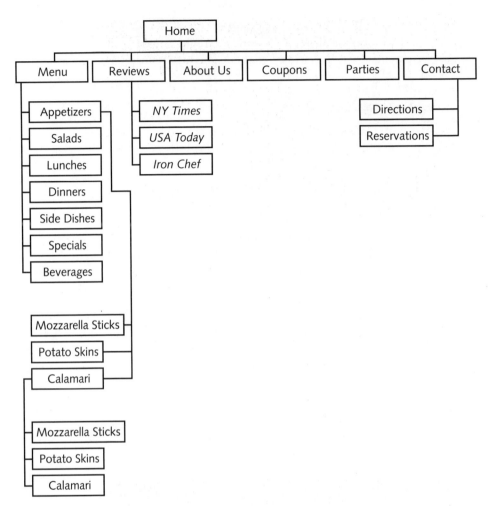

Figure 6-7 An updated schematic based on new information

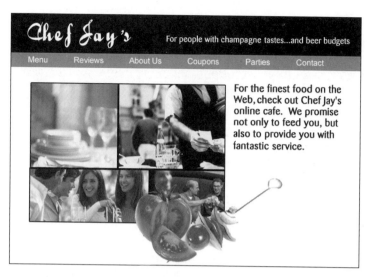

Figure 6-8   The home page with navigation based on the new schematic

Within the figure, there is no apparent link to return to the home page. Whether you include a home link on each page depends on your preference. Some sites have a Home button that links back to the home page, and other sites, such as Chef Jay's, make the corporate logo the link back to one. Web users have largely come to expect that clicking a site's logo will bring them back to the home page.

The new layout illustrated in Figure 6-8 has one problem: it more or less buries the main part of the site—the food—in with all the other categories. To fix this, you should build a new schematic that breaks the food topics out into their own main categories. Figure 6-9 shows how this adaptation looks on the home page.

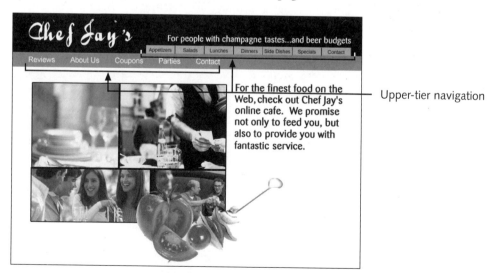

Figure 6-9   The home page adapted to highlight certain content using two upper-tier navigation structures

This time, there are *two* upper-tier navigation devices, because a distinction has been made between the types of categories. The food categories are treated and presented separately for two reasons. First, the navigation would be cumbersome if all the first-tier options were placed on one navigation device. Second, and more important, such layouts are considered acceptable and often useful when the main subject of a site, whether it relates to services, products, people, or, in this case, food, is broken out and highlighted separately.

Don't Program Yourself into a Corner

Imagine that you have this great idea for a navigational feature on your site. The navigation bar will be developed in Flash so that the upper-tier categories fold or unfold to reveal the second-tier categories as the user rolls the mouse on and off each category title. It would be a pretty innovative effect, and a unique tool, because you don't see that sort of thing every day.

So you build it, and after the site is launched, your client and manager agree that the navigation is fascinating. You are given a bonus and praised for your amazing combination of creative and programming prowess. Life is good; until the phone rings. It's your client, and she would like some changes made to the Web site. The Media page should be called Newsroom, the Special Discounts section should be removed completely, a new category called Innovations should be added after About Us, and a bunch of second-tier pages will need to be added. By the way, she wants it done today.

 As you learned in Chapter 5, you should be prepared for situations like this in terms of planning, billing, and completion. Web site development agreements should outline how many excess development hours clients are willing to pay toward the project, and turnaround time for changes should be predetermined.

Unfortunately, this sort of scenario happens all the time. Flash, DHTML, and other types of programming technology are highly useful and allow developers to be extremely innovative when creating their navigation. These technologies are especially useful in situations in which a lot of links would make a navigation more cumbersome than desirable. Before you implement such a design, consider how often the navigation is likely to change, and think about how difficult or easy implementing such changes will be. Not all employers or clients will want to wait days just for a category name to be changed—no matter how good it looks. Also, make sure that a team member is available at all times to make changes. Hiring a freelancer to build an unusual navigation device might save money in the short run, but there will be no one on hand to make revisions when the device needs to be changed in a hurry. That can end up costing more than was originally saved, or at least causing more trouble than it was originally worth.

Navigation Specifics

Although understanding the tiered system is the first and perhaps most important step in building your navigation, there are many nuances and subtleties that need to be incorporated. Strong navigation design incorporates the **three-click rule**, which specifies that a user should be able to get to any page from any other page within three clicks, without using the browser's Back button.

Placement of Links Within a Browser

You can put buttons and navigation elements anywhere on a Web page. However, being *able* to do something doesn't necessarily mean that you *should* or that it's a good idea.

One of the challenges of designing a Web site is that you never really know exactly how a user is going to see the page. In print design, if you create a printed brochure, you know that your reader will see exactly what you produce; the edges of the piece are finite, and the final size is nonadjustable after the printing is done. Because Web site users can have any of a variety of computing configurations, however, there is no standard for how your site will appear to the viewer.

Not knowing how your visitors will view your site is a problem that affects many aspects of site development. In terms of navigation, however, this problem has a very simple solution. No matter the size of the browser, or the resolution of a visitor's monitor, the upper-left corner of a browser window is always visible (at least until the user scrolls). If parts of your site are going to get cut off (so that the user has to scroll to see them), they will be cut off because they are on the right side or bottom of the browser window.

It's bad practice to make your visitors hunt around for primary navigation devices. Therefore, except in rare circumstances, you should place your upper- and second-tier navigation devices along the top or down the left side of the page whenever possible. Figure 6-10, on the next page, shows two sites that adhere to this rule.

Although most sites do adhere to the top and left structure, there are times when navigation features appear in other areas of a site. Many sites, especially those that were developed in the mid-to-late 1990s, have their navigation features at the top or left of the site. They then emulate that navigation at the bottom of each page, using blue underlined text. This redundancy provides flexibility for Web users who have older computers that don't display graphics, who deliberately turn off the ability to display Web graphics because of slow modems, or who have impaired vision. The text navigation feature allows these visitors to make their way through the site easily.

Today, you're more likely to find a game player with an old Atari than you are to find a Web surfer with a computer that can't display graphics. Still, keeping text links that emulate the main navigation is a good idea, especially if the pages are long and require a lot of scrolling. The extra navigation features will save your visitor the trouble of having to scroll back up to the top of the page to find the buttons.

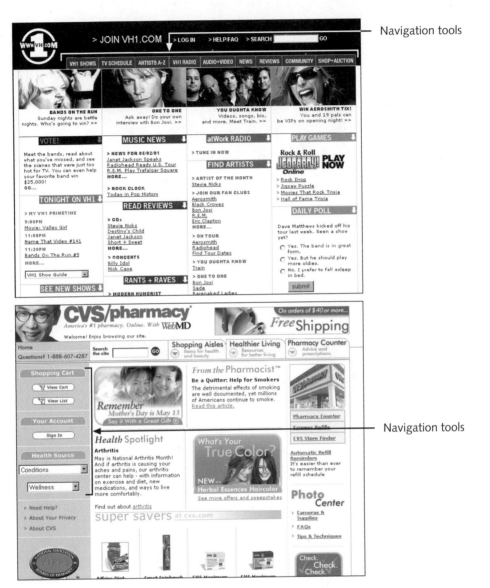

Figure 6-10 Upper- and second-tier navigation features located at the top or left side of the page

Sites that are developed entirely in Flash or Shockwave or that are created using frames might also have their primary navigation tools along the bottom or right side of the site. Frames divide a browser into distinct areas so that the user can change or navigate one or more portions of the site while other portions remain static and visible. The right-side navigation is acceptable, because in both cases, the size of the page itself can be pre-set. A Flash site can be set to a specific number of pixels to reduce any chance of browser scroll, and you can design a frames-based site so that a specific number of pixels on the bottom or the right can be reserved for content. This space is non-scrollable, regardless of the user's monitor resolution.

Navigation Consistency

Consistency is one of the underlying concepts for practically everything brand-related. Whether developing a brand, an advertising campaign, or a navigation system, consistency helps maintain organization and increase brand value.

Maintaining consistency in navigation is important from both design and placement considerations. Buttons that appear as graphic text on one page should not change in color, size, or style on the next page. Inconsistency in these areas hurts the brand image and confuses the user as he or she surfs from one page to the next. The same holds true for placement of navigation elements. As you learned earlier, having a clear and distinct navigation structure for various tiers of your site is necessary for organizing content. This organization depends on keeping each tier in the same place throughout the site. If the main navigation features appear at the top of some pages, keep them there on all pages. Do not move them to the bottom or to the side for certain areas of the site.

Although you should always maintain structural consistency throughout a site, it is acceptable to have the first-tier links appear differently on a home page than on other pages of the site.

Number of Links

Often, designers create sites with far too many links. They do this because of a lack of organizational skills (poor planning) or to make the site appear far larger than it really is. Figure 6-11 shows an old home page for one of northern New Jersey's larger newspapers, *The Record* (**www.bergen.com**), as it appeared in December 1999. Considering the massive amounts of content available and the popularity of the printed paper, this site should have enormous traffic. Beyond the home page, however, the only other pages that were getting any benefit from *The Record*'s 2.6 million hits per month were the sports and obituary pages.

Figure 6-11   An old home page of *The Record*

The reason that *The Record*'s Web pages got such little attention was that there were simply too many links on the home page, confusing visitors as to where to go next. Recognizing this to be a major problem, *The Record* changed its site completely. Figure 6-12 shows a recent version of *The Record*'s home page, in which the number of links has been reduced to broader, more maintainable categories. This layout serves information to the user far more successfully, even though it has an equal or greater amount of content with which to work.

Figure 6-12 *The Record's* updated home page is easier to navigate

Double Links and Dead Ends

Some sites, in an effort to seem larger, or in a misguided attempt to make information easier to find, create multiple links that lead to the same page. Make sure that visitors know where each link will take them. Visitors become frustrated when two or more buttons under different names lead to the same page of information.

When you create a page, make sure that each button is properly labeled and that you are not deliberately or inadvertently misleading visitors. Done properly, the navigation on your site should make all information simple to find. On each page, only one button should lead to any other page. This avoids multiple links to any particular piece of information.

Conversely, don't lead your visitors on a wild goose chase either. Pages that are "under construction" might be a necessary part of business on the Web, but make sure these are clearly indicated *before* your visitor reaches them, either by clearly indicating on the home page that some areas of the site have not yet been completed or by making the links to unfinished pages inactive. Following multiple links just to end up at a page that doesn't exist is a common complaint among Web users.

Search Engines

Search engines invite users to type in a word or phrase that they wish to search for within a site. After a search term has been entered into the search engine, the engine scours a database for words that match the words that are being sought. If the engine doesn't find any matching words, it returns a message to the user that no results were found. Simple search engines to help users find information within a site are fairly easy to build. Because of this, many sites have added them. After all, search engines look great on a site and give the impression that the site is sophisticated and large.

Too often though, the site is not large enough to justify the inclusion of a search engine. Users may find themselves entering key words to find information on a site, and nine times out of 10, ending up reading a message that no information could be found on their key words.

So how many pages will you need before a search engine is justified? It's a judgment call, really. If you believe that enough content exists on your site that a user who conducts a search will usually find results, it may be worthwhile. This is especially true if your site is so large that some information is buried deep into a low tier, where it may be inconvenient or unlikely to be found through searching by standard navigation.

Site Maps and Paths

It's kind of funny that you can "get lost" on a site when you have never moved from your chair, but it does happen. Site maps and flags to illustrate the path a visitor has taken to get to any particular place are easy to implement and exponentially increase the convenience factor of particularly large or database-driven Web sites.

In addition to adding these features, sites should embrace the default nature of the Web that changes the color of a link after a user has clicked it. This change of color is an easy way to let the user know that he or she has already visited a page. Amazingly, however, many site designers program their sites to bypass this feature and keep all links the same color after they have been clicked. As a result, site visitors may find themselves on a page they have been to time and time again—all for the lack of a simple reminder of where they had already visited.

Location Reminders

You should include page or category titles on each page, or at least highlight the area of the navigation system that got the visitor to his or her present location. It's fairly common for a user to forget what page or site section he or she is reading, even though he or she may have just clicked there only moments earlier. It's good practice to provide simple reminders to let users know at all times where they are within the confines of your Web site. This is often done by providing a path that shows users what page they are on and how they got to that page or by highlighting the name of the page or section on the navigation bar. The highlighted links shown in Figures 6-5 and 6-6 are examples of these indicators.

Easy Exits

Contrary to popular belief, letting visitors leave your Web site is not a negative act. In fact, it's considered good manners in standard netiquette. Visitors appreciate it when you provide links from your site onto other sites that may provide supporting information to what is on your site. Many broad-based search engines will even promote your site listing to a higher rank if you provide easy ways off your site and onto other areas of the Web.

At the very least, don't make the common mistake of creating your site in frames. This forces other sites to show up within your outer shell so that your own navigation and brand identities are retained. Doing so is typically considered bad practice, and users don't appreciate it.

Graphic Design and How it Relates to a Web Site

Regardless of how your site *works*, the way it looks is the first thing surfers will see and the first thing they'll use to judge the quality of your site. Animation, cool graphics, and other visual stimulators are exciting to site visitors and they keep the visitors coming back. That's why it's important to understand graphics and use them as best you can.

The term **graphics** refers to any visual feature of your Web site, including figures, buttons, and imagery. Graphics come in many sizes, shapes, and forms, and the way they are used largely depends on how you create them. The three main types of graphics that you need to understand are background graphics, inline graphics, and button graphics.

Background Graphics

One of the most noticeable design-related changes to have occurred on the Web is probably the change in the backgrounds of many sites. For a long time, unattractive wallpapered backgrounds plagued Web sites. That's okay if you're building a site for the local dog groomer, but not appropriate for corporate Web sites or any other site that wants to appeal to a large audience.

As designers and audiences became more sophisticated, so did the layout and design of most Web sites. Today, it's pretty rare to find many sites with any type of background at all (save the clever use of background brand advertising on sites like CBSMarketWatch.com, which was mentioned in Chapter 4). Savvy Web site developers and marketers have come to understand that legibility is second only to profitability on any site (and apparently, legibility is easier to achieve). Users come to a site to find information, and they want to find it quickly. They won't spend much time marveling at the great graphic work that went into creating a background or elaborate border design, so you should expend your design efforts on clean and logical presentations.

Consequently, most site backgrounds have **flat colors**. Flat colors are images or areas made up of fields of one or more single-tone colors, such as you might find in a comic strip. In comparison, photographic images combine far more colors and tonal ranges to give an image a photorealistic look.

Another background option is to use a very plain, flat color band either on the left side or toward the top of the page. Having anything on the site that gets in the way of the content is a definite taboo.

How Backgrounds Work in a Browser

Whether you are doing your own hard coding of a site or putting your site together with a program such as DreamWeaver or ImageReady, there are a few universal rules that apply to **background graphics** (which are any images in the Web browser that appear behind the content). It is a good idea to keep these guidelines in mind when setting up your site:

- Unlike inline images and others that are covered later in this chapter, the background image and/or color is set in the <BODY> tag of the HTML text. If you're using an image as part or all of your background, it's the only image that is referenced in this tag, and there can only be one.

- The background image is the only image that can be connected to (touch) the edge of the browser window. All other images will usually come no closer than 5 to 10 pixels to the edge of the browser window.

- It's *never* recommended that backgrounds be animated, because it adds little aesthetic appeal and is potentially a major distraction to the site visitor.

- Backgrounds don't appear on page printouts. If your background color or image is dark with white lettering, people who try to print your page get just white text on white paper. In other words, they'll get a blank sheet. You can solve this problem by adding a link to a printable version, in which the text is presented in black on a white background. Although the printable version is a potential solution, it's not as optimal as simply avoiding light text over a dark background in the first place. Having two sets of pages for each page of information—one for viewing and one for printing—can be cumbersome and can open the door to information discrepancies when the site is updated.

- Background images (as opposed to solid color states) don't appear only once in the browser window. Instead, the image is placed in the upper-left corner of the window and tiled (repeated) infinitely down and to the right. Figure 6-13 shows an example of a tiled background.

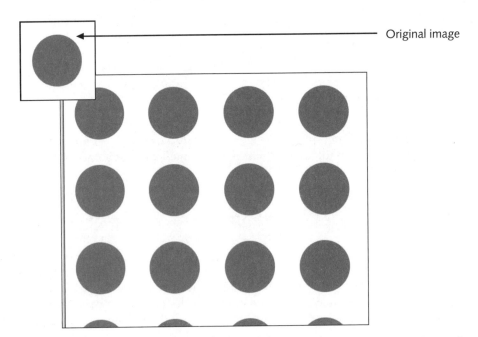

Original image

Figure 6-13   Background image appearing multiple times because of infinite tiling

Note that these guidelines apply to two-dimensional graphics that are saved in either JPEG or GIF file formats. Images that are created in other programs and saved as different formats may not adhere to traditional rules of background images. Applications such as Flash or Shockwave or sites that are created in DHTML and that use layers often work differently.

It used to be that tiling played a major role in how sites appeared on visitors' monitors. **Wallpapering** a background (another term for tiling) meant that designers would manipulate a small image to create the appearance of a much larger image when tiled in the browser window. The challenge of successful wallpapering is to carefully create the graphics so that there are no "seams" in the background. (Seams are the obvious lines that appear when the image repeats itself but is not lined up properly.) Figure 6-14 shows examples of seams that detract from the aesthetic appeal of a site and that create a distraction for the site visitor. Creating wallpaper can be a time-consuming process, even with specific tiling tools in the better graphics programs.

Figure 6-14   Wallpaper with visible seams

In the past, the size of the file that you used to create your background could be a problem. If the physical size of the tiled image was too small, the repetition would be obvious. Due to the small physical size of the graphic, the site visitor would often see the background load tile by tile as the site struggled to fill the browser window, even if the file size (in bytes) of the background graphic was small. On the other hand, if the image was too large, the file could eat up a significant amount of the total file size that you allocated for any one page, based on your site's lowest common denominator (LCD).

Thanks to increases in bandwidth and changing page design trends, background graphic size has become a nonissue in designing sites. Figure 6-15 shows an example of a Web site that successfully uses a tiled background.

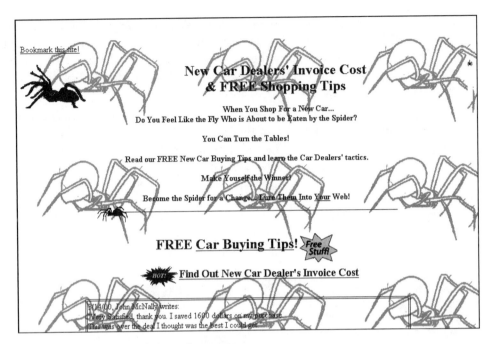

Figure 6-15   Tiled background on a site

Inline Graphics

Inline graphics are any graphics that appear in a Web site and that are not backgrounds or buttons. Product photos, images of a corporate headquarters, head shots of key personnel, or even pictures included for aesthetic value are just some of the types of pictures that adorn most Web sites.

Although many designers use Adobe Photoshop and similar graphics programs to create exciting images within a Web site, photographs are the graphics used most often. Designers can use custom photography that is captured with a digital camera, although many site developers—especially designers of brochure sites—prefer to use royalty-free images. **Royalty-free images** are sold by stock photo houses for a fee that allows anybody who pays for them to use them in their work. If you keep your eyes open, you'll start to notice the same images appearing over and over again on various Web sites. However, even if royalty-free images or custom photographs are used for a site, designers still will have to use Photoshop or some other program to edit the images, resize them, and make them smaller in file size.

Unless you're creating a site for personal reasons, it's important not to go overboard with graphics. Inline images are best used to show a product, place, or person. The Web is a highly visual medium, and as such, it benefits from colors and imagery that take it beyond a simple black-text-on-white-background presentation. In addition, because the Web is a digital medium, full-color photographic images are no more expensive to create than are black-and-white images—unlike print development, which is significantly more expensive if done in full color. However, because online color has no added expense and because the Web is so open to graphics use in general, Web designers are often tempted to overdo it, to the point that the graphic development overwhelms the site and detracts from the information that is being conveyed.

If you want to use images for purely aesthetic reasons, you should do so to enhance and emphasize a point. For example, a music entertainment site can easily stand to have a picture of a guitar adorn the pages. The guitar adds a visual clue for the user about the site's purpose.

Button Graphics

Button graphics have surpassed simple text hyperlinks as the preferred means of navigating between Web pages.

However, although the use of graphic buttons has grown significantly in popularity, this does not mean that simple text hyperlinks don't have their place in the Web world. Information within the body copy of a page that relates to information found elsewhere on the site still is presented typically as a link. As mentioned earlier, some people choose to turn off their browser's ability to display graphics. Web site programmers can use a simple piece of code to make text links available for users who can't or don't see graphics. These can be presented along with the graphic buttons for users who prefer more graphical links.

Because virtually any image on the Web can be turned into a hyperlink, most designers who understand the importance of clear navigation will create their linkable graphics to *look* like linkable graphics. Figure 6-16 shows a few button types that are common on the Web.

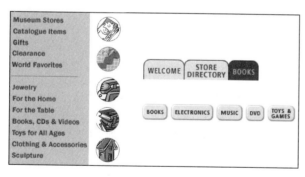

Figure 6-16   Various button designs

Designers can use **rollover** techniques to make it obvious that the buttons are navigation features. With a rollover feature, the button changes color or appears that it has been pushed in when the user either rolls the cursor over it or clicks it. Changing to look as though it's being pushed in is usually just a matter of changing the placement of the drop shadow (as though there were a light source hitting the button), if the button is designed with beveled edges, as shown in Figure 6-17.

Figure 6-17   Changing rollover states for beveled buttons makes them look pushed in

Although it can be tempting to create buttons with lots of graphics pizzazz, keep in mind that buttons and navigation are meant to be an innocuous tool, not the reason that a user comes to your site. Modern design standards lean toward simplicity in navigation graphics, with a basic and highly visible bar or column used to present the category page titles. **Image maps** often are used to achieve this effect. An image map is a single graphic element that allows a Web user to access different parts of the site, depending on which area of the graphic he or she clicks. In other words, although a simple button on a Web site is a graphic that acts as one hyperlink to one other page, an image map is one graphic that acts as multiple hyperlinks, with each hyperlink providing access to a different page.

Programmers create image maps by segmenting the graphic into coordinates on the X and Y axis and then determining to which page of the site each segment should lead. Figure 6-18 shows how one long vertical column has been created and divided so that each area on the graphic connects to a different page within a given Web site.

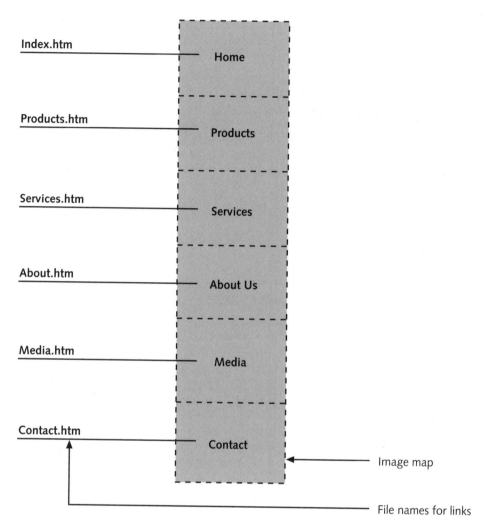

Figure 6-18   An image map is one graphic that links to multiple pages

UNIVERSAL DESIGN TIPS

In recent years, the most successful Web sites have relied on good graphic design to support their business operations. The following are tried and true tips on what flies and what fails in Web design:

- Don't go overboard with background graphics. The louder or more design-oriented your background is, the harder the copy is to read. Instead, try to use solid colors—white, gray, or black tend to be the most popular, and each does a good job of presenting information. These colors are easy on the eye and avoid the implications certain shades can have in various cultures. Be careful—solid colors can be loud too. Nobody wants to squint at pink text that sits on top of a neon orange background.

- You can write or download a script that keeps the background in position as you scroll down the site. Don't use it—it hurts viewers' eyes.

- You know that really cool introduction page or animation that you storyboarded and wanted to put on the site for the period of time before which users actually reach the home page? Resist the temptation and don't put it up. Visitors want to get right to the information they are seeking.

- Keep animation on a page to a minimum (it can be distracting) and don't have too many animations on different parts of the page. In fact, although it will really depend on the content and the audience for your site, it's rare that more than one will ever really be necessary. If children are your target market, you might find use for two or three.

- Overdone drop shadows, bevels, and embosses were popular in the late 1990s. Let's leave them there. Stark images and white space are the way to go.

- Give your reader a clear path to follow. Use your graphics in such a way that they lead your viewers' eyes to specific areas that you want them to see. The biggest mistake you can make is to overwhelm content with imagery.

TECHNICAL CONSIDERATIONS FOR WORKING WITH GRAPHICS

Graphics on the Web are displayed in one of two ways. **Bitmap graphics** are the most common, with vector graphics gaining in popularity. Vector graphics, used with animation programs, are composed of discrete objects that you can move independently. Bitmaps on the Web (not to be confused with the bitmap file format) are graphics that are built by a collection of one or more **pixels** that come together to create an image. A pixel is like a small dot that appears on your monitor screen, and each pixel is responsible for containing one color. These colors then combine to create an image.

Figure 6-19 shows a photograph at its normal size—100 percent. You can see that it is impossible to distinguish the different pixels individually because they are so small. The right side of Figure 6-19, however, shows a small portion of that photograph, magnified to 400 percent of its actual size. Note that the individual pixels are more apparent.

Figure 6-19 When magnified, you can see pixels that combine to make an image

Bitmaps are saved primarily in either the JPEG or GIF file formats. Designers have built careers out of knowing how to master difficult graphics programs like Adobe's Photoshop to properly manipulate imagery for the Web. Besides needing a creative eye and significant artistic insight, graphic designers have to be experts in colors, file size management, formatting issues, and other areas that determine whether their images will enhance a user's experience on a site or distract him or her from it.

Color and the Web

Students of graphic design learn that computers display colors by emitting red, green, and blue light. These colors are mixed in varying amounts on a computer monitor to achieve millions of colors. The range of colors that a computer can display is called its **RGB gamut**. Appendix C discusses color and how it works on the Web in more detail.

Today, most monitors can display thousands or millions of colors, so viewing photographic images typically is not a problem. That wasn't always the case—early browsers could display only 256 colors, and disparities between Mac and PC displays limited the ways in which Web site designers could use color. The Mac versus Windows problem still exists; however, most designers who use Macs know to take the color discrepancy into consideration when designing their sites.

Web Versus Television Displays

Designers face new hurdles as more people have the ability to see the Web on their television sets. Black text on a white background is easier to read on a computer, while white text on a black background is easier to see on TV. You should avoid using reds and yellows on television, as they tend to bleed, but both of these colors look fine on a computer monitor. Depending on the audience and how they will be viewing a site, developers will have to be increasingly aware of which colors they use and how they will be interpreted by the user's viewing device.

Brand Color Consistency

Ensuring consistency of the brand is the most significant design challenge faced by Web site developers. Consistency in color is a part of the overall branding effort, and designers must maintain this consistency between the paper-based and computer-based collateral efforts. It sounds like an easy enough task. However, as larger audiences gain access to monitors that show more colors, designers can be tempted to take advantage of the large RGB color gamut. Even if a Web developer works only on Web projects and never even looks at Quark Express (a popular program for print development), it's important for him or her to understand that color on a computer monitor is not the same as color on a printed piece. Far more colors can be achieved in the virtual RGB world (and in nature) than can be achieved in print. If the designer does not understand this, then he or she could build brand colors on a Web site that could never be matched by the company's printed collateral or marketing material. As such, inconsistency with the overall brand effort may result.

Resolution

The term **resolution** refers to the number of pixels that make up an image, usually measured in linear (straight) inches. The higher the resolution, the more pixels there are in an image.

Higher resolutions are better for most print pieces (because more pixels in an image means that there is more ink used and thus sharper detail in each image), while lower resolutions are fine for digital projects, such as Web design. (A Web page is shown on a screen built to display only 72 pixels per inch.)

Depending on the type of project on which you're working, you may work with up to three types of resolutions measurements: image size, pixels per inch, and dots per inch.

Image Size

The **image size** describes an image's physical size, such as 3 × 5 inches, when you print the image.

Pixels Per Inch (PPI)

Also referred to as the **image resolution**, **pixels per inch** (ppi) measures the number of pixels per inch in an image. Pixels can be added to or subtracted from each inch of your image without changing the image size. For example, your 3 × 5-inch picture can have 72 pixels per inch, or it can have 300 pixels per inch. It's still 3 × 5 inches in size. Because each pixel contains color information, there is more detail and clarity in print work if you have more pixels within each inch (it is higher in resolution). However, as you will soon learn, when creating a Web site, there is no benefit to using images with a high resolution.

Problems with Pixels When using a graphics program such as Photoshop, it is very easy to start an image with a high resolution and then reduce the resolution by subtracting pixels from the image. The opposite is not possible, however, without severely **pixelating** your image (ruining the quality by making it blurry).

Pixelation occurs because when you increase the resolution or the physical size, you're asking the graphics program to add pixels without telling it what information (colors) to use. The image becomes blurry as a result. Often times, smart Web site developers create all their Web graphics in a high-resolution version first and then archive the high-resolution (hi-res) files before reducing the resolution for the Web. That way, if they later need to create a brochure or other print piece with a design that is consistent with the Web site, they already have the hi-res files and don't have to re-create everything from scratch.

More pixels equals a higher resolution, and the extra color detail (provided by the additional pixels—remember that one pixel equals one color) increases the file size of the image, as compared with a lower resolution version. For example, consider two versions of a 1×1-inch image with different resolutions. At 72 ppi, there are 5184 pixels (72×72). At 300 ppi, however, there are 90,000 pixels (300×300). This huge difference explains the difference in the amount of detail and also the difference in file sizes.

6

Dots Per Inch

Also known as **monitor resolution**, **dots per inch** (dpi) refers to the number of pixels or dots that appear per inch on a monitor. Most monitors display 72 dots per inch. Therefore, if your image is 72 ppi, it will appear as its actual size when viewed at 100 percent—one monitor pixel for each image pixel.

Figure 6-20 shows two versions of the same image as they might appear on a computer monitor. In each version, the image is 6×4 inches and is displayed at 100 percent. However, the low-res version easily fits within the confines of the monitor screen, while the hi-res version is so big that you can see only a portion of it on the monitor. This discrepancy causes big trouble for designers.

low-res version

hi-res version

Figure 6-20   Low-res and hi-res versions of an image as seen in a browser

Because the monitor can display only 72 pixels per inch, the low-res 72 ppi image on the left can fit comfortably in the monitor since at 100 percent view. There is one image pixel for every monitor pixel. At 288 ppi, the higher-resolution image provides too many pixels per inch for the monitor to handle at the same 1:1 ratio. Therefore, the image appears larger on screen than it does on paper. In this case, the image resolution is 288 ppi. That's four times the 72 ppi that the monitor displays. The image appears on screen at four times its actual size, or, in this case at 24 × 16 inches. The monitor needs to be 24 inches wide to properly show all 432 horizontal pixels (6 inches × 72 dpi = 432).

Because Web surfers are using a computer monitor to view your site, you don't need to use graphics that are any more than 72 pixels per inch—which is one pixel per image for every pixel displayed on a monitor. If you use images that are higher in resolution than 72 ppi, they appear in a browser in much the same way as does the image in Figure 6-20. In addition, as we've seen earlier, higher-resolution images are also higher in file size and thus cause visitors to your site to have to wait longer for each image to download.

Although you should avoid using hi-res images on the public pages of your Web site, there is a place for hi-res images on the Web. Most notably, as you will see in Chapter 11, many companies that use public relations strategies to promote themselves typically employ a "cyber media room" on their Web sites, providing special access primarily to editors of newspapers, magazines, or other broadcast outlets, as well as to marketing and advertising firms. Among the other information that is provided in the cyber media room is typically an archive of hi-res photographs (including product shots and executive head shots) and logos that publications can download and use if they need to print a story about the company.

The only setting that you have to worry about when it comes to dpi is the resolution settings of the monitors that your audience will be using. Most standard monitors are set to display 800 × 600 pixels (800 pixels across by 600 down). Most modern-day monitor settings can be changed, however, to any number of other display sizes. (Other common settings are 640 × 480 and 1024 × 768.)

Because of the popularity of the default setting, most Web sites are designed for the 800 × 600 standard. They will fit the browser window at 800 pixels horizontally. The 600 pixel vertical measurement really means nothing if the site is meant to scroll. As Figure 6-21 shows, sites that are designed for 800 × 600 monitor displays are cut off on monitors that are set for 640 × 480, and they have extra space unaccounted for on monitors set for 1024 × 768. Unless you know that your specific audience is viewing your site at some alternative monitor resolution, you're best off designing for the 800 × 600 standard.

| 640 × 480 | 800 × 600 | 1024 × 768 |

Figure 6-21   Site appearance is affected by monitor resolution

Keep in mind that when you are designing for the 800 × 600 standard, the 800 pixels across goes for the entire monitor display area, not just the browser window. This means that when laying out the design for the site, you're going to have to factor in about 5 pixels on either side for the sides of the browser window. You'll also need to plan to allot another 5 pixels for the default space that most browsers place on either side between the browser window and the page itself. Lastly, if your page is going to scroll (and you should always assume that on some monitors, it *will* scroll), you'll have to account for about 40 pixels for the scroll bar. This means that your horizontal page measurement really shouldn't be any more than about 740 pixels.

If you are trying to get everything into the browser window without scrolling, or if you need certain information to be visible when the visitor first comes to your site, you'll have to do similar calculations to take the bottom and top of the browser window into consideration. The height of a Web site that will fit into a browser window on an 800 × 600 monitor is about 450 pixels. (The toolbars on most browsers take up quite a bit of space.)

Other types of resolution, such lines per inch (lpi), exist only for non-digital media, such as print. Explanations of lpi and complex print discussions are beyond the scope of this text.

File Formats

A file format is the way by which graphics are saved and compressed into manageable sizes. When it comes to flat, two-dimensional images, there are really only two file formats to consider: JPEG and GIF. A third, PNG, which was meant to be a combination of the other two, really hasn't gained popularity because browsers have been slow to recognize the format. (In other words, not all browsers and browser versions can display PNG images.)

Images that are rendered in 3-D development programs also will be presented as either JPEGs or GIFs, if they are meant to remain static (unmoving) pictures on the Web. If they are meant to have complex animation and interactivity (simple animation with fewer frames can be handled by GIFS), they may need to be in the format for Shockwave files. Even though PNG hasn't made a place for itself directly on the Web, it is a popular format among Flash developers when importing certain JPEG images into movies. PNGs prove useful in certain instances because the format supports partial transparency.

So what's the difference between the formats, and why would a Web designer choose one format over another? Table 6-1 provides a look at what makes each of them different.

Table 6-1 Differences between GIF and JPEG file formats

GIF Format	JPEG Format
GIF uses a color index, and only supports up to 256 colors	JPEG supports up to 16 million colors
Part or all of a GIF image can be made transparent	JPEG images cannot be made transparent
A series of GIF images can be bundled together as one image to create a basic animation	JPEG images cannot be made to animate
GIF is a considered *lossless*, meaning that the quality does not get worse each time that you save it	JPEG is a *lossy* compression format, meaning that each time you save an image, it will eliminate information that it considers to be useless, making the quality worse each time it is saved
GIF will display images better and have a lower file size for images that have flatter colors, color fields, and fewer gradations	JPEG will display images better and have a lower file size for images that are photographic and/or have lots of colors

Beyond the factors outlined in Table 6-1, there is little value in understanding the differences between the JPEG and GIF file formats in significant depth. In the not-so-distant past, when dial-up modems still made file size and download time a much more difficult hurdle to overcome, it was more important to have a better understanding of the two formats. Improvements in connection times and upgrades to Adobe Photoshop (the most widely used program for editing and saving images in one file format or the other) have made predicting how an image will appear within a browser and how long an image will take to download a simple task. Photoshop will calculate the image at different quality levels and report the download time it will take over various connection speeds.

Three things have taken the urgency out of needing technical knowledge of the popular figure formats: improved bandwidth, improved color capability on monitors, and ease of manipulation of formats.

Improved bandwidth conditions have made file size less of an issue than it used to be. File size and cumulative file size are still important considerations, but less so than in the early days of the Web.

Improvements in monitors mean that most people now see thousands or millions of colors on their monitors. In addition, the need to create GIFs to avoid unwanted color banding has been virtually eliminated. Color banding is an unattractive meshing of color that occurs when an image with many colors is presented on a monitor that can display only a few colors.

Most modern graphics programs, most notably Photoshop, have made it very easy to create images in either JPEG or GIF format. For the most part, intuitive dialog boxes do most of the work for you, reducing the creation time (for GIFs especially) from long minutes into scant seconds. Trial and error, which was a necessary evil with earlier versions of most graphics programs, has been eliminated. Now it is easy to achieve precision in image quality and reduced file size.

File Size and Download Time

When a Web surfer visits a site, the page downloads to the visitor's computer from the server where the site is located. The more data the page requires—including graphic elements, text elements, and images—the longer the surfer must wait to see the page. Some page elements, such as a limited amount of HTML-generated text or a simple background color, download instantaneously because the information (pixels or file size) contained within them is very small. Searches of large databases containing many fields and cells of information may take more time as compared to smaller databases, because the search request makes the server work harder to provide information.

Graphics and images also require more computing power and time to download, as compared to simple text. As you learned earlier, the more pixels that appear in an image, the higher the file size. The higher the file size, the longer the download time. Web users who still access the Internet through a dial-up modem can download only a limited amount of information (measured in *bytes per second*). The longer the visitor must wait, the higher the chance that he or she will get frustrated and move on to the next site.

Fortunately, as the Web matures, download time is becoming less of a concern for developers. Modem speed is still an issue, but hardly as limiting as it was in the late 1990s. Because more and more people report that their major use of the Web is from work, and with the steep increase of B2B Web sites, many developers are unconcerned about how heavy their Web sites are in file size. As design style has changed from the "in your face" approach of wild background colors to a more subdued "less is more" look, even reaching the 36.6-Kbps-modem user has become less of an issue.

Does that mean that you should go out and create graphics without any thought at all to their file size? Of course not. It just means that you have a lot more liberty to be creative, with fewer technical limitations to hold you back (depending, of course, on your audience).

Chapter Summary

- Above all else that is *important* when creating a site—the plan, the testing, and the technology—the elements that are the most *obvious* are the graphics and navigation. Their vital importance to the experience of a Web visitor stems from the fact that graphics and navigation both can add value to and can destroy a site. When developing, site creators need to keep in mind at all times that the main purpose of a site is to provide information to site visitors. Graphics and navigation should help, not hinder, that process.

❐ Setting up a tiered structure for the site is vital for organizing and categorizing content, no matter how broad that content is. The structure needs to be built in a way that allows for growth of the site and ease of access to all information. It's also important that your navigation doesn't confuse, frustrate, and possibly drive your visitors away. These pitfalls include using numerous dead-ends, making the navigational structure difficult to decipher, and having too many links.

❐ Graphics features offer many opportunities to take advantage of the aesthetic qualities of the Web. From buttons to backgrounds and inline images, graphic designers can have a field day designing graphics that will make a site pop out and come alive for site visitors. However, it's this urge to fill the Web's blank creative canvas that causes many designers to over-design a site, making pages take too long to download, buttons too difficult to recognize, and information too hard to read.

❐ Aside from knowing when to rein in the graphics, designers need to understand the many nuances of how graphics will appear within a browser window. This information includes having an understanding of color, the differences between platforms, and how file sizes affect the download time on various speed connections.

KEY TERMS

background graphics
bitmap graphics
dots per inch
flat colors
graphics
hyperlinks
image maps
image resolution
image size
inline graphics
monitor resolution
navigation
pixel
pixelating
pixels per inch
resolution
RGB gamut
rollover
royalty-free images
second-tier navigation
sticky
three-click rule

tier
upper-tier navigation
wallpapering

REVIEW QUESTIONS

1. The primary navigation features on a site usually _____.

   a. remain visible and accessible at all times

   b. remain visible and accessible until a link is clicked

   c. remain visible and accessible until the user reaches the third tier of the site

   d. aren't as important as other tiers

2. _____ is one of the main navigation pitfalls that you should consider before programming your site.

   a. Future changes to content that may affect the navigation

   b. Rollovers that may not work on a Web site

   c. Differences between browsers and how the differences may affect the navigation

   d. Whether users will be interested in the categories you have created

3. Because of monitor resolution scrolling issues, the best place to put navigation usually is _____.

4. A good way to remind users where they are within your site is to _____.

   a. change the color of the button on the navigation bar that leads to the page the user is on

   b. give each page a different background color that corresponds to the color of the button that got them there

   c. write text that indicates where the user is within the site

   d. display the current navigation tier along with any tiers above the current tier and highlight the current button

5. Which of the following would least likely be a primary navigation option for a bank?

   a. Open an Account

   b. About Our Bank

   c. Meet Our Staff

   d. Discover Bank Services

6. One of the only situations in which it is acceptable to change the placement of the primary navigation from one page to another is _____.

   a. between the home page and the rest of the site

   b. between the contact page and the rest of the site

   c. between the opening animation and the rest of the site

   d. It's never a good idea to change the placement of the primary navigation.

7. Background graphics appear in a browser window _____.

   a. by appearing 5 to 10 pixels away from the edge of the browser window

   b. by tiling infinitely down and to the right

   c. as JPEG images, regardless of the format in which they are saved

   d. Images don't appear as backgrounds.

8. _____ is one of the three most commonly used background colors.

   a. Green

   b. Maroon

   c. Navy blue

   d. Gray

9. In a normal, non-frame, HTML-generated Web site, the only graphic that can touch the browser window edge is _____.

10. An image that allows links to multiple pages is called a (n) _____.

    a. image map

    b. JPEG

    c. PNG

    d. button

11. If your image has a flat field of just a few colors, the best way to keep your file size low while getting good quality is to use a(n) _____.

    a. JPEG

    b. PNG

    c. GIF

    d. image map

12. If you want to make sure that both Windows and Mac users see the same colors, you should use a color palette that consists of _____ colors.

13. A color gamut refers to _____.

    a. the range of colors that are available in any one particular color model

    b. the specific colors that cannot be achieved in the CMYK color model

c. the colors that are available for Web use

d. the colors that Netscape Navigator and Microsoft Internet Explorer reserve to create their Web browsers

14. Web images do not need to exceed a resolution of _____.

15. An image that is 5×7 inches in size with a resolution of 150 PPI has _____ pixels.

16. Most Web sites are designed for monitors with settings of _____.

   a. 640×480 ppi

   b. 800×600 ppi

   c. 1072×740 ppi

   d. 1000×850 ppi

17. JPEG images handle _____ better than GIF images.

   a. animation

   b. transparency

   c. flat colors

   d. photographs

HANDS-ON PROJECTS

1. It's time to get back to building your Web business. Break out the business plan and gather your partners.

   a. With your partners, present a list of the site's content topics and describe how the information will be categorized within the site. How will that information be gathered? Provide reasons why you feel that the content you are providing will be relevant to your target audience.

   b. Create a schematic based on the content you will provide, clearly showing upper, second, and third tiers. If you think that more information might be needed later in the life of the site, indicate where this information might go and how it would be worked into the overall navigation.

   c. If you have graphic design experience (Photoshop or some other program), create a potential home page design for your site. If you do not know graphic design, sketch out a picture of how the home page might look. Provide the reasons why you chose the type of design and layout that you have sketched out.

2. On the Web, look through at least two of the major retail sites, such as **Amazon.com**, **BestBuy.com**, **Staples.com**, and **Walmart.com**. List good and bad points about the way each site has been set up. Answer the following questions as you search through each site:

    a. Can I find products easily?

    b. How many clicks do I think it will take to get from an advertised product to the product itself? How many clicks did it actually take?

    c. In my opinion, what is the main purpose of the site?

    d. Is the content current, and is the content important with respect to the site's purpose?

    e. Are the graphics helpful, or are they distracting? How long do they take to download with your connection speed?

    f. Is the navigation easy to follow? How many different tiers does the Web site have?

    Look through at least three online retail sites that have not been so heavily advertised and that are relatively more obscure. Try **lowestfare.com**, **superstargifts.com**, **smyrnacoin.com**, **fromthecellar.com**, **1800faceoff.com**, **charrette.com**, **homedecorator.com**, or **spoon.com**. Answer the same questions, and compare them to the answers developed for the major retail sites. What is your conclusion about major players versus smaller retailers and how both handle navigation?

3. You are building a site in which your client, who is not very Web savvy, wants the following information categories:

Contact Us	Product "A" Description	Company History
Links Page	Home	Product "B" Description
About Us	Philosophy	Products
Industry News	Press Releases	Product "C" Description
News Article 1	E-Mail Link	News Article 2
Employees	Mission Statement	Client List

Organize these categories into a full schematic drawing showing the upper, second, and third tiers of the Web site.

7

TESTING YOUR SITE FOR MAXIMUM PERFORMANCE

In this chapter, you will learn about:

♦ The various reasons for testing a Web site

♦ The four types of consumer testing

♦ The three types of business testing

♦ General testing tips

Consider the following scenario: you're taking a long driving trip alone, along some back roads that you've never traveled before. You have the route mapped out, and you're on your way to Brownsville. When you're about 50 miles from your destination, you come to a fork in the road. According to your map, you're supposed to take the road that leads to the east. However, a sign at the fork points west and reads, "Shortcut to Brownsville. 30 miles to the center of town."

Because you are tired of driving, you take the shortcut, only to find that it must have been put up by vandals as a joke—you've gone nearly 100 miles out of your way! Now you're angry, and you know one thing for certain— you won't fall for the same trick on your way back home, nor will you make that same mistake on any future trips. The mistake was bad, but the severity of the mistake was not such that you couldn't learn from it and make better decisions in the future as a result of the knowledge you gained.

Other mistakes, however, are much more grave—so much so that there are no second chances. Say you are back at the fork in the road. This time, suppose you take the shortcut only to find that the sign was placed by much more malicious vandals—it leads to a steep hill and eventually off a large cliff. You certainly won't be making *that* mistake again. In fact, your error was so bad that you won't be making *any* mistakes again.

Unfortunately, in business, mistakes can be measured in much the same way. Some set you back but are minor enough that you can learn from them and use the knowledge to take a different course of action the next time. This knowledge typically is defined as *wisdom*. Other mistakes are so bad that they're irreparable and drive you out of business.

Because customer loyalty is so hard to achieve on the Web and because leaving one site in favor of another is so easy, it is crucial to limit damage caused by errors at all stages of Web development. Avoiding errors requires employing a serious testing effort *before* your site launches and continuing those tests during the life of your site.

You use different types of tests at different times in development. For example, some tests make sure that the site is working from a technical perspective and that the design coincides with the brand. Other tests focus more on the user experience. These tests identify which elements are helpful and which are confusing. They also ensure that site development work stays on track with the market research that was done before you started constructing the site. See Chapter 2 for more information on market research.

INTRODUCTION TO SITE TESTING

The Web pages shown in Figures 7-1 and 7-2 illustrate the kinds of changes that sites may implement as a result of testing. The page in Figure 7-1 shows the cyber media room for JVC, which primarily is used by editors of publications looking for information for stories they are writing that include or are about JVC products.

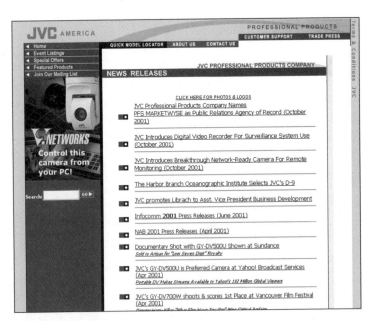

Figure 7-1   Original JVC cyber media room

The media room shown in the figure did what it was supposed to do—it presented news. However, it was less than ideal for editors, who sometimes had to dig around a bit to find the information they were seeking. Subsequent research and testing of the site found that editors would be more likely to include JVC in their stories if the page showed more information about each article, with dates and news categories highlighted. Based on the specific recommendations of this particular target audience, changes to the site were made, and the result appears in Figure 7-2.

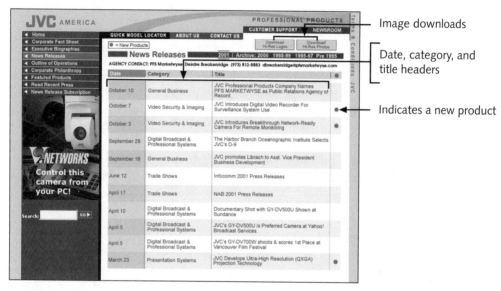

Figure 7-2 Revised JVC cyber media room

Notice that the center area of the revised page includes more details so that editors can quickly scan each news item by date, category, or title. Advanced programming on the site allows editors to sort the list by any of these topics for faster information gathering. Other changes include indicators for new products, as well as more obvious links for hi-res photos and logos.

It's not uncommon for a site developer or client company to misread the audience or be a little off the mark in terms of initial focus. Sometimes the people who are the most involved make the most errors, because they get too close to a topic or project to retain a clear view of it. It may take someone outside the project, who is less closely associated with what is being done, to give an accurate account of problems and potential solutions. This is where testing comes in.

Unfortunately, more often than not, testing is overlooked or done only at a minimum. It's disregarded in favor of publishing a Web site sooner rather than later. Although some testing measures may take a bit of time, the time that quality testing saves in the later stages of site production is well worth the energy and effort up front.

Site developers often wonder, "What if our testing reveals a problem that we can't immediately change?" There is no law that says all results of any given test *must* be acted on at that very moment—or at all. Based on testing feedback, you will probably want to make some changes as quickly as possible, but it's important to remember that Web sites are always a work in progress. They should be constantly evolving and improving over time. Many of these improvements are the result of ongoing testing that provides feedback into problem areas and that gives opportunities for site enhancement.

CONSUMER TESTING

Testing has various stages that you'll want to employ to make sure that the work you are doing stays in line with your initial concept and remains relevant to potential users. Although not all of the following types of testing are needed for every site, you should always do some testing. How much testing you do depends on factors that include the type of site you are creating and your available budget. Consumer tests fall into four general categories: concept, design, navigation, and beta. Testing usually is done by a sample of your site's target audience. These individuals work with test pages in a local environment. Typically, testers are seated at computer terminals and have a set schedule of items for which to look.

Concept Testing

Concept testing is the evaluation of audience reaction and response to the purpose of your site. It can apply to a portion of the site or to the entire site. Some elements of concept testing start during the market research phase of the site. The initial market research should give you insight into your potential audience and reveal information about your competition. A **competitive analysis** is a determination of key factors regarding competitors vying for your target market. This information may include their advertising strategies, perceptions in the marketplace, growth rates, market shares, and, most important, their exact products or services. You'll use this information to determine the concept for your site and how it will differ from those of your competitors.

The competitive analysis that you do when developing a Web site likely will be different from the competitive analysis that would be done for a traditional company, due to the access audiences have to your products or services. For example, say that you were going to open a small advertising agency to serve the local markets. Your competitive analysis would examine local competitors serving the size and type of companies that would be your potential clients. You wouldn't bother analyzing agencies like Young & Rubicam, Gray Advertising, or BBDO. They hardly would be considered competitors, with their multimillion dollar accounts and global marketing outlets. It's unlikely that many of your potential clients would ever consider retaining agencies like those, nor would those agencies likely be interested in retaining the local businesses that will comprise your clientele.

Now assume that your business venture is a Web site that reports on sports, with scores, updates, news, and other information. Your main source of revenue will be advertisers who are looking to reach your particular audience (as outlined in the demographic analysis from your market research). In this case, because the Web is so open to your audience, your site would be directly competing with sites like **ESPN.com** and **cbssportsline.com**. It's unlikely that your start-up site would have the funds to compete with established, big-budget sites like those on any level—marketing, development, content gathering, and so on. It's equally unlikely that if your site simply offered sports scores and updates an audience would bother coming to your site at all. They could just go straight to the big sites and get all that information—plus more.

What you need is a **hook**—something that makes your site different from the others and valuable in a unique way. Maybe the hook is a particularly opinionated sports writer who is funny and provides perspectives found only on your site, or maybe your site will focus more on "second tier" sports, such as arena football, that the big sports Web sites overlook. Whatever the hook is, it is the concept that will make or break your site.

The hook leads directly to concept testing. Before you work on your site, it's important to gather representatives from your target audience and test to determine whether your concept is valid. You know who your potential audience is from your initial market testing. Finding out exactly *how* that market will respond to the particular site you are planning and the precise information you'll be providing is another, equally important part of site preparation and is the goal of concept testing. For example, a Web site about growing better gardens would have a specific target audience. However, if your site promotes the idea that the only flowers worth growing are purple flowers, then a positive audience reaction to the site might not be guaranteed. It might seem great to you, but would your audience buy into it? Your testing must determine the following:

- Is the site unique or valuable enough to make anybody visit, stay, and come back a second time? If customers won't visit or return, why not?

- What can be done to enhance the concept and make it more enticing?

Testing the concept *before* the site is built may save you lots of disappointment later when the site is published and it's too late to do anything about the fact that nobody is really all that interested.

Design Testing

It's always a good idea to gauge audience reaction to the aesthetic aspects of your site. **Design testing** can determine this. Depending on the type of Web site you are planning, it may be difficult to make changes to the site design as development reaches the later stages. At the same time, as a marketer and developer, you are sometimes at risk of exhibiting two negative behaviors often demonstrated by people who work closely with site design: personal preference and boredom. Design testing helps keep you on track in terms of the look of your site.

Putting personal preference ahead of what would be most likely to work is a bad idea. In other words, you may like Web sites that have a sleek, futuristic design, with harsh edges and dark colors. You might even design your site this way—even if your audience would most likely relate to a much softer, brighter look.

Sometimes looking at the site too much causes you to become tired of it. This behavior is probably even more common than the tendency to act on personal preference. Boredom occurs when a developer looks at a site during the construction process day in and day out, so much so that he or she starts to nit-pick small aspects. Eventually, the developer may spend so much time on the site that he or she starts making radical and (most often) unnecessary design changes.

Having a set of design rules, which are determined by audience feedback gained from design testing, helps you maintain focus. The audience—not you—will be using the site most often, and it's this audience that you need to please in terms of page layout and design. Your audience won't be in a position to study and restudy the overall design to the point that they get bored with it. Chances are that they'll be at the site for a few minutes, each time they visit.

To make sure that they get the most of this time, it's important to test your design on your potential audience *before* the programming for the site really gets started. Because some programming is determined by the layout, which in turn is dictated by the design, you need to establish a **graphic template**, which is the basic layout that will be used for most pages within the site.

When testing the design of a site, most developers create a number of **comps**. Comps are sample design versions, or mock-ups, to show to a representative audience. These comps may be hand drawings of a site, non-working graphical representations, or fully developed single pages. Three to five comps are typically developed for review. The test audience is asked to review each comp based on different criteria and to comment on each one. This review might include having the audience rate the comps on a scale. When the results are tabulated, you will usually find that one or two designs stand out above the rest, although certain aspects of other designs may be rated highly as well. You then should consider all the feedback and rework up to three more comps that reflect the comments and ratings of the initial design test. These comps then go through one last review.

Although the initial three to five comps usually look very different from each other, the resulting three subsequent comps tend to look like variations of each other, with relatively minor differences among them. Figure 7-3 shows the initial three comps that were presented for testing for New York Yankee Derek Jeter's Turn 2 Foundation.

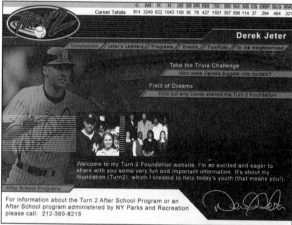

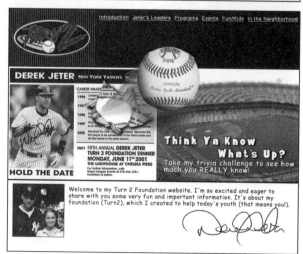

Figure 7-3   Original comps

Figure 7-4 shows the two comps that were designed based on the initial test feedback.

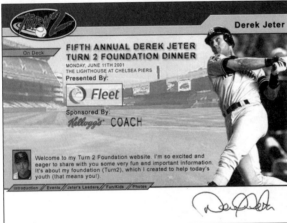

Figure 7-4   Revised comps

Figure 7-5 shows the final design.

Figure 7-5   Final design based on comp reviews

Notice that the designs in Figure 7-4 are similar to each other and combine aspects of the original comps. The final design is a variation on these revisions.

Navigation Testing

It may be easy for you as a developer to know intuitively where certain information is on your site. After all, you put it there in the first place! However, just because you know where something goes doesn't mean that it will be obvious to your audience.

Navigation testing ensures that your audience understands how to use the navigation system and that the destination of each link is obvious. Navigation testing of your site comes after programming of the site has taken place and enough of the infrastructure has been built to make some of the pages link together. However, it doesn't come so late in the process that you can't go back and make fundamental programming changes, if necessary.

Because implementation of the navigational structure is so vital to the success of your site, you should be sure to check the following:

- Clarity of the button graphics: Often, when a button and its title are composed from a graphic, the text used in the button's name may appear fuzzy, especially if it's small and compressed.

- Naming convention: The title for each button should let your audience know the information to which the button leads.

- Consistency of all navigation: The placement and button types should remain in the same place from page to page so that users are not hunting for them.

Also, check for slight shifts in the navigation graphics from page to page. Variations in one or two pixels can crop up.

- The correct tiers appear on the correct pages: You don't want third-tier navigation elements visible on the home page.

- Ease of navigation: Make sure that the user can easily get back to the home page, or to any other page, with just two or three clicks without using the browser's Back button.

You should first test the clarity of the graphics and the names of the buttons and links. Take the graphic buttons in Figure 7-6, for example. To some people, the picture of the briefcase could mean the link brings you to a page that describes business solutions. To other people, it could suggest a page that provides online forms to fill out.

This handshake could represent an agreement or a link to contact information

Figure 7-6 Sample navigation buttons with ambiguous meanings

Text links also may be ambiguous and misleading, allowing users to think a link means one thing while it actually means another. Testing the graphic and vocabulary representation of the links may help keep visitors from getting lost.

In the navigation test, the testing audience typically is asked to start at the home page and find specific information within the site, as though they were on the Web equivalent of a scavenger hunt. Ask your audience to use the available links over as many tiers as necessary. Encourage them to take notes and comment on the ease or difficulty of using the navigation tools to find the information for which they are looking.

At an early stage of development, you may ask users to navigate through the site, even without content on the pages, to discern what type of information they expect to find by clicking a specific link name. For example, an e-zine that provides information on television and entertainment may plan to create a first-tier navigational button called "Top Ten Lists" that would lead users to the top ten movies and TV shows for that week. However, in testing, the site might learn that site users who see that button expect to see a series of "Top Ten" lists from *The Late Show with David Letterman*. (David Letterman's Top Ten list is a popular segment on his late night talk show.) Your testers should take notes about the type of information they expect to find on various areas of the site based on the navigational pointers. Testers should also keep track of which paths would most likely be followed, based on their expectations.

Based on the testing results, you may not need to make any changes to the site. However, you might need to clarify links, add or remove buttons where needed, or otherwise make the site more easy for your audience to understand.

Channel Testing

If your site is particularly large and has more than eight first-tier navigational choices and many second-, third-, and even fourth-tier options below the first-tier options, you may want to construct a **channel test**. A channel test is an evaluation of one or more first-tier categories and their underlying navigational tiers. The test helps to highlight problem areas in complex navigational structures. Sites that are large enough to warrant an internal search engine, for example, would be likely candidates for conducting channel tests with their audiences.

For example, if you are part of a venture that will be building an online department store, you need to have an advanced searching mechanism to help people find products, reviews, and other information quickly and easily. Search engines, such as the ones used by **Walmart.com** and **BN.com**, allow users to do their searches on a number of categories, including books, CDs, electronics, and other products. The databases and programming for this type of engine can be very complex. Before your site's advanced programmer or database engineer develops this feature for all areas of the site, you should create one sample section, or channel, and test audience response to it. You then can analyze the feedback and make necessary changes. These changes then are incorporated into the programming for each of the other existing channels, as they may apply.

Beta Testing

When a site is near the final stages of development and is almost ready to go live, you should perform a **beta test**. The beta test is the final test of a nearly completed site or application. Beta tests are done by representatives of the target market for the purposes of discovering last-minute bugs and other incidental problems.

By the time you're ready to do beta testing, you have tested the concept and developed the site so that it stays consistent with the original focus. By this point, the interface has been established, tweaked, and implemented, as has the basic navigational structure. During the beta test, the sample audience reviews the site one last time. While earlier tests concentrated on fundamental issues, such as the overall concept of the site and whether the navigation is clear and leads users where they expect to go, the beta tests check for slight inconsistencies. At this point, the testers are looking for minor bugs or problems in the site.

In almost all cases, the beta tests are done in a **live environment**, which means that the site is working off the hosting server. In addition, testers are using the hardware (computers and modem connections) and software (browsers and plug-ins) that they ordinarily would use in their day-to-day Web surfing activities, as opposed to using local environments. By working in a live environment, the site developers can better learn how the site users will respond to the site. (Testers might love the site when working off a local environment—virtually eliminating any download time—but might not be as receptive to that same site when connecting through a slower modem connection.)

A broad-range live environment is accomplished utilizing a number of Internet connection configurations to make sure that every likely scenario is taken into consideration. For example, you might set up terminals so that some testers are using the site on a Macintosh with Netscape 3.0 browsers, while others are using Macs with 4.0 or higher-level browsers. Other users would be using a Mac workstation with various versions of the Microsoft Internet Explorer browser. Still others would be testing different browser environments while at Windows 98, 2000, or NT workstations. At the same time, you would use different modem speeds to account for usage lags so that you can help optimize the site for various connection speeds.

Beta tests often reveal slight flaws in programming, such as **broken links** (links that don't lead anywhere), slight shifts in graphic placement from page to page, and inoperable interactive applications—such as order forms or online calculators. You may also find inconsistencies in the site between different operating systems, different browsers, and different browser versions because some scripts and programming elements behave differently in different environments. Although you should have discovered and resolved most of these kinks by the time you conduct the consumer beta test, this last review gives you a final chance to eliminate glitches and make sure that your site contains as few errors as possible before it goes live.

What the audience is instructed to look for during a beta test depends largely on how the overall development and other tests have gone to that point. Although it's important not to "lead" your audience in one direction or another, especially in earlier tests in which you want the least biased results, it is helpful to provide direction at the beta test stage. The beta test audience may not be the same people who were involved in earlier tests. Your testers should know that feedback on certain issues is important, but that you are not looking to them to provide feedback on the overall concept or navigation. (Even though these features will have been built to reflect the results of earlier tests, you'll never completely please *everyone* who will use the site, and people who act as beta testers will often provide unsolicited opinions.)

The direction you provide depends on the issues with which you are most concerned as the programming draws to a close. Some sites are looking for some last-minute specifics, such as audience reaction to download speed, interactivity, and page transitions. Other sites use the beta tests as forums to allow users to randomly browse the site and take notes on final usability, success with concept follow-through, interest in the site, and other issues that the developers may need or want to change in the time left before the site is finally published.

Minor changes are really the only types of changes that should occur as a result of beta testing. Developers should be fairly certain that they have gotten most things as close to right as they can by this stage. If your beta tests uncover major problems, you may need to delay the site launch. However, in doing so, you may incur huge losses of time, money, and momentum. This is why it is crucial that earlier testing be done in a meaningful way.

BUSINESS TESTING

Testing your site for Web readiness goes beyond testing audience reaction. You also must consider company-related factors. For example, you must address your business's internal and functionality issues to ensure long-term usability for your customers. Internal testing tends to be less formal and organized than consumer testing. Business testing is done by designated internal employees of the company (or an outside agency) for whom the site was made, and it is an ongoing process to determine the success of three key elements: brand integrity, site functionality, and systems integration.

Brand Testing

Usually undertaken by an internal marketing department or outside branding agency, testing to ensure brand integrity is initiated during the design phase of site development. This **brand testing** continues throughout the life of the site, although the bulk of the work happens during and immediately after the initial site design. If your site is for a traditional brick-and-mortar company, it's important to make sure that the traditional brand has been properly translated to the Web. You must ensure that colors are used consistently in online and offline applications. Be sure to use the logo appropriately. The look and feel of the site should evoke thoughts and feelings that are consistent with the traditional brand identity. For example, if your company has a serious image and uses subtle, shadowed imagery on dark backgrounds, a Web site that has a title of floating bubble letters, brightly colored buttons, and animated GIFs would conflict with the corporate image.

If your site is a pure-com, the Web version of the brand is the only brand presence that the company has. Therefore, you must ensure that the brand is handled well and that it coincides with marketing or advertising strategies; this coordination is important to long-term branding efforts.

Unlike the formally structured user testing, the brand testing isn't as much of a "test" as it is a general review. Although the brand itself is almost always tested for audience reaction and feedback when it is first developed, it usually falls to the company's marketers to judge whether the online brand has been properly implemented. This usually is done by looking carefully at all areas of the site (or at comps that have been developed for the interface) and by judging the pages against the rest of the brand's characteristics.

Functionality Testing

When you add complex interactive elements to a site, such as search engines, back-end administration pages, and shopping cart systems, you should conduct **functionality testing** on a regular basis. Typically done by internal programming employees, this testing ensures that the elements are working, are efficient, and are doing what they are supposed to do. Functionality issues include basic elements such as a "thank you for shopping" page that

7

appears after a shopper makes a purchase. They also include the correct solution for variables calculated by an online calculator. These elements will be different for each site.

Functionality tests also address significantly more complex issues, such as ensuring that purchase orders are being sent to the correct internal department when an order is placed on the site and that the servers can handle expected increases in traffic. Many consumers might not notice slight pixel shifts of images (like mastheads and buttons) from page to page, but functionality testers should be on the lookout for consistency in these types of elements. The earlier navigation testing should also identify these kinds of problems. Broken links, error messages, and other such problems also are addressed in the functionality test.

Functionality tests can address elements of your Web site that are processed offline. For example, suppose that a user comes to your Web site and fills out a job application or a request for membership and is expecting an e-mail response. Functionality testers will make sure that the applications and requests arrive at the site, that the appropriate e-mail response goes back to the visitor, and that it contains all the proper information. Similarly, functionality testing evaluates e-mail messages that should be sent when a user forgets his or her password. It also ensures that no future e-mails are sent at all when a user requests that his or her name be taken off solicitation lists. Such e-mail messages are called **auto-responses** and are prewritten responses that are sent automatically by the server to a user.

Another important part of functionality testing is security testing. Security testing is the process of making sure that all client files remain private and that the server and any private files are safely protected from hackers or other unauthorized individuals who may try to gain access to the site. Security testing is sometimes treated separately from other functionality tests.

You should perform functionality tests a number of times at regularly scheduled intervals. The frequency with which you perform your tests depends on the level of interactivity and the amount of traffic on your site. Sites with large databases, search engines, integrated systems, and heavy site traffic need a fairly aggressive schedule of functionality testing. Sites with limited complex interactivity or smaller levels of site traffic can work on a reduced testing schedule. These tests should occur throughout the development of the site and throughout the life of the site.

Systems Integration Testing

Some parts of your site will never be seen by customers. Like the plumbing and heating systems of a corporate building, certain elements exist to keep the company functional, but they work in the background.

The programs that you develop for your site, such as shopping carts or internal purchase order systems, need to integrate well with other systems, programs, and databases that your company uses for an effective and efficient workflow. The types of systems that are integrated are largely a function of your site's type. For example, an electronic commerce site has a lot going on behind the scenes after a visitor places an order. If the order is paid by credit card, it needs to be processed by the appropriate third parties. At the same time, requisition requests need to be sent to a warehouse so that the order can be fulfilled, and the database has to be kept current so that a proper inventory accounting of the products ordered can be maintained. The accounts department needs to be aware of all orders placed. On sites that allow visitors to track their purchases, timely order status information must be available to users. They need an accurate accounting of where their orders are and when they will be received. Information about the customers needs to be kept, as does a history of their purchases (both for marketing purposes and for product returns or customer service needs).

Regardless of your type of business, testing the site to confirm that all the components and internal departments are properly integrated is vital throughout the development process to ensure that the whole organization works smoothly.

Systems integration testing usually is done by advanced programmers or network specialists with advanced knowledge of complex programming, hardware, and software. For example, the previously mentioned electronic commerce site needs to evaluate the following:

- After an order is placed, how is that order handled?

- Which person in which department handles the order and ensures that the order is fulfilled?

- Can the order be tracked, filed, and updated in real time so that it is not only accessible by internal sources but also trackable by the customer online?

- How is billing done?

- Can credit card payments or invoices be maintained and integrated with existing invoicing systems (assuming that the company is a brick-and-mortar business) or work with a newly developed invoicing system (for pure-coms)?

- Where are client profiles stored?

Sites that are less complex than a large-scale electronic commerce site, such as a brochure site or content-only site without electronic commerce capabilities, need to test aspects of the site such as back-end site administration pages (used to update the site so that changes are made quickly). They also need to provide tracking and accounting of all ads placed by advertisers.

Like functionality testing, you should perform systems integration tests frequently, usually at regularly scheduled intervals during site development, as well as after the site is launched. This is especially important as the site grows and new technology is implemented for different purposes.

ACHIEVING SIGN-OFF

Having a client "sign-off" on a project is a term to be taken literally. As you learned in Chapter 5, a **sign-off** is a written approval by the client (assuming that you are developing the site for another person or company) that indicates he or she is satisfied with the work and accepts the site as you have built it. You need to get sign-offs on tests and their results as part of the testing process.

Sign-offs may come in many forms. For a final site, some agencies simply ask that the client print the home page of the site, add his or her signature or initials, and fax it back. Agencies that are more careful have specific forms that a client needs to fill out to indicate satisfaction with the site. Although it may seem like a minor administrative point, achieving sign-off on each site development and testing phase has legal repercussions and could influence a verdict in a court of law, should the site ever become embroiled in a dispute.

This chapter has emphasized that the purpose of testing the site at so many different points of development is to ensure that visitors will respond well to the site, that they'll be able to find the information that they are looking for quickly and easily, and that the site will work smoothly with other internal systems. These are the primary reasons for testing. However, if the site is being built for a client, there is an additional motive for all this testing: absolution from responsibility should the site not achieve its intended success.

In all cases, it's important to ensure that sign-offs are received from the client in written form; in other words, you need a recognized representative of the client to apply ink to paper in such a way that the client understands that he or she is approving the work done on the site. Often, clients will simply e-mail approval, sending a short note to say that the site looks great. Unfortunately, in a court of law, that's not good enough. As of the end of 2001, e-mail acceptance of a site was not binding evidence in a court of law, and by allowing e-mail sign-offs, you may be opening the door for legal problems down the road.

When problems arise, some clients will go so far as to completely deny that they gave any verbal approval on a site—especially if it turns out that resolving the problems would cost them extra money. Verbal approvals are easily confused or misunderstood, and rarely, if ever, do they hold up in court. Take specific care to get sign-offs on as many aspects of the site as you can, and retain any documentation that shows that your clients have reviewed and approved of all testing methods and result analysis.

Presenting the results of each test to your client is good practice and legitimizes the reasons you have taken certain design and programming actions. After the results of a test (say, a test of the navigation) are provided to the client, the client should have to sign-off on a statement of approval before the results can be acted upon or before production on the site can continue. If your client or team is in a hurry (and they are *always* in a hurry) and they want to skip a test that you recommend, you should get sign-off on a statement saying that the client or team requires a certain test be skipped.

Tests are not the only items that require sign-off. The following list outlines some of the other elements of a site that ordinarily require a client's approval, although the specific list that you develop will likely vary depending on the client or the site:

- Schematic layout: This approval is extremely important to get as quickly and as early in the process as possible because the navigation you build will depend on this schematic. One change to the schematic can mean a programming nightmare later in development stages.

- Accepted site design: Usually a client must approve the home page layout design and one or more internal page samples. In accepting the overall site design, you may want individualized signatures on specific page elements, such as the following:
  - Colors used
  - Button design
  - Key graphics
  - Font sizes and styles

- Programming languages to be used

- Final site completion (mandatory before public launch)

You also may want to get specific sign-off on client changes during production. For example, assume that you have created the site according to the original schematic, on which the client signed off. A couple of weeks later, you receive a phone call from the client asking you to change the name of one first-tier button from "Products" to "Catalog." It's not a huge problem, but it will take you about two hours to make the change. Depending on your relationship with the client, you may or may not decide to charge him for the extra work. Assume further that you make the change and move on. A few weeks later, he changes his mind—he'd like the "Catalog" button changed back to "Products." Another two hours wasted. The savvy developer would have gotten the client to sign a form at the time of the first change, so that when he changed his mind again, the developer could avoid any conflicts over rebilling for the work. More important, because this scenario is not all that unrealistic, many changes may force you to miss promised deadlines. Sign-offs on each change request from the client will help clear you of responsibility for missed deadlines.

When development for the site (as contracted for) has been completed and the site is ready to go live, you should print a copy of the site's home page and have a qualified representative of the client company or development team provide a signature of approval. This signature indicates that the site is satisfactory in all respects as–is and that you have permission for the site to go live.

PRACTICAL CONSIDERATIONS FOR TESTING

You can conduct consumer tests in much the same way as you do the initial market research. You use one-on-one interviews, online and offline surveys, focus panels, and similar techniques. You should attempt to retain the same testing group throughout the testing cycle, because this consistency will give a better indication along the way whether you, as a developer, are implementing the feedback into the site in a way that is making the overall user experience better.

As with the original demographic research, you should ensure that respondents are not led any certain way (although there are instances, as we learned earlier, when it is wise and reasonable to give respondents direction). You also should ensure that testing questions and projects are not vague. Beyond that, you should remember that testing is a complex process that involves a subjective element—the human personality. It's easy to let testing distract you from your objectives.

Understanding Testing Systems

The practice of testing—whether you are evaluating products, marketing materials, or Web sites—is a unique science that involves various levels and mixtures of psychology, sociology, and mathematics. Some of this research and testing will be factual in nature; some will be more subjective. In fact, all the testing and research that you do will fall into two distinct categories: qualitative and quantitative.

Qualitative tests explore the nature and psychology of a specific group or market and don't involve statistics or mathematics at its foundation. These efforts test and study a respondent's reactions to specific elements on a site. The testing reveals what the subject likes and dislikes. You can also learn and consequently anticipate the sort of elements to which a respondent will likely respond. Although researchers can make educated estimations as to whether any given qualitative finding can be attributed to a larger audience beyond the respondent group, it is inaccurate to make mass generalizations based on qualitative testing results. Qualitative research is associated with psychographic analysis, which sketches the personality and emotional traits of a target market.

As the statistical side of research and testing, quantitative data takes a representative sample of a target or market and measures its findings in quantifiable results. Quantitative results can be applied to mass populations that reflect the sample tested. For example, if a study of 500 respondents that accurately reflects the target market shows that only 12 percent actually visited a specific area of a Web site, it can be expected that when the site is launched publicly, a similar percentage of the viewing population also will visit that area.

To understand both types of analysis, consider a political campaign scenario. Surveys, or quantitative research, done before the election show that 64 percent of registered voters will vote for candidate A, 30 percent will vote for candidate B, and the remaining 6 percent are undecided. (Statisticians typically present a margin of error of plus or minus a small amount of percentage points to allow for slight variations in their findings.) Even though the survey may have covered only 1000 or so respondents in a city of over 1,000,000, it is statistically acceptable to project that if the election were held that same day, the turnout would reflect the quantitative findings. However, this projection holds true only if the group of respondents accurately reflects the demographic composition of the city.

Probabilities and statistics classes often cover the deciphering of information obtained from testing. Testing can be an exacting practice with less than exact results, and before you take a serious stab at conducting a test, you need to know the questions that you want answered and have an understanding of the differences between the tests and how the results may apply to the success of your Web site. You then should study testing and result analysis processes before conducting further tests. (Once again, don't be afraid to take the probabilities and statistics classes!) Remember that incorrect result determinations can be as damaging as not testing a site at all.

Consider the Source

Although you value the input of the people who are testing your site, the involvement of the people who are analyzing that feedback is just as important. The data analysts should remember that although many people provide valuable feedback on projects, some inadvertently will throw a fence up in the road. People being tested sometimes give misleading or useless feedback, perhaps because they simply don't know enough about the Web to answer. They also might understand the Web and know how to do basic searches, but not know enough to give useful advice as to how you might make the site better or what specifically is wrong with the site that would keep it from being successful.

Other personalities are less than helpful in other ways: They want to make their mark on the site, so even if they really don't see any problems, they might invent a couple just to provide suggestions. They may also exaggerate actual problems. Recognizing these personalities and reading between the lines will help you get a more realistic idea of the scope of opinions.

Keep Your Goals in Sight

Of course, you're going to want to create the best Web site that you can in the hopes of gaining something, whether it be revenue, new employees, or some other goal. Both consumer and internal testing results will help you do that. However, don't allow the test results to keep you from completing the site, and don't let them cause you to exceed the budget trying to make upgrades and changes.

Suppose, for example, that consumer testing results show that many of the respondents would like for your site to broadcast live events using Webcasts on a regular basis. Well, that's a fine suggestion, but not a particularly inexpensive one to implement. It also would take extra time that you may not have. (You may have advertisers and media that are expecting a launch within a certain time frame.) Similarly, systems integration testers might recommend adding additional servers or newer technologies to increase the efficiencies of all systems. However, a careful **cost-benefit analysis** to weigh the potential benefit of expenditures against their cost may reveal that the benefit of adding more or better equipment does not promise a positive return on investment. Thus, the suggestions of the test may be ignored.

The point is that although you should take the results of all tests seriously, you must balance what you need to implement now with what can be implemented later—or maybe not at all.

CHAPTER SUMMARY

- The practice of testing a Web site is often overlooked, but it is an important part of site production. Consumer testing reveals problem areas in site concept, design, navigation, and channel planning. Beta tests confirm that your site is ready to launch. Business testing addresses the functionality, brand, and systems integration considerations of site development. When analyzing your test results, you should have a grasp of statistical analysis, but remember that subjective factors such as personalities can play into tester responses. Finally, don't let the results of testing distract you from your original goals. Test results give you an opportunity to make necessary changes before the launch of your site.

KEY TERMS

auto-response
beta test
brand testing
broken link
channel test
comp
competitive analysis
concept testing
cost-benefit analysis
design testing
functionality testing
graphic template
hook
live environment
navigation testing
sign-off

REVIEW QUESTIONS

1. When does testing for a Web site occur?

2. Concept testing usually starts _____.

   a. during the initial demographic analysis

   b. after the interface design has been established

   c. just before beta testing

   d. during systems integration testing

3. Results from testing _____.

   a. need to be acted on immediately to make the site as perfect as possible

   b. should be tempered with your budget and launch schedule

   c. should always be analyzed twice by outside agencies before being acted on

   d. shouldn't be acted on until a retest is taken

4. A competitive analysis for a small Web site that sells electronics would likely include _____.

   a. Web sites developed by local brick-and-mortar electronic stores

   b. Web sites for large, well-known electronics stores, such as Amazon.com, Circuit City.com, and others

   c. brick-and-mortar electronic shops that don't have Web sites

   d. a combination of local, smaller electronic shops with Web sites and Web sites of major electronic retailers

5. List two things that competitive analysis helps you determine.

6. During the design testing, the testers are usually presented with _____.

   a. three to five sample comps

   b. the final design, as determined in the concept test

   c. the complete navigation system as it will appear in the final Web site

   d. a full channel of the Web site

7. One of the best ways to test the navigation of a site is to _____.

8. By the time a site goes to beta test, _____.

   a. it should be nearly completed, with little left to fix

   b. it should be nearly completed, but way ahead of schedule, so that there is plenty of time for major revisions

   c. the interface design should be about to receive sign-off

   d. the systems integration test will be getting started

7

9. The beta test _____.
    a. takes place on standardized computers, so that the test can reflect that everyone has had the same experience
    b. takes place on multiple types of systems and browsers working off a local drive
    c. takes place on multiple types of systems and browsers working from a live server environment
    d. is completed by internal workers, to ensure that the final site integrates properly with all other systems

10. Making sure that _____ usually is not evaluated during functionality testing.
    a. automated e-mail is sent on schedule
    b. the navigation design is clear
    c. small issues that consumers wouldn't ordinarily notice are accounted for
    d. online calculators work properly

11. Systems integration testing helps to make sure that _____.
    a. the user can find his or her way around by using an internal search engine
    b. the internal accounting systems will work with the outside accountants' system
    c. taxes are properly calculated and charged
    d. the shipping software works with the accounts payable software

12. When are systems integration tests held?

13. A channel test tests a site's _____.
    a. navigation
    b. graphics
    c. Web brand
    d. None of the above.

14. Sign-off on a project from a authorized representative of a client company is just as good as _____.
    a. a verbal approval from that client
    b. a sign-off from the authorized representative's secretary
    c. a verbal okay from the art director on your team
    d. None of the above.

HANDS-ON PROJECTS

With testing, much of the work you'll do will be after the site development has already started. It will continue until the site goes live, and beyond that as well. This means that much of the testing will happen after the business plan has already been written, and you've begun to put development into motion. Thus, take this chapter off from your business plan. Instead, complete the following projects.

1. Create part of a Web site, such as an interface design, a fully developed concept, a navigation schematic, or a part that you feel you would best accomplish. Gather a testing group from your class, and test your work to see if it is usable on the Web. What type of questions will you ask as part of testing? Based on the responses, how would you change your design?

2. You are the head of a research and testing facility that has been hired by the following Web sites to perform specific tests for them. Visit each site and follow the directions for each:

   a. **www.cvs.com**: Create a test that determines how easy it is to find products, use the shopping cart, check out products, remove products, and anything else you can think of. Make sure your test takes the download times for searches and checkout procedures into account, as well as the amount of information provided about each product.

   b. **www.rockwell.com**: Create a navigation test to ensure that all of the links are obvious, and that they all work to make information easier to find.

   c. **www.recipenotes.com**: Create a concept test. Assuming that this site's target market comprises cooking enthusiasts, ensure that the purpose and content are relevant and interesting to a visitor. Compare recipenotes.com to other sites on the Web, such as **Cooking.com** and **Cookinglight.com**. How does it compare? The tests you create should determine what, if anything, recipenotes.com offers that is unique. If recipenotes.com does not offer anything unique, how can it fix this shortcoming?

Once your test questions and directives have been devised, put together a group of people to take the tests, either from within the class or from people you know outside of class. Since you likely won't have access to a room full of computers at which you can sit everyone down for a test all at once, you can provide the questions that you want answered on paper, and ask each person to take the test at his or her own computer. The number of people you ask is entirely up to you as long as you feel the you have enough information to get useful results. Write up all results in a short report.

7

3. Working off Project 2, this time take the perspective of a tester. You should be the person taking the test for at least one other person in the class. After you take his or her test, analyze the test and the questions that were asked. From the perspective of a tester, do you feel that the questions were leading in any way? Do you feel that the questions were relevant? What questions or types of questions did you feel were missing, or that the test could have benefited from? Summarize your analysis of the test.

8

DEVELOPING AND UNDERSTANDING THE BRAND

> **In this chapter, you will learn about:**
> ♦ The various aspects behind brand value, including brand promise, brand loyalty, and unique selling position
> ♦ How a brand can work against your business objectives
> ♦ The four core brand recognition elements: logos, colors, shapes, and tag lines
> ♦ Brand consistency and moving a brand onto the Web
> ♦ Special branding considerations for smaller companies
> ♦ Unique aspects of branding online

Have you gotten the idea that this whole book has been building up to this particular chapter? In a way it has—in every chapter so far, we've discussed the importance of the brand. Disregarding the brand has been the downfall of some well-known companies—both online and offline. The demise of Web sites that ignored branding has been more obvious because of the attention these failures have received by the media. Conversely, concentrating on brand has built some of the most successful firms.

When it comes to the Web, the concept of brand is often a source of major debate. Many company executives question whether you can brand on the Web. Is branding worth the effort? How can you translate an offline brand into an online brand, and vice-versa? Industry observers offer varying opinions on the subject of online branding. This chapter puts the debate into perspective, starting with an explanation of brands and branding and why a brand is so important when developing a Web site.

WHAT IS A BRAND?

In Chapter 1, we defined "brand" as the promise that a Web site, company, product, or service makes to its customers. In advertising, marketing, corporate identity, and similar industries, the terms brand and branding can take on multiple meanings. Some people think of the brand as a logo, a corporate color, or a tag line. This is a popular misconception. Defining a brand simply as a logo is like defining a car simply by the shape of its body. You'd be completely disregarding the engine, the electrical system, and other components that turn a complex combination of metal, rubber, wiring, and glass into a working automobile. The body, in this instance, is only a component of the car. Similarly, the logo is only a component of the brand. The brand itself is intangible—it's an inherent promise made from the company or product to the consumer that reflects what the consumer can expect in terms of overall quality. That promise is made up of a number of tangible and intangible elements, including the logo, the tag line, and the company's reputation. Consumers relate to brands through an impression that is formed through time, action, and interaction. This impression is based on consumer expectation and is shaped through deliberate messages delivered to a targeted audience.

Building the Brand and Keeping the Promise

Imagine that you make a new friend. We'll call him Chris. He's a nice enough guy, and he never misses a chance to offer his help or to remind you that he's there for you if you need him for anything. Chris has a good car, and typically, a pretty light schedule. Of course, having just met him, you're probably not going to be asking him for too many favors right away.

One day, you need a suit picked up from the dry cleaner for a function that night, but with your schedule, you won't have the time to get to it. You think of who might be able to help you out, and you remember that your new friend Chris has offered time and again to lend a hand whenever you might need one. The message has been sent. He has done his marketing, and from repetition, he has painted himself as a reliable source for assistance when you're in need. He has built his brand (or personality, which is the human equivalent): a nice guy with a good heart and a willingness to help a friend.

So, you call him and ask if he can do you a favor and pick up the suit. He'd love to help you out. With that reassurance, you get on with your regularly scheduled events for the day, secure in the knowledge that Chris is taking care of the trip to the dry cleaner for you. After all, he sold himself as a nice guy who is there to help you out.

When you get home later that day, you're surprised to see that your suit isn't there. You call Chris to ask him if he has it. As he picks up the phone, you can faintly hear the sounds of Nintendo games in the background. He almost sounds surprised to hear from you, and when you ask about the suit, he pauses a second. He gives a weak excuse about his car breaking down. You get the distinct impression that he simply forgot! He apologizes emphatically, and you give him the benefit of the doubt, making other, last-minute arrangements for a suit.

Chris continues to offer his services, and a few weeks later you ask him for help again. Although he happily accepts the chore, he once again fails to deliver. The next time that you need a favor, you think twice before asking Chris. Apparently he's great at making promises, but not so good at delivering on them.

On a basic level, brands are comparable to this scenario. Through corporate identity, advertising, public relations, and other marketing efforts, a company sends you its message: "Hey, this is what we're good at, this is what we can do, and this is why you should use our products or services." The company establishes its promise, and in some way, shape, or form, the company tries to get you, the consumer, to trust it. The company hopes that the message resonates enough to convince you to make a purchase. However, if you buy into the promotion and the claims, and purchase a product only to discover that the company has failed to live up to its promises, the brand becomes nothing more than an empty boast.

Suppose you run a Web site that provides travel information. If your site's brand message is that you offer more comprehensive information on remote destinations than any other travel site on the Web, then you should do that, or at least come close. If your site actually does offer more information on remote locations, but the information is categorically incorrect (oops—did we write that there are never any hurricanes in St. Thomas?), then the brand promise hasn't been fulfilled. Fulfilling a promise becomes a bigger problem for you than it is for the customer; regaining the customer's trust after the brand promise has not been delivered is practically impossible, regardless of how much money is spent on advertising.

Do consumers really give the brand only one chance to fail? It depends on the brand in question, and, although this is not always the case, it often comes down to longevity and history. Say, for example, that your new friend Chris actually had picked up your suit as asked, delivered it to your house, and waited until you arrived to make sure that you got it. In that case, he built a stock of trust by fulfilling his promise. As time goes on, he continues to fulfill his promises and proves himself to be reliable and good to his word. In other words, you know you can trust him. Then, one day, when he says he will do you a favor, he fails to do it. You brush it off as an isolated incident. Chris could fail a number of times in a row, and you'd still go back to him in the future. You might think that something was wrong. Maybe he's in a bit of a funk or a personal slump, but because he's been so reliable in the past, you still trust him. He would really have to slip up, and do it often, before you lost faith completely. That's because time and history played a crucial role in your fundamental opinion of him. First impressions can be important when building a successful brand.

The same is true in traditional business. Although it's typically a lot easier to lose consumer trust than it is to gain it in the first place, consumers will be forgiving based on your past performance. Look at Coca-Cola, one of the world's largest and most respected brands. Although its concoction of flavorings, soda water, and caffeine was one of the most popular drinks in the world, Coca-Cola took a chance in the mid-1980s and changed its formula. Coke drinkers hated it. "New Coke" has been considered one of the largest corporate missteps of the last century, but consumers didn't abandon the company and remain unforgiving. Instead, consumers were thrilled when Coca-Cola brought the old formula back under the name Coca-Cola Classic.

Now, if Coca-Cola had been a new company at the time of this experiment, the situation might have been different. Consumers might not have put faith in a company that switched its formula soon after its release, and they might have hesitated to go back. Coca-Cola, however, didn't have a history of radical product change. It had a history of stability and of being associated with fun and refreshment. That brand image was strong enough to endure an isolated misstep.

Using an example from the cyber world, look at how differently ToysRUs.com and eToys.com were treated by consumers. Both made major mistakes during the holiday season of 1999. Both promised a better Web toy-buying experience and reliable shipping. Both failed. Each site delivered a large number of toys to families *after* Christmas. In fact, in a side-by-side comparison, the eToys.com site was actually a little better than its rival—at least it was easier to use from a navigational and functionality standpoint. However, in the end, eToys.com lost out, closing its doors in March 2001 and selling its name to another toy retailer.

In contrast to eToys.com, ToysRUs.com earned a profit during the 2000 holidays. The sustainability of ToysRUs.com might be attributable to that company's deeper pockets, allowing it to weather any storm a little longer. The real story is that although electronic commerce traffic and sales were breaking records during the 2000 holiday season at ToysRUs.com, both were down considerably at eToys.com. ToysRUs.com enjoys an established brand promise that was built over a long period of time and that is strong enough that consumers forgave the company for the 1999 transgression. Without any real history of brand fulfillment, however, eToys.com's one big failure was all that consumers had to judge it by.

The Brand: Company, Product, or Both?

The word "brand" gets tossed around pretty liberally, as does "company." What exactly distinguishes one from the other? In fact, in many ways, the terms are interchangeable. Pepsi, for example, is a company. It is listed on the New York Stock Exchange, it employs tens of thousands of people, it owns some buildings, and it rents others. Pepsi pays taxes and is incorporated. The Pepsi company, however, also owns a product with the same name. Because they have the same name, the company and the product share a brand promise, identity, and personality in the perception of the public.

Other Pepsi holdings, whether they are products such as Diet Pepsi or Slice, or entire companies unto themselves, such as Taco Bell or Kentucky Fried Chicken, are brands in their own right. Although they have their own target markets and their own marketing strategies, these affiliates may still be affected negatively if the Pepsi parent missteps and does something to hurt the brand image.

In other instances, the relationship isn't quite as clear. Federated Department Stores, for example, isn't exactly a household name. However, the brands that it owns, such as Macy's and Bloomingdale's, are known as some of the largest and most popular department stores in the country. Each of Federated's brands reaches its own market demographic, each has its own promise, and each markets itself in its own fashion. Each department store chain runs itself as its own company.

Each chain is responsible for keeping up its own brand image and reaching and reacting to its own audience. If Macy's should misstep against its own brand by not keeping whatever it establishes as its brand promise, it's hard to imagine that problem reflecting on Bloomingdale's or other Federated-owned stores.

For what sort of brand promise and image is Federated itself responsible? Well, so few general consumers know the Federated name that it might not even have a brand promise to live up to. However, general consumers aren't the only people who matter. The Federated name might not mean a lot to the average consumer, but what about to investors? What about to vendors that supply Federated with material and other goods? Even if the only reputation that Federated needs to maintain is that it pays its bills on time and that it is constantly looking to increase its profits, it's important to maintain that image. If Federated makes an error that results in negative publicity for the company, the news may indeed reflect poorly on all its associated brands.

Building Brand Loyalty

When a branded item stands up against a non-branded competitor, the brand usually will win. If you put a Pepsi next to a generic brand of cola, most people will choose the Pepsi, even before tasting either soda. People tend to prefer a branded item because with a brand, they know what they're getting.

Brand Promise

The brand promise lets people know what they can expect from the item they are purchasing. When you consider that most companies claim to be "number one," "the largest," and to "use the best ingredients," the bond that consumers form with a brand is more than just an academic understanding, it's an emotion. For a brand to succeed, it must form an emotional tie with its core audience. That doesn't mean that consumers are expected to break down weeping at the mention of a Whopper Deluxe Value Meal. It means that consumers form, through subtle, positive, and emotional reactions to specific messages, a sense of personality and promise that they associate with a particular brand. Consequently, they are drawn to companies, products, and services that they find appealing on a personal level.

If you bring someone a gift of chocolate in the traditional gold-colored box that represents Godiva, he or she knows instinctively that you are giving a high quality, rich, delicate chocolate. Is the recipient simply associating the price with the gift? Partly. The price of a product is part of what constitutes its personality. The brand (including the box's gold color and ornately embossed emblem), the knowledge of what is in the box, and a conscious acknowledgment that most people think of Godiva as a high quality chocolate, have been combined to shape an emotional connection with the brand before the box is even opened.

This Godiva scenario, of course, assumes that the recipient has already heard of Godiva. If you have never heard of that particular brand, the chances are that you will still be able to form an opinion about the quality of the product by the style of the packaging. Even the elegant shapes of the chocolate pieces themselves (far different from the squared shape of most chocolates) work to create an initial judgment that the taste will be superior to the average chocolate. If you determine that to be true upon tasting it for the first time, Godiva has lived up to its promise.

Brand Connection

What kind of personality do you associate with a person who drives a Volkswagen? How does that personality compare with that of someone who drives a Lexus? The Lexus message, through advertising, logo design, and message style paints a deliberate picture. (A recent Lexus television advertisement was done in French, with violins playing in the background.) Lexus drivers are classy and stylish—not snobbish or middle-aged (as might be associated with drivers of other luxury models) but young sophisticates who enjoy the finer things in life. Volkswagen drivers, in comparison, are likely to be even younger and comparatively carefree—people who live life by the day and who have an almost quirky lifestyle.

Marketers don't expect that consumers are walking around thinking about their brands, but they do know that strong branding helps forge emotional connections between their brands and the targeted consumer. Marketers hope the brand association will translate into **brand loyalty**. Brand loyalty is a consumer's commitment to a brand and occurs when a consumer will go out of his or her way to buy specific brands that they trust, even if they are harder to find or more expensive than other available options. Consumers continue to support brands with which they feel comfortable. After brand loyalty has been established, it can be difficult for competitors to sway that consumer from his or her preferred brand.

A good example of brand loyalty can be seen with some computer users and their operating systems, especially proponents of Macintosh computers. Although Mac has significantly less market share when compared to its Windows counterpart, Mac has managed to build such brand loyalty among some members of its core market that their devotion to the platform sometimes reaches a cult-like quality. Focus groups run by competing computer manufacturers have shown that if a new Windows-based computer were introduced that ran twice as fast as the focus group's current computer and the new computer was priced competitively, Windows users in the group would have no problem abandoning their current computer for a faster one. Of the Mac users, almost none agreed to make the switch. When the Mac users were offered the faster Windows-based system for half the price of their Macs, they still refused to switch. The same held true if the computers were *given* away—the Mac enthusiasts still refused to leave their favorite brand.

The Mac example is an extreme illustration of brand loyalty. There is a distinct line between brand loyalty and fanaticism, but the example does underscore how strong an emotional connection can be between a brand and its consumer. For a competing Brand X to win over a consumer who is enamored with Brand Y, it may take a combination of giveaways, enticing promotional offers, and a long period of time just to get the consumer to try the product. Even then, there is no guarantee that the consumer will make the switch.

So, when does price become an issue? In Chapter 1, we recognized that one of the downsides of electronic commerce is that consumers can easily research prices on competing Web sites and make a purchase determination based on the best price available. To understand what role price plays in brand loyalty, we'll look at the different types of brand-conscious shoppers:

8

- Brand loyal: Shoppers who are committed to one brand, so much so that they will travel out of their way to get it. Price is rarely—if ever—going to take them away from a brand that they trust.

- Brand preferred: These shoppers prefer certain brands over others and will go a bit—but not far—out of their way to get them. They wouldn't switch to a competing brand if there is only a slight price differential, but they might be swayed if there is a significant price difference.

- Brand aware: These shoppers may like one brand over another—enough to recommend that brand to others—but they wouldn't go out of their way for it. Even slight price differentials in competing brands might sway their purchasing decisions.

- Brand conscious: These shoppers don't have a preference of one brand over another, and they wouldn't go out of their way for any brand in particular. Price values may be the determining factor in which products they choose. However, these shoppers still prefer to choose among brands that they know or about which they have formed an opinion (either through direct use or reputation). They stay away from brands that they don't know and avoid generic, unbranded products.

- Brand indifferent: Shoppers who base their decisions strictly on price and convenience. They are open to brands that they don't know and to generic, unbranded products.

Any one shopper can fall into more than one—or even all—of the categories. A consumer who is brand loyal to Ford cars, for example, may not care one way or another about what brand of dish soap he or she buys. A consumer's reaction to certain brands is not always such a conscious reality—a shopper in a grocery store might look for Philadelphia-brand cream cheese, for example, and not even bother looking at the price. To that shopper, nothing can substitute for the Philadelphia brand. If the store is out of it, he or she may not buy any cream cheese at all and wait to buy it at another time. That shopper is brand loyal to Philadelphia, but he or she might not even realize it. Brand loyalty doesn't always involve the same fanaticism that we saw earlier with Macintosh computers; few people wander the streets thinking longingly about their choice of cream cheese.

Brand Image

One more factor completes the brand equation. As we'll see later in this chapter, successful brands rely on a brand recognition component that helps make the brand instantly recognizable. For example, if you drive down the highway and see the Golden Arches on the horizon, you know that a McDonald's is near. In the same vein, if someone says that she is in the mood for McNuggets, you know that she is talking about a product that can be bought only at McDonald's.

The association of a brand with an image or something tangible is the third important general factor that drives the brand. Figure 8-1 shows how the three components (the brand promise, the brand personality/emotional connection, and the image/recognition factors) combine to build a strong brand.

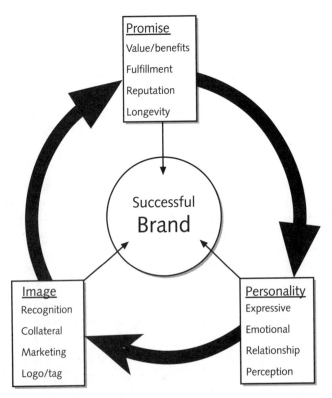

Figure 8-1   Components of a brand

A brand needs recognition to gain familiarity, an emotional connection to gain trust and association, and a promise (and a follow-through on that promise) to build the historic value at the heart of the brand. These don't have to happen in any specific order, nor does one necessarily lead to another, but these elements often happen simultaneously and continue over time as the brand grows stronger.

Establishing the Unique Selling Position

Without a need or desire for an item, consumers won't buy it. If there is a need, and a choice of brands, why would a buyer choose one product over another? Recall that brands and products distinguish themselves by having a unique selling position, or USP.

Assume that every bar of soap on a grocery store shelf looked exactly the same. Each was a plain white bar that came in a simple gray box, with each box saying that this particular soap was guaranteed to get you clean. Beyond that, the only thing that separated one product from another was the name. If the prices were exactly the same across all products, there wouldn't really be much of a choice to make. You could grab any bar of soap and feel relatively confident that it would do just as good of a job as any other bar.

One day, however, you walk into the store to buy soap, and one box jumps out at you. This one also is gray, but bright, green letters on the face of the carton announce "New, Fresh Scent!" The product stands out because it's unique. It is offering something that makes it different from the others. Thus, that fresh scent is that particular brand's USP.

You learned in Chapter 1 that the USP is what distinguishes one brand from another and that it tells the consumer the benefits of buying a product or hiring a particular service. The USP is different from the brand promise; the USP is more of a statement of fact, whereas the promise is an intangible element that takes a long time to develop and may incorporate many aspects of a product, service, or company. The brand promise is based on a leading attribute that strongly represents the product's biggest benefit to the consumer, but may also incorporate other benefits that are secondary in nature.

What happens if two or more brands develop the same USP? What if another brand of soap also promises a "New, Fresh Scent!"? Other attributes such as price may factor into the customer's purchase decision. However, deciding between the two similar products with similar USPs is where the personality of the brand comes into play. If two soaps both claim to have a new, fresh scent, and both are similarly priced, each might appeal to different consumer demographics, and the brand personality that resonates with each demographic group will be the one chosen. (For example, Soap X might advertise with comical commercials that feature college students fighting over the use of a bar of Soap X after a particularly sweaty football game. Soap Y's advertisements might be more serious, featuring businesspeople who choose Soap Y on the day of an important meeting.) If the brands are pursuing the same market, each consumer will make up his or her own mind based on any number of criteria, including past experiences with each brand, the color of the packaging, which advertisement they've seen last, or even which of the brands is within arm's reach.

Claims that are too generic or broad don't usually work as a USP. A claim by a pizza maker that it uses fresh ingredients, for example, would likely be ignored because fresh ingredients are a given. For example, DiGiorno Pizza's USP is that it provides consumers who enjoy the taste of traditional, freshly made pizza from a local pizzeria a cheaper, quicker, and more convenient alternative with the same results. DiGiorno's tag line "It's not Delivery, It's DiGiorno," along with the message sent in its commercials, promotes that USP by portraying DiGiorno as great-tasting frozen pizza that is indistinguishable from delivery pizza. The USP makes a brand unique and distinguishes it from its competition. This USP is not saying that DiGiorno uses "fresh ingredients," which doesn't do much to distinguish it from other store-bought pizzas or take-out places.

WHEN BRAND WORKS AGAINST YOU

Sometimes, a brand image can be so indelible in the mind of the public that it repels certain markets. Oldsmobile provides the perfect example. It had an image of reliability and sturdiness in its cars. Oldsmobiles were driven mostly by older men, and the brand became associated with being behind the times. Losing market share, Oldsmobile tried to use a new marketing campaign to change its brand image to appeal to a younger demographic group. Oldsmobile wanted to be more modern, more hip. The tag line "This is not your father's Oldsmobile" became one of the more famous in advertising history. Yet Oldsmobile wasn't able to reverse the brand image, failing in its attempt to attract a new market. The image was too closely associated with being stringent, old, reliable, and safe (but not safe in a good way). Oldsmobile was long past the time that it could convince a younger generation to take another look.

This didn't need to be the case. Oldsmobile could have started to take a more modern approach to branding a long time ago, slowly integrating younger imagery into the brand message over a long period of time, making the transition much less harsh and more believable.

Other companies have understood that a brand image can work against them, and they have taken successful steps to protect themselves from it. Toyota has always been thought of as a maker of everyday vehicles, as has Ford Motor Company. Although there are many vehicle models branded under the Toyota and Ford names, both brands have largely remained middle-of-the-road vehicles that the masses can afford. It's seldom mentioned by the media that Toyota owns the upscale Lexus line or that Ford is the proud owner of the Jaguar line of cars. The Toyota and Ford names don't appear on either line of their luxury-brand vehicles, because both manufacturers understand that associating upscale and expensive luxury automobiles with makers of everyday vehicles would tarnish the luxury brand images and make them less desirable in the luxury market.

Similarly, AT&T, which is a corporate giant and, because of its age, considered old and traditional, is not looked on very favorably by the desirable but hard-to-reach 18- to 24-year-old market. When AT&T marketed its entry for a 10-10 number to save money on long distance calls, it did so without ever mentioning the AT&T name in the advertisements. The association with the AT&T brand would have turned away the market it was seeking.

To avoid negative reaction because of an established brand image that may not speak to all markets, brands that wish to broaden their consumer base need to communicate with their primary audience, using varied messages that keep the promise intact but that acknowledge changing times as they happen. Some cartoon characters, like the Peanuts gang or the Simpsons, never grow older, but see their surroundings and situations change over the course of years or decades. Brands need to do the same thing. Coca-Cola was started in the late 1800s; yet it's not considered a drink for old people, nor is it looked on as an old, corporate giant. Coca-Cola has maintained its market share over decades because it's gone to great lengths to keep its image fresh and to maintain its brand promise and personality, all while keeping its youth market intact.

ELEMENTS THAT BUILD THE BRAND

8

Despite brand's definition as an intangible entity, there are a number of physical elements that are required to communicate the brand's message to the target audience. Before any brand material is developed, you should have defined the demographic and psychographic profiles of the target market through market research (as discussed in Chapter 2).

The first element that people think of when they think of a brand is the logo. In fact, many people who are unfamiliar with the concept of branding will confuse the logo *for* the brand. The logo colors, shapes, and tag line are components of the brand, but none of these items in particular is the brand itself.

Logos

Many people assume that a company's logo is equivalent to its brand because the logo is the key visual element used for brand association. The logo usually is a relatively simple design (because logos are often reduced when used in letterheads, business cards, and other material, and simple designs are easier to see). They are made up of no more than a couple colors because colors are expensive to print and more difficult to translate into black and white. Logos should be easily distinguished by customers at a quick glance.

Most often, the logo design is created so that the design itself says something about the company or the brand. The Nike swoosh, for example, gives the impression of speed and activity. Other logos are more challenging to decipher, because they have a more philosophical rationale. In some cases, the definition of what a logo stands for is made public and used as part of the branding campaign. In other cases, it's more for internal use, so that employees have an insightful understanding as to what the company is about. Visteon, an automotive supplier that was formerly part of Ford, launched its brand in 1997. Its logo, shown in Figure 8-2, is made of swirling dots.

Figure 8-2   The Visteon logo

In its announcement of the Visteon brand, the company described the logo as a swirl of "energy dots," suggesting motion and symbolizing the company's entrepreneurial energy, responsiveness to customers, and speed in designing and delivery products.

Branding to a company's own employees for reasons of loyalty and pride is as important as branding to the consumer. Although not all logos are developed with a deep meaning (some are adopted for their aesthetic value), they all act as icons that allow both employees and consumers to quickly associate a brand promise with a certain organization and its offerings. Figure 8-3 shows a number of familiar logos.

Figure 8-3   Well-established logos

Colors

Colors play a part in brand identity. High schools, colleges, and most sports teams associate themselves with certain colors, and brands often do too, creating unmistakable recognition for themselves. The orange and green of every Crayola crayon box and the red and white of Coca-Cola are standout examples of the way colors play a role in consumer brand recognition. A turquoise gift box with a white ribbon lets a person know immediately that the gift is from Tiffany & Co., creating instant recognition that the item inside will be elegant and valuable. The color of the box has worked as a brand recognition factor (it's from Tiffany's). The brand promise and history of promise fulfillment has created the expectation of the recognized brand (the item is valuable) as well as the personality of the brand (elegance).

Shapes

Logos and colors aren't the only means of brand identification. For many companies—and for their products in particular—there is significant brand identification in the packaging. Who can mistake a can of Pringles potato chips or the traditional Heinz ketchup bottle? If you wipe the name off a bar of Dove soap, people will still recognize it by the unusual shape.

 The number 57 appears on every one of Heinz's ketchup bottles. Although the number 57 is forever associated with Heinz, there really aren't 57 varieties. Founder H. J. Heinz just happened to like the number 57, and the mystique that has surrounded the strange and seemingly random appearance of this number on most of its products has been a large part of the company's brand presence.

Shapes and specific product features often play a defining role in the public's recognition of a brand. Although the Yahoo! logo is well known around the globe, the site design and layout are equally recognizable. Unlike other portal sites that cram as much information as possible onto their home pages, Yahoo!'s home page has remained relatively unchanged: a standard white background (notice how the color is immediately associated with the brand) with the search engine area toward the top of the page, just below the one banner ad. Major content areas, news subjects, and shopping sections are followed by more specialized links. It's a simple design, and users know that it's Yahoo! without needing to see the logo at the top of the page. Few other sites share this distinction.

The consistency of a brand's shape and design is important because people tend to feel more comfortable with things that they recognize and with which they are familiar. Like an old pair of jeans or a favorite blanket, Yahoo!'s instant recognition among its users makes it comfortable for them, and it is one factor that contributes to the audience coming back to the site time and again.

Tag Line

Although there are many other factors that go into creating core brand recognition, one of the most important is the **tag line**. The tag line is the brief statement used by most brands in advertisements or marketing campaigns that sends a quick message of summation to the audience.

"We Love to See You Smile" is the current tag line used by McDonald's, and it sends a quick, clear message about McDonald's. It doesn't say "We Make Hamburgers—Fast," because the audience already knows that. Through its previous brand recognition efforts, marketing, and history of keeping its brand promise, McDonald's has expanded its brand objectives. Branding efforts no longer inform people about what the company does. It's assumed by now that we *already* know what it does. By using the "We Love to See You Smile" tag line, McDonald's hopes that its customers will associate the fast food chain with quality customer service and a happy experience.

The tag line may change for a company, usually in conjunction with newly devised advertising campaign efforts. Consumer product and service companies are likely to change their tag lines more often than B2B companies. Changing a tag line doesn't mean that the USP or brand promise have been altered. It simply means that the company is delivering new messages about its brand that it believes will resonate with its target consumers.

Stages of the Brand

The McDonald's example brings up the issue of brand lifespan. At certain stages in a brand's life, it is better to deliver certain messages than other times. Companies need to establish themselves in their marketplaces before getting creative and unique in their messaging.

McDonald's "We Love to See You Smile" tag line works because we already understand what McDonald's does—McDonald's has been selling fast food for decades. What if that tag line were instead used by McLarry's? Your response might be: Mc*Who*?? What does McLarry's sell? Why would that company want to see me smile? The tag line and the current brand message work for McDonald's because its previous efforts have already created mass brand recognition and solidified the company's brand promise. For McLarry's to use "We Love to See You Smile" as part of its initial branding effort would be a big mistake because the company has no history of branding.

Similarly, Coca-Cola is safe in calling its soda "The Real Thing" because we already know that Coke is a refreshing soft drink. Coca-Cola's original tag line was a lot less ambiguous, though. "The Drink That Makes the Pause Effective" didn't exactly roll off the tongue, but it sure did send a message. The "pause" was a break in the day, or even a break from life, depending on how a consumer interpreted it, and drinking Coke made that pause all the better. The follow-up tag line of the early 1900s, "The Pause That Refreshes," continued the refreshing theme, as Coca-Cola no longer needed to let anybody know that it was a drink—that was common knowledge.

Today, the fact that Coca-Cola stands for refreshment is ingrained with its brand promise. Although Coca-Cola still uses the word "refresh" in some of its packaging and marketing messages, the company no longer relies on it as its primary message. Instead, Coca-Cola now concentrates on sending other messages, such as "It's the Real Thing" and "Coke Is It!"

Many of the early and already-forgotten pure-coms skipped the first—and maybe most important—steps of establishing their messages and of letting their audiences know what their brand promises were. Instead, they went for cheap laughs with imagery or messages that had nothing to do with what they were actually about. Shock value alone typically isn't enough to build a brand, especially at the very beginning stages.

As a counter example, look at an early Amazon.com campaign. The initial national push was a radio-heavy campaign (less expensive than television) featuring an Amazon.com representative calling large places such as the Pentagon, Buckingham Palace, and football stadiums in an attempt to rent space for the "world's largest bookstore." The ads were funny and promoted a particular brand personality, but they also sent a message—that Amazon.com was simply *huge* and offered the best book selection available. The ads resonated—Amazon got its message across, and as a result, it is the most popular bookseller on the Web.

BRANDING FOR SMALLER INDUSTRIES

Coca-Cola and McDonald's are obvious examples of the branding concept. Large general consumer companies like these need to reach practically anybody with dollars to spend to see their empires grow. What if the company you are branding is smaller, however, without the budget required for mass brand recognition? What if it is part of an industry with a much smaller customer base? Even in cases like these, branding measures are necessary for long-term success.

A company that makes switch gears for backup electrical power generation is not the kind of company that will be buying 30-second spots during *Friends*. The market for such a company consists of engineers and a few key decision makers at hospitals, utility centers, and other companies that would need this type of machinery. Even in industries such as these—which are so specialized, and B2B-oriented that the masses may never hear of their existence—brand promises play a major role in growth. In fact, because prices of many B2B transactions are negotiated at the time of purchase and because projects are customized based on current client need, brand loyalty may be even stronger in these relationships than in the general consumer market.

Brand Consistency

When it comes to marketing the brand, the most important rule is to remain consistent. Companies may spend a good part of their marketing budgets on **brand management** (efforts to promote a brand and ensure it's being used properly and effectively) to make sure that the integrity of the brand is upheld throughout all forms of public dissemination. The larger the company, the harder it is to maintain consistency because larger companies tend to have a greater global reach into one or more markets, may use multiple marketing and promotional agencies, and may be involved in a large number of promotional efforts at any one time.

Consider the following scenario. Someone who visits a brochure-style Web site immediately gets a sense of that company's brand from the layout, navigation, and copy of the site. If he or she is interested in what the company has to offer, the visitor might e-mail a request for more literature. When it arrives, the colors used in the materials are different from the colors used on the Web site. In addition, the Web site uses photographic imagery in dark backgrounds, while the printed pieces have cartoon-style illustrations against stark white backgrounds. The tag line "Build it Better. Build it With Us," which appears on the site, is nowhere to be found on the literature. The consumer might not notice the variance, but from the company's perspective, a perfect opportunity to drive the brand message home has been lost.

The potential customer may not notice the discrepancies. At worst, he or she does notice and thinks the company is disorganized. At best, the brand image hasn't been helped in the least. In fact, without the consistency between materials and messages, there has been no brand message established at all. The company is just another in a sea of competitors. Sure, there's a logo, but there's hardly a brand because the message hasn't been properly developed.

Remaining consistent throughout each medium a company utilizes is vital to ensuring strong penetration of the brand into the minds of its target market. In every aspect of life, from training a dog to learning to fly an airplane, consistency and repetition affect our behavior and help us form associations. The same is true for brands. Messages need to be repeated often and sustained without wavering. This means that if your company's logo is a specific shade of blue, it should appear in that shade on everything you do to promote your company. If the message is "We give great service" in radio commercials, the basic message should remain the same in the TV commercials. If the design style used in the print campaign is light and airy, it should be light and airy on the Web site. With the abundance of information that is constantly available, repetition is a key factor in reinforcing the message. Whether customers love you or hate you, at least they'll know that you exist, and they'll know what you stand for.

ONLINE BRANDING

Wait a second. Wasn't this supposed to be a book about Web sites? Why are we talking about the historical relevance and branding efforts of (mostly) traditional marketers, with barely a mention made of the cyber world? Well, it's important to understand the concept of brand building and development before we explore how the (relatively) new phenomenon of the Web factors into the branding equation. The rise of the Web has led to new questions about brand building. Specifically, does the formula for building a brand in the traditional world work in the cyber world? Does there really need to be a distinction between these worlds?

Although there are many opinions on these issues, marketers have largely divided themselves into three camps. The first camp believes that marketers make too much of an issue of cyber branding and that the Web should be treated just like any other medium (such as television or magazines) used to convey a promotional message. A second group views things slightly differently, holding that cyber branding is a vital component to an overall brand, but that it must be translated carefully to the Web under rules that are slightly different from those under which a traditional brand gets built. A third camp of marketers claims that there's no good reason to even concern oneself with cyber branding, because the nature of the Web prevents the very loyalty that brand efforts seek to establish.

We can safely disregard the view of the people who fall into the third group. No matter what camp you might side with, however (and examples can be derived to support each theory), the Web simply hasn't been around long enough to historically determine which brand outlook is correct. For the remainder of this chapter (and this book), though, we'll take the perspective of the second group of marketers. We'll examine how a brand can translate itself onto the Web, recognizing which traditional rules change along the way, which do not, and why.

Translating the Traditional Brand to the Web

As you'll see in Chapters 10 and 11, marketers use many different types of media to send messages to their audiences. Direct mail, television, radio, print advertising, and billboard advertising are just a few of the popular methods for promoting a brand. Each has unique aspects, including costs and expected benefits. Each marketer uses its own mix of marketing vehicles, often combining several methods into one cohesive campaign. Despite the differences in traditional methods, most share a few key similarities:

- Promotional efforts are finite; that is, their messages are in some way limited. A 30-second TV commercial can tell a story for only 30 seconds. An 8.5 × 11-inch print ad can say only as much as can be printed on the page.

- Promotional efforts speak to consumers as a group, not as individuals.

Neither of these media similarities are true of the Web. The Web, however, is more than just a new medium. It's a hybrid medium of sorts, in that the Web is something to advertise *for* (for example, a print ad might have a line at the bottom that says "check out our Web site") and something to advertise *on* (such as with banner ads). The Web changes some of the rules of brand building, offering more opportunity but also creating more marketing struggles. The following sections describe five distinct differences between the Web and other marketing media: the Web is a marketing hybrid, it provides individualized message delivery, it offers new market access, it provides brand reinforcement, and it reveals new competition. As you will see, these differences can be used to enhance the relationship between the brand and the consumer.

The Web's Hybrid Status

Other marketing methods are pushing a product or service; the Web, however, falls between the promotion and product sales processes. As the diagram in Figure 8-4 shows, a Web site can promote the brand and try to push consumers toward a product, just as a traditional marketing vehicle would do. Both exist for the purpose of getting a consumer to buy products or services. At the same time, though, traditional marketing vehicles may also try to push consumers to a Web site because the Web allows so much more space for information (as opposed to a print and or billboard that has only the space available on the page) and because it can be viewed for any length of time (as opposed to TV or radio, which is confined to a certain number of seconds or minutes). In effect, then, although both the traditional marketing campaign and the Web site may try to push products on their own, the traditional marketing campaign or effort may also try to push consumers toward the Web and allow the Web site to make the final sale. This is the first time that one marketing tool has been used in a major effort to promote what is essentially another marketing tool.

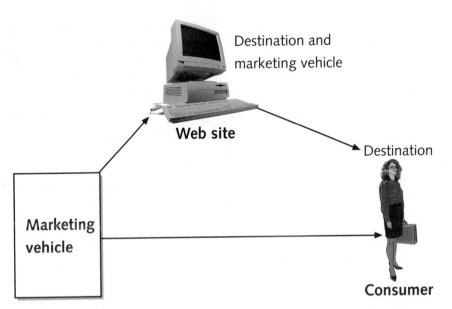

Figure 8-4   Web sites are both marketing tools and consumer destinations

Because the Web has a practically infinite capability to present information, it's become common practice for most other forms of advertising, which are limited in the amount of information they can relay, to provide "teaser" information only—just enough to get the audience interested. They then guide viewers to a Web site for more information. In addition, coordinated marketing efforts can be utilized with the Web to create more engaging and interactive relationships with consumers. You will learn more about this integration in Chapter 9.

Individual Message Delivery

The Web potentially speaks to each member of a given audience as individuals. Depending on how much technology is employed, Web sites can offer a heightened level of personalization, as you have already seen in previous chapters.

Traditional mass marketing tools and branding efforts have to consider the audience as a single entity, offering no flexibility to speak to individual members of a target market. A television commercial delivers one message, and all the audience can do is accept or reject the message. The commercial really has no way of reaching out to a particular member of the audience and saying, "Hi, John. Thanks for watching this commercial! What other information would you like to see?" The Web can create such tailored images.

Your site not only can greet each visitor with a personalized message, but also can make recommendations as to what information that visitor might want to access. This is two-way, instant communication between your visitors and your site. In terms of building a consumer relationship, it doesn't get closer than this! No other branding device allows you to receive such instant and tailored communication.

Why is this important? First of all, it allows far better customer service than was ever previously available. Users may be invited to provide feedback on the site, the product, or other aspects of the brand, and the marketer can collect this information quickly, with little expense, and use the results to make necessary alterations to the site, service, or product. Help with particular products, such as furniture that must be self-assembled or high-tech items that may confuse people, can be made available through e-mail correspondence, a search area, a F.A.Q. (frequently asked questions) area, or even during scheduled real-time chat sessions with customer service employees.

Another reason that the one-on-one interaction is important is that interaction creates a much stronger emotional bond between the brand and the consumer. A clothing site may allow you to choose a model in your particular size and see how different combinations of clothing would look together on someone the same size and from different angles. If done creatively, the site may even recommend items that would go together or recommend accessories when an outfit has been selected. The result is that the site becomes a virtual personal assistant.

Mattel does something similar to this concept, inviting young girls to visit the site and dress a virtual Barbie with a large selection of cyber clothing. The Web site promotes the Barbie line while allowing each individual user to explore her own creativity. The Barbie site helps create a bond between the customer and the brand that might otherwise be difficult to forge.

Surveys and similar interactive devices are other means in which a brand can engage its audience on the Web. These methods are discussed in further detail in Chapter 9.

Reaching New Markets

The obvious markets that may open up to a brand on the Web are geographical. Your Web site is available to anybody, anywhere in the world, who has access to the Internet. This allows you to reach potential consumers in areas in which you don't otherwise market or advertise. This is definitely a benefit, and marketers that already have global operations may gain access to remote regions that they had trouble penetrating offline.

Going live doesn't make you a global marketer with a worldwide audience. You still need to find ways to let your audience know that your site exists on the Web. You must also take into consideration the fact that some parts of the world have relatively few people with easy access to the Web (as compared to accessibility in the United States). You must also address language barriers if your site is to be truly international.

Geographical market expansion is only one of the ways brand penetration may increase. More importantly, the Web provides access to new, untapped demographics. Because most traditional marketing efforts are expensive to execute, trying to reach an audience outside the target demographic (as determined by the market research) could be a waste of money, but the same isn't true with the Web.

Consider the New York Philharmonic. Not known as a hotbed of entertainment for your average 16- to 28-year-old, its site is pretty ordinary, as shown in Figure 8-5. It gets right to the point on the home page, offering information about composers and upcoming dates. It does this instead of first providing any sort of introductory statement telling what the New York Philharmonic is all about. Because the information is presented without much introduction, it seems like the site was built for visitors who are already familiar with the Philharmonic. We can assume that unless the developer just wasn't doing a good job of planning the site, its target audience is mature adults who have had experience with orchestras and classical music.

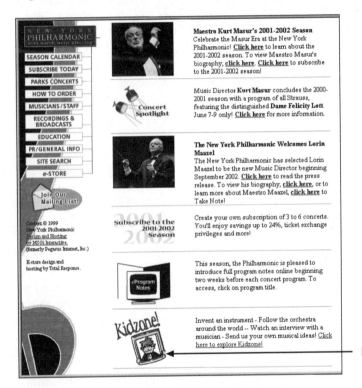

Link to kid-friendly features

Figure 8-5   The New York Philharmonic Web site

Although the site design doesn't stay very close to the brand image that the Philharmonic usually portrays (the orchestra typically presents a more sophisticated image than what is on its site, which is busy), the site does attempt to reach a younger demographic. Notice the link toward the bottom of the page. Clicking it brings you to the site shown in Figure 8-6, where kids can play games, take quizzes, and do other activities that are fun, and that teach them about music, especially classical music. In fact, this area of the site is better constructed than the main part of the site! Although the Philharmonic's typical marketing budget is spent primarily on attracting its core adult audience, it wisely uses the power, reach, and technology of the Web to reach out to a new market at a young age.

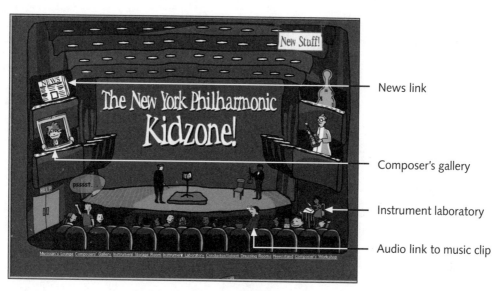

News link

Composer's gallery

Instrument laboratory

Audio link to music clip

Figure 8-6   The New York Philharmonic kids' page

What more could the New York Philharmonic do to pursue new markets? Although attracting a younger audience is a smart marketing move, it's questionable how much extra revenue the Philharmonic can bring in by targeting such young children. This disconnection becomes even more pronounced when you realize that the site does nothing to reach the kids as they become teenagers. The Philharmonic could add a page that tried to reach an young adult market. The site could add MP3 downloads of symphonic versions of popular music (such as the symphonic versions of pieces by Led Zeppelin, Metallica, or Aerosmith), and interviews with popular rock musicians who were influenced by classical music. The site doesn't have to push the New York Philharmonic too hard—just raise awareness and generate interest, potentially converting an untapped market into regular fans.

Brand Message Reinforcement

Because the Web is so dynamic and vast, it presents marketers with opportunities for creating brand images in subtle ways that weren't possible before the development of the Web. The Web allows a brand to enhance its image, reinforcing its promise even without consumers making a purchase.

Pampers.com, shown in Figure 8-7, provides the perfect example. Pampers has been protecting tender bottoms for decades, and the brand has long been trusted by concerned parents who want the best products for their children. Although the Pampers brand has evolved over the years (as do most products), it has never lost its focus on the brand promise or allowed its reputation to be tarnished in any way. The Pampers Web site continues that fulfillment of brand promise. Although the site provides a lot of information about the Pampers line of products, what really makes this site stand out are the prominent sections geared to providing parents with important information about raising a child. From tips on preventing Sudden Infant Death Syndrome (SIDS) to coping with the problem child, Pampers.com seeks to assist parents with the issues that they have to face on a day-to-day basis—issues that have nothing at all to do with Pampers or diaper use. In fact, Pampers.com goes so far as to allow parents to e-mail questions about pregnancy or child-rearing issues to a specialist.

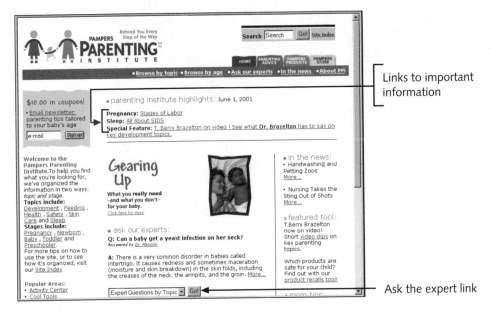

Figure 8-7   Pampers.com

Why would Pampers bother? The company is in business to sell a product, so what does it care about helping a parent whose six-year-old won't stop sucking his thumb? The reason is the difference between the product (what Pampers *sells*) and the brand (what Pampers *promises*). Yes, Pampers sells diapers, but that's hardly enough to form the emotional connection needed to secure brand loyalty. In that respect, Pampers does not make diapers. Rather, it makes safe, comfortable, reliable products because Pampers genuinely cares about your children. *That* is the brand promise. The Pampers.com Web site, by offering parents free information and help, is the company's subtle way of saying, "Hey, we're a company that cares, and we are here for you and your family." What parent would hesitate to purchase a diaper product from a company like that?

When translating your brand onto the Web, ask yourself (or better yet, ask your customers!) this question: "What type of information can we provide our audience, beyond our own product information?" If you're a greeting card company, you might offer tips on the perfect Valentine's Day date as February comes around. If you're a local car dealership (not all brands have to be national or global in scope), your site could offer driver safety tips, or better yet, a list of nearby scenic places to drive to on the weekend.

These efforts show your customers that you care about them. Obviously, customers realize that you exist as a company or as a Web site (or both) for the purposes of making money. For branding purposes, the emotional connection is made when you are *for* money but *about* people. Using the Web the right way can promote the idea that your brand understands its market and that it seeks a relationship that goes beyond just a dollar. It enters into something more important—trust.

New Competition Arenas

In the last chapter, we briefly discussed the competitive analysis that needs to go into your market research. Although it was discussed only briefly, the broad appeal of the Web and unexpected competition raise the bar for many brands, presenting them with new and stiffer competition that they may not have encountered in the traditional arena.

Smaller, local companies that launch a Web site in support of their brands will find themselves going up against large corporations that have deep pockets and far more resources than they do. Alternatively, large corporations will stand shoulder to shoulder on the Web with smaller companies that might be more in touch with consumers because their upper management is closer to the trenches. Because any one company is only a click away from any other, they each have to contend with what the other has to offer. Brand loyalty is one factor in company or product success, but the Web offers competition that may sway a consumer from one brand to another.

A local clothing manufacturer might have spectacular designs and sell its line through off-beat independent stores in a regional area. The company never had to worry about being on a shelf next to clothes made by DKNY or Tommy Hilfiger because the boutiques weren't interested in selling mass-produced clothes. Similarly, the large clothing brands didn't worry too much about the small local designers honing in on their turf because they already had the distribution system established to lock them out of the larger stores. Enter the Web. Now, both companies can be seen by anyone, anywhere, at any time. Does that mean that they will be competing equally? Of course not. The larger companies still have more money to spend on marketing and site enhancement than the smaller companies do. Likewise, the big players have the more widely established brand recognition. However, the *opportunity* for both brands to be seen by the same audience is now far more possible than it was when they remained in the traditional retail world. This increases the chances for competition among all brands.

Companies need to guard against their customers leaving their brands for another by taking actions to retain those customers. The consistency of the brand on the Web must be apparent, and it can't waver from the off line brand. Other important factors in retaining customer loyalty include site stickiness (a point that will be analyzed in Chapter 9) and the monitoring of competition on the Web (both before and after launch). These factors ensure that your site can offer something unique to its audience.

8

AMAZON.COM: BUILDING BRAND THE RIGHT WAY

You've undoubtedly noticed that Amazon gets mentioned a lot throughout this book. Regardless of whether it thrives and becomes one of the wealthiest global brands or whether it fails to ever make a dime and eventually closes shop, **Amazon.com** will remain a fascinating case study for years to come.

Amazon.com is largely given the credit for ushering in the age of commercial Web development. The fact that founder Jeff Bezos was able to rise out of obscurity and create an electronic commerce Web site with such mass appeal and keep almost no inventory sparked excitement in a lot of entrepreneurs. The story that Bezos thought up the Amazon.com concept while driving to Seattle with his family in a station wagon has become the stuff of legends—most people have no idea if the story is true, but it certainly made the rounds. If he could do it, then anybody could! And anybody tried.

Beyond its business concept, Amazon is also admired because of the speed with which it has been able to build a globally recognized and respected brand. A process that marketers know takes years—even decades—happened almost overnight for this online retailer. Its stock price was through the roof, and suddenly, millions of dollars in venture capital was provided to anyone with an idea. This didn't happen because Amazon.com did such a fantastic job in branding. The novelty of the Web and the Amazon.com concept created a buzz around the site that made people want to visit and even take part in it by buying something. Amazon.com was credited not only for its own remarkable steps on the Web, but also for helping to usher in the age of popular Web commercialization. The instant buzz helped build its promise (you can buy books from your home or office quickly over the Web with a greater selection than your local bookstore) and recognition (newspapers and publications everywhere covered Amazon.com as both a company and as the cornerstone of the New Economy).

Timing and publicity weren't the only reasons Amazon.com got so big so fast. The company also made a lot of the right moves. Unlike pure-coms to follow, Amazon sunk more of its money into internal development and less into high-cost television advertising. Amazon.com took certain and deliberate measures to make its customers feel at home, as discussed previously in this book.

Amazon.com cleverly devised an advertising method to help get its name and logo out in front of its market. The affiliate program, which you learned about in Chapter 4, allows Amazon's logo to appear on practically every page of Yahoo!. When a user performs a search on Yahoo!, a small Amazon banner appears next to the search results. The banner is a link to books on the search topic. These books are available on Amazon.com. An ad on every page of Yahoo! normally would be expensive, but it didn't cost Amazon a dime—not up front, anyway. Instead, Amazon.com paid Yahoo! based on how many people clicked through to the Amazon site. It was a higher rate than Amazon.com would have paid using the CPM method, but Amazon received significant branding benefit among all Yahoo! users who saw the ads but who *didn't* click through.

Amazon continues to build brand awareness and interest by adding new product categories such as electronics and household appliances. It even allows customers to create personal stores in which they can sell their own items. Amazon's marketing has continued with the off-beat feeling of its early advertising with new methods such as free shipping periods, discounts on one book if another is purchased, user reviews of books, personal book lists, and wish lists.

Where was Barnes & Noble through all of this? The rightful heir to the cyber-bookselling let an upstart get the better of it. Barnes & Noble's stumble helped to fuel business at Amazon.com by driving to the site people who wanted to see the new kid on the block. Barnes & Noble, with its **BN.com** Web site, has since tried to play catch up. Its site, which looks similar to Amazon.com's but with fewer perks for visitors, often has lower prices than its rival. However, it suffers from a latecomer image and the impression that it is a weaker copy of the original. Barnes & Noble has deep pockets, and it's catching up, but even if it outlasts and overtakes Amazon.com, it may be a long time before the Barnes & Noble name is associated with online bookselling.

Is having a well-developed brand enough to build a successful company? Not really. Even if the company keeps the brand promise, achieves immediate recognition of its identity among customers, and serves a truly unique purpose, success or profitability is not guaranteed.

For instance, Amazon.com has built its brand and given people a reason to come to the site and to keep coming back. Despite Amazon.com's brand recognition, popularity, and critical acclaim, however, it has yet to turn a profit. Internal problems have plagued the online retailer, the most devastating of which is a troubled distribution system. Orders for multiple books are often shipped in separate packages (sometimes even from separate distribution centers), even though Amazon.com charges the customer for shipping and handling costs only once. It's been estimated that, at times, Amazon.com loses over $2 *per order*. The high costs of infrastructure investments and marketing programs have added to its spending woes, and although CEO Jeff Bezos continually promises investors that a profit will be realized shortly, it's a promise that, as of 2001, continued to elude the marketer.

CHAPTER SUMMARY

- ❏ A brand is a promise that tells a target market what it can expect from a certain company, product, or service. Brands help a product or company form a relationship with a consumer. Continued sales and success are often influenced by how well the brand is built and received by its audience. Successful brand building requires time, patience, luck, and skill. Fulfillment of that promise shapes a company or product's reputation and can make or break a company or product's long-term survival.

- ❏ Along with promise, a brand needs to have a personality and to establish its USP—the unique selling position that sets it apart from competitors. These elements of the brand are relayed to the target audience through logos, colors, shapes, and tag lines.

❏ The Web offers a unique opportunity for a brand, in that it may open up new markets both geographically and within different demographic groups. Regardless of the market that is being sought, the goal for the brand is to establish its promise and then to continually fulfill that promise over time.

KEY TERMS

brand loyalty
brand management
tag line

REVIEW QUESTIONS

1. _____ is not a primary ingredient in the development of a successful brand.

   a. The brand promise

   b. A global presence

   c. An aspect that makes the brand unique from other brands

   d. Brand recognition by a target audience

2. In most cases, the one thing that is crucial to brand success is a _____.

   a. high marketing budget

   b. history of brand promise fulfillment

   c. logo that has an interesting story behind it

   d. memorable tag line

3. Which of the following best describes the personality of a particular brand?

   a. The brand is fun, lively, and meant to be enjoyed by people who love life.

   b. The branded product is of high quality and will last a very long time without breaking.

   c. The branded product is the top seller in its market.

   d. The brand has an interesting history and has been established over a number of decades.

4. _____ is the least likely to qualify as a viable USP for a chain that services automobiles.

   a. "We provide high quality service in less than an hour"

   b. "We always use the best parts"

   c. "We have experience with older vehicles"

   d. "We work on all foreign imports"

5. Ideally, a brand has success as a result of _____.

   a. severe price breaks and ongoing promotional rebates

   b. brand loyalty due to an emotional connection made between the brand and the audience

   c. the repetition of the brand message through exhaustive marketing efforts

   d. the collapse of competing brands

6. A brand that has, for over 30 years, been associated with teenage boys and rebelliousness may find the _____ market the most difficult to tap into, even with the development of new product lines.

   a. teenage girl

   b. college student

   c. businessmen over 30

   d. young male

7. Describe a tag line.

8. Consistency of a brand image has to happen _____.

   a. during the initial rollout of the brand, but may become more loose over time

   b. during the period of translation from traditional brand to cyber brand

   c. throughout the life of the brand

   d. internally for the benefit of brand employees

9. A company that manufactures hair care products could enhance the brand and further engage the audience on its Web site by _____.

   a. providing hair care tips and style guides for various occasions

   b. providing a page of printable coupons for its products

   c. providing a list of stores where the product is sold

   d. providing biographies of celebrities who use the products

10. Nike is an example of a _____.

    a. brand

    b. company

    c. Both A and B.

11. One of the most important new markets that a Web site offers a brand is _____.

    a. customers in far-off geographic markets

    b. customers who speak languages other than English

    c. customers who are brand loyal to competitors

    d. potential customers in other demographic categories

8

12. Name one attribute of a camera manufacturer that would be a good branding message or USP.

13. Give an example of a tag line currently used by a product or service that you think accurately reflects that company's primary brand image.

14. Provide an example of at least one product or company that has a brand image so set and established in its market that it might find it hard to break into another market. Explain why you chose that company for an example.

HANDS-ON PROJECTS

1. Get your in-class business group together. The most important aspect of your business plan is about to start.

   a. Decide what your site's particular USP will be. How will your brand be unique?

   b. What is your brand promise, and what steps will you need to take over time to fulfill that promise? How will the unique aspects of the Web help you in that endeavor?

   c. What is the personality of the brand? How will you create the personality of the brand to attract the Web site's target market?

   d. Create a logo and develop a tag line for the site or company. Identify the branding elements, such as corporate colors, fonts, styles, and imagery, that need to stay consistent and determine how your brand should use them.

2. Tag lines help you form an immediate association between a brand and an idea. Below are tag lines from famous brands:

   ❑ Mmmm, Mmmm, Good

   ❑ Just Do It

   ❑ The Quicker Picker Upper

   ❑ The Choice of a New Generation

   ❑ Snap, Crackle, Pop

   ❑ We Bring Good Things to Life

   ❑ Drivers Wanted

   ❑ Let Your Fingers Do the Walking

   ❑ When it Absolutely, Positively Has to be There Overnight

   ❑ When You Care Enough to Send the Very Best

   a. Name the brands that are associated with these tag lines. What do the tag lines say about the brand?

b. From your own knowledge of each company (either through use of their products or exposure to their marketing), what do you perceive each brand's promise to be? What about its USP? Are they different?

c. Based on their style and marketing, how would you describe the brand personalities?

3. Northeast Ski has decided to open an electronic commerce Web site. The company sells all major brands of skis and ski accessories and has a client base that keeps coming back. Northeast is known for its service and the product knowledge of its salespeople. The shop also has a wide product selection and a great return policy. A fireplace in the center of all Northeast stores is a draw for its customers, who enjoy the lodge-style atmosphere when they shop at this particular retailer.

a. By trying to sell online, what other competitors will Northeast have to consider that it didn't have to worry about when it was strictly a regional chain?

b. On a Web site, how can Northeast maintain the warm, homey atmosphere that has been such a draw for its stores?

c. What steps can the company take to provide online service similar to the service that customers appreciate in the stores?

d. Using techniques that rely less on direct sales than its current strategy, how else can Northeast further enhance the brand?

e. What steps can the company take to convert non-skiers into skiers with its Web site?

Assume that this company does not have a name, established brand, or tag line.

f. Come up with a name, brand promise, and tag line that will quickly let customers know what makes this particular chain different from its competitors.

8

9

MAKING YOUR SITE STICKY

In this chapter, you will learn about:
- The basic elements of Web site stickiness
- Ten methods that help make a site sticky
- How to let visitors know about your site's sticky features
- Two approaches to avoid when striving for stickiness

The word "sticky" makes you think of gum at the bottom of your shoe, extreme heat, and the floor of most movie theaters. In most parts of the free world, people try to avoid these things (although we've pretty much learned to live with the movie theater thing). So, if we strive to avoid "sticky situations," why would we want to make our Web sites sticky? Well, when it comes to Web site development, the word *sticky* takes on a far more positive meaning.

WEB SITE STICKINESS

As you learned in Chapter 5, a sticky site is one that keeps surfers coming back time and again. The brand loyalty discussed in Chapter 8 translates into stickiness on the Web. The stickier the site is, the more reasons a Web user has to return often.

Of course, not every site needs to be sticky. A corporate brochure site, for example, is hardly looking for visitors to return over and over again to read content that rarely changes. Instead, that site is looking for a user to visit once or twice and then pick up the phone to begin a relationship. However, sites that earn revenue through electronic commerce sales and banner advertising rely on users to come back on a regular basis—this boosts traffic, which in turn increases revenue.

In general, revenue generated from an existing customer base (users who buy or visit on an increasing basis) is less costly from a marketing perspective than trying to capture new users. Some Web sites have implemented sticky elements very effectively and have profited from them. Others haven't done such a great job and have suffered as a result.

WHAT MAKES A SITE STICKY

Think about what makes you return to any particular restaurant. Chances are that it's a combination of good food, good service, good atmosphere, and perceived value for the money spent. Why do you bring your car to get serviced at the same place that you took it to the last time? Maybe it was because the service provider was honest about the problems and costs of fixing the car, and the waiting room had a big screen television and a free soda machine. The reasons that you go back to a certain place a second time, or use a particular brand of a product over and over, are sticky elements.

Stickiness on the Web is different from physical brand loyalty only because in the online world, it is so much easier for users to shop for products or information at different places. Compared with the physical world, the Web is awash in examples of innovative, newer, cheaper, and more dynamic approaches to stickiness. Regardless of how sticky a site may be, brand-enabled customer retention and loyalty remain the primary requirements for success.

KEEPING USERS INTERESTED AND ENGAGED

Although it may seem obvious, the very first thing that makes a site sticky is the culmination of many of the things we have discussed already in this book. The content on your site needs to be relevant to the audience whom you want to attract, and the content has to be presented in a way that makes it easy to read.

Keep the following points in mind when creating a user-friendly Web site:

- Large bodies of text are often difficult to read on a monitor. Provide short blurbs about long articles or pieces of information to give a general overview of what a user can expect to get out of reading further. Most Americans get bored and become distracted after about 150 words if you haven't already captured their interest. After that point, they'll move on.

- Use large type for headlines to let users know immediately what the subject matter is. Keep the number of major headlines to a minimum so that some content takes precedence over other content.

- People are visually oriented. Use photographs and images liberally to accentuate the point of your information, but not so much so as to slow the downloading of the site.

- Bullet points help users absorb facts.

- Use marketing copy to engage readers. "The Top 5 Reasons Why You Should Use This Product" is a lot more likely to capture attention than a straight paragraph about why the product is so great. People love lists.

- Occasionally ask questions in your headlines—they can pique the curiosity of readers.

Figure 9-1 shows how **MSN.com** uses some of these techniques to immediately engage its visitors. Notice how you quickly can see which stories take precedence over other stories and how the headlines are written to make the reader curious enough to research further. MSN.com also provides a short summary of each article, allowing the visitor to decide whether the article is of interest.

9

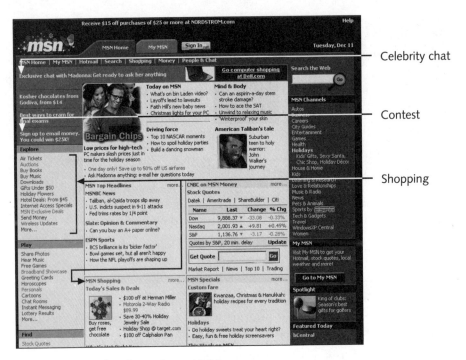

Celebrity chat

Contest

Shopping

Figure 9-1   Sticky elements on MSN.com

Keeping these pages consistent is also a key factor in retaining users. Much like the consistency factors that dictate the placement and usage of brand elements, navigation features, and design issues, you need consistency in general site layout and presentation.

Space.com, shown in Figure 9-2, is a good example of a site that remains consistent in its layout each day. Although this site's subject matter is too specific to appeal to a very general audience on a regular basis, Space.com has made the right moves in attempting to retain its audience. Screens from three consecutive days show the main story at the top of the page, along with an accompanying photograph. This is clearly the lead story. Other stories are presented, each with a different level of importance. The important thing is that a user can make an immediate association with the site and will not be confused as to where he or she should go on each successive visit.

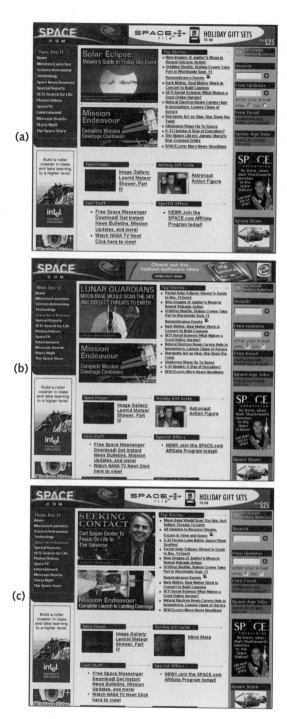

Figure 9-2   The Space.com site as it appeared on three consecutive days

Space.com's content doesn't appear to be attractive to a large audience on a repeat basis. If Space.com is otherwise doing everything right, why would it have trouble retaining an audience? If the site follows every guideline in this book and all other books on the topic, and if it employs every possible trick to being sticky, shouldn't it succeed?

The answer, unfortunately, is no. If people aren't interested in the initial content, then no amount of sticky efforts can help make it a success. Space and astronomy may hold obvious appeal for exciting the site's developers, but some knowledge of human nature is needed to make a site successful in the long term. Why are people interested in space? What types of stories will they find interesting? Will the masses lose interest if the site is too science-oriented, or will they lose interest if it is populated with stories about UFO sightings? This is not 1969, when Neil Armstrong walked on the moon as everyone watched the United States win the space race. This is the 21st century, where the space shuttle blasting off hardly makes the news at all.

Space.com may or may not still be alive by the time you read this book. Its chances for long-term success are at risk because of the narrow appeal—and subsequent lack of stickiness—of its subject matter.

The point, then, is that not all topics are going to be of interest to all people. If you are creating a site for yourself and don't expect to make a living from it, you can include whatever topics interest you. However, in a cyber business model that relies on advertiser dollars or electronic commerce revenue to earn a profit, real costs are involved in updating content on a regular basis, and the competition is more vast and more easily accessible to your audience.

STICKY FEATURES

In the previous chapters of this book, Amazon.com has been used as an example of a Web site that uses personalization and intuition to keep its customers coming back. There's a lot more to stickiness than these two features, however. Web sites attract visitors by engaging them in opinion activities, entertainment features, contests, and sweepstakes. Point-based rewards systems, games, and personalization also can help retain visitors. These various options can be used in combination for even greater appeal.

Voting, Polls, and Surveys

Polls and surveys are popular ways to allow your audience to have a voice on your site. People like to make their opinions known. At the same time, we like to know what others are thinking, who agrees with us, and who doesn't.

Although users aren't always willing to provide personal information such as names and phone numbers without a promise of security, many of them are more than happy to share their opinions. The following are some typical polls found at various sites:

- Who will be the this year's MVP? **(Baseball.com)**

- Uncle Junior of The Sopranos has teamed up with hip-hop crew Full Force. What other mob-tinged team-ups would you like to see? **(VH1.com)**

- Do you think religious clubs should be allowed to meet in public schools? **(CNN.com)**

The benefit of polls and surveys is two-fold. First, they give people a reason to come back to the site. If you voted for something or someone, or in some way voiced your opinion on a Web site, you might as well come back the next day to see the results. While you're there, you might as well respond to the next poll question and come back the next day to see the results. Second, online polls create a sense of community that allows your users to become a part of the site. They have a voice, and your site allows them to use it. It's the difference between your site speaking *with* them and speaking *at* them.

Some sites take the poll technique even further. You don't agree with the results of the poll? Who are all these people who disagree with you? Well, let them know how you feel in the bulletin board! Voice your opinion in your own words, or respond to other people's opinions. If simple polling brings visitors back for the poll results, bulletin board opinion postings give added incentive to return—and stick around. People love to see their real names or site user names displayed on a Web site, and they will return to see the names or to respond to posts others have made to their opinions. These staggered, virtual "conversations" keep people coming back to a site to remain involved. Unlike chat rooms, which are instantaneous, bulletin boards maintain a conversation only when someone responds to a posting. A few lines of conversation may take hours, days, or weeks to complete. Each time a participant returns to the site, the site has one more opportunity to get him or her to interact with the content—which might include spending money. From the site owner's perspective, each return visitor is another chance to convince advertisers that their ads will be viewed by many potential customers.

Figure 9-3 shows **Alloy.com**, a site geared toward teenage girls. Alloy.com uses polls and bulletin boards to create a community to which its audience responds.

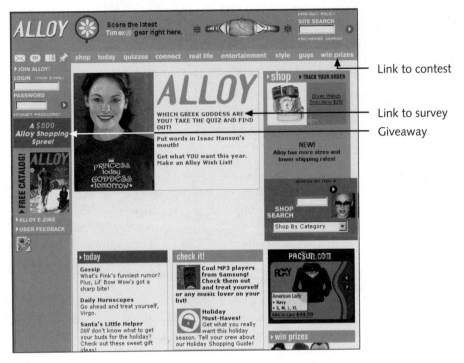

Link to contest

Link to survey

Giveaway

Figure 9-3   The Alloy.com site with sticky features

The many bulletin boards and opportunities for interaction give Alloy users more reason to return to the site. By returning, they not only can find out if others have responded to their comments, but also can get involved in newer, more timely discussions.

Entertainment

We all love to be entertained, and smart Web site developers use this basic fact to keep their visitors returning. Videos, Flash movies, games, and trivia can be used to keep visitors happy and eager to return to your site. However, including entertainment features makes sense only if the entertainment is not entirely superfluous and if it somehow relates to the content on the site.

BMW made headlines in 2001 with its release of a series of six short films that could be seen only on its Web site. Figure 9-4 shows stills from these innovative productions. Far from the standard, boring sales video, each segment of the BMW series was written as a real story, including fights and spy plots. Of course, each film had a gripping car chase featuring a BMW.

Figure 9-4 Stills from BMW.com's online movie

What was even more exciting for movie fans, though, was that BMW went all-out to hire top talent and popular names such as Madonna and Mickey Rourke for the starring roles and Ang Lee and John Frankenheimer as the directors. BMW obviously knew its audience and knew that high-impact, high-adventure entertainment would resonate with potential BMW buyers. Furthermore, most of BMW's target market had fast enough Web connections to view the movies without much trouble.

 BMW has a history of using film to further enhance its brand message. Although this was the first time that BMW used the Web as an entertainment and branding vehicle, the company introduced the Z3 roadster and the X5 sport utility vehicle in two James Bond films with great success.

About the same time that the BMW films were being released on the Web, **Burger King** was releasing a series of three Flash-animated movies that also was picking up some press (although not nearly as much as BMW). A scene from one of the Burger King movies is shown in Figure 9-5.

Figure 9-5   A scene from Burger King's online movie

Both entertainment campaigns helped make their respective Web sites sticky. With each one releasing a different movie each week, users kept coming back to the BMW and Burger King sites to see the additions to the collections.

The companies used different entertainment methods to reach their respective audiences. BMW used sleek, action-adventure films with high-profile casts to reach a sophisticated, affluent, and young audience, spending large sums of money to get the projects completed. Flash movies of cartoon characters driving BMWs wouldn't have effectively reached that particular audience. Burger King, on the other hand, didn't need Hollywood personalities in high-budget films to reach its audience of kids, teenagers, and young adults. Flash cartoons were more than enough to attract its audience by using off-beat humor.

Neither of these companies invented film or Flash. Both tools have been used on the Web by many other companies. So why did BMW and Burger King receive so much press? These instances were newsworthy because each was a high-profile example of how mainstream marketers could embrace the Web to promote their brands.

Online games are another source of entertainment on the Web that can help make a site sticky. Online gaming has become a large industry all its own, with games becoming standard content on many Web sites. Figures 9-6 and 9-7 show games that appear on **Hersheys.com** and **CBSSportsLine.com,** respectively. Both sites provide fun for the site visitors, while promoting the respective brands.

The Hersheys.com game, shown in Figure 9-6, is a maze in which the player uses Reese's pieces to navigate.

Figure 9-6   The Reese's maze on the Hershey's Web site

9

The CBSSportsLine.com game, shown in Figure 9-7, has players throwing a football through a swinging tire, which is reflective of the sports theme of its site.

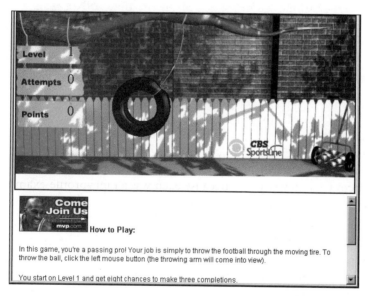

Figure 9-7   An arcade game from CBSSportsLine.com

Online gaming is still in its infancy, with the games being heavily affected by connectivity rates. Flash, Shockwave, Java Applets, and other technologies contribute to the growth of online gaming. Although there are some fun games out there and they are getting better each day, Web games are nowhere near the quality of Sony PlayStation, Sega, or Nintendo.

Despite these comparative shortcomings, online games have two benefits that non-Web games don't have: they're free, and they allow users to feel as though they're part of a community, with competition among players providing new challenges and interaction with other people.

How do Web games such as the ones shown in Figures 9-6 and 9-7 help make a Web site sticky? First of all, they're just fun, and they add an interactive component to the site. Second, they create a challenge by enticing users to come back repeatedly to try to beat their previous scores. Sites that are particularly clever and that have the money to develop databases can make this challenge more obvious, by posting the high scores of all users in a public game page for other players to see. Players will return frequently to try to beat their own scores and to defeat other people whom they've never even met.

Finally, online gaming holds an intrinsic marketing value that helps a site find new users. Multiple-player games ask one user to invite friends to the site to play, using one captured set of eyes to bring in other site visitors. E-mail chess is a perfect example. The game takes two people to play. Player One makes a move. The chess site e-mails Player One's friend, Player Two, to inform her that a move has been made by Player One. Player Two makes her move, and an e-mail is sent back to Player One telling him that it's now his move. The two players continue to come back to the site time and again, maybe over the course of months, to finish one game against each other. During that time, the players see dozens—maybe even hundreds—of ads, boosting traffic numbers for the game site.

Contests and Sweepstakes

Odds of 1 in 73 million never seem to deter people from buying lottery tickets. Regardless of the odds, people love a chance to get something for almost nothing, and online contests offer just that. Part of what makes online contests so enticing is their ease of entry. You don't even have to buy a product to play. (Although some traditional products have a "no purchase necessary" offer that allows people to enter a contest by standard mail, these are relatively few in number.) You also don't have to wait in line to buy a ticket, and entry is usually as easy as submitting vital statistics and contact information. Collecting this customer data is one of the benefits Web sites gain from developing the contests.

Contests have been run in different ways, on various Web sites, ranging from traditional to creative. Figure 9-8 shows the **WorldVillage** site, which features contests. As you can see, the contest part of the site is so important that it takes center stage on the home page.

Figure 9-8 A contest-oriented site

For some sites, merely providing your name and contact information is enough to be entered into a contest. Other sites may require more. A site that wants its visitors to look through the site as much as possible may, for example, run a virtual scavenger hunt. Such contests require that you look through the site to find a certain image hidden among the content. Other sites might have players gather information from the site to answer a short quiz for entry into a contest. Better yet, a content-oriented Web site may somehow get users to view advertiser's Web sites to enter a contest. Of course, the more work a user has to do, the less likely that user will want to bother with the contest at all.

Be aware of legal issues when it comes to running online contests. Making a user do any kind of work or requiring a set of skills to enter or win a contest may cross the fine line into gambling, and thus be deemed illegal. Legal issues regarding gambling and the Web can be especially precarious. The fact that some states have legalized gambling while others have not continues to fuel the debate of whether the gambling takes place in the state where the site's server is located or whether it takes place in the state in which the Web user is located. In general, a contest is in the gambling category if the Web users are required to put something at stake to play. It's also gambling if they incur a loss, such as money or points they may have earned. It is wise to seek legal counsel when undertaking such endeavors.

In a simple, daily Web contest, **Uproar.com** asks registered users to guess the lowest number for the day. It's as simple as that. You type a number greater than zero, and if no one else has guessed that number, you win $10. The prize is not much money, but the contest takes all of a second to enter (you register only once), and it's played daily. You can guess the number 1, but it likely wouldn't be the winner, as hundreds of other contestants would also guess the number 1. Sometimes the lowest number that nobody else guesses is in the teens; other times it's in the high hundreds. Thousands of people enter the contest every day, and those same thousands come back the next day to see the winning number and to find out if they won. While they're there, they might as well play again...and maybe even look through the rest of the site.

Corporations and sponsors of contests often get involved in the promotions by donating prizes. Anything from movie tickets to a new car, cash, or a vacation can be given as a prize online. Legitimate corporations always pay out, as required by law. Other contests promoted on the Web are less legitimate. They are run as scams or they use *extremely* small print to sell a product or to con a Web site user into providing a credit card number or some other personal information.

Integrated Promotions

Contests can successfully include both traditional and cyber methods to promote a site. This integration has the potential for dramatic results.

Suppose, for example, that Hometown Bank wants to increase its customers' use of debit cards for everyday purchases, while at the same time driving traffic to its Web site to promote online banking. The bank could run a contest that encourages bank customers to make purchases with their debit cards as often as possible and to retain the receipts. At the end of each month, Hometown Bank's customers could go to the bank's Web site and view three random winning numbers. If the last three digits from any customer's debit card receipt for that month match the winning numbers, that customer is a winner of a token prize.

Let's add more detail to this scenario and say that the winning numbers were 593 and that you had a receipt for a debit card purchase of $45.93. The final three numbers of the receipt would match the winning numbers and you would be a winner. Want to increase your chances of winning each month? Make more debit card purchases—each receipt becomes a lottery ticket. Of course, you need to come to the Web site to view the winning results—they won't be posted at the bank branches! The bank gains in two ways. It makes money each time a debit card is used, and it keeps people coming back to the site so that they can see bank services, mortgage rates, interests rates, and other reasons why they should use that bank.

This type of promotion can be expanded to get more corporate sponsors on board. Hallmeyer's Grocery store, for example, may want to get in on the action. If the winning receipt is from Hallmeyer's, then the winner not only gets the prize, but also a $1000 shopping spree. Hallmeyer's gets more customers—because customers will shop at Hallmeyer's rather than with a competitor who is not participating in the contest—and Hometown Bank gets to entice customers with another prize. Depending on the arrangements made between the bank and the grocer, Hallmeyer's may provide the shopping spree, the money to help promote the contest, or some other prize.

In Chapter 11, we'll review methods of integrating contests in a marketing campaign to promote a Web site and how different media can play a part in Web contest promotion.

Rewards Systems

One of the most effective loyalty programs ever developed is the **rewards system**, or points system, promoted by airlines. Continental's OnePass, for example, has led the way in this field, consistently ranking among the top in popularity. Travelers who use Continental sign up for OnePass at the gate, through a travel agent, or online, and then they earn "points"—typically one point for every mile traveled. A trip that spans 3000 miles is counted as 3000 points. Membership in the program costs nothing, and you have to sign up only once. Many airlines have developed similar programs.

What does the airline get out of offering the rewards system? Customer retention. For example, if you accumulate 25,000 points, you earn a free round-trip ticket to anywhere in the continental United States. So, if you already have 3000 miles from your last trip, and you're going across the country again, you might as well use Continental and be that much closer to free travel rewards.

Continental has moved its rewards system to its Web site as well. Along with offering lower rates for tickets purchased over the Web, Continental rewards visitors with an extra 1000 points for every e-ticket purchased. Continental would rather have customers buy online than by phone, because every e-ticket sold online is one less phone call that a field representative has to take, one less commission that Continental must pay to a travel agent, and one less person waiting in line to check in at the airport. These costs are higher than the 1000 air miles Continental is awarding in exchange. Continental is paying the customer to do work for the company. This system makes the company sticky— it gives you a reason to fly Continental, and it also gives you a reason to use the Web site for booking flights.

Other companies have affiliated themselves with Continental's OnePass points program. Every dollar spent on an American Express card, for example, equals one point toward a free ticket on Continental. This effort expands the loyalty franchise, giving Continental OnePass flyers reason to make purchases with their American Express cards, as opposed to other available payment methods. In the case of American Express, however, OnePass users don't have to use their points toward free air travel. If they wish, they can turn their points in for a variety of products from a special American Express catalog. Either way, it's a sticky means of keeping customers coming back to a brand.

Web sites use similar points systems for making their sites sticky, although few have been as successful as the airline models. The Web seems like an obvious platform for reward system success, but success has been elusive for some of the online points innovators.

9

Beenz.com, for example, shown in Figure 9-9, was a rewards Web site that tried to do the same basic thing as Continental OnePass, but with different industries. The concept was that users would come to the site and register to start their beenz account. They went to various sites that had affiliations with beenz.com, and they collected "beenz" (the company's name for points or reward units) for registering, taking surveys, making purchases, and so on. Users could return to beenz.com frequently and check on how many beenz they had in their account. They then could spend those beenz at participating Web sites.

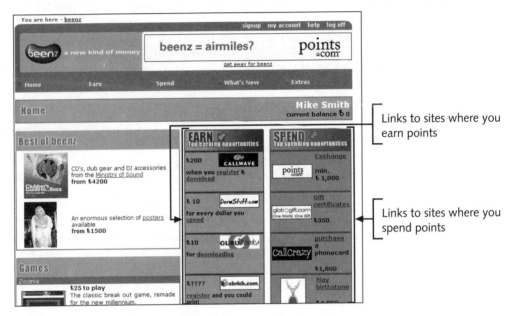

Figure 9-9   The beenz.com rewards site

The screen shown in the figure depicts beenz.com in its original concept as a general consumer site. Beenz.com was acquired by Carlson Marketing Group in October 2001. Carlson integrated the beenz.com technology and account information into the Carlson Gold Points Rewards customer loyalty program.

In concept, the beenz system sounds similar to the Continental OnePass program. Why, then, would it be less successful? For a points system to help make a Web site sticky, the rewards or benefits to the consumer must have some real perceived value. Free air travel through an established airline is a significant reward for doing something that a business traveler or vacationer is going to have to do anyway. Beenz.com, however, had some shortcomings:

- It did not offer strong affiliations with well-known brands. This point emphasizes the importance of brand recognition and loyalty factors. If you are going to bother registering for beenz so that you can get savings on books, for example, you want to redeem those savings at Amazon.com or BN.com—not GuruBooks.com, of which relatively few people have heard. The books might be the same, but the brand recognition of the partner is nonexistent. For this type of model to be more successful, the participation of Web partnerships needs to provide discounts from better-known brands and sites.

- When a participant signs up for programs such as OnePass, he or she is signing up with only one company—in this case, Continental. Beenz.com, however, whose business model relies on partner sites, required users to register with relatively unknown Web sites. In the user's mind, this translates into increased spam, junk mail, or telephone solicitations. It's a hassle few people want to put up with, and it remains a drawback on this site.

- OnePass gives you something that has a high dollar value—airline tickets. Everybody knows how expensive it can be to fly, and so the points are, in essence, a form of cash. Beenz.com and similar points systems on the Web never really *give* you anything for the work you've done to earn your points. What they do is allow you to redeem them for a *percentage off* a purchase. Thus, if a book at GuruBooks.com was $30, you could cash in a specified amount of "beenz" for 15 percent off the sale price. Big deal—that's a savings of $4.50. You still have to spend money to get anything with the points you've accumulated. In a situation like this, people realize pretty quickly that they're accumulating points for a coupon.

Despite the flaws in the beenz program, points systems and rewards *can* be an effective means of bringing people back to your site, if done correctly. Keep the following points in mind when developing a points system if you want your users to take advantage of it and keep coming back because of it:

- Offer something valuable and tangible. Depending on your budget, a good tangible prize can be tickets to a movie, show, or concert on the low end to a car or vacation on the high end. People appreciate value, and if you give them something to work toward, they'll take advantage of it and get involved. For long-lasting success, don't offer something cheap. You're promising users a reward for their loyalty—make it worthwhile. Doing less than that can be detrimental to the overall brand.

- Integrate your online rewards system with offline efforts. Most popular soda brands have created integrated points systems for short-term summer promotions. A popular "under the cap" game run by many soda companies allows customers to earn rewards by collecting points that are printed under the caps. They then redeem them on the soda company's Web site, where they can see what types of prizes they can get for various amounts of points. The draw here is obvious. Say a user drinks enough of a certain soda to collect 50 points. He or she goes to the site to see what can be acquired for 50 points, and, of course, sees an even better prize for 75 points. Because that's an attainable goal, the customer might as well wait and buy some more soda to accumulate more points and get the better prize.

- Seek third-party partnerships if your Web site wants to offer a points/reward system but doesn't have something of unique value to offer as a reward. Make sure that your partners have high brand recognition and reputation. This brings value to your site. Endurance is an important factor in a points system. It may take visitors a long time to build enough points for redemption. Users will be a lot more interested in building points on your site for a $100 Web shopping spree on **CircuitCity.com** than they will be for a $100 Web shopping spree on HalsElectronics.com. CircuitCity.com promises quality and customer service, and everyone knows it'll be around in the future so that the points can be used. The same may not be true for the unknown retailer.

- Make registering for the points easy. Filling out forms online can be a hassle. Make it as easy as possible for users to be part of the points system. At the same time, don't make the system itself too difficult to understand. Remember that OnePass gives one point for every mile traveled. That's pretty easy—and easy is what people want.

- Allow users easy access to review their accounts. Let participants check how many points they have, find out for what the points can be redeemed, see the last time they earned points, and so on. This feature is just one more way to make your site sticky.

Earlier in this chapter, we discussed using games as a source of entertainment to keep users coming back. Because they are on the Web, online games can be used as part of a points strategy. Depending on how your reward system is structured, the points earned while playing a game could be saved in a database and turned into credit toward rewards. You could award the high scorer of any given week a certain amount of points for accumulation in his or her account.

Some of these ideas for rewards may be difficult to implement because they require serious financial investments and complex programming. The market research that you do in the preliminary stages of the site design will let you know if the money that you invest will be well spent.

Personalization

Personalization gets a lot of coverage in this book, and for good reason. Personalization uses Web technology to its best advantage and can be a major sticky benefit to a Web site. As long as it doesn't make the visitor feel suffocated or watched, personalization can make a user feel welcomed to a site, as though the site were speaking to him or her on a personal level.

Aside from the cheery "Welcome Back, John" that may greet you upon entering a Web site, the personalization elements of sites such as MSN.com that you learned about in Chapter 3 also help make a site sticky. When you are allowed to arrange the content of a site in the order that you prefer, you know that the information that is pertinent to you will always be available when needed. It stands to reason that a user will want to return to this site on a regular basis, because the layout has been customized for his or her personal preferences.

LETTING USERS KNOW ABOUT STICKY CONTENT

The elements that go into making a site sticky are useless if no one knows they exist. You should design the home page of your site in such a way that updates and changes can be immediately noticed by visitors with even the shortest of attention spans.

Suppose, for example, that you have a home page that shows only a generic logo, a "Welcome to our Web page" message, and the basic navigation for the site. Your visitors might come to the site, look at the different pages, and then move on to the next site. A week goes by, during which you make significant content changes to each category within the site, but you don't reflect those changes on the home page. After all, the home page just serves up the navigation and a simple welcome message. When the user returns to your site, he or she will see that the home page hasn't changed and will have no reason to believe that any other content on the site has been updated. Chances are good that the visitor will leave without ever collecting the new information.

A simple way to avoid this is to add a line in a prominent position on the site that reads "Site last updated on [*date*]." This lets the user know that even though the home page looks the same, there are changes and new information *within* the site.

If you include contests, surveys, or other sticky features on your site, you should prominently display these elements on the home page. A survey, for example, should present the question, provide an area to answer the question, and offer a link to a page with results of the last survey. This will help visitors realize that there are new polls or surveys constantly being taken, and it will draw them further into the site to see how those questions were answered.

STICKINESS NO-NO'S

There are a few other, more technical ways of making your site stickier, but they're generally frowned upon and considered annoying or even rude. For stickiness to be successful, the site needs to entice visitors to come back or remain on the site longer by choice, without being forced into it.

Frames Retention

The lesser of the tech-sticky evils, **frames retention** is an older method of retention that was popular back in the early days of the Web, but it is rarely used now.

In short, frames were created by Netscape as a means for breaking up a Web site into different segments. Each segment acts as though it were its own browser, deriving information from different pages. Figure 9-10 illustrates how this works within the browser window.

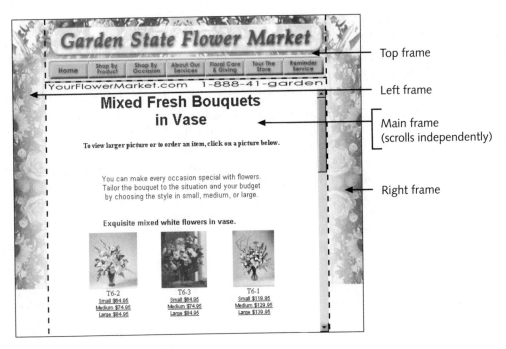

Figure 9-10 Frames retention

Although there was a lot of excitement over frames when they first came out, the negative aspects of frames soon outweighed the positives. Frames sometimes do not line up properly, causing printing troubles or preventing the site visitor from using his or her browser's Back button. This renders useless any effort to bookmark a page, retrace site visits, and so on. Consequently, the use of frames quickly diminished. However, frames are still used by some companies in an effort to allow users to exit their Web pages using hyperlinks to other sites without letting visitors venture too far away.

Mouse-Trapping

One of the most frustrating phenomena on the Web is mouse-trapping. It probably won't be long before some lawmaker somewhere makes mouse-trapping illegal (although enforcement will be a bit tough). Although most sites that mouse trap are of a seedier nature, other sites also use the technique to keep users from leaving.

In **mouse-trapping**, a user comes to the site either by typing in a URL or following a link from another site or from an e-mail solicitation. As soon as that user tries to leave the site—by closing the browser window, by typing in another URL, or by using the browser's Back button—the exit attempt launches up to three more browser windows, each showing a different page of the site or a different ad. Trying to close each of these windows may trigger up to three *more* windows to open, and so on. The user spends a frustrating amount of time trying to close all these windows from a site he or she no longer wants to be on. Eventually the user will get all the windows closed, but more often, it's faster just to quit the browser program and start over again from scratch.

Mouse-trapping and frames retention are each considered to be very short-term sticky devices. They may keep your visitors on your site for a bit longer than they intended to stay, but they do damage to respectable brands and hardly encourage return visits.

CHAPTER SUMMARY

❑ Getting people to come to your site the first time is a difficult chore, but getting them there is only part of the battle. You need to keep them there and keep them coming back. Integrating sticky elements into your site helps involve your user so that he or she has a reason to return on a regular basis. To do so, you can update content regularly, make sure that information is relevant and easy to find, and use polls, surveys, entertainment features, contests, rewards systems, and personalization. It's important to implement techniques that resonate with your audience and that make your site a regular destination, not just a flash in the pan.

❑ Make sure that the sticky features are obvious on your home page. Avoid using techniques such as frames and mouse-trapping, which only serve to annoy visitors.

9

KEY TERMS

frames retention
mouse-trapping
rewards system

REVIEW QUESTIONS

1. Which of the following would be the most effective example of a sticky element on a Web site?

   a. A biography of all the employees who are involved with the Web site, with a different biography released each week.

   b. Changing the background color of the Web site every day and taking a poll that lets visitors guess which color will appear the next day.

   c. Publishing an exciting and well-written novel and releasing a new chapter each week.

   d. Changing the layout of the site and challenging the visitors to find the information for which they're looking.

2. Stickiness on a Web site most closely relates to _____.

   a. market research

   b. brand loyalty

   c. unique selling position (USP)

   d. Flash programming elements

3. When people are reading text on a Web site, _____ will most likely catch their attention.

   a. making the text a nontraditional color

   b. bullet-pointing your copy

   c. using narrow columns

   d. using wide columns

4. Which of the following headlines would most likely make people continue reading a story?

   a. "A Brief History of Bad Business Mistakes"

   b. "The Seven Deadly Sins of Business Decisions"

   c. "Good Business Gone Bad"

   d. "How They Lost It All"

5. Which of the following scenarios would least likely get a potential user interested enough to join a site's rewards program?

   a. A traditional marketer offers points for searching its site, which can be redeemed for free merchandise at its brick-and-mortar locations.

   b. An unknown marketer offers points for registering with Web sites, and those points can be redeemed for deep discounts from a number of well-known and popular brands.

   c. A Web site offers points for every game that you play on its site, and those points can be cashed in to play even better games on their site for free.

   d. A content site offers points for every page you view, and accumulated points let you view more content.

6. One of the best ways to let users know that changes are being made on a regular basis is to _____.

   a. change the color of the site often

   b. change the layout of the home page

   c. welcome the visitor by name

   d. change the content on the home page

7. Give two reasons why online contests help draw people back to a Web site.

8. Bulletin boards are a good way to keep a site sticky, mostly because _____.

   a. they provide up-to-date information on current topics

   b. they allow readers to catch up on gossip provided by others

   c. they create a sense of community and a discussion that takes place over time

   d. they are easier to use than online games

9. Personalization on a Web site can be a sticky element primarily because
   _____.

   a. people like to see their names on a Web site

   b. personalization allows the user to conveniently access the information in which he or she is most interested

   c. personalization instills a sense of privacy

   d. on a site that utilizes frames, personalization allows a user to work outside the frames configuration

10. The best place to show off sticky elements that appear on your site is
    _____.

    a. on your site's home page

    b. in banner advertisements that appear on other sites

    c. in printed advertisements promoting the site

    d. on interior pages of the site

11. Describe two reasons why a site that uses a point system for stickiness might partner with other marketers.

12. Aside from making a site sticky, what other benefit does an online survey have? Describe at least one major benefit in detail.

13. Besides simple entertainment value, what are two other benefits of online games?

14. Describe mouse-trapping.

HANDS-ON PROJECTS

1. It's time to return to your Web site's business plan. With your business partners, discuss ways to make your site sticky. Describe the elements you will use to keep people coming back. Why did you choose some elements over others? Research how difficult these elements will be to create in terms of programming and whether you expect the benefit of those efforts to be worth the extra expense it will take to add them to your site. Describe how, if at all, those efforts will relate to the rest of the content provided on your site.

2. Find three sites (other than those described in this chapter) that have online contests. Describe what the contests offer and how large a role they play on the site. Would the contests on those sites be enticing enough to get you to provide them with your private contact information? If not, why not? What are the reasons that the contests on your chosen sites would or would not attract you for subsequent visits?

3. Consider your own experience on the Web. Are there any sites that you return to repeatedly? What is it about those sites that makes you come back so often? Write a description of the sticky elements of three sites that you visit frequently and why they cause you to return to them. Then visit a site that competes with each of the sites about which you wrote. What aspects of these competing sites are lacking compared to the sites you like to visit? What could these competing sites do to make you come back to them more often?

10

MARKETING STRATEGIES FOR WEB SITES

In this chapter, you will learn about:
- ♦ The different components of marketing and advertising
- ♦ Popular and effective methods of traditional marketing
- ♦ Popular and effective methods of cyber marketing

If the initial pure-com frenzy taught marketers anything, it's that high-budget television advertising alone is not the most successful way to market a Web site. One after another, Web start-ups poured investor money into weird, off-beat promotions in an attempt to claim a share of the Web audience.

The euphoric business atmosphere generated by a crop of overnight pure-com millionaires reflected not only a changing economy, but also a changing business environment. Business suits were out. Going to the office (often a converted warehouse or loft) in shorts and a t-shirt was in. Most pure-coms used television advertising to promote their sites, and the results were some of the strangest commercials ever produced. As you have learned, most of the commercials were innovative, but had no real branding message. Few ads delivered a sense of urgency, brand awareness, or a clear message.

Most of these efforts defied common sense and the established laws of brand building and marketing. Television ads alone were not the right vehicle for most of these new companies. Getting a message to the right audience needed a far more strategic approach, with an integration of various media and campaign directives. This chapter reviews marketing approaches that the owners of Web sites can use for long-term success.

UNDERSTANDING MARKETING

On a basic level, the term **marketing** means exactly what it implies: the act or process of bringing a company, product, or service to the market. Marketing, in all its forms, lets the public (the target audience as determined in the market research reviewed in Chapter 2) know that a specific product or service exists and entices them to purchase it.

Other terms also describe this process. In particular, the terms public relations and advertising are common. These terms are so widely used that they often overlap each other, causing confusion and misinterpretation. Within marketing circles, the specialties break out like this:

- **Public relations (PR)** deals primarily with spin—getting people to talk about certain products, companies, or items. As you learned in Chapter 5, PR professionals help announce, write, and promote stories about a client company. These stories are intended for distribution through the news media. PR may be handled by an entire firm or by a PR specialist within a creative agency. The PR company has the responsibility of informing the editors of appropriate magazines, for example, that its client has just released a new product, in the hopes that the editor will have a story written about it.

- **Advertising** primarily addresses efforts in which different media outlets are used to convey a message directly from the advertiser to its desired audience. Marketers purchase the ad space or time and control the message that the audience receives. Advertising agencies are responsible for developing the creative concept for a campaign, including the print ads that appear in magazines or newspapers and the commercials that are created for television or radio.

From a practical standpoint, public relations and advertising fall both under the marketing umbrella because they both are components of the marketing process. However, as you learned in Chapter 5, each specialty has separate responsibilities. This current chapter deals with advertising and integrated marketing issues; public relations is covered in Chapter 11.

MARKETING APPROACHES

Today's society is increasingly exposed to information; from scrolling news banners on the sides of buildings to stock reports broadcast directly to your mobile phone, there is no escaping the torrent of data that competes for our attention.

We live in a world with a growing number of marketers who are trying to reach an increasingly ambivalent audience. As our lives are more rushed, tolerance for advertising wears thin. In addition, as media become more extreme, we grow deaf to the message. When "shock jock" Howard Stern and others like him are considered commonplace, what is left that will grab our attention?

Because of information overload, marketers are challenged to create the best possible combination of traditional and online marketing. These marketers must also keep an open mind to unusual and innovative ways of getting a message in front of the target market.

As you learned earlier in this book, and as we'll see more specifically later in this chapter, marketing for a Web site is not only about using different media to send your message. It's also about innovation in promoting the company, product, service, or Web site.

Advertising Campaigns

The word **campaign** is used when discussing the marketing of a brand, product, or Web site. A campaign usually describes an organized effort of advertising and marketing for one or more distinct purposes, spread over one or more media outlets, and centered around a conceptualized theme. A campaign has four primary ingredients: message/purpose, theme/concept, time frame, and media.

Message/Purpose

The message or purpose of a campaign is the idea it conveys to a certain audience. General messages may be used to establish or underscore the brand promise, with the objective of increasing recognition of the brand name. Examples of messages are "We provide the healthiest recipes of any cooking site on the Web" and "You can find the product you are looking for more quickly and easily with our unique online shopping feature." Even if those messages aren't sent verbatim, but instead are delivered through imagery and copy, the viewer gets the same basic understanding. Other messages might be less brand oriented, and instead are intended to highlight one specific idea or promotion, such as "Half-price Wednesdays now through Christmas" or "Refer a friend to our Web site and receive a $50 gift certificate with his or her first purchase."

Theme/Concept

A theme is a secondary idea that supports the message, establishes the personality of a brand, and makes the brand more attractive to one audience versus another. Conceptual approaches create a theme that evolves over time and that is consistent throughout various media.

Earthlink, a large ISP that provides Web connectivity, built a campaign that played off Web users' desire for privacy. Earthlink aired a series of TV commercials featuring people who were faced with circumstances in which their privacy was breached. One ad depicted a man and a woman talking at a bar. The man said he would like to take the woman out, and he asked for her phone number. She gave it to him willingly. At the request of the bartender and another bar patron, the man sold her number to both of them for $5 apiece. Even though a computer never once appeared in the campaign, the message—privacy is important—was sent effectively. The bar/singles scene and subsequent betrayal of the woman provided the concept by which Earthlink conveyed its message. Earthlink delivered the message that it would keep customer information private—without being overt about it.

Time Frame

Campaigns may continue for a specific period of time, or simply continue until they have run their course. Typically, however, even for extended campaigns, marketers suspend the campaign at certain points so that they can do research and testing to measure its effectiveness. For example, marketers may want to know whether the campaign increased sales or traffic, or whether it increased brand recognition. Other questions might relate to timing of response. For example, if the campaign included six weeks worth of print advertising, what week seemed to have the most response? What week had the least? If the data measurements show that the campaign is having success, the campaign may continue until it is no longer effective.

Media

How the message and concept reach an audience depends on the media that are used in the campaign. Media options are vast, and each option has suboptions associated with it. For example, traditional media options include television, radio, print, outdoor, Web (banners and other), and direct mail.

Any place that a company can put an ad is considered media. As more advertisers try to find more creative ways to reach their audience, more media options have emerged. Today, ads can be found in the back seats of taxis, at the pumps in gas stations, and even at the bottom of the holes in golf courses.

Each type of media reaches different audiences, and within each media type are even more specific target audiences. For example, television ads and newspaper ads are geared toward different audiences. Furthermore, television ads that appear on reruns of *Murder, She Wrote* are geared toward a far different audience than are the ads on *Buffy the Vampire Slayer*. You will know who your audience is from your market research data.

Each media category has different things to offer to different audiences, and an effective campaign considers which media can most effectively reach a particular audience while allowing the marketer to relay its message properly. Often, a campaign will use more than one media at a time, and while it's usually desirable to maintain the same concept or theme throughout all media, it's not always possible.

Campaigns for Web Sites

Owners of Web sites in particular need to be careful about the campaigns they create, because, as you learned in Chapter 8, Web sites are both an advertising medium and an advertising subject.

Sites must be careful to deliver messages and concepts gradually. After your audience knows your site's name and its purpose, it is fine to deliver messages with extreme themes, also called conceptual campaigns. However, doing so too soon can lead to confusion for your customers. Products such as orange juice are straightforward, and even new brands of orange juice are fairly safe in introducing themselves with very conceptual campaigns because the idea of orange juice is not a mystery to anybody. At the time of its commercial takeoff, however, the Web was still a new medium to most people. Many early pure-coms were hurt, not helped, by using over-conceptualized campaigns for their unknown brands in this new medium. The Pets.com sock puppet is a classic example of the negative repercussions of over conceptualization. The highly recognizable sock puppet likely obscured the site's message—as a result, customers knew the puppet, but did not know why using Pets.com was better than just going to the pet store for supplies.

Instead of wasting money on ads that have little to do with their subject matter, new, unknown Web sites should spend marketing money on the areas of the site that really make a difference in the customers' experience. These areas include online customer service, better navigation, and more intuitive databases. Owners of sites should take their time about advertising and should build the brand gradually while retaining cash and improving the site. Without an established brand grounded in a firm business, a new Web site that promotes itself broadly through advertising will have only one chance at reaching its audience; an ad may draw a visitor to the site, but if he or she doesn't like what's there, no amount of advertising is going to get that visitor to come back.

Does this approach mean that no marketing is necessary, or that Web sites should never buy television time? No, it doesn't mean that at all. It just means that the marketing that does get done and the ad messages, concepts, and delivery vehicles that do get used need to make sense for the audience and medium. Table 10-1 shows guidelines for optimal timing for delivery of messages, depending on how long the brand has been in existence.

10

Table 10-1   Ad campaign time frame

Stages of Brand	Appropriate Actions
Stage 1 Brand infancy, just after inception through end of first successful campaign	• Campaign should focus on establishing the brand and building name recognition • Explain the brand promise • Make the USP obvious • Concept should be clear, not overly done so as to obscure the message • More marketing dollars should be spent to ensure the site is solid, functional, and beneficial to its audience
Stage 2 Early stages of a brand. Inroads have been made to achieve brand recognition in the market. A customer base has been established.	• Message should reinforce the brand, continuing to seek heightened brand recognition • Benefits of the brand should be highlighted, with the USP taking center stage in most efforts • Concept should be clear, although if research has shown that the company or product already is familiar to the core audience, the concept can begin to show more of the brand personality

Table 10-1   Ad campaign time frame (continued)

Stages of Brand	Appropriate Actions
Stage 3 Customer base is firmly established. Brand has successfully penetrated the market.	• Message can stray from mere brand recognition to promote particular aspects of the brand, product, or Web site • If research indicates that the USP has been understood and accepted by the market, then the message can promote beneficial aspects of the brand other than the USP • Concept can be largely personality driven, with heavy creative elements • Campaigns should revisit basic brand recognition (as outlined in Stage 1) if direction of the brand changes • Marketing to current customers should be a primary focus

Conceptual and Direct Approaches

Most successful campaigns have been conceptual in nature. A **conceptual approach** uses a story, a metaphor, an image, a joke, or another indirect means to send a message. A **direct approach** is a straightforward statement of the facts. The famed Charmin toilet tissue television ad campaign provides a good illustration. In the ads, Mr. Whipple had to beg his customers, "Please don't squeeze the Charmin." Shoppers just couldn't help themselves from squeezing the Charmin because it was so soft—a conceptual approach to relaying a message. In comparison, a 30-second TV commercial of text on the screen that says "Charmin bathroom tissue is very soft" is a direct approach. Conceptual campaigns can have the dual purpose of selling a product or service and establishing the brand personality at the same time.

INTEGRATED MARKETING

Bringing a product or company to market might seem like a fairly simple process: You make a TV commercial, maybe design a print ad, and then perhaps create a radio commercial. It might appear easy to do when you are looking at someone else's efforts in a magazine or on TV.

In reality, marketing a product or service can be an extremely complex process with endless choices. Any one decision may require three more decisions. Marketers must consider variables that can range from budget problems to actions by competitors before they can advance their promotional campaigns.

To produce a solid marketing or promotional campaign for a Web site, marketers can use multiple types of advertising media in conjunction with one another. As you will learn later in this chapter, options for advertising media include television, print, and the Web.

This multipronged approach is called **integrated marketing**. Using different media and marketing methods gives you an increased opportunity for market penetration, leading to brand recognition and sales.

Integrated marketing allows you to do the following:

- Reach more of your audience.

- Establish brand message consistency and recognition through repetitive message delivery.

- Take advantage of each marketing effort's strongest function. For example, in certain situations, a television commercial may work best for brand recognition, whereas a follow-up direct mail campaign provides a stronger call to action. The determination of which media outlet is best to use in your market (as discussed earlier) depends on the demographics of your audience, the costs associated with that outlet, and the objectives of your campaign.

Agenda for Development

To pull together a successful integrated marketing campaign, you must begin by creating an agenda for development of the campaign. Although agendas vary from one marketer to another, a rough agenda for development generally addresses campaign objectives, brand components, market research data, budget, message, theme, media choices, and ad production.

10

Campaign Objectives

Begin your advertising plan by determining whether the campaign is oriented toward making fast revenue gains, establishing brand awareness, or supporting ongoing brand awareness. Set goals for what you are trying to accomplish. Goals can include increased sales levels, increased traffic numbers, or increased brand awareness. For example, if your campaign's purpose is to drive traffic to your site, set a level that you'd like to reach, such as "500,000 visitors per month over the next three months" or "an increase in traffic of 30 percent over last month's traffic rate."

Brand Components

Every campaign must identify clearly the specific brand promise, brand personality, and universal selling position (USP) of the product or company being promoted. These three elements should be promoted consistently in all marketing efforts.

Market Research Data

Your agenda for development should make good use of the market research and competitive analysis information you have collected. Your audience profile provides the audience demographics and psychographics of the target market. This information helps you determine how your site differs from similar sites. Market data also helps you understand the messages to which the market is most likely to respond, your competitors' overall strategies, approaches that have succeeded for your competitors, and how you may either counter or improve on those efforts.

Budget

You need to establish a budget and a duration for your campaign. The budget should allow you to get the greatest mileage out of your money. If you have a $2 million ad budget you could buy one 30-second spot on the next Super Bowl broadcast, but that might not be the best bang for your buck. Your budget should balance circulation/market reach factors against the demographics you want to reach. The decisions you make regarding your budget relate closely to media choices, as described later. The time frame of your campaign also ties into budget. As you learned earlier, it is a good idea to suspend your campaign to assess its effectiveness. If you determine that your efforts have been successful, you may want to resume your strategy. If not, you probably ought to rethink your approach.

Message

Your campaign must have a message. Making a direct statement about the brand in general requires a different approach than promoting an upcoming event, such as a special sale, or a specific aspect of your site.

Theme

Determining the theme or concept is an important aspect of developing your campaign. This step often is integrated with the selection of the media, which is outlined in the next section of this chapter, because many ideas for campaigns cannot be developed fully without knowing exactly what media your campaign will use.

Media Choices

You have many options when it comes to determining which media should be used in your campaign. Options include television, radio banner ads, print outlets, outdoor or a combination of these options. Decide how these will be integrated. In developing the media plan, consider the location of the audience and budget constraints. For example, if the site that you are marketing is a resource for vacationers, using print ads in *Travel* magazine or television commercials on the Travel Channel may be very effective. When selecting media for your vacation site campaign, you must consider the ad space costs of these venues plus the cost of producing the TV commercial or a print ad. Remember that you must balance media selections against the limitations of your budget. If your first choices for media squeeze the budget very tight, you should explore alternate methods that are more cost effective.

Ad Production

The last element of the agenda for development is the production of the ads. You need to develop and produce all material for the campaign. Material includes the design and printing of direct mail pieces or advertisements, the production of TV or radio commercials, and the design of Web banner ads.

Creating an advertising campaign can be like playing a game of chess. At any point, you have multiple options and opportunities. Each step requires study and understanding of the surrounding environment, an anticipation of the effect of any decision, and the likely reaction of competitors to your efforts. Most important, each move can be a vital part of achieving the overall objective successfully or failing to do so at all.

Where to Advertise

Marketers have a vast range of media venues to use when delivering a message. Purchasing media typically involves buying time on television, space in print publications or in outdoor locations, and banner ad space and impressions on Web sites. The specific challenge in purchasing media is to correlate the marketer's audience (both demographics and psychographics) with the demographics of media outlets. This synchronization is typically the responsibility of the media strategist, as you learned in Chapter 5.

Every television show, magazine, and Web site that is selling advertising can provide a marketer or its agency with a demographic and psychographic breakdown of its audience. Those that fit the profile of the marketer's target audience are the ones that you should consider using. Budgetary restraints play a factor in narrowing down this field even further, until you decide on the ideal media for your campaign.

For the time being, an unavoidable distinction exists between online and offline marketing techniques. Eventually, the Web will be seen as just another marketing vehicle, but for now and for the next few years, all online marketing sources are segregated and considered to be their own unique category.

Offline marketing approaches include the traditional approaches of bringing a message to market. They include print, direct mail marketing, television and radio, and outdoor advertising. Each method has its own benefits and drawbacks, and each has the potential of reaching a market in a different way.

Print Advertising

In the early days of Web commercialization, many industry leaders predicted the demise of **print**, the medium that includes magazines, newspapers, circulars, and other paper-based advertising. Far from being dead, print is enjoying a renaissance of sorts, with print media still in high demand. The Web pundits who discounted print as a viable medium soon realized that they needed print not only for collateral material such as brochures and quality media kits, but also for driving traffic to their sites in the first place.

When marketers consider advertising in print, they are usually considering magazine or newspaper vehicles. These ads are sold in various sizes. National publications may sell space regionally for spot market penetration and to reduce overall costs to the advertiser.

Successful print ads designed to increase brand exposure tend to combine imagery with a creative headline followed by a little body copy to get the point across quickly. Marketers realize that people who see their ads usually do not read them in depth. It's rare for a print ad to play on deep emotions. Instead, ads that appear in print go for a quick hit using either conceptual or direct approaches to get a quick message to the reader. Print ads often use humor to gain an audience's attention. Figure 10-1 provides a few examples of non–Web, traditional print ads, with a main headline used to reinforce the images for a hard–hitting message.

Figure 10-1   Examples of traditional print advertising

Other ads, such as catalog-style ads used by supermarkets, car dealerships, jewelry stores, and computer outlets, are more direct. These ads are considered "call to action" ads because they are less geared toward building the brand and more oriented toward getting the audience to take immediate purchasing or viewing action. These ads involve significantly more copy and are used by readers almost as a catalog. Although these types of ads do not necessarily promote the brand image and may stand apart from a larger campaign, they are useful for moving consumers to take immediate action. Figure 10-2 shows an example.

Figure 10-2   Call-to-action ad

Figure 10-3 provides before and after examples of a print ad that appeared for a popular brand of professional movie cameras. The first ad (on the left) shows the camera and uses a large headline to announce that the advertiser is selling the camera at a lower price than are its competitors. A campaign that might be derived from the print ad could tie into the color used in the background of each subsequent ad, or it could use a similar layout.

Figure 10-3   Comparison of overt and subtle brand advertising

Note that the ad has little conceptual or brand-building message components. The message is "This is our camera. It's cheap. Buy it." The abundance of copy at the bottom of the ad doesn't add much value, and most people probably wouldn't bother to read it.

The second ad in Figure 10-3, on the right, never appeared in any printed publication, but provides an example of how that same message could be sent while reinforcing a brand personality. It shows the same camera in a separate layout, this time sporting a large price tag. The copy has been reduced significantly and includes the headline "Digital Etiquette: Leaving the price tag on to show off how little you've spent may be considered obnoxious." This ad also lets people know that the price of the item is lower than competing items. At the same time, however, it has a concept, an element of brand development, and the appearance of a personality through the use of humor.

Print ads are moderately targeted to specific audiences. For example, *Wall Street Journal* ads are geared toward business professionals, while *Good Housekeeping* is directed toward homemakers. Each publication has data outlining its demographics available for agencies and marketers. In addition, magazines often schedule issues focusing on specific topics in advance, so that agencies can identify good opportunities for advertising. For example, if an online trading site is the focus of an advertising campaign, and a certain business publication is dedicating its November cover story to online trading's role in the markets, that issue might provide a good opportunity for the marketer to buy ad space.

In magazines and in some newspapers, print ads are purchased by a specific percentage of a page: ads can be bought as a full page, half page, quarter page, and so on. More aggressive print campaigns may encompass two-page spreads, fold-outs, or even multiple-page layouts that emulate a brochure or feature story within the publication. (Publications typically label these sections as "special advertising sections" so that the reader does not mistake the paid information for unbiased journalism.)

Other venues, especially newspapers, sell ad space by the column inch. If a media buyer has a choice, he or she will try to get the advertising on a right-side page, which is where the reader's eye naturally falls when scanning over a two-page spread.

Conceptual, campaign style print ads can be a benefit to the marketer either as a direct call to action or as a brand builder. A contest or announcement of an upcoming sale or a coupon to clip from the bottom of the ad could serve as a direct call to action within a branded message. A simple message that correlates with an image or images can work to promote the brand. Web sites can benefit from both types of promotions simultaneously if they are done well. Because the name of the company is usually also the name of the URL (for example, Web surfers find Amazon by going to **Amazon.com**), any ad that appears in print can create a brand awareness with the hope that a reader might find his or her way to the site.

As with other media, Web sites seem to have taken one of two directions in their marketing concepts: either humor to the point of absurdity, or extreme and sometimes off-beat high-tech imagery. As we've discussed and will look at again toward the end of this chapter, the use of extreme concepts strictly for shock value has hurt rather than helped some brands.

Figures 10-4 and 10-5 show Web print ads that are typical of the industry. It is almost impossible to tell from looking at the ads what the advertised Web sites do or what they offer. Few people will take the time to read the lengthy text and find out what TouchScape (in Figure 10-4) is or why they should bother to investigate it. In addition, the lack of any real text or headline in the **Polaroid.com** ad in Figure 10-5 makes the ad's message or subject difficult to determine.

Figure 10-4   TouchScape print ad

Figure 10-5   Polaroid.com print ad

Direct Mail Advertising

Direct mail is advertising that is sent through standard U.S. mail or courier services such as UPS or Federal Express. Direct mail is one of the more targeted marketing approaches of all the traditional methods. It forces the audience to interact with the advertisement, even if that interaction is limited to simply throwing it out. Marketers develop lists of recipients by using sign-in forms on their Web sites, by keeping track of customers, by purchasing lists from other marketers who reach out to similar audiences, or by purchasing lists from list companies that specialize in creating current lists of various demographic groups.

Marketers send direct mail pieces directly to people on a list. These campaigns can consist of postcards or printed brochures, or higher-cost items such as calendars, magnets, pens, or other pieces that will keep the marketer's name and message in the mind of the recipient. Because marketers can tailor their mailing lists to practically any demographic group, direct mail is a highly targeted form of advertising. It's also one of the less potent. Typically, advertisers are thrilled with a return rate of 1.5 percent to 2 percent for a direct mail effort. A return rate higher than that is considered a home run.

Unlike print advertising, which adheres to the specific page size and audience of any given publication, direct mail has more possibilities. Marketers can develop their campaigns based strictly on budget, audience, and creativity factors. Postal regulations as to what can be sent through the U.S. mail narrow some direct mail options, but only slightly.

10

When developing a direct mail marketing campaign, the factors you need to consider include the audience, personalization, the number of recipients, the number of pieces in the campaign, and the size/shape of the item you are mailing.

Audience   Because direct mail campaigns don't have a predetermined demographic (unlike the print medium), the audience is really up to you. Suppose you have a Web site that sells cookware, ingredients, and utensils. Is the purpose of the campaign to rejuvenate interest among previous and existing customers? If that's the case, you already have the audience's vital information, such as names and addresses. Is the main purpose to generate interest among potential customers? If that's the case, you'll need to get (or more typically *buy*) a **mail list**. Mail list companies have access to numerous sorted consumer lists. You specify the type of audience for which you are looking, and the mail list company compiles a list based on your criteria. Another option is to purchase subscriber lists from magazines and newspapers that are targeted to your specific market (in this case, *Gourmet* magazine would be a good option). These media may customize a mailing for you for a certain price.

Personalization   Most direct mail pieces are geared to an audience *en masse*. A direct mail piece such as a postcard delivers the same targeted, conceptual message to everyone on the mail list (which is predetermined to be made up of people interested in cooking).

Although this approach is highly focused, you can create an even more specific direct mail message using a relatively new phenomenon called **digital printing**. Popularized in the mid 1990s, digital presses have evolved to produce printing that is equal in quality to that of traditional commercial presses. Digitally printed pieces are more expensive than traditionally printed pieces per unit, but offer two distinct advantages. First they can be cost-effective to produce high-quality, four-color work in small quantities, unlike commercial printers. Second, and most important to the direct mail marketer, digital printing allows for personalization. Each piece can include the same message and same image, and also the recipient's name printed in the body copy or body copy that discusses a certain aspect of the site that might appeal to a particular recipient.

Consider the two following bodies of copy directed to a recipient named Julie Smith. You know through market research interviews that she is an avid cooking fan, spends a lot of time in her kitchen, and often likes to have guests over for large dinner parties:

> *"Dear Cooking Lover:*
> *We know you like to cook. E-Cookware.com is the one-stop shop on*
> *the Web for every appliance and ingredient that you need. Let us help*
> *you prepare that special meal for your family or Saturday night's party*
> *with our wide array of stainless steel utensils, cookbooks, and more, all at*
> *15 percent off at E-Cookware.com."*

or

> *"Dear Julie,*
> *For the best dinner party, you need the best utensils! E-Cookware.com has*
> *everything for the next time you're entertaining. We're the one-stop shop on*
> *the Web for every appliance and ingredient that you need. So, Julie, let us*
> *help you prepare that special meal with an exciting 15 percent off every-*
> *thing at E-Cookware.com, especially for entertaining enthusiasts!"*

Both pieces say essentially the same thing, but the second option is more personal, using the person's name and her particular fondness for dinner parties to speak to her on a one-to-one level. Digital printing makes that personalization possible.

Number of Recipients   The number of people to receive a direct mail campaign is affected by your budget and your audience. A Web site that sells small items such as electronics and that is meant to appeal to the general public needs to reach a large audience. In contrast, a Web site that generates revenue by selling personalized investment advice to C-level executives (CEO, COO, CFO, and so on) has a much smaller audience.

The number of recipients affects the cost of the mail list, the cost of the printing (more recipients means more pieces to print), the cost of administrative work to label and mail all the pieces, and the cost of postage.

Number of Pieces in the Campaign   A direct mail campaign that uses multiple pieces sent over a pre-set number of weeks has a higher likelihood of audience penetration than a single, one-time attempt. Multiple pieces help increase the percentage of people who actually read the pieces and also help increase the brand penetration among those who do not read it, but who glance at it as they throw it out.

Additionally, you can use unusual mailings—not just brochures or letters—in your direct mail campaigns to get a point across. In one particularly well-executed campaign, direct response marketing expert GWJ executed an effort for Bell Labs in 1999. The campaign was targeted to C-level executives of Fortune 1000 companies and highlighted Bell Labs' expertise in Y2K preparation. The campaign used a dinosaur theme to warn that companies that did not take the Y2K threat seriously would end up extinct. Three separate print pieces were sent, each with a different dinosaur image, headline, and message, as well as a calendar counting down the days to Y2K. The fourth and final piece was a package containing a silk tie with an elegant dinosaur print for the male recipients and a silk scarf with a similar print for the female recipients. The result was a memorable direct mail campaign with an anchor piece that recipients weren't likely to discard. Furthermore, it created a good segue for salespeople, allowing them to call on the recipients to get their reactions. The campaign was so successful that a large number of recipients called the advertiser directly.

Variety of Pieces   The only restrictions on items that can be part of a direct mail campaign are dictated by budget and laws. Although print is the cheapest and therefore most popular item to create, other creative ideas can prove useful. CD-ROMs, and particularly the new Cyber Cards (business card-sized CD-ROMs that hold 40 MB of data), have a lot of potential for marketing Web sites. Although study results vary, it's widely accepted that people who receive a Cyber Card in the mail are more likely to play it than they are to read a direct mail printed letter, because their standard makes them a novelty.

Like the Web sites they are marketing, CD-ROMs and Cyber Cards are dynamic. You can include a guided tour of your product or company, complete with narration and music, on a CD. You can also provide e-mail links and launch a direct connection to the site itself.

Although direct mail's rate of return may be unhappily low, it is a good branding tool, and, done right, can go a long way toward keeping a Web site or brand on the mind of an audience.

Television and Radio

The most dynamic of standard advertising vehicles—television and radio—give the advertiser a specific amount of time to tell a story. Unlike other, two-dimensional advertising techniques, TV and radio can play on the audience's emotions by using vocal inflections, and, in the case of television, facial expression and body language. Lighting, sound effects, and setting also play a big part in conveying an idea to an audience.

Campbell's Soup ran a television ad that opened with a social worker and a foster child standing on a porch, ringing a doorbell on a dreary day. The social worker looked down at the child, and asked, "Are you ready to meet your new mommy?" The girl, tightly clutching her teddy bear, looked away. Even after meeting her foster mother, the child remained silent. Trying to make the little girl happy, the disheartened woman made the girl a bowl of Campbell's soup and brought it to her in the girl's new room. The girl sipped it, and, as the sad-looking foster mother turned to leave, said softly, "My mommy used to make me this soup." The foster mother turned around with an understanding smile and said, "So did mine."

How many people's eyes welled up at each repetition of this commercial? Plenty. Campbell's used the campaign to forge an amazing brand message for its soup: warmth, family, bonding, and memories. Everything from the acting to the set to the situation played a part in reinforcing a brand identity in a way that no other vehicle could possibly accomplish.

Web efforts to take advantage of television have largely avoided emotional or subtle approaches, going for laughs and just plain weirdness. Television and radio can be powerful media, but they are not effective if the concept behind the ad is weak and has little to do with the Web site being advertised.

The Super Bowl George Orwell's *1984* is known as one of the best anti-utopian novels ever written. It was also the title and premise of what is commonly considered to be the best television commercial ever to air. A 60-second piece to introduce Apple Computer's Macintosh, the commercial featured a downtrodden society of colorless, lifeless people, ruled by Big Brother. Although appearing to be a friend to the people, Big Brother was an oppressive dictator out for power and limitless control. The ad implied that Big Brother was a representation of IBM, the leading computer maker at the time. The hero of the ad maintained hidden journal entries in hopes of one day joining a fabled underground rebellion. The computer he used in hiding was the Apple Macintosh, with its blue tinted screen gleaming brightly against the dreary backdrop of the anti-utopian society.

Although it aired only one time, that particular commercial left two distinct marks. It created tremendous appeal for the Macintosh, making the computer a household name almost overnight. The ad also established the Super Bowl as the preeminent advertising vehicle on television. Advertising producers began to view the Super Bowl as a canvas upon which to create some of advertising's most unique and memorable spots and campaigns.

The Super Bowl has become more than just a simple football game. It consistently draws the largest television viewing audience each year, with audiences tuning in from all over the globe, according to Nielsen Media Research. Many people, in fact, tune into the game as much for the advertisements as for the game itself. A huge range of ads, including the likes of the Bud Bowl and Ray Charles and the Diet Pepsi Girls (who later toured in concert, thanks to popularity they gained from their Super Bowl ads), have appeared during the Super Bowl, and many have gone down in the annals of advertising greatness.

While the Super Bowl is full of surprises, nothing in advertising raised more eyebrows than Super Bowl XXXIV, which was played in 2000. Instead of the standard advertisers that the world had come to expect, the field was dominated by newcomers: pure-coms were all over the game, from sponsorships to 30-second commercials. At over $2 million per spot, the New Economy players were using television's greatest advertising vehicle to solidify themselves, legitimizing the Web as the next great communications medium. In a way, Web sites' ads seemed to be confirming media reports about the gluttony and power of the Web while simultaneously attempting to convince viewers that investing in Web sites was good business. Of course, that was hardly what happened. By the next Super Bowl, only two pure-coms, **Monster.com** and **E-Trade**, were buying commercial time during the game. More alarmingly, of the 13 sites that laid out big money purchases for Super Bowl XXXIV, only five were in business a year later, and three of those were running out of money fast.

The Super Bowl remains television's ultimate advertising venue. Companies who thought that recreating Apple's original Macintosh magic was as simple as making a 30-second, $2 million purchase learned a hard lesson. The lesson was a reaffirmation of brand importance for companies and Web sites looking to survive in the long term. Traditional marketers have long relied on their affiliation with the Super Bowl to build on their brands, to launch a product or company, or to continue a specific campaign. However, neither television nor the mighty Super Bowl alone are enough to establish an entire brand.

Outdoor Advertising

Outdoor advertising encompasses billboards, the sides of buses, train platforms, the backs of park benches, and similar types of fixed locations. The advantages of outdoor advertising include its broad exposure to a captive audience (anyone sitting in traffic will check out your ad as a distraction) and its relative cost-effectiveness compared with print and television. However, outdoor advertising is not targeted.

Standard Online Marketing Approaches

Although Web sites use traditional methods such as those we have reviewed in integrated, conceptual campaigns to attract visitors, sites may also use other Web sites to help in that effort. Chapter 4 covered a number of methods of online advertising, including banner advertising, interstitial ads, embedded ads that appear within the body of text on a site, and pop-up windows that appear in front of or behind the browser window. Web advertising is a source of revenue for some sites that sell space on their pages, but for other sites and marketers, the Web offers one more way to get a message across to an audience.

Web ads need to maintain a look, feel, and concept consistent with the overall campaign if they are part of an integrated marketing effort. At the end of 2001, right before the Christmas shopping season, **adiamondisforever.com** ran an aggressive ad campaign that involved television, print, and Web advertising. The design of each ad remained consistent, featuring diamond rings displayed against a deep black background, and the message was about falling in love all over again. The Web ads, done mostly in Flash, added a bit of dynamics, with a small magnifying glass image floating across the Web page and landing on the image of a diamond ring in the banner ad. All ads invited the user to visit adiamondisforever.com and to create the perfect ring.

Banner ads can be a powerful component in a campaign, as you will see in this section. In addition, the Internet offers other valuable means of promotion beyond advertising, with permission-based e-mail marketing being foremost among the alternative methods.

Banner Ads

Banner ads have begun to push the limits of what they can do and how they can appear on a page. In fact, ads have begun to take up more space within the browser, possibly testing the limits of viewer irritation. An embedded ad that debuted for MSN.com in 2001, for example, displayed the MSN logo within a large box. The MSN multicolored butterfly grew within the box, continually flapping its wings. When it reached a certain size, the butterfly left the confines of the box and flew around the screen, obscuring the page content. If the viewer tried to click anywhere within the page while the butterfly was flying, the butterfly would fly in front of the cursor, and the viewer would be taken to MSN.com instead of to the page he or she actually wanted to visit.

Time will tell how far, how large, and how intrusive ads can get before users get fed up and abandon the sites on which the offensive ads appear. In 2001, a survey[1] showed that most Web users were dealing with the ads and understood that the ads, although intrusive and annoying, were an acceptable tradeoff for free content.

Web ads don't have to be annoying to be effective. Flash technology can build a site within an ad, allowing buttons and e-mail links to be included within the body of the ad. They also can offer a fair amount of interactivity, such as the clever ad for Absolut vodka, in which a bottle of Absolut, standing alone as it does in its print ads, is seen wrapped in an orange peel. When a viewer dragged his or her cursor over the ad, the cursor became a peeler, and as the cursor was dragged over the bottle, the peel was removed to unmask the bottle underneath. The tag line "Absolut Citrus" appeared under the bottle.

Other forms of interactivity can help ads lead audiences to the places within the advertisers' sites that will most likely appeal to the audience. For example, a standard banner ad for an online bank could promote lower mortgage rates with a link to the bank's home page. A more effective version of that ad could allow the user to enter his or her current payment data and other variables directly into the ad. Then, a link to a calculations page within the bank's site would show how much money the visitor could save by refinancing through the advertised bank.

The Web offers significant opportunity to create interactivity and personalization in ways that no other medium could even hope for. The characteristics "bigger and more annoying" can give way to "clever and targeted."

Permission-Based E-Mail Marketing

Permission-based marketing is the cyber version of direct mail marketing. Among the many differences, though, is the claim by e-mail marketers that the response to e-mail efforts exceeds 17 percent—a significant increase over direct mail's average 1.5 percent rate of return. Whether this figure is legitimate is too early to tell. For the time being, it seems that permission-based e-mail marketing is showing some real promise. One of the reasons that it has a higher rate of return is that, unlike traditional direct mail and random e-mail marketing (called *spam*), permission-based e-mail marketing has a valuable

[1] Source: *Adweek*, October 12, 2001.

new component: permission. In other words, the recipient of the e-mail advertisement has told the marketer that it's okay to solicit him or her through e-mail. In fact, in some cases, customers have requested that e-mail updates and marketing information be sent to them.

How is the permission received? This is one of the areas for debate in terms of success rate. When people visit a Web site, make a purchase, obtain a subscription, or in some other way complete an online form, Web pages often include some text toward the bottom of the form that says "Would you like to receive updates and announcements about our site by e-mail?" or something similar. This text is followed by two option buttons, marked "Yes" and "No." People who click the "Yes" button have granted the Web site permission to send them regular solicitations by e-mail. However, in most cases, the default for the option buttons is for the "Yes" button to be selected automatically. If you don't switch the button setting to off, you give the site your permission to send you information. Many people inadvertently grant permission to send e-mail solicitations simply because they didn't read the form carefully.

The law requires that all e-mail solicitations also include a viable return address that allows the recipient to request that his or her name be removed from the marketer's e-mail list. In 2001, a precedent-setting court ruling awarded a judgment in the amount of $34 to a woman who sued an e-mail marketer because after she requested to be removed from its e-mail list, the company sent her an e-mail to confirm her request to be removed, and included an advertisement along with it.

Many permission-givers genuinely want to receive e-mail advertising, making permission-based e-mail a great opportunity for the marketer to reach out to interested clients. Although this approach is more effective for retention-based efforts than for new client conversion efforts, it is just as important, and is often far easier and more cost efficient than trying to reach those same recipients using print or direct mail methods.

One of the best parts about most permission-based e-mail marketing programs is that they can be extremely targeted. The original form that the user filled out to grant permission typically includes optional demographic and psychographic survey questions. Sites want such information to help keep track of who their audiences are and whether those audiences are changing in their description, needs, or wants.

Most people will skip over a form survey unless there is some enticement offered for completing it. A Web site usually offers something worthwhile, like free shipping on the customer's next order or 10 percent off a purchase, in return for completing the survey.

The questions vary depending on the type of information that the marketer seeks. Customer age, gender, income, marital status, and other facts are among the most common things marketers want to know. Other highly sought information includes data about visitors' careers, interests (such as sports, traveling, or boating), types of magazines that they read, TV shows that they watch, and so on. The marketer then can compile these facts into a database and use this information to run specific e-mail campaigns directed toward groups of people who fall into similar demographic and psychographic categories. Databases allow for a relatively easy distribution of personalized e-mails to a very large number of recipients.

The e-mail messages vary in design and message depending on the demographic groups marketers are trying to reach. Unlike plain text e-mails that you might receive from friends or coworkers, most e-mail marketing efforts are more dynamically designed, with graphic headlines and other features. The example shown in Figure 10-6 shows that permission-based e-mails can look more like a flyer than a standard e-mail.

Figure 10-6   An example of a well-designed permission-based e-mail marketing effort

Finally, a great benefit to the e-mail marketer is the ease with which the campaign can be tracked. Each e-mail marketing effort usually includes plenty of links to the marketer's Web site. Because of advancements in technology, marketers can easily track how many people—and which people in particular—have responded to any given e-mail in a campaign. Appendix A briefly discusses the technologies that make this possible.

Viral Marketing

Gaining momentum in the early part of the century, **viral marketing** (marketing that is done when a message is funny, unique, or outstanding enough that one recipient feels compelled to pass the message on to others) is growing in desirability among marketers.

As elusive as it is popular, in viral marketing, customers or the public do the bulk of marketing work by spreading news and information to each other. In addition to having the advantage of word-of-mouth buzz, viral marketing is inexpensive—it does not require purchasing ad space. Getting the general public to do your marketing for you isn't all that easy. However, if it works, viral marketing can be a huge brand builder and traffic driver for a Web site or for a traditional marketer.

Perhaps the best example of a viral marketing campaign wasn't expected to become so popular. In a Budweiser beer television ad that took the marketing world by storm, a few guys simply yelled "What's up?" to each other in person and over the telephone. The ad became an instant cultural icon. Kids were imitating the guys in the ad at schools, concerts, sporting events, and any other place where they were with their friends. The "What's up?" craze hit the Web in a big way. Creative people took the audio track from the commercial and placed it over short clips from other media sources, such as old cartoons and even news clips of the 2000 FBI seizure of Elian Gonzales. This video was manipulated to show characters mouthing "What's up?" The resulting spoofs were often very funny. The makers of the short clips sent them to their friends, each of whom sent them to several of their friends, and so on. Eventually, it seemed that everybody with an e-mail address had seen at least one version of the takeoff, and Budweiser's brand went infinitely further than its original media buy ever could have. Most of the people who created and originally passed on the Web clips of the "What's up?" ads did so on their own just for fun. The viral marketing addition to Budweiser's television campaign was an unintentional bonus for the brand.

10

Unfortunately, viral marketing is not practiced only by advertisers or hobbyists with genuine senses of humor. Other forms of viral marketing that existed long before the Web have found new life in e-mail. Chain letters are a common occurrence on the Web. The subjects of such letters range from being simply ridiculous ("Send this letter to at least 10 people you know within the next three days or you'll have bad luck for the rest of your life") to being in poor taste ("A young boy is dying of cancer and his last wish is to break the world's record for the highest number of e-mails received—please send this letter to everyone you know and help make his wish come true"). These are nothing new. Such efforts made the rounds years ago by way of U.S. mail. Urban legends, rumors, and petitions to get local or federal laws changed also are common viral forms. (The fact that you need actual written signatures and not just e-mailed names in order to validate a petition doesn't seem to matter much to the petition originators, nor to those who sign them and pass them on.)

Whatever the purpose, the power of digital word-of-mouth has not been lost on marketers, who try to create messages in such a way that recipients will want to pass them along to others. Unfortunately, this is a very hard thing to accomplish on purpose. Once in a while something is funny enough, surprising enough, or entertaining enough to capture someone's attention. If the interested party sends it to a bunch of friends, the cycle begins.

Viral marketing isn't limited to the Web and e-mail. Beer brands have been known to "plant" customers at a bar to promote a particular brand of beer. The two will order their beers and sit next to other bar patrons and engage them in conversation or discuss between themselves (within earshot of legitimate customers) the outstanding qualities of that particular brand. Of course, they'll do so in such a way that they won't make it obvious that they are anything other than customers themselves. The idea is to convince bar patrons to try a particular brand by making it seem that others around them are doing so.

Other forms of viral marketing also exist, but they don't rely on humor as much as the "What's up?" example does. The quid pro quo method works in theory, although in practice, it has had mixed results. This oft-tried method encourages visitors to a Web site to spread the word by providing the Web site with e-mail addresses of acquaintances that the site could contact in exchange for some reward to the original visitor. Another version provides visitors with incentives to get friends and family to visit the site on their own. In return for the data, the site usually offers free shipping, free products, or some other motivation for the visitor.

Does this sound familiar? It should. This type of viral marketing has been used by traditional companies for years. Chances are that you've received an offer from Columbia House to buy 12 CDs for a penny (as long as you promise to buy seven more at regular prices). For every friend you get to sign up as a member, you receive four more free CDs. Get a friend to sign up with AOL, and get a free month of service. These are examples of viral marketing. The viral marketing method is widely used and is sometimes known by the names *commission* or *pyramid scheme*. The challenge of viral marketing falls on the shoulders of the marketers, who need to create a message that people find interesting enough to spread.

Guerrilla Marketing

The fact that the public is inundated with advertisements makes it much more difficult for marketers to get their message through to their audiences. How often do you actually take the time to read an ad that appears in a magazine compared to the amount of times that you just turn the page to get past the ad? Even worse for marketers is the speed with which most people throw out direct mail advertisements. Marketer's messages are everywhere, and so it's often necessary to be more creative or more aggressive when it comes to getting the message across. The term **guerrilla marketing** describes marketing tactics that are aggressive and "in your face." People standing on street corners and passing leaflets to anyone who passes by are engaging in guerrilla marketing methods. So are people who walk around parking lots at malls or concerts putting business cards and flyers under windshield wipers or who slide menus, coupons, and other ads under doors of dormitories or apartments.

With pressure on marketers to gain exposure among a glut of Web start-ups, pure-coms paved the way for even more innovative means of guerrilla marketing. Car wraps became a popular fad in the late 1990s, and have not entirely faded away. A car wrap provides a motorist (anyone with a legal driver's license may apply) with a free car to drive for a specified length of time. Typically the applicant has to prove he or she spends significant time driving on crowded highways or city streets, and not through quiet rural towns. The catch is that the car is wrapped completely in advertising for the Web site that is running the campaign. As it makes its way around town, the car becomes a moving billboard for anyone around to see, as shown in Figure 10-7.

Figure 10-7   A car wrap that promotes Go.com

The biggest benefit of guerrilla marketing is that it reaches people and that it is fairly inexpensive to do. Having flyers or coupon books handed out on a street corner usually doesn't cost more than minimum wage plus the costs for the flyer. In addition, like direct marketing, people are forced to interact with guerilla marketing efforts—even if only to throw it out or pass it on the highway. The downside of guerrilla marketing is that it is almost completely untargeted. There is no guarantee that much of your target market will be among those who see or receive your message. Similarly, a relatively small audience will be reached with each effort. If you have 1000 flyers to hand out, you're only reaching 1000 people, plus the few that find the flyers on the ground after the original recipients throw them away. Nevertheless, for a site that needs to get a message out quickly and inexpensively, guerrilla marketing can play a significant role in a campaign.

CHAPTER SUMMARY

- The best site on the Web is useless unless people know it's there. Marketers have an open canvas to attract attention to a Web site, with virtually no limit on how to send a message to their audiences. However, as we have seen in this and earlier chapters, brand development is an important part of long-term success. What the marketers tell their audiences needs to be tempered with how new the brand is and how familiar the audience is with what the company does.

- Campaigns that integrate several marketing methods to help build awareness around a brand have four main components. The message/purpose is what the marketer wants to tell the audience. The theme/concept is the unique way the marketer chooses to relay that message. The concept then remains consistent throughout all of the media used, whenever possible. The time frame is the expected amount of time that the campaign will run, and the media are the outlets that are used to convey the message.

❏ Traditional marketing venues include print, direct mail, television, outdoor, and radio. These methods can be demographically targeted and typically incorporate a concept to play off the audience's emotions. Unlike conceptual approaches, direct approaches are factual and straightforward statements. Online approaches use banner ads, permission-based e-mail, viral marketing, and guerilla marketing. Integrated marketers use more than one of these media simultaneously to reach their market from a number of different approaches, and they use the strengths of different methods to achieve a more complete branding effect.

❏ Conceptual, integrated marketing campaigns work to bring a developed message to the market and to put your URL in front of people's eyes, while at the same time, they help to build the brand. The tricky part is finding the right message to send, and then finding the best way to send it.

KEY TERMS

advertising

campaign

conceptual approach

digital printing

direct approach

direct mail

guerrilla marketing

integrated marketing

mail list

marketing

permission-based marketing

print

public relations

viral marketing

REVIEW QUESTIONS

1. _____ is the best example of an integrated marketing campaign.

    a. A print ad campaign that spans three different types of magazines over a period of two months

    b. A two-piece direct mail campaign that follows a series of regional television and radio spots

    c. Six weeks worth of banner ads on Yahoo!, Excite, and MSN along with the distribution of a monthly e-mail newsletter

    d. A man in a monkey suit standing in front of a crowded theater, handing out flyers

2. Describe the difference between a marketing message and the marketing concept within a campaign.

3. Media outlets are chosen primarily based on _____.

   a. budgetary constraints and demographics

   b. space/time availability

   c. budgetary constraints and creative theme

   d. brand promise and USP

4. A new Web site that does not have an established brand name would be wise to _____.

   a. spend a small portion of the budget on television commercials, and spend the lion's share of funding on Web banner advertising

   b. spend its money on print advertising and direct mail until most funding has been spent

   c. spend its money on infrastructure and internal innovations with less expensive initial marketing efforts, saving some cash for later when the brand is more established

   d. not spend any money on marketing, allowing viral marketing to drive traffic

5. A campaign's time frame should _____.

   a. not exceed six months

   b. last as long as the ad is effective

   c. be reassessed on a regular basis

   d. Both B and C

6. The Super Bowl has long been the best television advertising outlet for growth because _____.

   a. the NFC always wins

   b. it traditionally gets more viewers than any other broadcast

   c. the prices for a 30-second spot are among the most affordable on television

   d. sports advertising has always been effective

7. The main reason that many TV commercials for pure-com Web sites failed is that they _____.

   a. cost too much money to run a long, memorable campaign

   b. didn't carry a relevant message

   c. had no follow-up print advertising

   d. weren't memorable

10

8. A funny Flash movie that gets sent around the Web by e-mail is an example of
   _____.

   a. permission-based e-mail marketing

   b. direct mail marketing

   c. viral marketing

   d. branding

9. One advantage of running a direct mail campaign through a digital press is that
   _____.

   a. it's cheaper per unit printed

   b. it can be tracked so that the marketer knows which recipient has responded

   c. it's the best way to produce over 5000 units

   d. each piece can be personalized to the recipient

10. In an integrated marketing campaign, it is important that the _____
    stay(s) consistent.

    a. vehicles for delivering the message

    b. message being delivered

    c. follow-up efforts

    d tracking techniques for success analysis

11. _____ is the best example of guerilla marketing.

    a. Billboards at a sports stadium that are seen by the live audience and the TV audience

    b. A company logo appearing on the side of a race car at the Indy 500

    c. Advertising that appears on the placemat of a local deli

    d. A person standing on a street corner handing out coupons to a local shoe store

12. Give three reasons why viral marketing can be a huge success.

13. Permission-based e-mail marketing can be effective mostly because
    _____.

    a. recipients have requested to receive information from your company and/or Web site

    b. e-mail is the cyber version of traditional direct mail, which has been proven to be the most effective form of advertising

    c. users are likely to pass along e-mail messages to friends, turning the e-mail into a viral marketing campaign

    d. it is quicker to develop an e-mail advertisement than a print advertisement

14. Describe why it is important to set budget and time restraints in an integrated marketing campaign.

HANDS-ON PROJECTS

1. Sit down with the business partners for the site you are developing. Considering the demographic profile of the target market you are trying to reach, create a marketing/advertising plan and detail the following in your business plan:

   a. Develop the message of your campaign. What is it that you will be trying to tell your audience?

   b. Create a campaign that uses conceptual methods of relaying your message. Describe the concept that you will create, and why you chose that concept.

   c. Which media outlets will you use? Find out the demographics of various media outlets.

   d. Describe what other marketing techniques you would use to promote your Web site.

   e. If possible, talk to advertising agencies, local advertisers, or media outlets to determine the approximate cost of launching your marketing strategy.

2. Find two Web companies that advertised during Super Bowl XXXIV and that are no longer in business. You may find their campaigns on the Web, at the *Adweek* (**www.adweek.com**) or *Brandweek* (**www.brandweek.com**) Web sites, or by calling the Museum of Television and Radio in New York (212-621-6600). Answer the following questions for each site.

   a. What kind of message did the site try to send, and how would you describe the concept used to send that message?

   b. Was the campaign successful in sending its message? Don't immediately assume that the answer is "no" just because the company is no longer in business—companies do not live and die by their advertising efforts alone. A successful ad campaign that drives significant traffic to a Web site can't help other internal or funding problems that the company might be experiencing. Explain why you think the campaign was successful or not.

   c. Watch TV and find a current commercial for a Web site. How does the message and method used differ from the Super Bowl ads that you reviewed? How has the demise of many sites contributed to the advertising concepts being used by today's Web sites?

10

3. Viral marketing is marketing in which the word is spread from one person to another. The success of a viral marketing campaign relies on the message or the way the message is presented. Maybe even without realizing it, you have received and even passed along a viral marketing campaign.

a. Describe three Web-based viral marketing campaigns that you have seen and that you thought were successful. A successful effort will be one that not only caught your attention, but also that you passed along to someone else. Explain why you thought the effort was successful.

b. Describe three other Web-based viral marketing campaigns that you did not find to be successful. Explain why you did not feel compelled to pass the marketing campaign along to others.

11

MORE ON MARKETING: PR AND NONTRADITIONAL PROMOTIONS

> **In this chapter, you will learn about:**
> ♦ The basic concepts behind PR
> ♦ Practicing PR online
> ♦ Working with the news media
> ♦ 14 tips for practicing PR
> ♦ Nontraditional marketing methods

In Chapter 10, you learned about marketing and advertising and how they complement each other and can help drive traffic to a Web site. Public relations (PR) is another promotional method that conveys a specific message to a specific audience.

To some, PR is the most important and most effective means of marketing—and the most complex. Unlike any other type of marketing, PR has the least concrete results. Successful PR takes a combination of experience, writing skills, knowledge of human nature, and an understanding of working with the news media. Marketers often use traditional PR and advertising methods in conjunction with nontraditional approaches to publicize a product, company, or Web site. This chapter describes PR, how to practice PR using the Web, and what the PR professional needs to know to succeed. You will also learn about nontraditional marketing approaches.

PR OVERVIEW

As you learned in previous chapters, PR is a set of actions taken to persuade or improve the general public's ideas, opinions, or attitude regarding a particular individual, organization, product, company, or Web site. In many cases, PR is executed through the manufacturing of news. By having a story reported through the media, or through editorial coverage, a company's message becomes news, not advertising. This kind of third-party reporting is seen as unbiased and is more meaningful to customers than messages delivered through advertising.

PR Basics

A large percentage of the news you read or see is generated through the efforts of PR personnel. When you hear about a new Microsoft product upgrade, the latest Madonna CD, or even that your city's mayor is running for re-election, chances are that the information began its life as a PR objective.

The primary functions of PR include arranging for special events (including parties and product launches), making news announcements in the form of news releases (including the distribution of background video and photography), and facilitating interviews, news conferences, trade shows, and seminar appearances. In addition to spreading good news, PR professionals must be prepared to respond to negative events, such as product liability issues and accidents. The management of bad publicity is called **damage control**. This chapter, however, focuses on what to do to get your company positive coverage. Recall that PR is often handled by a PR specialist within a marketing or creative firm. Many companies also have their own internal PR departments.

The following scenario provides an overview of the kind of activities that PR encompasses. Say you run a Web site called WebSearch.com. WebSearch.com is a pure-com that has developed a new way of allowing people to search the Web. Using a graphical interface, users can come to your site, type in specific keywords, and be presented with a 3-D rendering of page icons along a time line. The time line shows the user the subject of each area of information and the time at which it was last updated. This is a revolutionary way of searching for information, and you have high hopes of changing the Web!

You want the world to know about WebSearch.com, but where do you start? You need to get news of the site out to the public so that people will know it exists and will come to see for themselves how amazing the new technology is. Sure, you could buy some banner ad space, but you're only reaching the tip of the iceberg that way. You'd be better off using PR professionals to produce a full-featured campaign.

To get the word out, WebSearch.com hires a marketing/PR agency to publicize the site. Your agency's first step is to arrange a party to unveil the Web site. Invitees include many prominent magazine and newspaper editors, as well as reporters for publications, television programs, and radio shows that deal with technology, business, the Web, entrepreneurship, and related topics. Prominent businesspeople, friends, family, investors, and other interested parties also are invited. The party invitation includes an announcement, called a news release, explaining that a new, earth-shattering technology is to be introduced. The party features a band, food, drinks, and a speech from your company's president and CEO, all of which are planned by your agency. The agency also is responsible for choosing the event location, writing the speeches, setting the event agenda, and making all other preparations. The agency's most difficult task is to ensure that the media representatives, who have invitations to at least a half dozen other events for the same night, make it to your event.

After the party, which goes flawlessly, much of the media in attendance are impressed enough with the site that they write or air stories about it. Some publications make only small mentions of the site, whereas others run feature-length stories about it. In addition, many broadcasters air segments about the site. Your president and CEO receives many requests for interviews. The interviews go smoothly because the agency prepares him for such appearances.

After the WebSearch.com launch party, the agency continues to keep the name of the site in the public eye by writing news releases about the site on a regular basis, whenever your company has newsworthy information to report. For example, one week your site might experience record-breaking traffic. Another week, a news release alerts the media that a new chief financial officer has been hired. Some media outlets ignore the releases, but others find them interesting and write stories, columns, or mentions about the site, its employees, or the technology.

11

Along with the news releases, the agency drums up public interest by sending WebSearch.com's CEO and president, as well as other designated representatives, on an aggressive seminar tour. These tours allow the site executives to talk directly to the public about how the site will change the way the world browses the Web. Of course, the media are invited to attend and cover each seminar as well.

Over the course of a few months, a reasonable number of magazines show interest in the site and give WebSearch.com coverage in their pages. Exposure changes from month to month, but overall, the effort works: the WebSearch.com name seems always to be in the news and in front of surfers' faces.

And then it happens. Your company is hit with a lawsuit from an independent programmer who says that WebSearch.com stole his code and that he was the original genius behind the technology. According to his story, he presented the idea for the search engine to WebSearch.com many months ago, and the company rejected his ideas. Now he wants $10,000,000 in damages.

The media, of course, love it. The same reporters who praised the site and wrote stories about its innovations are equally eager to report the lawsuit. Now your agency really has its hands full—not in sending out news releases, but in doing damage control.

The WebSearch.com anecdote illustrates the basic aspects of PR. In reality, PR can consume seemingly endless time, energy, and dollars, with results that are nearly impossible to measure. Despite the intangibility of PR results, it does work.

Why PR Works

As the previous scenario illustrates, PR is a behind-the-scenes way to influence public opinion. The biggest benefit of PR is that a marketer's message seems to come from neutral sources. Advertising is direct and not subtle; a print ad for a Web site that says the site is great works only if it promises something that the reader already needs or wants. Audiences know that advertising claims are biased—if not exaggerated—because the messages come directly from the marketer. Furthermore, superlative claims of being "the best" fall on deaf ears—we've heard it all before.

In comparison, statements that proclaim a site to be great or a product to be useful are far more believable if they come from an impartial news source. If you are reading an article on Web sites that offer the widest selection of products, and a certain Web site is mentioned or featured, you're more likely to take note. The Web site didn't pay for that mention. Rather, an editor knowledgeable on the subject deemed it newsworthy, and the praise therefore is seen as unbiased and more believable. The believability factor is one reason that aggressive PR campaigns are a popular marketing method.

Wide exposure is another reason that companies use PR. One event or news release may be covered by any number of media outlets—far more than might be financially possible in which to advertise.

For example, a news release announcing the launch of a Web site for music downloads might be picked up by *Billboard*, *Rolling Stone*, *Spin*, *ZDTV*, *Good Morning America*, and other smaller publications and shows. Although some of the mentions may be relatively small (sometimes only a line or two in a "New and Noteworthy" feature), the minimal effort of writing and sending the release has resulted in wide exposure to a large audience. To buy advertising space and time in all the media outlets that carried the story would break the bank. PR, for this reason, is often referred to as "free advertising."

Although the news mentions may be brief, they take advantage of the association with the brand reputation of the media source. If readers believe *Rolling Stone* is a credible source of music news (based on the brand it has built) and a *Rolling Stone* writer discusses a new music site in a positive way, the reader believes that the site must be good.

Because of the potential for wider exposure and increased credibility from third-party sources, PR is a strong weapon in brand building. When integrated with advertising and other marketing tactics, PR has the potential to create a stronger relationship between the Web site and the consumer. This relationship enhancement occurs because the benefits of the site and the value to the user are relayed from a supposedly unbiased source, rather than from the company itself. As you learned earlier, a brand is a promise, and building a successful brand involves fulfilling that promise, which translates into your reputation. Advertising alone can tell the audience what the promise is, but an editorial mention about how that promise is being fulfilled helps build and pass along the reputation.

PR Challenges

What makes PR more difficult than other types of marketing is the fact that it is relationship based. In comparison, buying media for a print ad campaign is a strictly financial deal. You pick up the phone, negotiate a price for space, send the publication the ad materials, and mail a check. It's up to you where to place the ads; it's a one-sided process.

PR differs from advertising in that the PR agency writes the news release and sends it to the desired media outlets. The release then sits on the editor's desk, among countless other news releases that also claim to contain newsworthy information. The editor obviously can't print or write about everything, so he or she must choose the stories that are the most interesting or would be most appealing to his or her audience. For all the work that an agency might do to write and send the release, the ultimate decision for exposure lies in the hands of someone completely unassociated with the agency or the company that is the subject of the news. The fact that the editor is a stranger to the PR representative makes PR daunting. Later in this chapter, you will learn about ways in which PR agents effectively work with the media.

Working with Media

Although technology advancements provide more tools and opportunities for practicing PR, the basic principles have not changed. PR still needs to be handled with sensitivity, because the human relationship between the PR agent and the editor can mean the difference between getting exposure and not getting exposure. The person who sells advertising for a magazine will likely take your money for the space, regardless of how you approach the subject of buying it. The editor is not going to give up his or her editorial space so easily.

Before we discuss some of the intricacies of running a PR campaign and working with the media, we first should look at the reality behind what is often a taboo topic. Some might argue that PR isn't really free advertising—editors can and do cover whatever they want in their space. Editors and news outlets do not get paid to respond favorably to a news release.

However, the way the news industry works is more complex than it seems. Traditionally, major news media such as the *New York Times*, *Forbes* magazine, the *Today* show, and others of that caliber really do make a clear distinction between news and advertising. The big-name media outlets aren't your only resources for PR, though. In fact, it's more likely that smaller, niche publications or industry magazines comprise more of your target PR audience than do the big names. You will find that with many of these smaller publications, the line between news and advertising becomes blurry.

You will never be told, "Buy advertising space from us, or we won't run your story." However, if a company or a Web site is spending ad dollars in a specific publication, that's going to be the first publication that a PR agency will look to for coverage when it is commencing a PR campaign. The implication is this: "We spend a lot of money in your

11

publication, so we'd appreciate some editorial coverage." Of course, it works the other way as well. A news release that is sent to a certain publication might be followed up by a phone call from an advertising sales representative from that publication, wondering if you'd be interested in buying ad space at some point in the near future. The implications are strong.

This does not mean that all PR is generated by ad dollars. Generally speaking, releases of valid and interesting news are picked up regardless of whether the company advertises. Still, it's important to be aware that the quid pro quo scenario exists in the real world of marketing.

Making Your News Stand Out

As mentioned earlier, every news release that is sent to an editor competes for that editor's attention, along with dozens of others that land on his or her desk every day. The first ones that an editor considers are those that are written correctly, have a purpose, and are of interest given that editor's position, audience, and area of coverage. The following sections explain how to shape and perfect your announcements for maximum effectiveness.

The News Release

Arguably the most important tool in a PR person's repertoire is the **news release**. This announcement of news is both a flag to editors—as in, "Hey, XYZ Company has news! Please cover us!"—and a statement of the news. A news release is brief—a few paragraphs should do it—and presents the facts in a clear, organized fashion. Be sure to include the five W's: Who, What, Where, When, and Why. Avoid hype or jargon—editors will see it for what it is. Include pertinent details, such as that your site logged a 60 percent traffic gain in one month, and be able to prove your facts. Include contact information, including your PR representative's name, telephone number, e-mail address, and fax number.

When putting together a news release, be sure it is customized relative to its news content. News releases should never be formulaic or adapted from a template. Experienced editors quickly pick out templated news releases and typically avoid them. The release should provide contact information so that a recipient can make a follow-up call. It should also provide a clear headline announcing the topic of the release, a brief, concise body of copy that details the news, and a boilerplate paragraph at the end of the release that gives vital information about the company.

A sample news release promoting the benefits of a Web site called CaseMatch is shown in Figure 11-1.

Notice the structure of the release: it has a headline, prominent contact information, and a release date. It is brief and straightforward—almost news-like—in its tone. A release should make its point quickly and provide all the information an editor needs.

CONTACT:
Deirdre K. Breakenridge
PFS Marketwyse™
973.812.8883
dbreakenridge@pfsmarketwyse.com
www.pfsmarketwyse.com

FOR IMMEDIATE RELEASE

LHN ROLLS OUT CASEMATCH.COM NATIONALLY - ANNOUNCES NEW CEO

KEARNY, NJ (October 1999) – Lawyers Homepage Network (LHN) announced that its patented CaseMatch service will be available to businesses and consumers in all 50 states by January 15, 2000. The site matches consumers and their case information with appropriate lawyers in a requested geographical location.

Now, with over 480,000 lawyers in its database, CaseMatch, a free service, can assist businesses or consumers anywhere in the U.S. who need legal help with anything from bankruptcies or divorce, to wills and testaments. The revolutionary e-mail technology used by CaseMatch protects the online user's anonymity until they choose to contact the attorney themselves. Finding an experienced attorney is as easy as a click of a mouse.

In preparation for the national rollout, top jobs at the company have shifted. Michael J. Custode, former head of business development and capital funding for LHN, is named new CEO. Custode was the founder and former CEO of Execu-Flow Systems in Edison, New Jersey. David Rizzo, founder of Lawyers Homepage Network and former CEO, continues as president, and will direct the sales and marketing divisions.

Custode has been elated with the initial response to CaseMatch in New Jersey, which began its online service last year. "Choosing an attorney can be very intimidating, and everyone wants a lawyer who knows how to protect and fight for their rights," he said. "We've received hundreds of e-mails from people who said that CaseMatch made the search process less painful and more productive. It saved them the time and stress of trying to find a reputable attorney on their own, and allowed them to correspond with attorneys from the privacy and safety of their own homes." He adds that there is no other service like this available on the Internet. "It's the first product that proactively seeks out clients for our lawyer members and provides a valuable service to the public. Small firms or solo practitioners couldn't ask for a better marketing tool."

For more information, consumers can visit www.casematch.com. Attorneys, law experts and support services can find more information on membership packages at www.lawyershomepage.com, or e-mail sales@lawyershomepage.com. Or, call 1-888-LAW-WEBB, ext. 50.

###

Figure 11-1   A news release for a Web site

Figure 11-2 shows a magazine article that was written based on the release.

New Jersey Law Journal

VOL. CLVIII – NO. 3 – INDEX 177   OCTOBER 18, 1999   ESTABLISHED 1878

Matching Lawyer to Client Online

Internet service lets lawyers shop themselves to the world by practice area and geography, but there are just a few caveats

By Tim O'Brien

In recent years, companies have been trying to lure lawyers via the Internet, offering everything from research, bulletin boards and legal news to networking and business opportunities. Now comes the ultimate lure: the chance to find new clients.

The latest venture is CaseMatch, a cross between a cyber-auction operation like eBay and an online dating service. It attempts to give consumers a place to shop their cases and lawyers a place to prospect, or at least be viable.

CaseMatch is the latest product of a fledgling, New Jersey-based Internet firm, Lawyers Homepage Network Inc., which hopes to use the new service to bring lawyers to their own home page.

That home page is a portal offering a smorgasbord of benefits, such as searches for experts and support services, case law databases, general postings and even job hunts.

It is also a place for vendors to sell stuff to lawyers — from legal software, phone and credit card deals to courier services, office supplies and legal books. Last week, lawyer members received e-mails offering them Xerox copier paper at a discount from an office supply company that is an LHN sponsor.

"We are the only portal in the world that provides a business-to-business opportunity for lawyers on the Web," says David Rizzo, founder and head of LHN. The home page is at *www.lawyershomepage.com*, while CaseMatch is at *www.casematch.com*.

Rizzo, a nonpracticing Massachusetts lawyer who just turned 33, explains that his company makes money primarily through advertising and its affiliations with its advertisers and sponsors. Specifically, while members get discounts on all the goods and services offered, Rizzo's company gets a cut of every sale.

However, lawyers do pay for membership if they let LHN build them a Web page. The cost ranges from $195 to $395 annually, with $150 for yearly renewals.

However, in an obvious move to avoid violating New Jersey's, and other states', attorney advertising and ethics rules, CaseMatch is free to lawyers, as it is to the lawyer-hunting public. In fact, more than 100,000 lawyers in five states — New Jersey, New York, Pennsylvania, Connecticut and Massachusetts — are in the CaseMatch database, categorized by practice area and geography.

By letting lawyers sign on for free, and by not giving any guarantee or warranty for the legal work, or even a voucher for the truthfulness of the firms' brief biographies, CaseMatch ensures that it is not a referral service. It is, according to the disclaimer of the service, the consumer who browses, contacts, negotiates and ultimately retains a lawyer, with the service not getting any portion of the fee or any per-case remuneration.

In addition, the case information given by the potential client is kept confidential, and the consumer remains anonymous until and unless he or she responds to a lawyer's response.

Israel Dubin, secretary for both committees, says he has not reviewed CaseMatch. But in general, he says, there is no violation of ethics rules if a service is simply matching the public to a lawyers' directory, if the lawyers do not pay, or split their fee and if the service does not engage in making determinations of the merits of the cases, or their likelihood of success.

In fact, he adds, a service that narrows the directory listing by state, as well as by practice areas, "gives me a comfort level" because a potential client is not being invited to contact out-of-state lawyers on a state law matter, or lawyers with no expertise in the area of their legal problem. ∎

NO NEED TO PAY TO PLAY: To avoid violating New Jersey's and other states' attorney advertising and ethics rules, CaseMatch founder David Rizzo makes his service free to lawyers and to the lawyer-hunting public.

Figure 11-2   An article that resulted from distribution of a news release

The Pitch

When you present or propose a story idea to an editor, you need a way to grab that editor's attention. This attention-getting effort is called a **pitch**. The pitch is the angle with which you present a story in a way that is meant to be of interest to the editors. Suppose, for example, that a local architectural firm recently completed a municipal building project in its community. The fact that the building went up at all may hardly be news for the local papers—a news release on the construction is not likely to get much attention. However, if the building was completed a month ahead of schedule and 10 percent below budget, you can present the building story with an angle that is a lot more interesting to an editor. The timeliness and expense savings to the municipality becomes the pitch—the draw that gets an editor interested.

Your pitch should include all the information the editor will need. The pitch should be to the point—not a lot of fluff. It should always answer the following questions:

- Why is the company or Web site you are promoting better than or different from its competitors? Or why is the update so interesting that it needs to be reported? If there is nothing unique about the site, or if the site doesn't do anything that hasn't been done before, why would a publication or program want to report on it?

- What specific trends in the industry does the site address? What services does it perform for its audience?

- Who is the target audience for the site?

- Who are the key executive personnel at the company you are pitching? What are their backgrounds relative to their positions in the company?

Know Your Contact

In addition to knowing its client company, the smart PR agent will also know some things about the editors being approached. A successful PR agent would never send a news release without first having a strong understanding of the following:

- The audience that the publication or broadcast is trying to reach. It's irresponsible to send a news release to an editor of a publication if you have never actually picked up and at least thumbed through the pages of that publication to get a feel for it. Understanding the audience also means understanding the demographics and psychographics of that audience. News outlets have media kits that provide audience information. These kits are available on request or are downloadable from the outlet's Web site.

- The type of story typically covered. There is a difference between a publication that concentrates on headline news and one that reports on more "inside scoop" topics. You should be aware of any style (for example, fun, serious, or sensational) that a news outlet uses and tailor your release accordingly.

11

- Special subject coverage. A news outlet may be planning coverage dealing specifically with the topics you are promoting. Most publications can provide you with an editorial calendar of the coming year so that you can prepare well in advance. Target your PR efforts to coincide with such coverage.

- The details of the story you are trying to report. If you do generate media interest, chances are good that the editor will contact you for details. The last thing he or she will want to hear is "Wow, that's a great question! I have no idea what the answer is, but I'll find out and get back to you."

It's important to do your homework *before* you send out the news release or try to attract the media's attention. If you make an error, the editor will remember that you wasted his or her time and will likely ignore your subsequent efforts to grab his or her attention.

Keeping Coverage Fresh

What if your company has nothing new to report? Not every company has a new development each week. Despite a lack of news, you shouldn't let the company or Web site's name stay out of the news for very long. PR agencies sometimes create news. These efforts either allow the agency to generate news releases around them or put something in the public eye so that the media will cover it on their own. **PR stunt** is a term typically used to describe such events.

Consider the Calvin Klein clothing company. Nearly every year, the company purchases a billboard in New York's Times Square and posts controversial images of beautiful young people in little more than Calvin Klein underwear. Every time Calvin Klein does this, some parents' group gets upset about it, gets a petition signed, and writes letters to the media to complain. Then, as usual, the media cover the story, flashing pictures of the offending ads on major newscasts across the nation for a couple days. After a few days, Calvin Klein inevitably removes the billboard in an act of contrition. By the time that happens, the ad has already become a PR homerun. A billboard that might have reached a few hundred thousand people out of the corner of their eye in Manhattan now has reached a few million people across the country.

Similar approaches can be less offensive or shocking. Maybe the Web site you are promoting specializes in appraising and auctioning fine art. A good PR agent might arrange with an art publisher for a book deal about how the Web has affected the fine art market to be written by the CEO or president of the Web site. The published book is now a new source of interest that can be promoted through a news release, pitched to magazines, and even discussed on local or morning television shows.

While keeping your company in the news is an important matter when building a brand and keeping your site's name in your audience's mind, be cautious of PR stunts that can backfire. A small advertising agency distributed a news release in December 2001, announcing that hackers had broken into the agency's site. Editors later learned that the agency, Nail, had invented the site, calling it Marron, Hadsell & Neilan. Figure 11-3 shows the original site on the left, and what the "vandals" did to the site on the right.

The "hackers" renamed the site Moron, Hack & Not There, and used the pages to attack and mock large ad agencies as out of touch and greedy. The site led visitors to an alternative—Nail. Papers and publications picked up on the original e-vandalism story, sending traffic to the site, before it was determined that the site had never been hacked at all. It didn't take long for the news to get out that the agency itself made the changes and faked the releases that claimed the site had been attacked. The people at Nail will have to hope that the editors who covered the story have good senses of humor: writing a news release about something that didn't really happen and tricking editors into writing articles about the non-event can be a sure-fire way to ensure that no publication will pick up on a news release from that company again.

Before   After

Figure 11-3   The "hacking" of this Web site was the subject of a news release

You can generate media interest by having magician David Blaine encased in ice for 24 hours while promoting your company, by trying to jet ski across the Atlantic, or by simply developing a new aspect to your site that media would be likely to cover. However you do it, keeping your site in the news in some way that is positive and interesting is vital to developing a brand and building traffic.

Online PR

Marketers often treat the Web as its own entity rather than thinking of it as just another marketing medium. Instead of segregating the Web as a medium, smart promoters think of it as another, more dynamic media outlet. Web technology offers new opportunities for reaching both the news media and the general public, and marketers should be taking advantage of these unique ways of disseminating their messages. It's important to realize that the technology has changed in terms of practicing PR, but the tactics themselves remain the same.

Specifically, the Web allows for chat rooms, video distribution, and e-mail distribution of news releases. Cyber media rooms are a new phenomena that have great potential for effectively practicing PR online. The Web also has spawned two new specialty media areas: reporters who cover the Web as a topic, and editors who are in charge of news Web sites.

Chat rooms give site visitors a sense of having a one-on-one relationship with people who may otherwise be hard to reach. If the CEO of a company wants to reach consumers, being the featured guest in a chat room gives that executive and the company increased exposure.

Video distribution capabilities provide many ways that sites can reach out to their audiences. PR tactics can include distribution of video backgrounds and product demonstrations. **Webcast** news conferences—which are broadcast by streaming video and audio over the Web—can reach reporters anywhere on the globe. Executives can conduct interviews with far-away news media. Online video does not have to be served to the public through a media source such as a news-related Web site. The video can play on the company's own Web site for all visitors to see.

Distributing news releases by e-mail might sound like a good idea, and in most cases, it is. As you will learn later in this chapter, savvy PR people distribute news in the format that is most convenient for each contact, whether it be by e-mail, regular mail, or fax.

The example of WebSearch.com, used earlier in this chapter, described a traditional PR approach for a news conference (allowing the CEO or other company representative to be available for a question and answer period) in which the basic goal has remained the same as it always has (to get as much information to an audience as possible through a live interview session). The Web allows companies to go beyond the traditional methods of achieving this goal. Now companies can use the Web for live online interviews and discussion from various locations, rather than assembling editors or journalists in one place to ask the company or Web site representative questions in person.

Print editors and TV and radio broadcasters are joined by Web reporters and broadcasters as potential recipients of PR efforts. Furthermore, editors who can't attend live events can still cover a story if you set up a Webcast of the event. The responsibilities of the PR agent are more broad as a result of having to organize the video production and to ensure that the desired editors watch. However, the increase in coverage can be much greater than without such efforts.

Web sites that pick up on news releases can reach more people than a printed publication or a television show. Additionally, it is much easier to archive stories on the Web, making historical information more likely to be read. Microfiche machines for print archives are hard to use and archaic in comparison.

Thanks to the Web, companies can take their news *directly* to their audiences. Before the Web, if you wanted the latest information on a company, you had to find a news source that had written about it or call the company directly. Now you can simply go to the company's site and download a file.

The Cyber Media Room

Even companies that have only a brochure Web site to promote their products and services can use their site as an integrated and interactive part of an overall marketing effort. Specially segmented areas of a Web site specifically set up for the media are becoming an important and necessary aspect of sites for companies that seek third-party coverage.

A **cyber media room** is an area of a site where a company can post current and past news releases so that editors and broadcasters can research the company. Often when an editor receives a news release of interest, his or her first action is to visit the company's Web site to gather more information. In addition, the cyber media room may also be of interest to non-media visitors, such as potential customers and employees, who want the most recent news about the company.

Cyber media rooms can vary in complexity. The simplest cyber media rooms offer just a list of news release headlines that act as hyperlinks to the full news release. Even in these most basic rooms, the headlines should indicate the release's subject and the date that the release was written. Other cyber media rooms can be more interactive, making the editor's job far easier—a definite plus for the company that is seeking coverage.

Figure 11-4 shows a cyber media room for JVC Professional Products. This simple page allowed the editors to review only the most recent news releases (within the past year). Most of the titles incorporated the date of the release at the very end, although some releases didn't include the date at all.

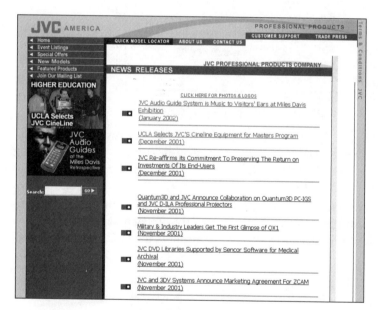

Figure 11-4   A cyber media room for JVC

Figure 11-5 shows the next generation of JVC's cyber media room. This page is considerably more detailed, but is easier for editors to use. The media room has been segmented into categories to make information easy to search. Category headings list the date the release was issued, the release title, the type of JVC product or business featured in the release, a symbol indicating whether the release is about a new product, and a symbol indicating whether a photograph of the product is available by means of a related hyperlink. Editors can sort the information by clicking any of the category titles;

for example, clicking the Date title arranges all the releases in date order, starting with the most recent, while clicking the large dot brings all the releases about new products to the top of the list.

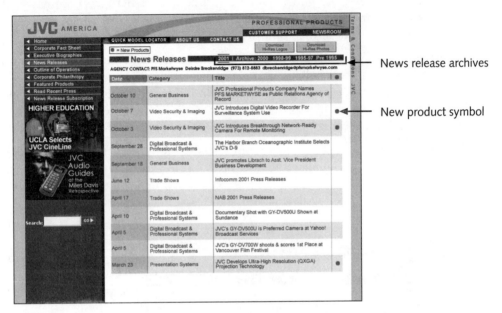

Figure 11-5   JVC's next-generation cyber media room

The new structure of JVC's cyber media room gives editors easy access to all of the information that they'll need to cover certain stories. Visitors can search through a complete archive of releases. Corporate fact sheets explaining the company's goals are provided, along with links to imagery.

Photo resources are important to include in cyber media rooms. Figures 11-6 and 11-7 show pages for photographs and logos, respectively. Each page provides a thumbnail depiction of official product shots or logo treatments for JVC and its various products.

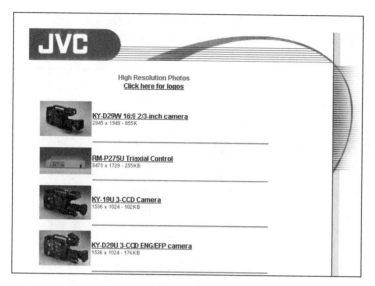

Figure 11-6   Hi-res photography from the JVC cyber media room

Each thumbnail acts as a link to a hi-res version of the image that is suitable for printing. This helps editors find useful images to support their stories and helps the company save time and money by not having to make and mail transparencies of photographs to interested publications.

11

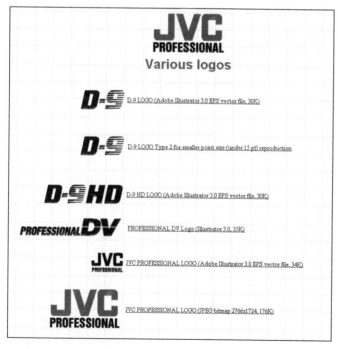

Figure 11-7   Logos available in the JVC cyber media room

A clear link to the cyber media room should be available in the first-level navigation that appears on all the site's pages, making it easy to find. In addition, sites often put the titles of their most recent news releases on their home pages. This lets visitors see the most recent news as soon as they come to the site, so that even if they never make it to the cyber media room, they will have an idea of the company's latest developments. This also allows the home page of a site to change on a regular basis, alerting visitors to the fact that there is new information within the site.

Tips Every PR Professional Should Know

Because a human is in control of the PR destiny of any release, PR can be tricky. In fact, because PR agents often work with clients for long periods of time, they typically send news releases to a regular list of contacts. Over time, PR agents develop an A list and a B list of media. The lists group contacts that are most likely to pick up on a given story or that are the most desirable for coverage.

The human-to-human factor makes PR a relationship-based form of marketing. The most important news could be ignored by an editor because of a bad relationship with a PR agent or because a release violated the standard, acceptable, and universally understood "rules" of PR and the agent/editor relationship. Bear in mind the following suggestions when developing relationships with editors:

- Keep the news release centered around the facts—in other words, have a point and keep to it. The release should be as short as possible without sacrificing important details.

- Do not send frivolous news releases for the sake of keeping the name of the site or company in the editor's mind. If it's not news, don't report it.

- Be realistic. If you tout an online bookseller as "the biggest online bookseller on the Web," chances are that any editor who has heard of Amazon.com will ignore the release completely. Exaggerating a point will eliminate your credibility.

- Don't send the same release to different reporters or editors of the same publication.

- Make sure that you are available to answer questions that a reporter might ask as follow-up to a news release. If you're not there to answer questions, he or she may simply move on to the next release in that huge pile.

- Keep phone calls to the editor to a minimum. Calling every day is considered disruptive, annoying, and downright rude. This is especially true if the journalist is on a deadline—that is the last time he or she wants to be interrupted.

- Ask your contacts how they want to receive their news releases. Preferred methods are usually either e-mail, fax, or U.S. mail. If it's through e-mail, don't let the ease of transmission lure you into sending loads of unwanted releases; this is considered spamming. In addition, resist the temptation to send file attachments. In surveys, most editors were adamant in their distaste for e-mail attachments.

- Make sure that the site for the company that you are promoting is as current as possible before a news release is sent. The editors you are contacting will likely visit the site for the most recent updates. It can be embarrassing if the information they find there is outdated.

- Allow editors some sort of direct entrance to the Web site of the company being promoted. No editor is going to spend the time to complete online registration forms to access further information.

- Be sure of your facts. An editor who reports erroneous information based on your news release can be sued for libel. That editor will probably never forgive such a transgression.

You should also bear in mind the following:

- The point of PR is to inform the public and to create a positive impression of a brand. Ultimately, it is up to the media and the public to interpret the information disseminated by PR efforts.

- PR is not only about news releases. It encompasses any means (such as having executives appear at speaking engagements or holding public events) that brings the company and its Web site closer to the public for a more personal relationship.

- Advertising copy is not the same as the text in a news release. In other words, don't treat your PR campaign as you would any other type of marketing campaign. Unlike catchy advertising copy that is written for a general audience and a quick reaction, news releases are written for a specific audience of writers, editors, and broadcasters who want facts.

NONTRADITIONAL MARKETING METHODS

Beyond the traditional means of print, television, radio, and billboard advertising and PR efforts, nontraditional methods of gaining the public's attention can be quite effective. As is fitting their roles as business innovators, many Web sites are adopting or creating nontraditional methods of promoting themselves. The rest of this chapter will look at some of the more outstanding nontraditional efforts—both successful and not-so-successful.

Some of the original nontraditional methods of marketing have become so popular that it is wrong to call them "nontraditional." The **Monster.com** blimp, for example, which can often be seen floating over various sports facilities during a game, is nothing more than a play off the Goodyear blimp, which debuted decades ago and has long been a presence at major athletic competitions.

In Chapter 10, you learned about car wraps, which became popular with the digital revolution and have become fairly commonplace. Web sites have overused this marketing method, which allows people to drive a car for free, as long as they don't mind that the

11

car is one big advertisement with a dot-com logo plastered all over it. From the bottoms of cups in golf holes to flat-screen ad monitors in the backs of cabs, today's marketers are always on the lookout for creative locations to place a message. Half.com and Cuervo tequila are two marketers that have gone to extremes to publicize themselves, as you will learn in the next sections.

Half.com

When it comes to innovation, **Half.com**, which sells a variety of products over a number of categories ranging from books to electronics, is a true leader. Half.com promises to save you money with each purchase. Although documenting the effectiveness of its particular innovations is difficult (in terms of driving traffic to the site or getting customers to spend real dollars), the company is, if nothing else, creative.

On a small scale, Half.com has tried to put its name in any unusual place where it has a captive audience. The top of Figure 11-8, for example, shows the front of a standard fortune cookie fortune, such as you might get in any Chinese restaurant. The back of the fortune, however, has a message different from what you usually get in a fortune cookie, as displayed in the lower part of Figure 11-8.

Figure 11-8   Half.com fortune cookie ad

Next to a large announcement of "$5 Off," the text reads: "Save a fortune at Half.com." The marketing wizards at Half.com know that they are sending a message in a place where there is little other advertising to compete for your attention and that a message on the back of a fortune will be unique enough to make the first-time reader pay attention.

Fortune cookie ads are nothing compared with Half.com's *real* innovation. In a far bolder move, the Web company has paid the local government of Halfway, Oregon, to name its town Half.com, becoming the country's first town to be named after a dot-com. Half.com is now not only a Web site, but a place to raise a family. What did this stunt gain the company? The result was a lot of free publicity on television and radio talk shows and coverage in newspapers and magazines by journalists who saw an interesting story in such a unique method of marketing.

Beyond the initial media interest, it's tough to see how Half.com, Oregon, will be an ongoing publicity source for the Half.com Web site, unless the town stays in the news or is used by the company in a marketing campaign. A traditional marketer used a similar technique, but with longer lasting results, as you'll see next.

Cuervo Island

Jose Cuervo tequila has made a unique effort to maintain its brand image as a fun drink for fun people. To help promote that image, the drink maker bought an autonomous island. Cuervo Island is an independent country. The company spent a ridiculous amount of money, but gained tremendous media exposure for its unprecedented marketing strategy.

The Cuervo Island stunt, which took place years before Half.com became a town, differs from Half.com's similar action in several ways. From a strictly marketing standpoint, Cuervo and Half.com each achieved a basic goal: they did something unique enough to gain significant headlines in mainstream media. Talk shows, newspapers, and major magazines covered both marketers' acquisitions at great length. Thus, from a PR perspective, each venture can be considered a success.

Like many other pure-coms, Half.com seemed to be acting impulsively by paying the town to change its name. If PR was the goal, there likely were less costly ways of going about it. Half.com did stir up a media frenzy in the period of time that followed the deal, culminating with a live broadcast from the town by NBC's *Today* show when the town officially changed its name. However, considering that the Web site provides visitors a deep savings on electronic commerce purchases, and that its corporate headquarters are located in Pennsylvania, it's difficult to see the correlation of a town with the brand promise. What does one have to do with the other? As a Web surfer and potential customer, what message or brand promise do you derive from a town being named after the site? True, the name may sink into your consciousness because of the uniqueness of the idea and the widespread coverage it gained. However, beyond that, you know nothing about Half.com as a company.

Unlike the Half.com town name purchase, the Cuervo Island purchase made sense for its brand. A tropical resort island is a perfect association with the Cuervo brand—after all, what appeals to fun-seeking young adults more than a tropical resort? In addition, Cuervo Island has turned into an alternate revenue source for the company, as it markets the island as a vacation resort to spring breakers, recent graduates, and others within its target market.

In addition, because Cuervo Island is an autonomous country with its own constitution, it regularly makes headlines when it applies to the United Nations for nation status, with the hope of entering a team in the Olympics. Even if it never happens, it's still a source of ongoing PR that the town of Half.com won't ever be able to match.

Lastly, the Jose Cuervo company uses the island (originally just a PR stunt) in integrated marketing campaigns that also promotes its Web site. In a joint effort with **CDNow.com**, Jose Cuervo held a contest in 2001 in which participants could register on the

Cuervo.com Web site (driving traffic to the site) for a chance to win a full-week trip to—you guessed it—Cuervo Island. The campaign spanned banner ads, print ads, and radio, and brought attention to the drink, the resort, and the Web site—all within one integrated campaign. The affiliation gave CDNow.com access to a specific target market and a chance to associate its brand with the same fun image as Cuervo.

Somehow, a vacation in the town of Half.com doesn't sound quite as appealing.

Other Innovators

They may be shameless attempts to capture a restless public's attention, or maybe they're ingenious methods of separating their names from the horde of others, but forward-thinking marketers are always looking for a way to promote themselves that is beyond the ordinary. Some ideas are just silly, others are impressive, but all of them, in one way or another, get their market's attention. The following are some standout examples of innovative marketing endeavors:

- Taco Bell: In early 2001, the Soviet space station Mir had ended its extended stay in orbit and was scheduled to be destroyed. The plan was to bring the craft back into Earth's orbit, where it would burn up in the atmosphere, with the remnants landing harmlessly in the Pacific Ocean. As a promotional stunt, Taco Bell sent a 40-foot raft into the Pacific Ocean with a target painted on it. If any piece of the debris hit the target, Taco Bell promised to give everyone in the United States a free taco. Of course, given how large the Pacific Ocean is, Taco Bell was well aware that the odds of a piece of space station hitting the target were slim to none. However, if the target *were* hit, the fast food chain would not suffer much by giving away food. Considering that a taco costs very little to produce, the company would have easily made up the lost cost by selling drinks and side items. In addition, Taco Bell would have exposed a tremendous amount of people to its product and gotten as much free publicity as it could handle. As it were, the company received plenty of exposure just for creating the stunt in the first place.

- In what was likely a very clever PR stunt, one pure-com promoted an offer before the 2001 Super Bowl: it would pay $1000 per second to anyone who was seen on television with a t-shirt, hat, or a sign that clearly showed the pure-com's name. Anybody wanting to claim the prize would have to prove that he or she were on television by producing a videotape of himself or herself during the Super Bowl. Mathematically, this worked to the company's advantage: even if the site was able to get only 30 seconds of exposure, the most it would have to pay would be $30,000. This amount is a far lower price than the $2 million and up that other companies were paying for a 30-second commercial spot on the broadcast. As it turned out, the company didn't pay a dime, but ended up getting maximum exposure, anyway. The NFL, upon learning of the program, sent a cease and desist letter to the Web site, claiming that the site was unauthorized to run such a promotion and that it would be sued if the site pressed on with its plans. In addition, the NFL stated that people caught at the Super Bowl participating in the contest would be removed from the stadium. The Web site backed down immediately—but it was in a no-lose situation. If the NFL had not protested, the company would have received advertising during the game at a fraction of what it would ordinarily cost to have signage on the field. However, even with the NFL's protest, the offending pure-com could spin the story in its favor. The news media seized the story. On one hand, the Web site was obviously trying to steal time from the Super Bowl, but on the other hand, people don't get thrown out of the game for wearing a Nike logo on a t-shirt, which also is a form of free advertising. Freedom of speech became the issue at hand, and little money was spent to start the buzz.

- DotComGuy: Taking a cue from the reality TV phenomenon, Mitch Maddox, a 26-year-old former human resource manager, legally changed his name to DotComGuy. On January 1, 2000, DotComGuy moved into a house in Dallas, Texas, that was devoid of any amenities except his computer and a connection to the Web (and a whole lot of Web cameras to stream his life to interested spectators across the globe 24 hours per day). The point? DotComGuy was going to prove that man could live by Web alone. People watched as DotComGuy bought everything online—food, furniture, toiletries, entertainment, and his entire wardrobe. The media regularly checked in to report on how DotComGuy was progressing. Web sites that wanted to be part of the hype jumped to sponsor him in his endeavor, including Network Solutions, the entity that sells and reserves domain names to companies that want their own dot-com domain name. For Network Solutions, the pairing was a perfect fit. The company promoted the same message that DotComGuy was promoting: the Web makes life easier and more convenient. However, like most PR stunts, DotComGuy's appeal was limited, and after a few months, most of the sponsors decided that the excitement had run its course. Most failed to sign on for further sponsorships. It is unclear whether any Web entity that got involved with DotComGuy actually saw any positive returns from its association with him, but there is no question that the promotional efforts were enough to get the names in front of the public, which is exactly where it wanted it to be.

11

Marketing Partnerships

Because so many marketers try to reach audiences with similar demographics, it makes sense for certain marketers to partner with one other. Companies that team up for specific promotions may enjoy the following benefits:

- Reduced marketing costs
- Wider media exposure and PR interest
- Greater interest by the target market

Companies may identify potential partners based on a number of criteria. These criteria include a similar demographic audience but lack of direct competition (characteristics shared by companies such as *Shape* magazine and Nike, for example), a similar marketing philosophy, a well-known and well-respected brand name in the marketplace, and available funding for promotional efforts.

The Web often plays a role in marketing partnerships between companies as it makes interaction with the audience easier and helps to drive traffic to a site. An interesting partnership in the summer of 2001 involved television network VH1 and BMW's Z3 Roadster. This contest (many marketing partnerships take the form of contests) enticed viewers to watch VH1 every night between 9:00 and midnight during July. A different keyword was provided each night. Participants then could visit the **VH1.com** Web site, register, and enter the keyword for a chance to win. A new Z3 Roadster was awarded each night, and the trunk of each contained VH1's top 100 CDs.

Both entities got terrific exposure from the campaign. VH1 gave people a reason to watch its channel for three hours a night and drove people to its Web site on a regular basis. BMW provided the prizes and gained great exposure in VH1's demographic audience of young, professional, active adults.

Because of hyperlinks, the Web makes a great breeding ground for affiliations. Promotions ranging from contests and sweepstakes to content sharing and simple advertising allow partnering Web sites to take advantage of each site's strengths to gain and retain similar audiences.

The best opportunity for Web partnership success probably comes from affiliations between traditional brick-and-mortar marketers (also known as **click-and-mortars**, which are brick-and-mortar companies that have added a Web component) and large Web brands. For example, because eBay has become such a powerhouse in the auction industry, many traditional auctioneers have become eBay partners to take advantage of the huge audience that eBay draws and the site's more advanced Web technology.

Chapter Summary

- ❏ PR is the process of influencing public opinion and bringing a positive image to the brand. The PR agency typically takes on many chores to make this happen, including setting up events, scheduling seminar tours, arranging interviews, and writing and distributing news releases. Editors and broadcasters pick up on these releases as source material for stories when the release has something important to say and may be newsworthy.

- ❏ PR can be the most effective of the marketing methods—but also the most difficult. Because success relies on the whims and decisions of people who are not connected with the account, the company, or the agency, PR requires finesse and structure. It's important to understand the audience of the media you are trying to pitch and to present the information to that media in a concise, comprehensive way.

❏ Although the general intent and practice of PR has not changed with the popularization of the Internet, some of the tools and methods have broadened. The Web adds two new facets to PR. First, the Web offers new ways to distribute news, including Webcasts, chat rooms, and cyber media rooms. The Web also has spawned a group of editors (both online and traditional) who cover news about the Web. It also provides news sites that act as media outlets.

❏ Nontraditional marketing methods are innovative and extreme ways of gaining an audience for a company. These methods go beyond the boundaries of typical advertising and PR efforts.

❏ Marketing partnerships bring together noncompeting sites and companies in different businesses but with similar demographic markets. Benefits of partnering include reduced marketing costs, increased publicity, and increased interest by the target market.

KEY TERMS

click-and-mortar
cyber media room
damage control
news release
pitch
PR stunt
Webcast

11

REVIEW QUESTIONS

1. PR is best described as a(n): _____.
    a. effort to reach the public through the purchase of general media
    b. effort to influence public opinion through positive news coverage
    c. way for corporate executives to get their names and faces out in public
    d. bridge between traditional and cyber marketing

2. The Web has made PR _____.
    a. more time consuming, due to the expanded media contacts that are available
    b. less desirable, as few people actually read news online
    c. broader, as news release distribution, Webcasts, and other technology make PR more flexible
    d. no different in practice than it was prior to the popularization of the Web

3. _____ is a new Web development that helps PR professionals get their messages out to editors and reporters.

   a. Banner advertising

   b. A cyber media room

   c. HTML

   d. An e-mail file attachment

4. The biggest benefit to PR in a marketing campaign is that _____.

   a. agencies charge lower fees for PR than for other forms of marketing

   b. to the general public, company news comes from an unbiased third party

   c. people remember what they read in articles more than what they see in a print ad

   d. when you make friends in the media, they are less likely to report bad news about you or your client

5. One of the toughest challenges about running a successful PR campaign is that _____.

   a. it takes at least several weeks to execute a PR campaign

   b. most editors are skeptical—they don't really believe what a news release says

   c. a PR agent needs to have many facts about the site they are promoting to make a decent pitch

   d. the success of an effort relies on the decision of a person who is unassociated with the account

6. The cyber media room is important to include on a company's Web site because _____.

   a. people like to see current data on companies

   b. it keeps site developers busy

   c. most editors prefer to find news by looking on the site rather than by receiving news releases in the mail

   d. when an editor receives a pitch, he or she is likely to look at the site of the company being promoted before doing anything else

7. When contacting an editor or reporter, it's most important to know _____.

   a. the demographics of the audience that the publication or broadcast reaches

   b. the advertising campaigns that will accompany the PR effort

   c. the details of all previous news releases

   d. how many more news releases you will be sending as part of the campaign

8. Creating an event for a company helps in the PR effort because
_____.

   a. it shows the general public that the company is active

   b. it gives the company a reason to produce a Web cast

   c. it's a way of creating news

   d. it helps to keep the media entertained

9. A pitch should _____.

   a. provide every last detail that an editor could want

   b. be sent through e-mail as an attachment

   c. be concise, factual, and interesting

   d. exaggerate the company being promoted so that it stands out among the other releases on the editor's desk

10. Describe at least three elements that should be a part of a Web site's cyber media room.

11. Which news release headline would most likely get an editor's attention?

   a. SomeWebSite.com Provides the Best Customer Service on the Web

   b. SomeWebSite.com Unveils New Shopping Cart Technology for Easier Online Shopping

   c. SomeWebSite.com Offers More Products Than Leading Online Competitors

   d. SomeWebSite.com Stands for Quality of Service and Customer Satisfaction

12. Name three publications or broadcasts that would likely pick up on a news release about a Web site introducing new technology.

13. Explain why PR may be more or less effective than traditional advertising methods such as print or television advertising.

14. Can PR be a targeted marketing effort? If so, explain how.

Hands-on Projects

1. With your partners, create a series of three news releases for your Web company. In each, make sure to include a headline that summarizes the information the recipients can expect to find by reading the release.

   a. Write the first release as an announcement of the site or company and its offerings to the market.

   b. Write the second release as a backgrounder promoting you and your partners, gearing it as a public interest story on the people behind the site.

11

   c. Write the final release to highlight any one aspect of your site that you feel is newsworthy.

   d. Come up with a list of at least 10 media outlets to approach with your releases (these can include print, broadcast, or Web media). Why did you choose these media? Will you approach different media for each of the different releases? Why or why not?

   e. Come up with a plan for an event that coordinates with your company announcement (the first release). This event can be a party, straight news conference, or PR stunt. Detail your plan and explain why you are going with the approach you selected.

2. Pick up a magazine that focuses on the Web, such as *Yahoo!* or *Wired*, and find a short article that mentions a specific Web site. Don't use the feature article or an article that focuses on one site in particular, but instead choose an article that mentions a site briefly. The mention might be in a "What's New" column or could be a short review of a site. Based on the article's content, write a news release for the site that may have led the writer to mention it in his or her article.

3. Come up with three potential business partnerships between well-known companies or industries. Explain why the pairings make sense. At least two of your proposals should include at least one Web site as a partner.

12

CUSTOMER SERVICE AND PUTTING IT ALL TOGETHER

In this chapter, you will learn about:

♦ The key components of customer service

♦ How to provide customer service for online customers

♦ How to enhance your Web business using customer service features

Action taken by a company, Web site, or salesperson to provide support or assistance to customers, either as individual efforts or as a general approach, is called **customer service**. Part of customer service is understanding what your audience would experience in the traditional world and replicating that experience on your Web site.

This chapter explains the importance of customer service and describes steps that Web sites can take to provide better service for their customers. We'll also take a look at ways sites are providing customer service. Finally, you will learn how customer service can affect customers' perception of a brand.

Customer service works with the overall branding and marketing campaign to create a customer-effective Web site and brand presence. A site that is **customer-effective** is one with a brand message that emphasizes high-quality customer service. Such sites are built specifically for ease of customer use.

CUSTOMER SERVICE TODAY

Most people—whether they are retailers or consumers—agree that the quality of customer service has deteriorated over the past few years. The phrase "the customer is always right" was once a staple of successful business practice, but is about as valid in today's world as a used typewriter shop. Consumers are coming to expect poor service, although most of us aren't happy about it.

Unfortunately, customer service comes down to simple mathematics: companies can compute how much it would cost to train salespeople, pay better employees, and take other measures to provide their customers with better service. They then can compare this figure to the amount of revenue that would be lost when a percentage of their customer base is lost because of poor service. If the revenue lost is not equal to or greater than the cost of implementing better customer service, it is unlikely that additional service improvements will be made.

Poor service can reflect on the brand. Consider the bankruptcy filing by Kmart, America's third-largest discount retailer, in early 2002. Among other reasons for its demise, polls showed that customers who frequented discount stores, including Kmart, Walmart, and Target, consistently described Kmart as having the worst customer service. In some cases, they described cashiers and salespeople as rude. The poor service drove many of these shoppers to other stores. Many of these customers stated that after so many bad experiences, they were unlikely to return to Kmart in the near future.

One place that poor customer service is not accepted is the Web. We may deal with rude, uncaring attitudes at a store because it's too much of a hassle to leave and go elsewhere. However, the Web's vast selection makes it easy for us to check out a competitor—and with the right incentive, shoppers will do just that, waving goodbye to sites that don't provide good service. Customer service on the Web was lacking for a long time, but it is starting to come of age as companies realize that cyber service is an integral part of sales and brand image.

CUSTOMER SERVICE OVERVIEW

Before you can understand how to improve the customer service experience, it is helpful to understand what an ideal customer service experience entails. In short, Web sites should create a presence in which the following is true:

- Customers feel that all their questions about the site are answered.
- Customers can find what they are looking for with ease.
- There is little worry that the security of customers' money or privacy is threatened when using the site.

- Customers can do what they need to do on the site with as little aggravation as possible.

- Problems are resolved easily and quickly.

- The site will work with customers in the present and in the future to create as pleasurable an experience as possible.

We will begin by explaining when customer service begins. Then you will learn how to use customer service to your advantage, so that you can treat your customers appropriately.

When Customer Service Begins

Many managers—of both Web and brick-and-mortar stores—don't begin the customer service experience at the right point in time, which is one reason that customer service has suffered in recent history. In actuality, customer service begins as soon as the user arrives at a store—either electronic or physical.

Unfortunately, many people running businesses seem to think that customer service starts when the customer complains that the wrong item was shipped or gripes that the company's Web site collapsed while he or she was performing an important transaction. The term "customer service" has become misunderstood and confused with the efforts taken to alleviate the stress and concern felt by disgruntled customers. These steps are a reaction to a bad situation. Instead, customer service should be proactive and serve the customer in such a way that attention and innovative experiences are provided from the outset.

Some of the major themes of this book, including market research, brand development, site navigation, and stickiness, are components of customer service. Each of these elements, done right, provides a better experience for the site visitor. This experience plays a major role in how the brand is perceived, whether customers return, and the ultimate success of your venture.

12

Components of Customer Service

Customer service starts with an understanding of what your visitors will want (which you should know from effective market research). You then provide them with it in the most reasonable manner possible. Retail stores and brick-and-mortar companies need to provide comfort and entertainment for their customers. For example, Barnes & Noble has in-store cafés, organizes writing groups for customers, and features speakers or musicians at the stores. The books almost seem like an afterthought. IKEA, the furniture retailer, has an on-site restaurant and offers babysitting. Each restaurant in the Fudruckers hamburger chain boasts a game room in which you can spend some time if you get tired of looking at the restaurant's neon lights while waiting for your meal.

These features make sense for physical businesses. People in the retail world are stimulated by many senses, and their experience with a store, restaurant, or other business is determined by how well those companies understand and provide for their customers' needs and wants.

All too often, though, Web sites follow the brick-and-mortar example too closely, substituting dazzling imagery for appropriate functionality. Consider the graphics and navigation of a site and their roles in customer service. Yahoo! is one of the most customer-friendly sites on the Web, but nobody is going to mistake it for the prettiest. Yahoo does not have a highly charged Flash introduction. It doesn't have eye-catching graphics or showy animations. It's simple and to-the-point. Yahoo's appearance serves its customers well, unlike many other sites that are impressive to look at, but that leave you unsure as to what the company does. Remember that while entertaining visitors is an important part of stickiness, unless your site is an entertainment-specific one, entertainment should be placed in specific areas of the site. These areas include games and movie links. In terms of navigation for customer service, people really want information with ease and convenience.

Being Proactive

Customer service is often seen as the steps taken *after* a customer has a question, comment, or complaint. This narrow approach means that customer service is seen as an afterthought and expenditure—that is, a cost with no quantifiable return. Customer service representatives who answer questions or field complaints from customers are not doing any actual selling, so they are viewed as non-revenue generating expenses to their companies.

A bad experience with a Web site will leave a lasting, negative impression on a customer, and the value of that negative effect is hard to quantify. In comparison, it is easy to tally the money a site is spending on its customer service efforts. Because of this inappropriate comparison, shortsighted companies often reduce their expenditures in customer relations in an effort to save dollars in the present, without regard to the overall effect it will have on the consumer relationship in the future.

Value Your Customers

Many companies try to provide the greatest amount of service while spending the least amount of money. Marketing data has allowed companies to compute the monetary value of each customer. In some cases, companies will not spend more than a certain amount in customer service per customer if the customer's "value" does not warrant the expenditure.

Therefore, employees in customer service departments often make relatively low salaries, with the median wage at about $10.60 per hour in 2001. The customer service field also experiences high turnover rates, with some companies turning over all their service-related employees each year. This turnover means that employees do not truly understand the Web sites they serve, nor are they intimately familiar with the needs and wants of the customer. These employees do not have the time or the financial incentive to really get to know the product or service very well.

When customer service is viewed as an expense, companies measure success by how quickly they can deal with a customer—regardless of how satisfied the customer is. Obviously, this approach does little to truly serve customers. Customers should not be viewed strictly as demographic data and statistics or expenses with dollar signs attached. They also should not be treated as though they were not worth time and energy because they have not spent a certain amount of money with your company. As you learned in Chapter 8, brand building is relationship building. Although shoppers are primarily price shoppers, minor differences in price between sites may not be enough to compensate for poorer quality customer service.

Web technology provides sites the tools to automatically deliver good customer service and one-on-one relationships with audiences. Computers, data tracking, and information-on-demand allow consumers to be treated as individuals, but far too many sites reject a personal way of relating to customers in favor of a generic approach that treats each shopper as part of a large demographic and not as an important individual buyer.

Broad Solutions for Online Customer Service

One effective way to deliver good customer service is to use any complaint, question, or comment as a resource to help improve the site. This can be done instead of simply providing a one-time solution to an individual's problem. To do this successfully, however, your company must have good communication among customer service representatives, site developers, and marketers. Sites that don't endorse communication among these departments won't realize the full potential of their customer service efforts.

A good approach is for customer service departments to keep a record of customer contact and to pass this information on to the designers and programmers. Sites that have a larger budget can use specialized software to sort complaints using keywords. The programmers can address the problem using technology or navigation improvements—for example, by creating a more intuitive, easier-to-use shopping cart. Not only will this change entice more people to complete their purchases, but also it might reduce the number of hours the customer service staff must deal with customer complaints.

A good experience for the customer translates to a positive view of the brand. This positive perception of the brand then results in repeat visits to the site. The only way customers will have good experiences is if the customer service angle is considered during the site development process.

Suppose, for example, that of 10,000 phone calls and e-mails that a site's customer service department receives in a given month, 6500 are complaints that the user had trouble figuring out how to remove certain items from the shopping cart (resulting in him or her abandoning the entire purchase). Customer service representatives could respond to the 6500 individuals, explaining the best way to remove items, and those who complained would be appeased. However, the following month, thousands more customers would have similar complaints—not including the untold number of people who had the same problem, but never bothered to e-mail the site about it. While solving the problem individually results in a short-term solution, fixing the site means that *all* customers will have better experiences.

Sometimes a site has a problem that is severe enough to create a negative impression of the brand and may keep users from returning (or even worse, unhappy customers will pass along negative information to other potential users). In such situations, the marketing department might get involved, boosting the brand with advertising that highlights site improvements in the hope of drawing disgruntled former customers back to the site.

The diagram in Figure 12-1 shows the pattern of communication and development that sites should use to properly respond to customer complaints. Unfortunately, site evolution based on feedback rarely occurs as described here. Because many sites keep their customer service centers and development areas in separate locations, regular communication between departments can be difficult or even nonexistent. Costs, including tracking technology (to track users and traffic) and competent service employees who can categorize feedback, may prove too costly to allow for the best evolution of the site.

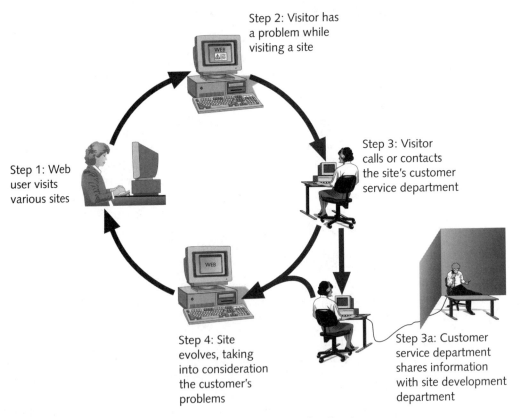

Figure 12-1   Ideal site evolution based on customer feedback

The level of customer service that your site offers depends on the type of site you are providing. Sites that offer low-level services (for example, brochure-style sites) don't need to provide sophisticated customer service options, but sites that are performing more complicated functions, such as electronic commerce, do need customer service that is in line with the site's functionality. For example, assume your site allows users to make reservations at local restaurants. A customer who arrives at a restaurant to find out that the online reservation was never confirmed with the restaurant would not need to do much more than send an angry e-mail to the site to resolve his or her customer service issue. However, a site that allows you to reserve airline tickets for a vacation or business trip needs to provide better customer service in the event that the traveler gets to the airport and discovers that the airline has no record of the ticket or reservation. Because of the severity of the problem and potential of extreme inconvenience, the site would have to take strong steps to compensate for its error. Such steps might include instant rebooking or free travel vouchers. Without such measures, unhappy customers will never return to the site.

Next, you will learn about some of the key ways in which sites can provide their customers with good service—including how to preempt problems wherever possible and deal with trouble when it does occur.

RESPONDING TO CUSTOMERS

When customers need to communicate with your company, whether it's because of a problem or just to ask a question, it's important that they have a reliable way to do so. Web site developers have a number of options that they can employ to help them communicate with their visitors and respond to their needs, problems, and inquiries. Methods such as telephone response systems, e-mail interaction, fill-in forms, FAQ pages, and online chat are some of the more popular ways that customer-oriented Web sites communicate with their users.

Interactive Voice Response Systems

Probably one of the most over-used and most annoying developments in customer service over the past decade has the been the automated telephone response system, or **interactive voice response (IVR)** system. Most people find the "…If you would like to continue in English, press 8. If today is Tuesday, press 9…" type of systems extremely frustrating.

Consumers have started to press 0 from the time the system answers in the hopes of reaching a live operator who can provide assistance. In the business world, we may no longer need to have face-to-face meetings to feel comfortable with each other, but we have not yet reached the point at which we can completely do away with human interaction. Because most customer service calls are either to ask a question or lodge a complaint, talking to a machine is not an acceptable resolution for most people.

12

Despite the public's distaste for them, IVRs should not be ignored by companies. Even though 40 percent of calls to IVRs end in the user dialing 0 to try to reach a human, 12 percent of callers hang up and abandon the call completely, and studies show that consumers are generally frustrated with the systems. However, a call handled by an IVR costs a company approximately $0.45. In comparison, it costs a company $7.60 on average to have a human being handle that same call.

With costs like that, it's easy to understand how any company that views customer service as both a necessary evil and a brand-building opportunity would not hesitate to implement an IVR. In a sense, the IVR is really a way to transfer the burden of customer service back to the customer. IVRs give customers the sense that companies are saying, "Sorry, we really don't have the time or desire to deal with you, so here is a nifty set of menu options that you can use to figure out the solution to your problems on your own." That is not exactly a customer-oriented attitude.

Not all IVRs are problematic. If done correctly, they can be beneficial to the consumer. **Bank of New York**, for example, allows customers to check their accounts through the Web site or by automated phone teller. The IVR instructs the caller to enter his or her Social Security number and a PIN (personal information number), and it then provides the account balance information. A simple menu provides access to other services and information from the telephone touch pad, with each option being distinct, obvious, and straightforward.

Be prepared to spend upwards of $75,000 for an IVR system if you are going to provide automated telephone service for users of your Web site. The following suggestions provide maximum benefit to the consumer:

- Always allow the user to dial 0 for the operator. 0 is universally known as the key to push to reach an operator. Make sure that an operator is always available to take a call. The most frustrating IVRs are the ones that start over from the beginning of the menu if the caller dials 0.

- Keep the options short and simple. Three levels of options with no more than four choices in each level is the optimal configuration, according to many customer service experts. Make each option distinct. Will the caller know the difference between "Account Information" and "Order Status"? Maybe, but maybe not. Ambiguous categories make the IVR more difficult to navigate.

- Don't repeat yourself. If your Web site provides customers with a tracking number for shipments of products ordered, the customer might be asked by the IVR to key in the tracking number to continue the call. When the customer finally reaches a human being, don't make him or her repeat that information.

Web sites that are really interested in serving their customers may want to consider setting up a toll-free line for users to call to ask questions of a real person. This system can support the IVR or even bypass it altogether. This is particularly important if your site deals with sensitive personal financial information. For example, sites that allow users to trade stocks online and/or bank online would likely need to provide some way for users to reach company representatives by phone if there were problems with their account.

Product-related Web sites can also benefit from a call-in center to handle returns, product problems, and so on.

Unfortunately, providing telephone access for customers can lead to problems, hassles, and expenses for a site. Once Web surfers realize that a phone number is available, many will opt for the immediacy of phone interaction over the less immediate option of e-mail correspondence, especially since many sites have built a reputation for being slower than desirable when it comes to responding to e-mail inquiries (detailed further in the following section).

Regardless of why people are calling, they need to be treated with respect. Callers are the ones with the problems, and they are using their own time to interact with your company. Long hold times, for example, can leave callers feeling more annoyed than they were before they called. Reducing hold times and accepting more calls means employing more people to work the phones, which means more telephones, more office space, more salaries, and more office equipment—all of which means more money. The trade-off for this expenditure is more business. Studies show that Web surfers are 45 percent more likely to travel to sites that offer customer service phone numbers. To reduce the potentially massive costs that can accrue by establishing a call center, many Web sites outsource their customer service calls to overseas corporations, particularly those in India and neighboring parts of Asia. Wages in India are typically lower than in the United States, as are most other business-related expenses. Many qualified Indian employees are fluent in multiple languages, which helps the site serve many different customers.

E-Mail and Response Time

By far the most popular way to enact customer service communication is to funnel all correspondence through e-mail. E-mail is far less expensive than having to employ a room full of people on telephones (even if you do use low-wage overseas employment). However, the impersonal nature of e-mail may not be worth the cost savings it provides.

Sites can provide customer service e-mail interactions in two ways. The first is to simply provide an e-mail link to a customer service representative so that the customer can correspond with someone at the site in his or her own words. The advantage of this link is that it requires almost no programming on the part of the Web site. A simple e-mail link takes five seconds to program in HTML. In addition, the e-mail option lets the user feel that he or she has an opportunity to completely vent or explain his or her questions or comments.

The same freedom of expression that makes open e-mail correspondence an advantage can also create a disadvantage for the site. People who are given the opportunity to say whatever they want may not get right to the point, and rambling e-mail messages take longer to read. Even worse, e-mail correspondence for customer service issues may be so incoherently written that you have no idea what the problem is.

The second option for providing customer service through e-mail is a fill-in form. Forms take a bit more programming than e-mail links (they require a database that supports

12

each field of the form), but they help site staff better understand the specific requests being made. Forms can guide a site visitor so that his or her correspondence is more explanatory. A form may also require that the user complete fields that provide valuable information about the user's experience on the site.

A good customer service form will not be too long (one screen is usually sufficient), nor will it keep the user from getting his or her point across. **Staples.com** provides a good example of how a customer service form should be written so that it extracts the necessary information while not being too burdensome for the user. Figure 12-2 shows a sample of the form that Staples.com uses.

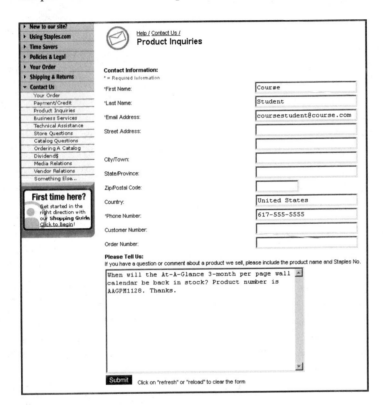

Figure 12-2   Staples.com's customer service form

The best forms start by allowing the user to select a general topic of concern, such as one of the following:

- Comment on site performance
- Request further information
- Notify site of a discrepancy
- Give general complaint or compliment

- Request account information

- Make other requests or concerns

The topic selected provides the user with a series of questions, written specifically for that category. Depending on how they are written, questions or fill-in areas allow for any combination of the following general types of options:

- Option buttons (which allow a user to choose only one answer), such as:

  Overall, did you have a good experience on our site:

  ◉ YES   ◉ NO

- Check boxes (which allow a user to choose as many answers as needed), such as:

  What were your reasons for coming to our site (select all that apply):

  ☑ Purchase products   ☑ Get product information

  ☑ Get industry information   ☑ Get contact information

  ☑ Other

- Fill-in areas, such as:

  Please explain briefly any questions or comments that you have about our site:

  _____ .

As you can tell from the last bullet point, freedom of expression is not suppressed with fill-in forms. People may still explain their thoughts in their own words. However, you can limit the number of words that the user can enter in these areas so that respondents must be concise.

12

Web sites often make two mistakes when dealing with customer correspondence. The first is to send out generic, templated responses that say relatively little except to acknowledge that the customer has attempted to contact the site. Don't assume that your customer won't be able to tell the difference between a customized response and a generic one. Generic responses will likely be met with irritation, and they will have less likelihood of answering the user's question.

Part of the reason that generic responses are ineffective is that most sites that use them employ keyword recognition software to answer e-mail. This software reads the letter or form and recognizes certain keywords. From these keywords, the software guesses the general topic of the correspondence and constructs a generic reply from a database of prewritten e-mail responses, sending the one that is the best fit for the keywords. This type of software can't recognize inflection of voice in a consumer letter, nor can it detect the mood of a correspondence. Customers like to feel as though there is a real customer-company relationship, and they want to be treated as individuals. Generic e-mails don't accomplish that. Instead, you should make sure that customers receive a response that directly addresses their specific concerns. Ideally, this is done by a customer service representative writing a customized response to every e-mail.

The second mistake sites make when responding to customer e-mails is related to speed of response. Although nobody expects Amazon.com CEO Jeff Bezos to respond to an e-mail inquiry as to why the latest Harry Potter book hasn't arrived, shoppers do expect that Web sites answer e-mails in a timely fashion. In the cyber world, "timely fashion" takes on a different meaning than in the brick-and-mortar world. E-mails can be sent around the world in an instant; therefore, slow responses to inquiries are unacceptable.

The definition of "timely" really depends on the site. Immediate responses are not possible unless computer-generated generic responses are issued, of the sort that we just warned against. However, while you should avoid generic responses, it is a good idea to implement an auto-response system that lets the e-mail sender know that his or her e-mail has been received. The e-mail should provide a time frame in which a response may be expected. The following text is an example of such a message:

> *Your request for service has been received. Thank you for taking the time to contact us. Although we get a high volume of e-mail correspondence from our Web site users on a daily basis, we will make every effort to review your request as quickly as possible. You can expect to receive a reply from one of our customer service specialists within 24 hours. We appreciate your patience and look forward to serving you now and in the future.*

The length of time to provide a personalized response will vary. Depending on the type of site you have, the number of people on staff to answer inquiries, and the marketing promises that your site makes, your site may take hours or days to respond. Medical, health-related, and pharmacy sites need to answer e-mails in a very short amount of time (typically less than 24 hours). Other sites, such as those that deal with banking issues or stock markets, also need to provide quick responses to customer service issues.

Regardless of the type of site you are running, the accepted rule for response time is that you should never exceed the response time that you promise. In 1998, **Drugstore.com** got bombarded with heavy criticism when its marketing promotion promised responses to e-mail questions within a 24-hour period; in reality, the average response time was over five days.

FAQ Pages

Most Web sites use a Frequently Asked Questions area, better known as an **FAQ page**, to address their audiences' most basic and common questions. These pages are set up to answer questions that the site frequently receives from visitors.

While some sites, such as **FedEx** and **Bank of America**, do a good job of summarizing general queries into their FAQ pages, those sites are the exception. These pages are often lacking in depth, and in some cases, they are essentially useless.

On some sites, it seems unlikely that anyone would ask some of the questions displayed. Some sites list manufactured FAQs about company executives. These FAQs are marketing efforts—not true FAQs. FAQ pages shouldn't be used as marketing propaganda—rather, they should try to answer some real questions that a user might have. Of course, most of the questions on the site will be specific to the site's subject area and not specific to a user's individual query. The FedEx site uses its FAQ pages to answer common user queries. Figure 12-3 shows FedEx's specific Package Status/Tracking FAQ page—one of several topics for which FedEx provides an FAQ page.

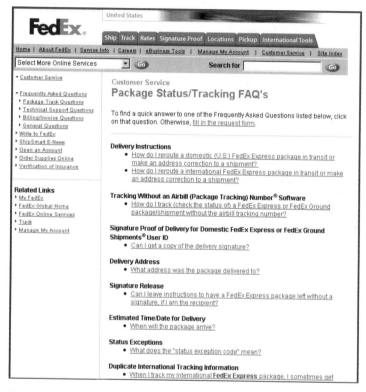

Figure 12-3 The FedEx tracking FAQ area

These kind of basic questions do provide your customers with valuable information. If your site uses tracking software to monitor traffic (as discussed in Chapter 4), you can determine how many people actually visit your FAQ page. Furthermore, if each question is a link to a separate page, you can even determine which questions are being viewed with the greatest frequency.

Although an FAQ page is not going to solve all your customer service issues, you probably should include one, since it may be conspicuous by its absence. An FAQ page is well worth the time it takes to put together.

Online Chat

Online "chatting" is similar to combining e-mail and speaking on the telephone. Chat rooms allow people to have live online discussions through typed, real-time dialog. Chat rooms, such as the one shown in Figure 12-4, can involve any number of people, can be used as an open forum for discussion, and can be made topical for more specific conversation.

Although most chat rooms on the Web are used for social reasons—to allow many people to meet and get to know each other in a casual setting—chat rooms do have viable business applications. Customer service initiatives could benefit from online chat sessions in which site visitors could discuss their problems or questions with a customer service representative while still on the site. This system helps keep representatives off the telephone. It also can help many people at once and is a faster solution than e-mail.

Although chat rooms have been popular among Web surfers and have a great deal of potential in customer service applications, the technology hasn't made much of an impact in the customer service area as of yet. The music site shown in Figure 12-4 illustrates how chat rooms work.

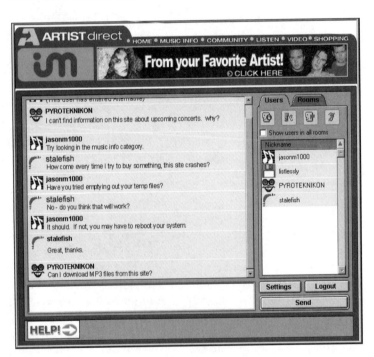

Figure 12-4   An example of a chat room

As with other types of customer service efforts, running a chat room for customer service means having the room staffed at all times. Another disadvantage is that chat rooms offer little privacy, and customers from different areas of the site and with different problems may all be in the chat room at once, reading one another's comments and the site's responses to those comments. The moderator of the chat room might have trouble juggling multiple conversations at once, and someone may feel left out.

A better way to provide instant online service comes in the form of the increasingly popular **instant message (IM)** system. IMs, provided as a free service from AOL, MSN, Yahoo!, and other companies, allow people on the Internet to communicate privately with one another instantaneously by typing. In a sense, they have conversations as though they were talking on the phone. Companies are beginning to take a serious look at these methods because they offer multiple benefits, including the following:

- **Privacy**: IMs are private, one-on-one conversations between two entities.

- **Cost efficiency**: Like chat rooms, they cost nothing in phone charges for either the company or its customer.

- **Personnel efficiency**: Customer service representatives can interact with more than one customer at a time without any of them knowing that he or she is not getting exclusive attention.

SERVICE THROUGHOUT THE SITE

Customer service is not something that should wait until the site visitor becomes so lost, confused, or frustrated that he or she needs to call your corporate headquarters. Your site should incorporate elements that will help make the site customer friendly. For instance, it could make recommendations about products or articles of interest based on previous visits, make sure that you provide adequate detail on everything that you sell (assuming yours is an electronic commerce site), and make the checkout process as simple and as easy as possible.

12

Making Recommendations

Although Chapters 3 and 10 cover recommendations in detail, it is worth mentioning the topic as a customer service subject. Recommending certain products or areas of information to a customer based on the past surfing or purchasing history of that person is a great way to help the customer. Appropriate recommendations are convenient for customers and are likely to be appreciated. In addition, offering tailored product or content information helps a site achieve its marketing and sales goals. Making recommendations is an example of proactive customer service—in other words, you are anticipating customer needs, not just reacting to problems or complaints.

Detailing the Facts

When you are running an electronic commerce site that sells products or are putting together a content site of a specific nature, be prepared to provide your customers with as many details as possible. The kind of information that each site requires will vary by type, but general guidelines for electronic commerce and content sites are helpful.

Details on Electronic Commerce Sites

Assume you are selling footwear through your electronic commerce site. It's not enough to offer a pair of "fuzzy bunny slippers." Shoppers need to know in what colors the slippers are available. They should also be able to select their own size. In addition, they'll need to know the kind of material of which the slippers are made, the washing instructions, and other similar details. Are the soles leather or rubber? Do the bunnies have whiskers? Floppy ears? Cottony tails? These are the kinds of details customers want when ordering products they can't examine in person.

As you learned earlier, part of customer service is understanding and recreating the experience your customer would be having in a physical store. Your site visitors are giving up the ability to touch the items they are shopping for in exchange for the convenience of the Web. That convenience won't exist if the information is not there to review. Product dimensions, colors, fabrics, number of units per container, and similar facts need to be included so that your audience know exactly what they can expect from their purchases.

Details on Content Sites

Sites that deal with information rather than with products need to be comprehensive in their reporting. It's not good enough to simply report that the Yankees beat the Red Sox 9 to 3. After all, ESPN.com has a full account of the game. Every story should be covered and presented in full.

Processing Online Orders

Order processing is one of the trickiest parts of any electronic transaction. Shopping carts, tax and shipping calculations, inventory tracking, and e-mail order confirmation are just some of the elements that must work together to provide a positive buying experience for customers. A breakdown in one of these elements can mean unhappy customers.

If visitors to your site are paying for anything—such as products or subscriptions—you need to alert them to every charge that they are paying. This includes surcharges, taxes, shipping, handling, and other fees. You also need to give them the anticipated delivery date, the durations of the subscriptions, and similar information.

Tracking Orders

Although online shoppers may accept giving up their ability to touch a product before they purchase it, it's harder to give up walking out of the store with a product and owning it as soon as it's purchased. For the electronic commerce site, an important part of customer service is letting the customer feel close to his or her purchase.

To do this, start by letting the user know how long it will take for an item to ship. This means making it clear as soon as possible whether the item is in stock. The out-of-stock alert needs to be obvious at the outset, when interest in the product is first generated. When the item has been put in the shopping cart and the customer clicks the checkout link is not the right time to display a page that says "Item is unavailable." This better-late-than-never approach discredits the site and leads to frustration for the shopper. If the customer has selected products that are in stock but that have varying shipping times, each product should be marked at the point of selection with an indication of how long shipping will take.

Figure 12-5 shows a screen shot of Staples.com, which does this notification very well. If all products are to leave the warehouse at the same time, the site should post the expected arrival date for that shipment and keep to that time frame.

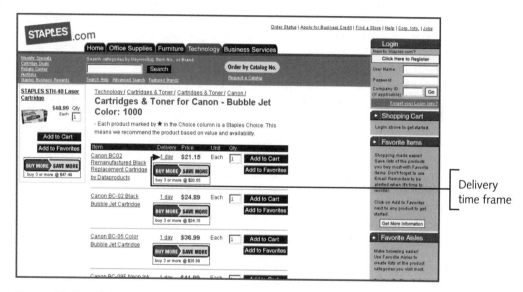

Figure 12-5   Shipment timing information shown on Staples.com

Sophisticated sites should provide a tracking system that allows shoppers to enter a tracking number and see where in the shipping process a particular order is. Such systems also should show any delays and the expected arrival date.

Returning Products

Inevitably, some orders will not be satisfactory, often through no fault of the site or the customer. Electronic commerce sites must be prepared to handle returns quickly and conveniently as part of providing customer service.

Suppose you order an American Eagles rugby jersey from an electronic commerce site that sells rugby merchandise. You specify the size, provide your credit card number and contact information, and upon placing the order, you are told that your jersey should be arriving in approximately five days. On the fifth day, a package arrives, and you open it to discover that instead of the American Eagles jersey, the company sent you the New Zealand All Blacks jersey. Although it may be an attractive shirt, it's not what you ordered, and so you decide to send it back.

How do you go about this? Sending back a heavy, long-sleeved shirt certainly won't be cheap, and why should you pay for it to be shipped back anyway? After all, it wasn't your fault the company sent you the wrong item. You could just keep it, but then your credit card would be charged for it. Even if you were going to send it back, where would you send it? To whom would you address the return, and would the company be able to fix the mix-up and send you the right item? Suddenly, shopping on the Web site seems very mysterious. You've made a purchase from a store that has no real physical existence. It's not even as "real" as a printed catalog that can at least be held.

Understandably, it can be somewhat confusing to deal with a company whose physical presence is hard to pinpoint. Sites deal with returns in a variety of ways. In the event that they sent you the wrong item (even if you ordered the wrong item accidentally), some of the less-organized sites will instruct you to simply keep it because they don't have the ability to accept and restock returns. Other sites will ask that you package the item and have it shipped back to them. Return postage is often printed on the shipping cartons. Of course, this solution requires the consumer to go out of his or her way to bring the item to the post office.

Sites should establish a return policy that is revealed to the customer in advance of processing an order. This policy should be based on options that are economically logical for the products being sold. For example, if an item's value is less than its shipping cost, it might make more sense for the customer to keep the item. In addition, the policy should be balanced against solutions that will most effectively serve customers. For instance, sites can arrange for courier pick up of returned items, include prepaid postage, and so on. The policy should be featured prominently in an easy-to-find area of the Web site so that there are no surprises if customers do need to make a return.

Retailers that have both online and traditional outlets enjoy a unique type of return policy. Companies such as **Staples, Kmart, Old Navy, Barnes & Noble, Circuit City,** and others allow shoppers to buy merchandise from the site and return or exchange it at their local retail outlets. Surprisingly, this approach has been slow to catch on with many consumers. While only a relatively small number of consumers have taken advantage of this benefit to date, this trend probably will change, and consumers will quickly recognize the value of such policies.

Customer service is just one consideration in developing a Web site. The next section summarizes the general things sites must do to achieve success.

SUCCESSFUL WEB SITES: PUTTING IT ALL TOGETHER

Building a successful Web site takes far more than an understanding of graphic design and programming. As you have learned, site developers need to understand business, design, and technology and how to put them together for maximum effect.

The Web market has changed drastically from the late 1990s, when the commercialization of the Web reached tremendous highs. Following the bursting of the Web bubble, a leveling-off of the Web economy brought more realistic business plans, better growth strategies, and smarter branding efforts. Whether they are electronic commerce sites that sell products, information-based sites that provide updated content in the hope of generating advertising income, or brochure-style sites that support existing companies in reaching prospective customers, Web sites share vital elements that can affect ultimate success. These common elements include the following:

- **Shared development**: Unless the site is unusually small, site development is a team effort, with team members offering talent in different disciplines.

- **Detailed market research**: Research data reveals what the market is looking for, what customers will respond to, and how the competition is doing business. This information helps companies design their sites to meet customer requirements and to differentiate themselves from competitors. Market research should be started before the first line of code for your site is ever written; learning too late that the results of market research conflict with the site's development direction can lead to disaster.

- **A solid design featuring substance over style**: Graphics and flash are not as important on a Web site as is a sound navigational system. Dividing site content into logical categories helps users find the information that they need as quickly as possible. This ease of use reduces frustration for visitors when using and understanding your site. Graphics should be simple and support the content without confusing the user. Their style should remain consistent throughout the site and be consistent with other brand material that your company or Web site has developed.

- **Brand development**: Ultimately, the success of a Web site can be significantly affected by how well the brand is developed and delivered to the target audience. The brand is the inherent promise that the company or site makes to its target audience. A brand takes time to build—it can't be bought overnight. Customers need to think of the brand as one that is reliable and one that keeps its brand promise. Without brand promise fulfillment, the brand becomes little more than a smokescreen; customers will easily see through the charade and abandon the brand. The brand that you create for your Web site should also have a personality that resonates with one or more specific audiences and that remains consistent throughout all media used in delivering the brand message.

- **Sticky site components**: Marketing of your Web site begins with the site itself. Sticky elements can generate return visits by an existing user base; marketing to existing customers is typically less expensive and more effective than new customer acquisition. Sticky marketing elements include personalization, permission-based e-mail, contests, and games.

- **Integrated marketing**: Successful marketing efforts often take an integrated approach, using multiple advertising media to send a message. The messages sent will vary in concept based on how well the brand is known by the target audience. Public relations (PR) is an important part of the marketing for a site. PR allows messages about the benefits and updates of a site to be

12

delivered through an impartial third party, the media. Communicating to editors is a precise process that requires different skills than communicating through other forms of advertising.

- **Effective customer service processes**: Customer service is as important in the cyber world as it is in the traditional world. Sites take steps to make sure that their visitors can find what they need easily, and in the case of a problem, that they have a clear way to communicate with the site for timely answers to questions and concerns.

Regardless of your site's ultimate goal—whether it be to generate income through electronic commerce or simply to increase brand awareness for your company—the Web plays an increasingly important role in modern communication and commerce. Despite the global attention that the Web has gotten over the past few years, the Internet as a whole is still in its infancy. Many new changes and evolutions are surely on the horizon, and they will reveal new opportunities for growth. The core principles of careful site planning, development, and marketing will comprise the foundation for limitless success for these future developments.

CHAPTER SUMMARY

- ❏ Customer service is an important part of business for companies operating both online and offline. In the Web environment, sites must take steps to provide care for their customers; to ignore customer service concerns is to risk losing customers to competition that is just a click away.

- ❏ Customer service starts by ensuring that users can easily find the information they seek. Making suggestions or recommendations to customers based on their previous visits or purchases is another proactive means of serving customers. FAQ pages, which provide detailed information, and allowing users to track their orders are other ways of ensuring positive customer experiences. When a user has a comment or question that requires specific attention by the site, the site needs to provide a communication method, typically e-mail, telephone, online chat, or instant messaging. Responses to customer inquiries must be both accurate and timely.

- ❏ How the customer feels about your site is a direct reflection on your brand, and this customer perception shapes the reputation of your site. A user's bad experience with a site will turn into a bad memory, and that can lead to negative word-of-mouth. A good experience will be remembered positively and is likely to translate into future visits.

- ❏ The key components for Web site success are shared development, detailed market research, sound site design, a well-developed brand, sticky site components, integrated marketing, and good customer service. The execution of these aspects can have a significant impact on your site's chances for success.

KEY TERMS

customer-effective
customer service
FAQ page
instant message (IM)
interactive voice response (IVR)

REVIEW QUESTIONS

1. Customer service starts when a user _____.

   a. first hears about the site

   b. first comes to the site

   c. buys a product

   d. has a question, comment, or problem

2. Most sites treat customer service as though it starts when a user _____.

   a. first hears about the site

   b. first comes to the site

   c. buys a product

   d. has a question, comment, or problem

3. One of the reasons IVRs are used for customer service is that human-operated systems cost about _____ as much per call.

   a. twice

   b. five times

   c. 17 times

   d. 20 times

4. In terms of design, sites interested in customer service should _____.

   a. weave entertainment features into the site wherever appropriate

   b. use as many Photoshop filter effects and design styles as possible

   c. keep the site clean and to the point, without sacrificing the aesthetics of the site for content

   d. include a splashy Flash introduction

12

5. Which of the following options is the most desirable auto-response e-mail?

    a. "Thank you for getting in touch with us. We have received your e-mail and will get back to you as soon as possible."

    b. "Thank you for getting in touch with us. Please allow 48 hours for us to review your inquiry and prepare a satisfactory response."

    c. "Thank you for getting in touch with us. Have you checked our FAQ area? You might find the information that you are looking for there."

    d. "Thank you for getting in touch with us. Please complete the attached form so that we may better serve you."

6. To fully utilize customer service efforts efficiently, a Web site should _____.

    a. deal with each problem and user individually

    b. deal with each problem and user individually and communicate problems to the development professionals so that the site can evolve

    c. deal with problems and users as groups, waiting until enough of the same type of comment occurs, and then sending a generic e-mail to all of them at one time

    d. create a larger FAQ section

7. A good IRV system should have no more than _____ levels of menu options.

    a. 10

    b. 7

    c. 5

    d. 3

8. One of the benefits of using customer service e-mail forms is that _____.

    a. they are easier to program than e-mail links

    b. you can create fields and questions that make user comments seem more positive than negative

    c. you can direct customers to make their points more concisely

    d. they are faster for the customer to use

9. Instant messaging is usually better than chat for conducting customer service because it _____.

    a. allows the customer service representative to handle multiple customers simultaneously

    b. allows for private conversations between customer service representatives and customers

    c. is faster

    d. Both A and B.

10. If your site is selling backpacks, which of the following is true?

    a. You need to tell your customers how large the backpacks are, their product weight, and their storage capacity. You also need to answer questions regarding their use as quickly as possible.

    b. You need to tell customers how many of each style you have sold.

    c. You need to tell customers when their order will arrive and how to return it, if necessary.

    d. Both A and C.

11. The letters FAQ stand for _____.

    a. Fully Automatic Questionnaire

    b. Fast Answers to Questions

    c. Frequently Asked Questions

    d. Find Answers Quickly

12. Describe two ways that a Web site can provide good customer service *before* problems or questions arise.

13. Describe why poor customer service may reflect poorly on an overall brand image.

14. A good customer service form will _____.

    a. consist of only yes or no questions

    b. be relatively short and to the point

    c. provide ample space for customers to detail all their problems with the site

    d. be required to be filled out before customers can check out and purchase their products

12

HANDS-ON PROJECTS

1. Your business plan is almost complete. Work with your partners to outline the steps that you plan to take to offer customer service to your site visitors. Explain what measures you will take to provide support for them online, as well as what they can expect in terms of offline support. Based on the type of site you are developing, do you feel that there will be more, less, or as much of a need for offline support (such as phone contact) as there will be for online support? State a case explaining why you plan to use the specific customer service measures that you are outlining. If possible, do some research into the costs of the customer service efforts you wish to employ.

2. Continuing on with your own site, assume that you and your partners will develop an FAQ page to help site visitors. The FAQ page should have no fewer than 10 questions, but can include as many FAQs as you feel are necessary. Is your site simple enough that only a minimal FAQ area will be required, or is it complex to the point that so many questions will likely arise that you may need to create categories of questions? Write the FAQ page as it should appear on your site.

   a. List the questions that you anticipate will be asked.

   b. Provide answers for the FAQs listed in Step a.

3. Find three sites—one electronic commerce site, one content-oriented magazine-style site, and one brochure site—and analyze their customer service efforts. Outline and describe the customer service steps that each site has taken. Write each site an e-mail asking a question about the site or its content.

   a. How long did it take for the e-mail to be answered?

   b. How important was it that the answer be provided quickly? Was the timing of the response appropriate?

   c. Was the quality of the answer satisfactory?

   d. List at least three positive aspects of each site's customer service efforts.

   e. List at least three negative aspects of each site's customer service efforts and provide suggestions for improvement.

4. Find three electronic commerce sites (do not use the electronic commerce sites you analyzed in Hands-on Project 3) and compare their return policies.

   a. How easy was the policy to find?

   b. How easy was the policy to read (was the language straightforward or complicated)?

   c. Does each site's return policy make buying from the site more or less attractive?

A

WEB TECHNOLOGIES

Each Web site uses a different combination of Web development languages and programs. A site's chosen technologies depend on the site's objectives. For example, an entertainment site's technological requirements will differ from those of a brochure-style site. The rapid development of programs gives Web site developers many options from which to choose. This appendix provides an overview of the more popular technologies in use as of 2001.

DESIGN PROGRAMS

Graphic design programs are used to create or manipulate images within a Web site. These images include photographs, logos, buttons, and so on. This category is dominated by Adobe Photoshop, although a few other programs are available.

Adobe Photoshop

The Adobe Photoshop graphic design program remains the leader in its category, offering the greatest functionality in terms of overall features and intuitive control. Designers can use it to do anything from simple color retouching to the development of exciting original creations. However, with each new version, Photoshop becomes more difficult for the new designer to understand, and it often takes weeks of practice just to scratch the surface of Photoshop's capabilities.

In 2001, Adobe released Photoshop 6.0. Web designers might find it more useful to stick with version 5.5, which was created primarily for use on the Web.

The interface for Photoshop 6.0 is shown in Figure A-1. What makes Photoshop particularly unique is its ability to create layers. With layers, designers can create composite pieces or special effects, without having to worry about doing permanent damage to the original image.

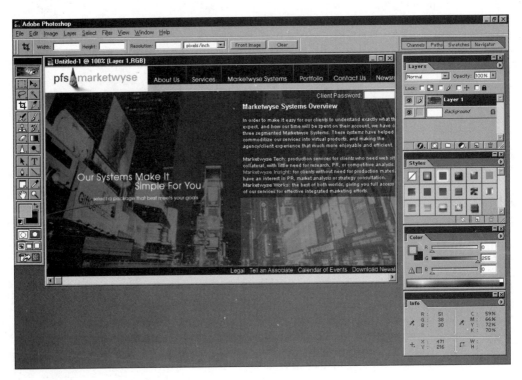

Figure A-1 The Photoshop user interface

Corel Draw

A lesser-known design program than Photoshop, Draw, from Corel, lets designers create graphics that are just as good as those created with its rival. However, the interface isn't as good, and complex designs are usually more difficult and slower to create, although learning the program can be a bit easier.

Microsoft Paint Shop Pro

The simplest of the three to learn, Microsoft Paint Shop Pro allows novice designers to jump right into their work. The overall quality of Paint Shop Pro and its features and capabilities are eclipsed by Photoshop's offerings.

Macromedia Fireworks

Macromedia Fireworks is a design program created specifically for developing Web graphics. However, because of the popularity of Photoshop, many designers do not use it for this purpose. What many designers *do* use it for, however, is to help compress files. Fireworks does a better job than most programs at compressing files to a very small file size without diminishing the quality of the image.

INTERACTIVE PROGRAMS

Interactivity on the Web has grown from a nice add-on feature to a recognized means of marketing and retaining an audience. Interactivity allows sites to provide personalized experiences for their site visitors.

Macromedia Flash

What began as a neat way to add animation to Web sites has launched a veritable revolution in development. Flash is a vector-based program from Macromedia that allows for quick-loading animation, interactivity, audio support, drag-and-drop features, game development, and database integration.

To view Flash movies online, users need to have a Flash plug-in loaded into the Plug-Ins folder of their browser. Most browsers that are version 4.0 or higher already have the Flash plug-in installed (which indicates just how widespread Flash development has become). When a user comes to a Flash site, but does not have the plug-in installed, he or she either sees nothing on the site or is led to another site (likely the Macromedia Web site) from which to download the plug-in. Downloading and installation, regardless of modem speed, is usually a quick process.

Flash has become popular with developers—perhaps too popular. Many site critics and surfers complain about sites that feature long, pointless introductory movies having little value relative to the site's content. These intros can make the collection of data more time-consuming. Flash animation should be used to enhance a Web site and make it more interesting or useful. Flash animation should not detract from the purpose a person has in coming to visit your site.

To see samples of Flash animation, go to **www.flashkit.com**.

Macromedia Shockwave

Also made by Macromedia, Shockwave allows designers to create sophisticated animations and interactivity. Shockwave converts Director files into a Web-compatible format. Director, also a Macromedia product, lets you build CD-ROM and DVD interfaces, and it is also gaining popularity for use as a Web site development program; however, its lengthy download time makes it less popular than Flash.

To see examples of Flash and Shockwave, go to **www.shockwave.com**.

Like Flash, Shockwave requires users to load a plug-in program to view applications in a browser. At the present, none of the popular browsers come equipped with a Shockwave plug-in installed.

WEB ASSEMBLY PROGRAMS

Although some developers still like to code their sites manually, WYSIWYG (What You See Is What You Get) programs have grown tremendously in popularity. These programs let developers lay out the images on each page without having to do too much manual programming.

Macromedia Dreamweaver

For many professional Web site developers, Dreamweaver has become the tool of choice for laying out Web sites. Easy to use but also loaded with a lot of features, Dreamweaver is not too difficult to learn, integrates well with various image formats, and offers a wide variety of functionality and options. The interface for Dreamweaver is shown in Figure A-2.

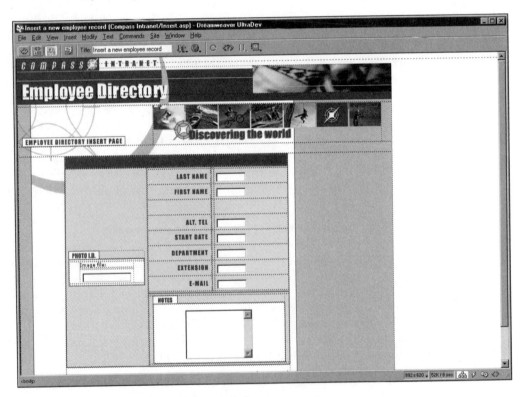

Figure A-2 The Dreamweaver user interface

Dreamweaver allows designers to reconfigure original Photoshop page composites and automatically reassemble them on the Web.

Microsoft FrontPage

Microsoft's entry in the WYSIWYG category is FrontPage. It is more limited in features and less functional and intuitive than Dreamweaver. Because it is relatively inexpensive, FrontPage has become popular with do-it-yourselfers and Web hobbyists, while most professional developers prefer to use Dreamweaver.

MARKUP LANGUAGES

Markup languages have grown in sophistication and extent of capabilities, expanding beyond the basic features of the original HTML described in Chapter 3.

HTML

HTML (Hypertext Markup Language) is the basic Web programming language used to build sites. HTML requires site developers to use tags around particular words to give them meaning in terms of page formatting and style definition. Tags are often used in pairs to indicate the beginning and ending of formatting styles. For example, `<CENTER>` is a tag that indicates that the text that follows should be centered on the Web page. The HTML code `<CENTER>Planning, Developing, and Marketing Successful Web Sites </CENTER>` would center the text (the title of this book) as it appears within the Web browser. HTML tags can also refer to graphics and their appearance.

Not a downloadable language or program like other programming tools, HTML comprises a standard set of tags that browsers recognize. To program in HTML, you need to type in a text file the words or graphic references that you want to appear on a page. You then use HTML tags to indicate the desired formatting of the text and graphics.

Web site developers and browser companies often develop new tags. These new tags that are recognized by browsers are released as updated versions of HTML. Implementing new tags doesn't require buying a program or downloading anything. It simply requires adding the new tags to the list of existing ones.

Programs such as Dreamweaver write the HTML code for you. In some form, HTML is still the foundation for all Web sites, even if newer, more advanced languages and applications have gotten more headlines as the Web begins to mature.

Figure A-3 shows HTML code for a relatively simple Web page.

```
<html>
<head>
<title>NCPP - National Council on Public Polls</title>
<meta http-equiv="Content-Type" content="text/html; charset=iso-8859-1">
</head>
<body bgcolor="#FFFFFF" LEFTMARGIN="0" TOPMARGIN="0" TEXT="#000000" LINK="#660000"
VLINK="#660000"onLoad="MM_preloadImages('images/pre%20down.gif','#959888601317');MM_preloadImages('images/
post%20down.gif','#959888623630')">
<TABLE BORDER="0" CELLPADDING="0" CELLSPACING="0" width="274">
    <!--row 1-->
<TR><TD width="182"><img src="images/01.gif"></TD>
      <TD width="75"><img src="images/02.gif"></TD>
      <TD width="71"><img src="images/03.gif"></TD>
      <TD width="88"><img src="images/04.gif"></TD>
      <TD WIDTH="65"><img src="images/05.gif"></TD>
      <TD ROWSPAN="3" width="121"><img src="images/06.gif"></TD></TR>
<!--row 2-->
<TR><TD COLSPAN="5">
<TABLE BORDER="0" CELLPADDING="0" CELLSPACING="0" WIDTH="479">
<TR><TD WIDTH="181"><A HREF="update.htm"><img src="images/07.gif" BORDER="0"></A></TD>
<TD WIDTH="298"><A HREF="qajsa.htm"><img src="images/08.gif" BORDER="0"></A></TD>
</TR></TABLE></TD></TR>
<!--row 3-->
<TR><TD COLSPAN="5">  CELLSPACING="0">
      <TABLE BORDER="0" CELLPADDING="0" CELLSPACING="0">
        <TR> <TD colspan="3"><img src="images/navbar.gif" width="479" height="28" usemap="#navbar" border="0"><map
name="navbar"><area shape="rect" coords="26,6,159,23" href="faq.htm"><area shape="rect" coords="172,4,270,23"
href="press.htm"><area shape="rect" coords="285,5,417,23" href="presspost.htm"></map></TD>
        </TR></TABLE>
</TD></TR>
<!--row 4-->
<TR><TD COLSPAN="6">
      <TABLE BORDER="0" CELLPADDING="0" CELLSPACING="0" width="100%">
<TR><TD width="101"><a href="disclosure.htm"><img src="images/12.gif" BORDER="0"></a></TD>
            <TD width="14"><img src="images/13.gif" BORDER="0"></TD>
            <TD BACKGROUND="images/14.gif" COLSPAN="5" width="488"> </TD>
</TR></TABLE>
</TD></TR>
<!--left nav-->
<TR><TD width="182" VALIGN="top">
<TABLE CELLPADDING="0" CELLSPACING="0" BORDER="0" WIDTH="101">
<TR><TD WIDTH="101"><A HREF="home.htm"><img src="images/15.gif" BORDER="0"></A></TD></TR>
<TR><TD WIDTH="101"><A HREF="officers.htm"><img src="images/17.gif" BORDER="0"></A></TD></TR>
<TR><TD WIDTH="101"><A HREF="members.htm"><img src="images/18.gif" BORDER="0"></A></TD></TR>
<TR><TD WIDTH="101"><A HREF="benefits.htm"><img src="images/19.gif" BORDER="0"></A></TD></TR>
<TR><TD WIDTH="101"><A HREF="join.htm"><img src="images/20.gif" BORDER="0"></A></TD></TR>
<TR><TD WIDTH="101"><A HREF="links.htm"><img src="images/21.gif" BORDER="0"></A></TD></TR>
<TR><TD WIDTH="101"><A HREF="contact.htm"><img src="images/22.gif" BORDER="0"></A></TD></TR>
<TR><TD WIDTH="101"><img src="images/23.gif" BORDER="0"></TD></TR>
<TR><TD WIDTH="101"><img src="images/24.gif" BORDER="0"></TD></TR>
</TABLE></TD>
      <TD VALIGN="top" COLSPAN="5"> <FONT FACE="arial, helvetica, sans-serif" SIZE="2">
        <!--heading--> </FONT> <font face="arial, helvetica, sans-serif" size="4" color="#5D4765">Press
        Releases</font><font face="arial, helvetica, sans-serif" size="4"> </font><FONT FACE="arial, helvetica, sans-serif"
SIZE="2"><BR>
        </FONT>
        <table width="252" border="0" height="36">
          <TR>
          <td width="109" height="47"><a href="presspre.htm" onMouseOut="MM_swapImgRestore()"
onMouseOver="MM_swapImage('document.Image24','document.Image24','images/pre%20down.gif','#959888601317')">
<img name="Image24" border="0" src="images/pre.gif" width="108" height="27"></a></td>
          <td width="28" height="47"> </td>
          <td width="109" height="47"><a href="presspost.htm" onMouseOut="MM_swapImgRestore()"
onMouseOver="MM_swapImage('document.Image25','document.Image25','images/post%20down.gif','#959888623630')">
<img name="Image25" border="0" src="images/post.gif" width="108" height="27"></a></td></tr>
          <tr><td height="166" colspan="3"><img src="images/looking.jpg" width="252" height="170"></td>
          </tr></table>
        <FONT FACE="arial, helvetica, sans-serif" SIZE="2"><BR>
        <B>For more information, please contact us at <A HREF="mailto:info@ncpp.org">info@ncpp.org</A>.
        </B> </FONT> <BR>
        <BR>
        <img src="images/wwb.gif" align="RIGHT" border="0"> </TD>
</TR></TABLE>
</body>
</html>
```

Figure A-3   HTML sample code

The Web page that results from the code shown in Figure A-3 is shown in Figure A-4.

Figure A-4   Page based on HTML sample code

XML

XML (eXtensible Markup Language) is a popular language that allows developers to have greater flexibility in their creation of Web sites. Unlike HTML, which is fixed and has a rigid set of commands that can be used in development, XML is a *metalanguage* (a language for describing other languages). In general terms, XML allows developers to create their own tags so that they can have limitless abilities to create various types of documents.

XML looks a lot like HTML and uses similar types of commands; however, the commands inside the < and the > can be commands that the developer makes up. Much of XML's abilities are far greater than HTML's, and they allow sites to be developed faster and to be more customizable to an audience. Sites written in XML can even run and load more efficiently than their HTML counterparts. Unfortunately, many browsers are still new to XML, and not all Web sites using XML can be read by all browsers.

For more information on XML, go to **www.ucc.ie/xml**.

DHTML

DHTML (Dynamic Hypertext Markup Language) was created by Microsoft as a proprietary language. DHTML's main function is to help add movement to a page, without using Flash. It allows certain portions of the browser to animate and aids in the creation of interactive games. It does this by supporting layers, which allow for more exact and real-time positioning of images.

Another popular use for DHTML is to alter the function of tags, depending on the activity occurring outside the browser. The activity might include a time or date change, a mouse click, and so on. This aspect of DHTML allows developers to control the appearance or occurrence of information and actions on a site based on the completion of a specific sequence of outside events.

Because DHTML is a language developed by Microsoft, Internet Explorer and Netscape each read DHTML a little differently, which can cause some problems for site developers who wish to use DHTML. Developers also need to implement scripts into their DHTML coding, which are usually written in JavaScript or VBScript, both of which are described later in this appendix.

FUNCTIONALITY LANGUAGES AND HOW THEY RELATE TO HOSTING ISSUES

Many languages are available to add functionality to a site. You should consider the project's parameters when determining which languages you'll need to use in development. This is especially true if you work for an agency or a traditional marketer that does not host sites in-house, but that instead has a third-party provider hosting the sites.

CGI

CGI (Common Gateway Interface) is a program used for transferring information between a Web server and a client. CGI programs can be written in most programming languages, although Perl and Visual Basic are among the more common.

CGI is used most frequently in processing online forms, allowing HTML-based pages to pass and process information collected in these forms. CGI formats the information in each field as categorized data. In comparison, simply passing the form information through e-mail does not allow for organization of data into categories.

CGI can reduce the speed of site loading, and the use of CGI opens a door for hackers to gain access to a server during the time that the CGI program is running.

Java

A programming language developed by Sun Microsystems, Java has gained widespread support. Intended to be multiplatform, Java can be used to develop full-scale applications and other smaller programs, which are known as applets.

The fact that it can be used anywhere is what has really launched Java into popularity. On the Web, Java is most often used to create online calculators, unusual animation, or unique effects that are more showy than useful. Java is difficult for the beginning programmer to learn, though for C++ programmers, it's a fairly easy transition.

A

JavaScript

Although many developers confuse JavaScript with Java, their names are the only thing these languages have in common. While Java is a complicated language that can create non-Web applications, JavaScript comprises a set of simpler commands. JavaScript programs can be viewed only in a browser environment. JavaScript was developed by Netscape and is used to add excitement to Web sites, allowing users to view stock charts, play games, and engage in other interactive and dynamic online applications.

SQL

SQL (Structured Query Language) is used for requesting information from a database. SQL (pronounced "sequel") is supported by PC database systems and can read data from databases that are spread out over multiple computer systems. This lets many users on a local area network access the same database at one time.

Visual Basic

One of the easier general programming languages to learn, Microsoft Visual Basic is also one of the most popular (although more experienced programmers often prefer C++). Visual Basic can be used for creating Web applications, although many developers see Visual Basic as the Microsoft FrontPage of programming. It is slower and less efficient than C++, and it does not work on all platforms.

VBScript

A Microsoft-developed language based on Visual Basic, VBScript is used to create Active Server Page (ASP) programs that run on a server and appear in a browser. VB Script is not as popular as JavaScript, but it is still widely used because of its close association with Visual Basic.

B

SAMPLE BUSINESS PLAN

The following is the framework of a business plan for a Web site that was launched in 1999. As the company is not a public company, the company name, site name, and the names of the individuals involved have been fictionalized. Many of the sections of this sample plan have been shortened; this appendix is intended to illustrate the general structure of a business plan, but because of the specific nature of each individual business, details have been reduced in this sample.

This plan was constructed in 1999 with the objective of attracting venture capital funding for the development of a Web site that provides interactive games. The site has a boardwalk-style theme, allowing users to experience the boardwalk experience from their homes. The games, therefore, are mostly boardwalk-style carnival games. The site's primary financial objective is to gain revenue through selling advertising space on the site.

EXECUTIVE SUMMARY

Boardwalk.com was seeking first round financing of $2.2 million to fund the development and launch of its premier online boardwalk gaming Web site in Fall 2000. A further $3.2 million round in Fall 2001 was required to increase sales and marketing and to support game development. Boardwalk intends to gross approximately $10.2 million by the end of year two and over $17 million by the end of year three.

Founded in 1999, Boardwalk.com was created as a community to provide the finest in online gaming, with its Web site consisting of boardwalk-style entertainment for children, teens, and adults.

Mission Statement

Boardwalk.com has a two-fold mission: to entertain and accommodate users while attracting advertisers. For families, it offers children, teenagers, and adults a fun and safe online entertainment source. Through game playing, prize winning, and boardwalk-style shopping, Boardwalk.com allows audiences to enjoy the experience of a seaside, carnival atmosphere for an endless summer vacation.

To aid advertisers and partners, Boardwalk.com visitors must click banner ads to acquire tokens for game playing. This strategy provides advertisers with direct traffic to their sites, resulting in increased product sales. The site also provides advertisers with unique promotional opportunities, including boardwalk-style stores and "flying airplane banners" that are consistent with the seaside, amusement pier theme. The primary business objective is to promote brand extension and site stickiness and to develop new revenue opportunities for contributors.

The Market

According to the 1999 Forrester Technographics Field Study, 60 percent of all online gamers are women, and 63 percent are between the ages of 25 and 44. The Forrester study also estimates that more than 100 million consumers like to play traditional games. Forrester research predicts online gaming will soar, and it expects Internet game revenue to explode to $1.5 billion by the year 2001.

The Games

Boardwalk.com consists of unique boardwalk-style games developed in Shockwave animation to target adult women, who are the majority of online gamers. It also targets adult men, teenagers, and children. The site is geared to look like a real amusement pier, complete with game booths, arcades, boardwalk shops, and carnival rides. Games like Frog Bog, Ring Fling, and Stray Cat Strut attract all audiences, and the game parlor, which consists of games like King of the Boardwalk Trivia, Surfside Keno, and Beach Bingo, are geared to attract adult audiences. Players can accumulate points to use toward prizes. The top five scorers in each game will receive monthly prizes.

A new game will be introduced each month after the site launch in Fall 2000. Teasers will generate interest to maintain Boardwalk.com's stickiness, keeping audiences coming back for more. In order to navigate the site, users are required to click advertisers' sites to play games.

Revenue Streams

Boardwalk.com will gross approximately $2 million by year one. That will rise to over $17 million by year three through aggressive marketing and advertising campaigns. These campaigns will attract companies across the United States that will have the opportunity to advertise on the Boardwalk.com site. Advertising includes unique and strategic positioning of banner ads, sponsorships, affiliate programs, and electronic commerce stores throughout the Boardwalk site. These advertising opportunities afford advertisers maximum exposure to Boardwalk audiences, who are required to click banner ads and other forms of advertising to play the boardwalk-style games.

Competition

Boardwalk.com is unique. Currently, there are no other boardwalk game sites on the Internet like Boardwalk.com.

The Company

Boardwalk.com is the brainchild of Jim Smith and Jane Brown. Smith, who is president/CEO of the company, has worked as a business consultant over the past seven years assisting many entrepreneurs in opening and operating their own successful small businesses. Smith has developed and built a Web-based company, Boardwalk. Brown has spent 17 years as a contract sales manager and independent sales representative in the window treatment industry.

Technology Plan

In line with Boardwalk's originality, 3D Studio Max is used to make the site more realistic. Using this technology, which is unusual for most Web sites, allows for more flexibility in vantage points and viewing angles. It also creates new and unique advertising opportunities. Other graphic design programs that will be used in the development of the site include Photoshop and Flash.

Schedule

Since its founding in 1999, Boardwalk.com has recruited an advertising/communications firm to build a 3-D, animated gaming Web site to produce collateral material to publicize the site, and to launch a public relations (PR) campaign. A sales team is also in place to populate the site with advertisers of "beachy" types of products, and other products that appeal to the target audiences. Boardwalk.com will be hiring a chief financial officer (CFO) with an extensive, corporate accounting background to distribute funds. The CFO will be Internet/technical savvy to assist in launching the site. A chief operating officer (COO) will also be hired to run Boardwalk's operations.

The production is scheduled to have nine games in place at the time of launch in September 2000, and it will continue to develop a new game each month.

Boardwalk.com anticipates an initial public offering 12–18 months after the launch of the Web site.

MARKET OVERVIEW

Market Size

According to the 1999 Forrester study, 60 percent of online gamers are women, and 63 percent are between the ages of 25 and 44. The study also estimates that more than 100 million consumers like to play traditional games.

Market Life-Cycle

The game industry is dynamic and constantly growing, with innovation coming from all corners of the globe. The game industry's total sales will overcome those of the movie business this year. Jon Peddie Associates predicts that there will be about 1 billion Internet-enabled, 3D-enabled devices in the market by 2004. As the Internet market grows, it can be expected that online gaming will have VCR-like penetration of the home market.

Competition

Figure B-1 outlines Boardwalk.com in comparison to its competition.

NabiscoWorld (All Shockwave)

(Site description)

Uproar (Shockwave)

(Site description)

Boardwalk.com Competitive Analysis					
	Boardwalk.com	NabiscoWorld	Boxerjam	Won.net	Uproar
Games:					
Boardwalk Theme	yes	yes	no	no	no
Amusement Park Games	yes	yes	no	no	no
Card Games	yes	no	no	yes	no
Trivia Games	yes	no	yes	no	yes
Classic Games	no	yes	no	yes	yes
Casino Games	no	no	no	yes	yes
Traditional Games	yes	yes	yes	yes	yes
Game Shows	no	no	yes	yes	yes
Sports Games	no	yes	yes	yes	yes
Graphics	yes	yes	yes	yes	yes
Prizes	yes	yes (Gameboys/Palm Pilots)	yes	yes	yes
Advertising	yes	no (corporate site)	yes	yes	yes
Demographics	n/a	n/a	80% female/20%male ("shopping moms")	68% male/32% female (median age 25-44)	54% Female/ 46% Male
Shockwave	n/a	yes	n/a	n/a	yes
Users per month	n/a	n/a	900,000+	300,000 (2.5 million registered)	6.2 million registered (3.6 million unique)
Newsletter	n/a	no	yes	no	no
Shopping Links	n/a	yes	yes	yes	yes

Figure B-1 Competitive analysis

THE SERVICE

Description of the Site

The site is geared to look like a real boardwalk amusement pier, complete with game booths and stores on the left side, the beach on the right side, and an amusement park in the background. Patrons "walking the boards" can enter stores by clicking them. The stores link to other Web sites as an alternative to the typical advertisement banner on the edges of the screen. In addition, the strategic placement of various types of advertisements along the boardwalk provides more room for the main screen.

Boardwalk users can play games for free. The only requirement on the site is that visitors must click advertisements to receive "tokens." This is a win-win situation for all parties involved. The user gets to play free games and win actual prizes, the advertiser's name is viewed by many people through a highly trafficked Web site, and the owners of the site gain revenue by customers clicking their advertisements.

Currently under development are seven boardwalk-style games and six parlor-style games. The mix will include both trivia and traditional games.

The Games

The Frog Bog

This game is highly symbolic because its main character is also the Web site's mascot. The frog's name will be determined through a sponsored contest played by visitors. The frog and the Boardwalk.com logo will be printed on stickers, temporary tattoos, flying discs, and other promotional items that can be distributed at the beach, at colleges, and at baseball games and other public locales.

Each player receives five frogs for each token. The player picks up a frog using the mouse and then places it on the end of a catapult. The other end has a target, and the player hits it with a mallet. A meter shows force percentage. When the player is satisfied with the force he or she is using, the catapult is struck with a mallet. The 3D-rendered frog is sent sailing through the air into the pond. The object is to land the frogs onto the flowered part of a lily pad. Each of the four lily pads is on a turntable in the water. The player scores points when a frog successfully lands in a flowered part of a lily.

Ideas to be incorporated into the development of the site: The site will have Cajun swamp music in the background. It will also include croaking and mosquito sounds. Occasionally, the frogs waiting their turn will zap a fly with their tongue.

Shoot the Moon

(Game description)

Hot Shot B-Ball

(Game description)

Ring Fling

(Game description)

The Wheel of Prizes

(Game description)

Stray Cat Strut

(Game description)

Wild Wild West Shooting Gallery

(Game description)

Boardwalk Game Parlor

There will be six games added to the Web site. They will be geared more toward an intellectual audience and will include a concentration game, a trivia game, backgammon, Keno, bingo, and chess/checkers. The Boardwalk Game Parlor will have a social atmosphere where sophisticated players can be challenged by interactive games.

Once again, players collect tokens to play games by clicking an advertisement. In addition, there will be chat rooms in the parlor where users can hang out or challenge others to a duel of mental brawn. The games will be named:

- (Who Wants to Be) King of the Boardwalk
- Concentration Game
- Surfside Keno
- Beach Bingo
- Beachgammon
- Chess/Checkers

Other Ideas to be Incorporated into the Site

- Arcade (play traditional video games)
- Test of strength (hit the target to ring the bell)
- Fishing game

Commerce Opportunities

There are many creative ways that an advertiser can splash a company name across the screen instead of only in the basic banner or box. With Boardwalk.com, advertisements can be camouflaged within the scenery in places such as airplane banners, storefronts, lamp posts, beach huts, and boats.

The most appropriate advertisers are those whose products coincide with the ambiance of summer. These businesses include retailers of sunscreen, surf boards and accessories, clothing, sunglasses, soft drinks, consumer electronics, and ice cream. Other advertisements could include those from amusement parks and shore resorts.

Areas of Interest

This Web site would catch the attention of people who are seeking clean, wholesome entertainment as well as those who are looking to win some prizes. The major appeal of Boardwalk.com is that it allows users to experience the summertime all year. It also allows dwellers of the Midwest, or other locations not near the beach, to be introduced to the shore and to pier culture.

Boardwalk.com also serves another purpose: It provides valuable information to vacationers and families by providing shore resort destination information, restaurant listings, travel agency information, maps, and online stores.

Added Value

Besides promoting an "endless summer" theme, visitors do not have to spend any money to have fun. They also get access to entertaining sites without trying to decipher search engine results. In addition, they can become "famous" and "immortal" by having their names posted on a high scorer's list.

The advertiser benefits as well because the player has no choice but to click advertisement banners and store fronts to receive game tokens. It is also a less-expensive way to have a store in a virtual mall because there are so many companies at the site sharing the expense. Another major benefit to the advertiser is that the price to display its name varies, based on the size of it.

REVENUE STREAMS

Boardwalk.com will gross a total of $2 million by year one, rising to $17 million by year three through aggressive marketing and advertising campaigns. These campaigns will attract companies across the United States who want the opportunity to advertise on the Boardwalk.com site. They will benefit from the unique and strategic positioning of banner ads, sponsorships, affiliate programs, and electronic commerce stores integrated throughout the Boardwalk site. These advertising opportunities afford advertisers maximum exposure to Boardwalk's audiences.

Boardwalk offers the following types of advertising:

Banner Ad Sales

General Site Banner Ads

- Framed HTML banners
- Billboard site banner ads with these pixel sizes: 800 × 373 (hanging sign), 610 × 153, and 612 × 800 (poster)
- Airplane sign banner ads
- Lamp post banner ads
- Storefront banners ads along the boardwalk/amusement pier
- Random banners including boardwalk posts, garbage cans, and newspaper dispensers

Game Interior Banners

- Top banner ads within the interior of each of game

- Bottom banner ads within the interior of each game

Sponsorship Programs

- Full package game sponsors will sponsor game awning advertisements, score-board advertising, and poster advertising on game counters. The site will incorporate sponsor's product(s) into challenges to game players.

- Page sponsors will sponsor e-mails to Boardwalk players who opt to have information and news updates sent to them.

- Contest sponsors will have their names and logos appear on the portion of the site that has game players involved in contests. For example, they can name the "Frog Bog" frog. Sponsors will also be integrated into any promotional material for contests.

- Pre-game sponsors will be prominently displayed while pre-games run for Boardwalk users as they wait for games to download.

- Post card sponsors will appear on post cards that can be e-mailed to friends from the Boardwalk site.

Affiliate Programs

Affiliate programs will be available to the following types of advertisers:

- Video game retailers

- Music retailers

- Movie retailers

Retailers will have the opportunity to be a part of Boardwalk's program to sell products through the site. They can use a kiosk, with Boardwalk receiving approximately 5 percent of the sales.

Electronic Commerce

Upon launch of the site, Boardwalk.com will have boardwalk storefronts prominently displaying the names and logos of advertisers. Because Boardwalk visitors are required to click banner ads, they will do so. When they click storefront banners, they will immediately be taken to the advertiser's site, where they will view the advertiser's catalog of products. This affords the advertiser the opportunity to drive more traffic to its site from Boardwalk. Eventually, as a part of Phase II of the Boardwalk launch, electronic commerce will be developed into the Boardwalk site, in which case, advertisers can incorporate their own directories and Web sites for electronic commerce sales.

The types of electronic commerce stores Boardwalk is seeking include Ron Jon's surf items, Coppertone tanning products, J. Crew beach towels, and L.L. Bean lounge chairs. It also includes national advertisers, such as soft drink manufacturers, candy companies, and swimwear manufacturers.

Additional Expansion

Boardwalk.com will continue to expand on the development of its games, especially as the industry grows and changes. Future game development will include entertainment on the cutting edge of technology that specifically appeals to Boardwalk audiences.

THE COMPANY

Founded in 1999, Boardwalk.com of Anytown, New Jersey, was created to provide the finest in online gaming. Its Web site consists of boardwalk-style entertainment for children, teens, and adults. Families can "walk the boards" and find a host of games, arcades, and electronic commerce shopping outlets for their endless summer pleasure.

Boardwalk.com Mission Statement

Boardwalk.com has a two-fold mission: to entertain and accommodate users while attracting advertisers.

Executive Team

- Jim Smith: President/CEO
- Jane Brown: Vice President, Sales

STRATEGIC PLAN

Overview of Site

The foremost objective of Boardwalk.com's business strategy is to brand the site as *the* online boardwalk game site. At launch, Boardwalk.com will be unique and distinguished and completely recognizable to beachgoers, gamers, and those who have never even seen an ocean. Qualities such as online shopping correlating to the endless summer theme will allow it to stand above the rest. Boardwalk.com is not limited to promoting gaming components; users will be able to purchase beach attire and several products related to the beach/boardwalk theme.

Initially, the advertising will be done on a regional basis through various channels, and it will spread out nationally and internationally after gaining enough revenue to support such advertising. Acting as a "new wave" in online gaming, Boardwalk.com plans to attract 750,000 users within the first year through advertising efforts, and it expects gross revenues to exceed $2 million within the first year.

Focus

Overall, the Web site has many different "rooms" intended to retain a user's interest. There are seven carnival-like games. Stores along the boardwalk allow visitors to shop as if they were walking along an authentic boardwalk.

On the advertising side, Boardwalk.com supports and facilitates electronic commerce between many businesses, including clothing stores, sunscreen manufacturers, sunglass manufacturers, ice cream stores, and any other store related to summer.

Positioning

What allows Boardwalk.com to stand above the competition is its plan to be the first to promote an endless summer theme. Although boardwalks are typically part of East Coast culture, knowledge of Boardwalk.com's existence will spread across the country through advertising, PR, and word of mouth.

Site Use

The main function of Boardwalk.com is entertainment. The main screen will be attractive to draw in potential consumers and deliver a "game fix." The integrated theme of combined gaming and shopping will be another reason for success of this site. This idea brings users of all ages to Boardwalk.com, but it caters to women in their 30s who comprise the majority of online gamers. Methods of site stickiness will be implemented to attract and retain customers. Strategies such as animated e-mail postcards will persuade users to draw in additional gamers to Boardwalk.com.

Phases of Game Development

Initially, the site will be released with five "boardwalk" and two "parlor" games so that it is available to the public by Labor Day weekend 2000. Phase II will introduce more games as the site grows. This method keeps users coming back to try new games as they are introduced. "Teasers" will be implemented to pique the curiosity of prospective consumers.

Relationship Between Advertising and Branding

A major reason that Boardwalk.com will undergo an extensive marketing campaign is that studies have confirmed that advertising leads to an increase in revenue.

Boardwalk.com intends to be *the* online boardwalk game site. The idea is to brand the site so that when consumers think of an amusement pier, they immediately associate it with Boardwalk.com. By saturating the market using print, television, radio, outdoor billboard, and guerilla marketing, Boardwalk.com intends to be a household name.

MARKETING PLAN

The Boardwalk.com marketing plan is designed to target its primary audiences, including female shoppers age 30 and over, game-playing youngsters age 7 to 12, and teenagers/young adults age 13 to 22. This is done in an effort to drive traffic to the Boardwalk Web site and to give advertisers increased exposure to these audiences.

The marketing plan is broken into two phases, with Phase I to be launched Labor Day weekend (2000 or just prior to that date). Phase II will kick off approximately six months to one year later (after the initial launch date of Boardwalk.com). Phase I will concentrate on prominent areas with boardwalk and amusement pier entertainment. In addition, strong cyber and traditional marketing campaigns (with an extra PR push to drive traffic) will move Boardwalk into Phase II with a favorable position to advertise on a national basis, in both print and broadcast media.

Online Marketing

- Banner ad trade-offs (Phase I)
- Link exchanges (Phase I)
- Kiosks (Phase II)
- Banner ad campaign (Phase II)
- Sponsoring of e-mails (Phase II)
- Viral marketing (Phase I)

Radio Advertising

- Local markets (Phase I)
- Major markets (Phase II)

B

Print Advertising

- Regional consumer publications (Phase I)
- Sunday newspaper inserts (Phase I)
- Women's interest magazines (Phase II)
- Teen publications (Phase II)
- Internet publications (Phase II)
- Music publications (Phase II)
- Comic books (Phase II)
- Gaming magazines (Phase II)

Guerilla Marketing and Promotional Items

- Promotional hand-outs (Phase I)
- Airplane beach banners (Phase I)
- Charity events (Phase I)
- Independent league baseball (Phase II)
- Beach'nBillboard™ devices, such as a sand roller (Phase II)
- New Jersey Balloon Festival (Phase II)

PR Campaign

- Regional (Phase II)
- National (Phase II)

Television Advertising (Phase II)

- Weekend programming for kids
- Weeknight programming
- Morning talk shows
- Sports
- Music
- Others

Charity Events

(Description of events)

Sponsors/Prizes

(Description of items)

Additional Information on the Web Site

(Description of information)

Kiosks for Charitable Raffles

(Description of kiosks)

Boardwalk Contests

(Description of contests)

TECHNOLOGY PLAN

Boardwalk.com will use a multitude of technological applications to bring it to life graphically and to make it functional for both advertisers and Web visitors alike.

Overview

Boardwalk.com will be a unique Web site from a graphical and functional standpoint. The following is a brief rundown of protocol from a functionality perspective for a participating Web visitor:

- The user visits the site (the first time) and enters his or her name and other information. This information is stored in a SQL Server database. 50 credits are placed into the user's account upon registration.

- The user visits advertisers by clicking banners or other ad vehicles. Each click on a new advertisement adds 50 more credits into the user's "account."

- The user can spend credits in boardwalk stores for discounts on online purchases and game playing.

- The user can spend credits to play Boardwalk.com games, such as the Ring Fling or Frog Bog. Each game played will deduct a certain number of credits from the user's account in the database.

- The game is played to completion. The score is tallied and recorded in the user's database area. As more games are played, the score in the database accumulates.

- Each week, the user receives auto-generated e-mail with the top 20 scores for that given month and is encouraged to return to the site to continue competing.

- At the end of each month, all scores are reviewed by the server, and the top five users with the highest score receive prizes.

- User credits and scores will be eliminated and started fresh at the start of each new month.

The following list records the predominant technological programming devices used for Boardwalk.com:

- 3D Studio Max

- Director 8

- SQL Server

FINANCIAL SECTION

Boardwalk income is projected annually over a period of three years. The company expects to generate revenue from the following sources:

Banner Ads

Banner ads will make up approximately 50 percent of the total revenue stream. Banner ad opportunities will increase per year as more games and commerce are brought into the site. Banner ad prices will range from $10 CPM for random ads on the boardwalk to highly targeted ads including airplane banners at $45 CPM, storefront banners at $25 CPM, and HTML banners embedded in the framework of the site at $60 CPM. At launch, advertisers will receive two months free advertising if they commit to a six-month contract. Also at launch, minimum advertising per month is $1000.

Sponsorship Programs

Sponsorship programs will allow advertisers to sponsor an individual game for a three-month minimum contract to a six-month maximum contract. Sponsorship programs will strategically place an advertiser's name and logo in various spots within a game. The advertiser's products will also become a part of the game challenges for increased exposure. The full sponsorship package is $10,000 per month. Sponsorship programs will make up approximately 25 percent of Boardwalk.com's annual revenues.

Electronic Commerce

Advertisers can place banner ads on the Boardwalk site with links to their own Web sites. Through Boardwalk, these advertisers will have increased exposure as game-playing visitors enter their sites and afford them the opportunity to sell products. Advertisers will give Boardwalk 10 percent of the sales of their products. Electronic commerce will generate approximately 10 percent of Boardwalk's revenues.

Customized Sites

Customized sites will allow advertisers to be listed in directories, build Web pages, and have electronic commerce sites within the Boardwalk game site. For approximately $150 a month, an advertiser can participate in an electronic commerce program and sell products through this Boardwalk offering. Customized sites will generate approximately 10 percent of Boardwalk's annual revenues.

Affiliate Programs

Advertisers will participate in affiliate programs that allow them to sell products off the Boardwalk site. Boardwalk will receive a 5 percent commission on any product that is sold through its own Web site. Affiliate programs comprise nearly 5 percent of Boardwalk's annual revenues.

Expense Assumptions

Boardwalk's marketing and PR campaigns will be intense programs at launch and continue through the life of the site. The purpose of a strong promotional program is two-fold: to generate interest and drive consumer traffic for game playing and to attract national advertisers to participate in any of the banner ad, sponsorship, electronic commerce, or affiliate programs. The marketing and PR efforts will increase over 40 percent between year one and year three. This will amount to significant visibility and branding in all forms of print and broadcast media, online marketing, and guerilla marketing and promotional efforts (especially as new games are developed and launched).

Corporate expenses include all expenses associated with technology. They will be outsourced to a Web development company that will handle the development of boardwalk games, provide maintenance to the site, and coordinate all ASP and hosting services. Personnel expenses, including executive team and administrative salaries and benefits, accounting and legal fees (in-house and outsourced), and other fixed and variable costs are also included.

Figure B-2 outlines the financial aspects of Boardwalk.com.

Boardwalk.com	Year 1	Year 2	Year 3	Total
Revenues				
Banner ad sales	$982,340	$4,460,000	$8,547,000	$13,989,340
Sponsorship programs	$650,200	$3,950,000	$5,630,000	$10,230,200
Customized sites	$154,850	$1,367,000	$2,100,000	$3,621,850
Affiliate programs	$55,900	$124,950	$190,990	$371,840
Electronic commerce	$180,625	$380,980	$559,070	$1,120,675
Total Revenues	**$2,023,915**	**$10,282,930**	**$17,027,060**	**$29,333,905**
Expense Projections				
Outsource Traditional Marketing/PR				
Print advertising	$330,000	$429,000	$471,900	$1,230,900
Television advertising	$236,000	$318,600	$350,460	$905,060
Outdoor billboard	$128,000	$172,800	$190,080	$490,880
Radio advertising	$154,000	$207,900	$228,690	$590,590
Guerilla marketing & promotion	$85,000	$114,750	$126,225	$325,975
PR/ad campaign fees	$143,500	$193,725	$213,098	$550,323
Total Traditional Marketing/PR	**$1,076,500**	**$1,436,775**	**$1,580,453**	**$4,093,728**
Outsource Online Marketing				
Banner ad campaign	$115,000	$155,250	$170,775	$441,025
E-mail sponsorship	$51,000	$68,850	$75,735	$195,585
Total Online Marketing	**$166,000**	**$224,100**	**$246,510**	**$636,610**
Total Marketing/PR Expense	**$1,242,500**	**$1,660,875**	**$1,826,963**	**$4,730,338**
Corporate				
Outsource Web technology/MIS	$185,000	$240,000	$280,000	$705,000
ASP Web	$245,000	$520,000	$590,000	$1,355,000
Web service provider	$45,000	$180,000	$220,000	$445,000
Total Technology Expense	**$475,000**	**$940,000**	**$1,090,000**	**$2,505,000**
Personnel				
Executive	$385,000	$435,000	$445,000	$1,265,000
Administrative	n/a	$35,000	$45,000	$80,000
Payroll taxes	$16,095	$22,620	$28,710	$67,425
Insurance	$6,000	$6,600	$7,200	$19,800
Workman's comp insurance	$8,000	$10,000	$14,000	$32,000
Total Personnel	**$415,095**	**$509,220**	**$539,910**	**$1,464,225**
General Overhead				
Furniture & fixtures	$10,000	$3,000	$3,000	$16,000
Office rent	$24,000	$24,000	$24,000	$72,000
Office equipment/computers	$10,000	$5,000	$5,000	$20,000
Utilities & telephone	$17,000	$12,000	$14,000	$43,000
Professional fees/legal	$20,000	$10,000	$10,000	$40,000
Office supplies	$7,200	$8,400	$9,600	$25,200
General contingency	$10,000	$12,000	$14,000	$36,000
Total General Overhead	**$98,200**	**$74,400**	**$79,600**	**$252,200**
Expense Total	**$2,230,795**	**$3,184,495**	**$3,536,473**	**$8,951,763**
Net Income	**($206,880)**	**$7,098,435**	**$13,490,588**	**$20,382,143**

Figure B-2 Financial overview

C

COLOR ON THE WEB

Because of the way computers represent colors, and because of variances in computer platforms, it is important to understand a few basic facts about using color when designing Web sites.

When light from the sun or some other source reflects off the surface of an object, the light that you see is processed in your eyes by cones in your retinas. This light is a mix of all available colors in the spectrum, as seen through a prism. The cones in your retina filter the light into red, green, or blue, depending on the chemical composition of the object off which the light is reflecting. When light filters into all cones at maximum intensity, you see white. When light is filtered as only red and blue, you see purple. When the chemical composition of an object absorbs light and does not allow light to reflect from the object, you see the object as black.

Depending on the amount of red, green, and blue being filtered, the brain can perceive millions of variations of colors. While the cones in the retinas see the range of different colors (*hues*), other areas of the retina, called rods, responds to light levels, allowing us to see ranges of light and dark for each color, creating variation of shades.

Computer monitors, TV screens, and other such devices work in conjunction with the cones in your eyes. With the use of red, green, and blue phosphors that emit light, your eye sees pixels on these monitors the same way that they see other elements in nature. A purple color on a monitor screen is a mixture of red and blue light emanating from the screen.

Because the Web is typically presented on a computer monitor, Web site designers can use within their design any color that is a mixture of red, green, and blue. This color variety is called the *RGB color model*, and the range of colors that can be seen within the color model is called a *gamut*. While the RGB color model does not allow as many colors to be seen on a computer screen as we can see in nature (nature can provide varying levels of brightness that computer monitors can't replicate), the RGB color model is wider than most other color models; another popular color model, CMYK (Cyan, Magenta, Yellow, and Black), which is used for printing, has a far smaller gamut of color.

You may need to simulate some of the colors that appear on a Web site in a printed piece, such as a brochure. Because RGB has a larger color gamut than the CMYK color gamut, be aware that you may be using a color on your Web page that can be seen on a monitor, but that can't be represented on paper because it falls outside the CMYK color gamut. This could cause problems if you are trying to build a brand and need to remain consistent with key colors throughout all material.

You may hear the term "Web-safe colors" used. This term was more common in the mid-to-late 1990s, when more people had older computer monitors that only allowed them to see 256 colors. Photographic-style imagery can use thousands of colors to show an image, far exceeding the 256-color limit of some older monitors. Web-safe colors are colors that can be seen by those 256-color monitors. Those colors appear exactly the same on monitor to monitor, regardless of the monitor manufacturer, and whether they are being seen on a Macintosh computer or a Windows PC. Today, however, the 256-color monitor is so outdated that it's hardly a consideration, reducing the role that Web-safe colors play in Web design. However, Web-safe colors are still used in instances when it is of vital importance that a particular color be seen exactly the same by all Web users.

While most monitors today have no difficulty displaying millions of colors, Windows computers generally display all colors a few shades darker than do Macintosh computers. A Web site designer who is working on a Macintosh and who is using a very dark blue in his or her design can expect that color to appear almost black to a Web user who uses a Windows computer and monitor.

Glossary

account executive — Web site development team member; the key figure heading up the team effort.

account management site — A site that lets people supervise their personal financial, utility, and other types of accounts.

ad serving program — Software that places and tracks banner ads on Web sites.

advanced programmer — A Web site development team member; responsible for incorporating Web site technology and programming.

advertising — The branch of marketing in which different media outlets are used to convey a message directly from the advertiser to its desired audience. Marketers purchase the ad space or time and control the message that the audience receives.

art director — A Web site development team member; a graphics expert who typically reports to the creative director and who is responsible for overseeing and directing the graphic designers in the creation and design of the site itself and its support materials.

auto-response — A prewritten response to a user inquiry that is sent automatically by the server.

background graphics — Images in the Web browser that appear behind the site content.

banner ad — The thin horizontal or vertical ad that appears at the edges of many Web pages.

basic site programmer — A Web site development team member; sets up the client's Web site, implementing the graphics elements, content, and hyperlinks into one cohesive page or site.

beta test — The final test of a nearly completed site or application to discover last-minute bugs and other incidental problems.

bitmap graphics — Graphics that are composed of one or more pixels that come together to create an image.

brand — The promise that a Web site, company, product or service makes to its customers.

brand ad — A Web ad that becomes a subtle part of a site's background.

brand loyalty — A consumer's commitment to a brand that occurs when a consumer will go out of his or her way to buy specific brands that they trust, even if they are harder to find or more expensive than other available options.

brand management — Efforts to promote a brand and ensure it is being used properly and effectively.

brand recognition effort — An advertisement that promotes a brand name, making the audience associate that brand with a feeling, lifestyle, or philosophy.

brand testing — Testing to ensure brand integrity is initiated during the design phase of site development.

brick-and-mortar store — A business that exists only in a physical location.

broken link — A link that doesn't lead anywhere.

business plan — An outline of a site's concept, market, anticipated revenue structure, marketing strategy, and technology plans.

business-to-business electronic commerce (B2B) — Sites servicing the business sector.

business-to-consumer electronic commerce (B2C) — Online retail sales by a commercial site to a general consumer; B2C accounts for most Web site sales.

call to action — An advertisement that requires an immediate customer response (such as calling the company to order the advertised product) to be successful.

campaign — An organized effort of advertising and marketing to promote a distinct product or entity that is spread over one or more media outlets and is centered around a conceptualized theme.

channel test — An evaluation of only one or more first-tier Web site categories and their underlying navigational tiers; helps to highlight problem areas in complex navigational structures.

click-and-mortar — A brick-and-mortar company that has a Web version of its business.

click-and-mortar landscape — The combination of online and traditional economic structures.

click-through — The number of times Web site visitors click an ad to link to the advertiser's site.

comp — A design sample.

competitive analysis — A determination of key factors regarding competitors vying for your target market.

concept testing — The evaluation of audience reaction and response to the purpose of your site.

conceptual approach — An advertising effort that uses a story, metaphor, image, joke, or other indirect means to send a message.

content developer/copywriter — A Web site development team member; responsible for either deriving original content that is pertinent to the site and target market or adapting client-provided content for a Web audience.

content manager — A Web site development team member; organizes and distributes a site's content.

content site — A Web site that offers unique information.

cost-benefit analysis — An analysis that weighs the potential benefit of expenditures against their cost.

cost per thousand (CPM) — the most widely used structure for quantifying Web ad placement.

creative director — A Web site development team member; the artistic force behind the design and structure of the site who develops concepts and ideas for the site and its support.

cumulative page weight — The total file size, in bytes, of any Web page when the file size for all the page's graphics are added together.

customer-effective — A description of a site that is built specifically for ease of customer use and that has a brand message that emphasizes high-quality customer service.

customer retention — The measure of how long a customer remains on a Web site or how frequently a customer returns to a site.

customer service — Action taken by a company, Web site, or salesperson to provide support or assistance to customers.

cyber media room — An area of a site where a company can post current and past news releases and other company information geared toward the news media; it also can contain photography and other art work.

damage control — The management of negative publicity.

database engineer — A Web site development team member; responsible for incorporating Web site technology and programming.

day trading — The act of buying stocks and selling them that same day after making a quick profit.

demographics — Physical characteristics of a population.

design testing — Tests that evaluate audience reaction to the aesthetic aspects of a site.

digital printing — A computerized print method that is equal in quality to traditional commercial press output. Digitally printed pieces can be personalized and are cost-effective for producing high-quality, four-color work in small quantities.

direct approach — An advertisement that is a straightforward statement of the facts.

direct gain site — A Web site that seeks to make profit from a visitor.

direct mail — Advertising that is sent through standard U.S. mail or courier services such as UPS or Federal Express.

dot-com — An online business that can be either a pure-com or owned by a traditional business.

dots per inch (dpi) — A measurement of the number of pixels or dots that appear per inch on a monitor.

e-tailer — An online retailer.

e-zine — A magazine published on the Web.

electronic commerce (e-commerce) — Online business.

embedded ad — A square advertising box on a Web page, making the page look like a standard newspaper or magazine page.

FAQ (frequently asked questions) page — An area of a Web site that displays frequently asked questions and their answers.

flat colors — Images or areas made up of fields of one or more single tone colors.

frames retention — The use of frames to break up a Web site into different segments. Each segment acts as though it were its own browser, deriving information from different pages and making it difficult for the user to leave the page.

freelancer — An outsourced employee of any type who provides services on a temporary basis.

functionality testing — Testing done on a regular basis to ensure that all site elements are working, are efficient, and are doing what they are supposed to do.

go public — The listing of a site on one of the major stock indexes so that its shares can be traded on the open market.

graphic designer — A Web site development team member; responsible for building the interface and graphic elements used in Web sites.

graphic template — The basic layout that is used for most pages in a site.

graphics — Any visual feature of a Web site, including figures, buttons, and imagery.

gross sales — Total dollars earned by sales before costs have been subcontracted.

guerrilla marketing — Aggressive marketing tactics, such as people handing leaflets to passers-by.

hard costs — Money paid to outside firms or entities for goods or services.

hit — Each individual Web page item that is downloaded from a site.

hook — Something that makes your site different from others and valuable in a unique way.

hyperlinks — A technical term for navigation elements.

Hypertext Markup Language (HTML) — A simple Web programming language made up of various tags that instruct browser software how to lay out a Web page for display on a monitor, where to find certain graphic images and other pages to which to hyperlink.

image map — Single graphic elements that allow Web users to access different parts of the site depending on which area of the graphics they click.

image resolution — (pixels per inch or ppi) Measures the number of pixels per inch in an image.

image size — An image's physical size.

impression — An appearance of an advertisement on any Web site.

in-house — Work done by internal company employees.

inline graphics — Any graphics that appear in a Web site that are not either backgrounds or buttons.

instant message (IM) — An Internet-based system by which people can communicate privately and instantaneously with one another by typing. They have conversations on a computer screen as though they were talking on the phone.

integrated marketing — Multiple types of advertising media used in conjunction with one another.

interactive developer — A Web site development team member; guides and directs the graphic designers in creating usable images for various interactive programs, including Flash and Shockwave.

interactive voice response (IVR) system — An automated telephone answering system that uses menus to direct callers to the information that they are seeking.

interstitial ad — Ads that appear behind a browser window and persist as the user moves from site to site. Sometimes interstitials work in conjunction with pop-ups.

live environment — A testing environment in which the test site is working off the hosting server and testers are using the hardware and software that they would ordinarily use in their day-to-day Web surfing activities.

lowest common denominator (LCD) — The minimum set of technical variables that need to be programmed so that the largest audience possible can see the Web site.

mailing list — an organized list of people and their contact information, categorized into various demographic groups, which is used primarily for direct mail marketing efforts.

market research specialist — A Web site development team member; determines the characteristics of site visitors by outlining audience demographics and psychographics; responsible for site planning tasks related to audience definition.

marketing — The act or process of bringing a company, product, or service to the market.

marketing strategy — A site or company's plan to gain customers and revenue.

marketshare — The percentage of the overall market for an industry that buys its products or services from a given company.

media buyer — A Web site development team member; responsible for purchasing desired advertising space based on the media planner/strategist's recommendations.

media planner/strategist — A Web site development team member; responsible for determining which means to use to deliver the site message to the prospective audience.

membership — A revenue model in which users pay a certain price (typically per visit, per week, or per month) to gain access to certain information on the site. Also known as a subscription.

merchant account — An account with a bank or bank-affiliated entity that processes credit cards and that allows purchases to be made online in real-time.

mirror — A duplicate of a site located on a separate server.

mission statement — A brief summary of a company's goals.

monetary gain site — A site that sells products or services online; also known as retail or electronic commerce sites.

monitor resolution — (dots per inch or dpi) The number of pixels or dots that appear per inch on a monitor.

mouse-trapping — The launching of multiple browser windows when a user tries to leave a Web site; it's an annoying means of preventing users from leaving certain sites.

navigation — Elements that allow the user to link from one page to another.

navigation testing — Tests that ensure that your audience understands how to use the navigation system and that the destination of each link is obvious and correct.

net profit — The difference between sales and costs.

New Economy — The economic environment beginning in the 1990s in which instant data, endless opportunity, and instantaneous decision-making are economic factors and in which the average American is an informed and active participant.

news release — An announcement of news that is brief, factual, and well-organized. A news release should include the five W's: Who, What, Where, When, and Why.

Old Economy — The pre-Web economic environment in which fewer than 5 percent of American households owned stock.

outsource — The subcontracting of work to a freelancer or specialist in a specific area.

page view — The number of pages within a site that have been visited by site users.

path through site — A measurement of site usage that shows the route visitors take to get to a site.

pay-per-click — An advertising method in which advertisers pay for their ads only when site visitors click them.

pay-per-purchase — An advertising method in which advertisers pay nothing for the ad impression, but in which they pay a premium (usually a percentage of the sale) if the Web user makes a purchase from the advertised site.

permission-based marketing — E-mail-based marketing delivered to recipients who have indicated an interest in receiving the marketer's promotional information.

pitch — An attention-getting angle used to present a story in a way that is interesting to editors.

pixel — A small dot on a monitor that contains one color.

pixelating — Ruining the quality of an image by making it blurry as a result of enlarging it.

pixels per inch (ppi) — A measurement of the number of pixels in an image.

pop-up ad — An advertising window that appears on top of a Web page loaded in a browser.

PR stunt — An event, often outrageous or innovative, staged by a company in an attempt to gain publicity.

print — The advertising medium that includes magazines, newspapers, circulars, and other paper-based methods.

production house — A small creative agency specializing in Web site production.

profit margin — The difference between what a product or service costs to produce and how much it can be sold for.

project manager — A Web site development team member; acts as liaison between the account executive and the rest of the site development team; responsible for various details of site development and coordination of efforts of all team members.

psychographics — Personality characteristics of a population.

public relations (PR) — The branch of marketing that gets people talking about certain products, companies, or items. PR is usually done by sending announcements of news for coverage by the media.

public relations (PR) specialist — A Web site development team member; responsible for publicizing the site through non-advertising means; often has direct contact with the client.

pure-com — A business that exists only online.

rate card price — The published price at which a media outlet offers ad space or time.

resolution — The number of pixels that make up an image, usually measured in linear (straight) inches.

rewards system — A loyalty program that awards points for visiting a site, spending money, or spending time on a site. Participants can put points toward merchandise, better content, free shipping, or other items of value.

RGB gamut — The range of colors that a computer can display.

rollover — The state in which a navigation feature changes color or appears that it is being pushed in when the user either rolls the mouse pointer over it or clicks it.

round — A cycle of venture capital funding.

royalty-free images — Images sold for a fee by stock photo houses that allow anybody who pays for them to use them in their work.

sample — A few representatives of a target market.

schematic — A rough sketch that approximates a site's various pages and navigation structure.

second-tier navigation — Navigation items that are directly beneath the upper-tier categories.

shoe-string budget — A very small budget.

shopping cart — a Web site feature that consumers use to collect items that they may want to purchase.

sign-off — Written approval by the client.

skyscraper ad — An ad that runs vertically down the side of a site

spider site — A site that searches the Web for user-defined products and that generates a list of the sites that offer the lowest price for that product.

sponsorship — advertising that allows content to be brought to you by a specific company.

static — A Web site that doesn't change frequently and that has no interactivity features.

sticky — Features that keep visitors returning to a site.

style guide — A set of rules that describes logo, colors, fonts, and other brand identity elements.

subscription — a revenue model in which users pay a certain price (typically per visit, per week, or per month) to gain access to certain information on the site. Also known as a membership.

tag line — The brief statement used by most brands in advertisements or marketing campaigns that sends a quick message of summation to the audience.

target market — The group of visitors that a Web site intends to attract.

three-click rule — A rule that states that a user should be able to get to any page from any other page within three clicks without using the browser's Back button.

tiers — Levels of navigation.

time line — A projected schedule for creating a site.

unique selling position (USP) — The distinctive aspect that any company, product, or service must have in order to appeal to a consumer.

up-sale — A higher-priced item or an accessory to the item in which a shopper is interested.

upper-tier navigation — The main information categories on a site.

venture capitalists — Providers of funding for site growth.

viral marketing — Marketing that is done when a message is funny, unique, or outstanding enough that a recipient feels compelled to pass the message on to others.

visitor — Unique users who have come to a Web site.

visitor session — The number of times a visitor views a Web site.

wallpapering — The horizontal and vertical repetition of an image used to create a Web site background. Also known as tiling.

Web start-up — Businesses that exist only online.

Webcast — A live broadcast of audio and/or video distributed over the Web.

Index